Beginning film studies

Beginnings
Series editors: Peter Barry and Helen Carr

'**Beginnings**' is a series of books designed to give practical help to students beginning to tackle recent developments in English, Literary Studies and Cultural Studies. The books in the series

- demonstrate and encourage a questioning engagement with the new;
- give essential information about the context and history of each topic covered;
- show how to develop a practice which is up-to-date and informed by theory.

Each book focuses uncompromisingly upon the needs of its readers, who have the right to expect lucidity and clarity to be the distinctive feature of a book which includes the word 'beginning' in its title.

Each aims to lay a firm foundation of well understood initial principles as a basis for further study and is committed to explaining new aspects of the discipline without over-simplification, but in a manner appropriate to the needs of beginners.

Each book, finally, aims to be both an introduction and a contribution to the topic area it discusses.

Also in the series

Beginning
film studies

Second edition

Andrew Dix

Manchester University Press

Published by Manchester University Press
Altrincham Street, Manchester M1 7JA

www.manchesteruniversitypress.co.uk

British Library Cataloguing-in-Publication Data
A catalogue record for this book is available from the British Library

Library of Congress Cataloging-in-Publication Data applied for

ISBN   978 1 7849 9138 8 paperback

First published 2016

Typeset by
Servis Filmsetting Ltd, Stockport, Cheshire
Printed in Great Britain by
Bell & Bain Ltd, Glasgow

For Karen

Contents

List of figures

Preface to the second edition

The first edition of *Beginning Film Studies* appeared in 2008. While its structure is largely replicated here, this second edition has afforded opportunities in other respects for significant revision and updating. New or expanded case studies have been provided for every chapter. Additional material has been introduced to register and evaluate emerging areas of interest for film studies, including the role played increasingly by social media in film publicity (Chapter 5) and in the fashioning of star personas (Chapter 7). By extending coverage of subjects such as the significance of characters in cinematic narrative (Chapter 4), this edition of the book also offers fuller assessment than did its predecessor of the impact upon film studies of cognitive approaches. Finally, film references and further reading suggestions have been updated throughout.

Acknowledgements

This book would not have been written without the friendship, support and advice of many people in the School of the Arts, English and Drama, Loughborough University: in particular, Brian Jarvis, Paul Jenner and Pete Templeton. For enlightening discussions of film, not least consideration of the star persona of Jennifer Lawrence discussed in Chapter 7, I would like to thank Jen Nicol, Teresa O'Rourke and Tosha Taylor. Much gratitude is owed, too, to David McGowan. Coverage of Bollywood cinema in Chapter 9 benefited greatly from conversations with Aman Nijjer and Anwara Tarafdar.

Staff at the Ronald Grant Archive offered guidance in selecting some of the book's visual illustrations. For help with accessing materials on Loughborough's cinema history for Chapter 10's case study, I am grateful to members of staff supporting the Local Studies Reference Collection of Loughborough Library. I am indebted, too, to pioneering research in this subject by Mervyn Gould.

Special thanks are owed to Russell Wilson, who provided the diagrams in Chapter 2 of continuity editing's 30-degree and 180-degree rules. For their great support I am also grateful to Julie Bunce, Bill Kennedy, Cynthia Kennedy, Mandi Ridding, Abi Smith, Andy Smith, Gill Smith and James Smith. The friendship and encouragement of Regula Biggins, Steve Biggins, Frank Mitchell and Julie Mitchell made the writing of the book much easier; it is a great sadness that Steve, always a vivid and funny conversationalist about film, did not live to see publication of this second edition.

Working with Manchester University Press has been a consistently happy experience, and thanks are due especially to Matthew

Frost for his warm commitment towards this project from the start and to Rachel Winterbottom for inviting me to produce a second edition and for her support during its writing. John Banks has been an exemplary copyeditor, helping to sharpen the argument of the book as well as its presentation and accuracy.

The biggest debts are owed to my parents, dedicatees of the first edition, and to Karen Kennedy, dedicatee of this one. Without them, neither version of *Beginning Film Studies* would have appeared.

Introduction

The coming of film

'Then came the film', wrote the German cultural theorist Walter Benjamin in the 1930s, recalling with excitement the arrival of a new art form at the end of the nineteenth century. For Benjamin, film's techniques such as slow motion and the close-up held the promise of reconfiguring time and space, thus blowing apart the 'prison-world' of previous daily life (1999: 229). In his account, film is not only liberating but a medium that can be differentiated clearly from earlier forms of visual culture. A number of other scholars, however, have taken issue with Benjamin and described the late-Victorian emergence of film less as a singular event than as a synthesis and modification of multiple existing technologies and practices. Simply to cite the names initially bestowed upon this art form is, Rick Altman argues, to recognise its conservation and appropriation of what came before, rather than its revolutionary newness: *photoplay*, *electric theatre*, *living photographs*, *pictorial vaudeville* and so on (2004: 19–20).

How long a story should film studies tell about the emergence of the medium with which it is concerned? Although, traditionally, the founding moment was taken to be the Lumière brothers' first public demonstration of their cinematograph in Paris shortly after Christmas 1895, this is much too straightforward a birth-narrative. Instead, genealogists of film have constructed extensive timelines. For the French director Abel Gance and the American critic and poet Vachel Lindsay, both writing early in the twentieth century, film actually descends from ancient visual

forms like Egyptian hieroglyphics. While Laurent Mannoni does
not look back quite so far in his magisterial history of film's emergence, *The Great Art of Light and Shadow*, he nevertheless finds an
early 'cinema' in the experiments conducted by thirteenth-century
scholars who projected images in a darkened room by reflecting
light from outside through a small aperture (2000: 5). Mannoni's
book goes on to detail a host of technologies of image capture and
projection that appeared in succeeding centuries. The best-known
of these is *the magic lantern* (see Figure 1), a device which peaked
in popularity during the Victorian period and enthralled spectators by projecting slides of variously picturesque, wondrous and
terrifying images upon a wall, curtain or even primitive screen.
Many other optical machines, however, also contained in miniature aspects of the future cinematic experience. Consider, for
example, the Phenakistoscope, invented in the 1830s and consisting of a disk decorated with pictures which was spun in front
of a mirror so as to produce a sense of movement comparable
to later cinematic animation. Or, from roughly the same period,

1 A magic lantern, one of film's precursor technologies

think of the Zoetrope, memorialised in the name of American director Francis Ford Coppola's production company and comprising a drum rotated at sufficiently high speed for the pictures painted on its interior surface to cohere in a film-like sequence. To explore nineteenth-century visual culture is thus to enter what Michael Wood calls 'a cabinet of wonders' (2012: 16), with other fantastically named inventions such as the Photobioscope, Phasmatrope and Praxinoscope also requiring placement somewhere in film's many-branched family tree. And so, too, do waxworks, dioramas, panoramic paintings, theatre and, of course, photography.

The early intertwining of film with other forms that is disclosed here provides a starting point for this book. In recalling this media overlap, however, we do not simply indulge historical curiosity, but witness something that eerily foreshadows the visual culture of our own moment. Much of the twentieth century saw attempts by film criticism and, later, by a more academicised film studies to demarcate securely its object of attention. Enthusiasts and students of film alike sought to identify and evaluate a distinct body of work produced for public delight, excitement and reflection by capturing light on a series of photographic frames and projecting the results so as to generate a sense of movement. Now, however, the assumptions underlying this enterprise are increasingly subject to challenge. In the first instance, as Tom Gunning writes, film is in the process of being 'dispersed into a number of new image technologies. The last modern art seems to be dissolving into a postmodern haze' (2000: 317). A moment's reflection on the irrepressible visuality of contemporary life – at least in economically privileged societies – bears out Gunning's contention. The primary works with which film criticism has traditionally been preoccupied have unstable boundaries now with a host of other spectacles, including video games, internet sites, TV shows, advertisements and amusement park simulations. Second, major changes to long-established ways of thinking about film are prompted by the progressive replacement of the medium's photochemical basis by *digital imaging*. Some of the challenges this latter development poses to familiar areas and protocols of film studies are raised during the course of this book and reviewed in detail in its Conclusion.

To dwell at the start of a text such as this upon film's instability and mutability might seem self-defeating, even suicidal. This is not so, however: the point is simply to acknowledge that now, just as earlier in its history, film studies takes as its object of inquiry something which is messy rather than pristine, in flux rather than fixed, and entangled with other cultural forms rather than self-sufficient. Alain Badiou, one of a number of major French philosophers to have been highly engaged by film, speaks in this vein of 'the fundamental impurity of cinema' (2013: 7). Gunning, too, is unfazed by suggestions that film's 'contemporary crisis threatens an established sacral identity'; there is, he says, 'no single identity to guard' (2000: 327). In the wake of the medium's own multiplicity, film studies itself should be understood as plural and contentious, not settled or monolithic. Hence, of course, the discipline's great intellectual excitement and its ongoing life.

The invention of film studies

From its beginnings, film has precipitated not only sensory stimulation but intellectual inquiry. A significant wave of recent scholarship has returned to the first discourse about film, produced early in the twentieth century, and has registered how it asked fundamental questions about the new medium's artistic parameters, ideological implications and cultural effects. Was film 'science or was it art', for example (Elsaesser and Hagener, 2010: 1)? With respect to audiences, was it likely to 'elevate and educate, or distract and corrupt' (1)? Film's earliest students included major figures from other creative fields such as literature and painting, repelled by its mechanical and chemical constituents but also drawn to it for its exhilarating modernity and for the elasticity of its presentation of time and space. Virginia Woolf was among these founding intellectuals of film, sustaining a complex engagement with the new art form across diary entries and novels as well as, more overtly, in her essay 'The Cinema' (1926). And, if a number of writers of fiction and poetry were driven to reflect on film, so too were figures from a background in the visual arts. In the United States, Victor Freeburg, for example, drew at times upon established precepts of art criticism when responding to the new medium in *The Art of Photoplay Making*

(1918) and *Pictorial Beauty on the Screen* (1923). At the same time, however, Freeburg had to acknowledge 'a quality of movement in film which was radically different to that of the other visual and plastic arts' (Marcus, 2007: 215).

While early critics such as these prioritised aesthetic investigation – seeking to identify film's distinctiveness as an art form – other writers approached the medium with different concerns in mind. So, for example, Hugo Münsterberg aimed in a pioneering book of 1916 to uncover and analyse the psychological activity initiated by what he continued to call 'the photoplay'. His interest, as he phrased it, was in 'the means by which the photoplay influences the mind of the spectator [...] We analyze the mental processes which this spe-cific form of mental endeavor produces in us' (Münsterberg, 2002: 65). The type of psychological inquiry developed by Münsterberg was not always a rarefied intellectual activity in this early period: on the contrary, it was also practised by government agencies on both sides of the Atlantic, anxious about the social effects of the psycho-logical reconditioning produced by film. Hollywood, too, took an interest in this strand of early film scholarship, sensing commercial value in research into exactly what goes on in the spectator's cortex during the viewing process. An adequate account of the first work on film has to acknowledge, then, that it was characterised by a range of intellectual orientations and carried out by a multiplicity of agencies and institutions.

All of this varied activity in the early decades of the twentieth century occurred, however, before the emergence of film studies as a named and demarcated subject area. 'Film was studied before 1935', Dana Polan writes, 'but largely without disciplinary solidi-fication into an academic tradition' (2007: 19). The first degree in film studies, in fact, was that offered by the University of Southern California from 1933 onwards. While, initially, the student intake on this and some other university programmes in the United States was dominated not by young scholars drawn to the subject for its intellectual challenges but by Hollywood technicians aiming to upscale their skills, film studies gradually disavowed any vocational bias. The subject was also internationalised, emerging as an accred-ited academic discipline not only in the United States but in such locations as Britain and continental Europe.

This is, of course, not the place for a detailed history of film studies. Interested readers can find fascinating accounts of the gradual disciplinisation of this field of study in texts such as Dana Polan's *Scenes of Instruction: The Beginnings of the U.S. Study of Film* (2007) and Lee Grieveson's and Haidee Wasson's edited collection, *Inventing Film Studies* (2008). However, two points might be made briefly. The first is to emphasise that, compared with subjects such as history, philosophy, theology and even literary study, film studies as a discipline is relatively youthful. Thus the work on film that readers of this book will do themselves is a contribution to a field not yet as thickly accreted with existing scholarship as some others. Second, it is important not to condescend to early film studies, despite its fragmented and diffuse aspects. This body of work, in fact, holds valuable lessons for us in our own moment, both in the range of projects and approaches it entertained and in its tendency to ask the most searching questions about film's nature, purpose and effect.

About this book

This volume offers readers a critical introduction to key subjects, concepts and methodologies in film studies. Specifically, it aims to provide:

- a knowledge of conceptual shifts in twentieth- and twenty-first-century film studies
- a vocabulary for the analysis of film form and style
- a sense of the ideological dimensions of film
- an awareness of key *post-textual* or *extra-textual* domains of film studies
- a prospectus of possible directions for film studies in the future.

Running throughout the book is the conviction that film studies is less a single set of orthodoxies for its participants to master and repeat than a field of diverse activities to engage in and extend. At times, it is true, particular critical and theoretical positions have come close to supplying the discipline with received wisdoms. The two strongest candidates to date are the director-centred auteur theory that emerged from France in the late 1950s and early 1960s (discussed in Chapter 6) and the composite of Marxist, psycho-analytic, feminist and semiotic approaches that started to form a decade later (discussed in Chapter 8). Even during the period of rule of each of these critical doctrines, however, dissenting voices could still be heard, hinting at other valuable and interesting ways in which to do film studies. The book will assess the benefits of these 'strong' conceptual frameworks while welcoming the fact of their relaxation to the point whereby film studies at present is hospitable to a wide range of research projects.

The organisation of chapters can be regarded as a set of concentric circles, at the centre of the smallest of which is found the film text itself. Chapters 1–3 assume that knowledge of film's stylistic repertoire as it has developed from the late nineteenth century to the present is indispensable for any work in film studies (whatever its focus). These chapters aim, therefore, to equip readers with resources for cataloguing and evaluating aspects of mise-en-scène (film's visual field), editing and soundtrack. From early, predisciplinary days, film studies has understandably been interested in assessing in detail the formal qualities of films themselves. Such narrowing of focus has not been without costs. Charles Acland suggests wittily that 'the problem with film studies has been *film*, that is, the use of a medium in order to designate the boundaries of a discipline' (2003: 46). At times, Acland's withdrawal of interest from the particularities of film texts is so complete that he resembles a literature professor who has stopped reading books in order to discuss instead the economics of publishing or the design of Kindles. Nevertheless, his critique of an 'artifactual approach to film' (52) is bracing, and helps to guard against the kind of formalism that reads a film minutely but has no awareness of the dense contexts of production and consumption in which it is enmeshed.

If the book's first three chapters focus closely on film stylistics, Chapters 4–8 move outwards, while continuing to promote detailed engagement with the film text itself. They are concerned respectively with film narrative, film genre, film authorship, film stars and the ideologies – class, gender, sexual and racial – of film representation. In each of these chapters, the text is less a self-enclosed, impermeable thing than a prism reflective of a host of real-world concerns that range from genre's importance in film industry economics to mutations of film authorship in the digital era, or from questions of social power raised by film narrative to cinema's role in the stereotyping of non-white or non-straight identities.

Chapters 9 and 10, however, decentre the film text more thoroughly, along the lines proposed by Acland and some other contemporary critics. For these writers, film studies has now mined the last seams of a textual approach and can renew itself only by other kinds of research. This desire to turn away from 'readings' of the primary material and do something radically different is not unique to contemporary film studies. Franco Moretti – whose work on genre features in Chapter 5 – urges a similar change of direction for his own field of literary study. Instead of focusing upon 'concrete, individual works' (2005: 1), or restricting itself to 'separate bits of knowledge about individual cases' (4), literary criticism in Moretti's view should take as its proper object of inquiry 'a collective system, that should be grasped as such, as a whole' (4). In film studies, systemically oriented work of this type aims to provide ever more detailed accounts of production, distribution and consumption. *Extra-textual* or *post-textual* scholarship might focus, say, on the mechanisms by which 'global Hollywood' extends the commercial reach of its products, or on the cultural politics of watching films in multiplexes. Chapters 9 and 10 welcome and review these emerging lines of inquiry, while arguing that the best work in film studies will combine savviness about broad institutional forces with sensitivity still to how these play themselves out in the detail of specific films.

Three other things should be said briefly at this stage. Firstly, some readers new to the subject may be anxious that film's manifold pleasures will be lost as a result of cultivating an analytical habit. What happens to the thrill we feel at the kinetics of a chase sequence, or at the star's beauty on screen, once films are watched in a resolutely critical and theoretical spirit? One (weak) answer is that the absorptive power of much cinema is such as potentially to deflect earnest interrogation until after each act of viewing. However, a stronger response is to emphasise the pleasures bound up in engagement with film criticism and theory themselves – gratifications different from sensuous reward by the screen, it is true, but not to be belittled by comparison. As well as introducing a wide range of critical models and theoretical vocabularies, the book includes many

'Stop and Think' sections that encourage readers to recognise not only the explanatory power but also the intellectual exhilaration of these frameworks.

Secondly, a word might be said about the language of film studies. Drawn from such disparate fields as narratology, genre study, Marxist theory, psychoanalysis and so on, the terminology employed by the discipline may sometimes seem off-puttingly abstract. It certainly did to the great Spanish director Luis Buñuel. Given his subversive, Surrealist imagination exhibited across half-a-century of work, Buñuel was hardly a maker of briskly common-sensical films; nevertheless, in his autobiography he tells the story of encountering 'a young man in a suit and tie' at a film studies centre in Mexico City: 'When I asked him what he taught, he replied "The Semiology of the Clonic Image."' Buñuel adds: 'I could have murdered him on the spot' (1985: 222). But while absorbing the lesson here about a self-regarding or rebarbative jargon, we should not rush to abandon abstract discourse in itself. The critic Peter Wollen puts the case well for film studies' specialised language: 'clearly any kind of serious critical work must involve a distance, a gap between the film and the criticism, the text and the meta-text. It is as though meteorologists were reproached for getting away from the "lived experience" of walking in the rain or sunbathing' (1998: 115).

Finally, attention should be drawn to the book's choice of films to support its discussion. For the most part, the case studies that conclude each chapter are taken from the strain of recent, popular American cinema with which most readers will be especially familiar. This should not, however, be taken as uncritical endorsement of Hollywood's current global hegemony. Instead, these already known primary materials have been selected so as to facilitate more readily readers' work with a range of critical models that may be being encountered here for the first time. Elsewhere, however, the book is committed to a wide geographical remit. While regrettable lacunae remain – for example, African cinema both north and south of the Sahara – the films drawn upon across the chapters originate in nations ranging from Spain to South Korea, Iran to Chile, India to Uruguay. Chronologically, too, the book aspires to breadth, aiming not only to be up-to-the-minute but also to venture beyond the recent and contemporary into such earlier filmmaking as the first single-shot documentaries, the radical Soviet experiments of the 1920s and Hollywood film noir of World War II and its aftermath.

A note on references

Film studies is an activity not only of serious watching but of serious *reading*. In this spirit the book is dialogical, interacting with many written sources. These are referenced here in author/date style, with the full set of 'References' placed at the end of the book. Some of these texts appear also in the annotated lists of 'Selected reading' that conclude each chapter. Dates of all films when first mentioned are given in parentheses; where a film appears without a date, this has been supplied earlier. Following the practice of a number of other texts, the titles of foreign films, where these are very familiar in English, are given as such. Again, this is intended only to enhance the book's accessibility, and should certainly not be read as proselytising for an Anglocentric film culture or a monolingual film studies. Finally, every effort has been made to check the viability of websites listed in the text: all URLs are correct at the time of publication.

Selected reading

Grieveson, Lee and Haidee Wasson (eds) (2008), *Inventing Film Studies* (Durham, NC: Duke University Press).
Substantial collection of essays on the discipline's plural and dispersed origins.
Mannoni, Laurent (2000), *The Great Art of Light and Shadow: Archaeology of the Cinema* (Exeter: University of Exeter Press).
A mighty scholarly achievement, placing the cinematic apparatus in a densely recovered history of optical experiments beginning as early as the thirteenth century.
Marcus, Laura (2007), *The Tenth Muse: Writing about Cinema in the Modernist Period* (Oxford: Oxford University Press).
Dense and absorbing study of attempts by modernist writers, early in the twentieth century, to uncover the artistic, cultural and political potentials of film.
Polan, Dana (2007), *Scenes of Instruction: The Beginnings of the U.S. Study of Film* (Berkeley: University of California Press).

Lucid, scrupulously researched account of disparate early twentieth-century American ventures in the study of film, prior to film studies' consolidation as a discipline.

Online resources

'Early Cinema', http://earlycinema.com.

Well-maintained site on cinema's inaugural decade from 1895 to 1905.

'Invention of Entertainment: The Early Motion Pictures and Sound Recordings of the Edison Companies', Library of Congress, www.loc.gov/collections/edison-company-motion-pictures-and-sound-recordings/.

Helpful introduction to the emergence of American cinema, featuring scholarly articles alongside many examples of early short films.

'Who's Who of Victorian Cinema', http://victorian-cinema.net/.

Excellent, scholarly resource on the personalities and technologies involved in cinema's beginnings from the 1870s to the end of the nineteenth century.

1

Seeing film:
mise-en-scène

In starting to think about film's distinctiveness as a medium, it might seem perverse to take instruction from study of another art form. However, the American New Critics, influential in mid-twentieth-century literary scholarship, are valuable to us in identifying a sin they call 'heresy of paraphrase'. New Critics have in mind here readings of a piece of poetry or prose which attempt prematurely to say *what* it means and show, by contrast, little interest in or even knowledge of precisely *how* it means. Thus the paraphrasing heretic asserts what a Shakespeare sonnet is expressing about true love, but fails to consider how the poem's thematic implications only emerge through its complex work of versification, rhyme, metaphor and syntax. The result is a disembodied kind of literary criticism, curiously inattentive to the specificities and textures of its own object of study.

Much of the discussion of film with which we are most familiar is weakened by similar insensitivity towards the particularities of the medium itself. The reader of newspaper film reviews and the viewer of TV programmes on cinema tend to encounter, precisely, heresies of paraphrase. Such discourse typically summarises a film's narrative turns, or discusses its characters, but leaves unaddressed its material distinctiveness: its modes of cinematography, say, or its key editing choices, or its layerings of sound. Yet to be concerned with such issues of cinematic form is not indulgent, or somehow minor in relation to more essential things we should be doing as students of film. On the contrary, any attempt to ask larger cultural or ideological questions about a film is inadequate if it does not include some reckoning with the work's formal dimensions. These visual and auditory repertoires should not be set aside, but, instead, actively explored as devices for the generation of meaning. 'The meaning of art', according to two Russian critics early in the twentieth century who were as absorbed by cinema as they were by literature, 'is completely inseparable from all the details of its material body' (Bakhtin and Medvedev, 1978: 12).

Film's 'material body' is thus the subject of this book's first three chapters. Before turning in Chapters 2 and 3 to editing and soundtrack, we begin with an account of film's visual properties, grouped together under the French term *mise-en-scène*.

Defining mise-en-scène

'What is mise-en-scène?' asks Jacques Rivette, a key member of the New Wave, that group of filmmaker-critics which energised French cinema in the late 1950s and 1960s. 'My apologies for asking such a hazardous question with neither preparation nor preamble, particularly when I have no intention of answering it. Only, should this question not always inform our deliberations?' (Hillier, 1985: 134). While Rivette's disinclination to define mise-en-scène is alarming, he valuably insists here upon the fundamental importance for film studies of engagement with particularities of visual style. What, exactly, is it that we see and give significance to as we watch films?

Consider the start of Sam Mendes's *American Beauty* (1999), as a fade-in takes the viewer from a black screen disclosing nothing to a scene abundant in visual information. As the sequence begins, we see a young woman lying on a bed. While this figure remains silent and inert, the spectator begins interpretative work, making provisional assessments of the significance of her location, appearance and posture. Lit harshly rather than flatteringly, the woman is without both make-up and stylish clothing, hinting at some disregard for normative Western femininity. For the moment, we may be concerned just to register and process this sort of visual detail, utilising the categories of setting, props, costume and lighting. To these critical subdivisions should be added that of acting or performance, even while the woman lies motionless. However, our eyes may be more mobile and inquisitive still, taking in not merely the figure on the bed but also the distinctive ways in which shots of her are composed. What are the implications of the camera's close proximity to her, admitting no other human presence into the visual field? And what seems connoted by the roughened texture of the image itself, shot on grainy video rather than 35mm film?

In carrying out interpretative work of this kind on a film's visual specificities, the spectator is considering mise-en-scène. As Rivette says, however, the term is 'hazardous', open to several competing definitions. It translates from French as 'staging' or 'putting into the scene', indicating its origins in theatre rather than cinema. The theatrical bias of the word is apparent even in the most recent edition of the *Oxford English Dictionary*, which offers a primary definition of 'staging of a play; the scenery and properties of a stage production; the stage setting', but gives no acknowledgement of the appropriation of mise-en-scène as a term in cinematic analysis. The shadow cast by the theatre extends into film studies itself, where some scholars – notably, David Bordwell and Kristin Thompson in their influential *Film Art: An Introduction* – choose to define filmic mise-en-scène exclusively by what it has in common with theatrical staging: setting, props, costume, lighting and acting. Were we to arrest our analysis of *American Beauty* after considering such visual properties as the abrasive lighting or the woman's stillness, we would be doing mise-en-scène work of this circumscribed, theatrically derived kind. But if the spectator goes on to acknowledge and evaluate other information offered to the eye – the camera's framing of the woman, say, or the video footage's imperfect quality – then he or she is pursuing instead that more expansive and satisfactory approach to mise-en-scène which embraces not merely the elements cinema shares with theatre but also visual regimes that are distinctive to film as a medium: all those things summarised by John Gibbs as 'framing, camera movement, the particular lens employed and other photographic decisions' (2002: 5).

This chapter adopts the broader of these two understandings of mise-en-scène. After first discussing the elements that film carries across from theatrical staging, it goes on to consider aspects of cinematography. Even such an expansive definition of filmic mise-en-scène is open to dispute as narrow and arbitrary. Jean-Luc Godard, another major figure in the French New Wave, writes with regard to a particular editing practice that 'montage is above all an integral part of mise-en-scène' (Narboni and Milne, 1972: 39). Bernard F. Dick, in a much-used textbook in film studies, suggests somewhat eccentrically that sound, too, should be accounted an element of mise-en-scène (2002: 19). While sound's contribution to the sum of a film's meanings is fundamental – in the scene from *American Beauty*, a man's voice from off-camera modifies the sense of isolation that is visually implied – the proposition which Dick makes is one, for the moment, to resist in the interests of isolating the peculiarly visual components of cinema. Similarly, while Godard shows a proper distaste for any approach to film that underplays the effect of *combining* shots, the approach to mise-en-scène that is elaborated in this chapter still finds it valuable to identify visual elements that may be uncovered even in a single shot and thus to reserve until later the discussion of editing.

Pro-filmic elements of mise-en-scène

Coined in the 1950s by the French philosopher of aesthetics Etienne Souriau, the term *pro-filmic* refers to those components of a film's visual field that are considered to exist prior to and independent of the camera's activity: namely, the elements of setting, props, costume, lighting and acting (or performance) which cinema shares with forms of staged spectacle such as theatre, opera and dance. The artificiality of separating these things from cinematography is immediately apparent: Jennifer Lawrence's looks of concern for her endangered sister in *The Hunger Games* (2012) – instances of performance, therefore pro-filmic – would not signify so vividly were it not for the film's close-ups and close shots of her (examples of cinematography). Nevertheless, with the proviso that ultimately they will be reintegrated with cinematography itself, we begin here by separately considering film's pro-filmic strands.

Setting

Cinematic settings vary in scale from the vertiginous interplanetary spaces confronting Sandra Bullock at the outset of *Gravity* (2013; see Figure 2) to the coffin that, patchily illuminated by a cigarette lighter and the glow of his phone, confines the protagonist

2 Interplanetary space as setting: Sandra Bullock in *Gravity* (2013)

in Rodrigo Cortés's *Buried* (2010). In opulence they stretch from the Roman palaces of epics or the sumptuous interiors of Wes Anderson's *The Grand Budapest Hotel* (2014) to the hellish lavatory that Renton occupies in *Trainspotting* (1996). While some film settings advertise their artificiality, others, by contrast, evoke what Roland Barthes calls 'the reality effect': at one end of the spectrum, the fantastical Yellow Brick Road in *The Wizard of Oz* (1939); at the other, teeming city streets that have been exploited throughout cinema history (from brief 'actuality' films made in France by the Lumière brothers during the 1890s, through Italian neo-realism of the 1940s and early 1950s, to instances of modern Latin American cinema such as *Amores perros* (2000) and *City of God* (2002)).

Whether expansive or narrow, magnificent or squalid, artificial or naturalistic, film settings compel our attention. They are not merely inert containers of or backdrops to action, but are themselves charged with significance. At the most basic level, locations serve in narrative cinema to reinforce the plausibility of particular kinds of story. An American urban crime drama would be sterile and unconvincing without the run-down street, the neighbourhood diner, the dimly lit bar; similarly, to guarantee the integrity of its fantastical story-world, Peter Jackson's *Lord of the Rings* trilogy (2001–3) requires enchanted forests, shimmering lakes and towering precipices. As these brief examples suggest, setting also functions as an index of a film's generic status. Chapter 5 will return to the question of setting's role in genre classification; for the moment, we simply note that particular spaces have become associated with certain film genres rather than with others. When Sergio Leone's *For a Few Dollars More* (1965) opens with an extreme long shot of rocky desert terrain, the spectator can make a reasonable, if still tentative assumption that the film is a western (albeit one that proves to have a playful relationship to the western's conventions as codified by Hollywood). The fact that in this scene we also observe a lone horseman, looking insignificant against immensities of sand and sky, alerts us to another basic function of setting in narrative cinema: its revelatory power with respect to character. As well as serving in quite obvious ways to specify the geographical co-ordinates and socio-economic positioning of film protagonists, settings may also work more subtly to evoke their psychological condition. Such symbolic use of space is especially vivid in German Expressionist cinema, which flourished after World War I. To take just one example: when the vampiric protagonist in F. W. Murnau's *Nosferatu* (1922) is seen in one shot standing behind the latticed window of an apartment block, we learn not just matter-of-factly about his living arrangements, but, more profoundly, of his sense of incarceration by conformist Weimar society. While highly developed spatial symbolism is a signature of this particular cinematic tradition, the spectator should also be sensitive to expressionistic settings elsewhere in film.

Props

Setting's functions of substantiating narrative, signalling genre and revealing character are also performed by props: objects of whatever dimensions that appear on screen. Like particular spaces, certain props are correlated with some genres more than with others (again a topic for development in Chapter 5). If a parachute appears on screen, it is a fair bet we are not watching a western (unless of a surreal sort); if a cigarette flares atmospherically into life in close-up, the film noir fan is liable to experience a greater thrill of anticipation than the devotee of epic. And, like settings, props also perform an informational role in narrative cinema with respect to character. Sometimes this function will be limited to confirming socio-economic and occupational status (a reporter's notebook, a businessman's briefcase); elsewhere, however, props may take on expressionistic power. When Travis Bickle drops an

Alka-Seltzer into water in Martin Scorsese's *Taxi Driver* (1976), the fizzing tablet seems not just one tiny component of his material world but indicative of his synaptic disturbance to the point of explosion (this effect enhanced by use of extreme close-up and non-naturalistic sound).

Props – or, speaking less technically, *things* – have also been at the centre of long-running theoretical debates over film's realism or otherwise as a medium. For key texts in a broadly realist tradition, including André Bazin's *What Is Cinema?* (1958–62) and Siegfried Kracauer's *Theory of Film* (first published in 1960), cinema shares with photography a vocation to reveal with heightened vividness the material world that we inhabit. From this perspective, the chief value of showing a cigarette or a parachute is to represent it in all its detailed particularity (a vision which, to be sure, may surpass that of everyday eyesight because of the camera's capacity for close-up). Yet for writers from other theoretical positions, cinema valuably *frees* objects like these from their material circumstantiality and instead endows them with other, non-realist potentialities. Luis Buñuel deplores the fact that for Italian neo-realists – favourite filmmakers, not coincidentally, of Bazin and Kracauer – 'a glass is a glass and nothing more' (Hammond, 2000: 115). In his 1918 essay 'On Décor', the French Surrealist author Louis Aragon positively revels in the elusive and multiple significances of film props: 'on the screen objects that were a few moments ago sticks of furniture or books of cloakroom tickets are transformed to the point where they take on menacing or enigmatic meanings' (Hammond, 2000: 52).

In thinking about the use of props in film, there is no need to be committed exclusively to either of these opposing perspectives. Depending on context, exactly the same object on screen may be a thing valued for its concrete particularities, *or* its narrative suggestiveness, *or* its symbolic density. 'Sometimes', as Freud is famously said to have remarked, 'a cigar is just a cigar'; at other times, though, it may be more or other than this (a phallic symbol, most obviously). The television set that figures in *Silver Linings Playbook* (2012) as an unremarkable detail of a realistically fashioned Middle American home becomes in *The Truman Show* (1998) an ominous sign of a society of surveillance.

Costume

Like setting and props, costume, which also includes make-up and hairstyle, has a wide range of functions and significances. Particular garments index historical period, national origin, class status, sub-group affiliation, gender identity, emotional and psychological condition and so on. In addition, costumes on screen may encourage the spectator to make assumptions about a film's genre. If we see figures wearing space suits, we might reasonably conclude that we have missed the martial arts movie. Similarly, the fact that Bickle in *Taxi Driver* transgresses norms of costuming – wearing military fatigues incongruous in a contemporary New York setting – suggests that what we are actually watching is a contribution to the sub-genre of the Vietnam War film.

Pioneering studies such as Roland Barthes's *The Fashion System* (1967) have long habituated us to consider costume as a structured set of signs replete with connotations. Barthes treats each item of clothing as a signifier from which, in quite orderly fashion, particular 'signifieds', or meanings, may be read off. To be adequate to the task of assessing costume in film, however, such a semiotic approach needs to be co-ordinated with sensitivity to matters of history and geography. For example, the top hat that signifies a boss's arrogance and a system of class exploitation in *Strike* (1924) – a revolutionary Soviet film discussed in Chapter 2 – communicates dandyish lightness and charisma when it is worn by Fred Astaire in 1930s American musicals. In both these instances, costume combines harmoniously with other pro-filmic elements – first with the boss's corpulence and huge cigar, second with Astaire's slimness and lithe movement – so as to reinforce already established meanings. However, there are other cinematic cases where costume is excessive in style or colour, thereby clashing with, rather than simply confirming, other aspects of a film's visual scheme. Jane Gaines argues that certain 1950s US melodramas exhibit such overdevelopment of what she calls 'the vestural code' (from *vesture*, or 'garment'). Rather like Buñuel and Aragon speaking about props, Gaines welcomes this heightened visibility of clothing in film, its freeing from the relatively mundane functions of supporting the realism of character and story. In these 1950s examples, extravagant clothing hints at desires not otherwise expressible in a conformist milieu. For Alfred Hitchcock, by

contrast, such costumes are 'eye-catchers' that dangerously distract
the spectator from the key task of following narrative line (Gaines,
1991: 203–11).

Lighting

In his remarks on costume, Hitchcock is worried that a pro-filmic
element may become autonomous and draw undue attention to
itself. Similar concern has sometimes been expressed by film practitioners about the over-promotion of lighting. One technical manual
much used by new entrants to the industry states that 'most skilled
lighting is self-effacing. The more subtle the treatment, the more
natural or "obvious" it appears to be' (Millerson, 2013: 236). From
this perspective, the ideal film lighting is inconspicuous, contributing significantly to the fashioning of cinematic illusions that absorb
the spectator to the point where he or she responds to them as to
natural phenomena and fails to recognise their artifice. However,
we should resist becoming such critically unaware viewers. Without
repressing the pleasure yielded by our vivid sensory investment in
the screen, we need also to be attentive to the manifold practices
by which this pleasure is generated. These practices include well-
established lighting conventions.

   This is not the place to describe in detail film's uses of key
lighting, fill lighting, backlighting, sidelighting, underlighting and
top lighting so as to achieve different patterns of brightness and
shadow. Anyone seeking specialised technical knowledge of this
kind can readily find it in manuals such as Millerson's. But it is
important to note the distinction between two basic lighting schemas in film: *high-key* (or *low-ratio*) and *low-key* (or *high-ratio*), the
latter sometimes called *chiaroscuro* (a term first applied to Italian
Renaissance paintings that included major portions of darkness).
High-key describes an even diffusion of lighting across a shot,
resulting in low contrast between relatively brighter and darker
areas and quite full detailing of what is shown; under a regime of
low-key lighting, on the other hand, there is much higher contrast
between bright and dark, with less penetrable areas of shadow.
If these two lighting types are approached in semiotic fashion as
signifying systems, then it might seem as if particular meanings
can be straightforwardly attached to each of them. Whereas high-

key lighting tends to evoke a sense of clarity and optimism, low-key lighting, by contrast, may induce feelings of moral ambiguity, anxiety, even terror. Yet, as with the assessment of particular props or costumes, this broad hypothesis needs to be tested in analyses of how exactly lighting functions in specific cases. High-key lighting could, for example, disperse such brightness across a scene as to become monotonous and oppressive, generating a sense less of well-being than of nausea (again *The Truman Show* comes to mind). Low-key lighting, similarly, may be nuanced or multiple in its effects. Certainly it evokes foreboding where it is deployed, again in signature fashion, in German Expressionist cinema and then in one of Expressionism's stylistic descendants: classic Hollywood film noir of the 1940s and 1950s. Even in a noirish work like *The Big Sleep* (1946), however, strongly contrasted light and shade connote mystery and romanticism as much as they do existential dread. And when contemporary noir continues to utilise a low-key lighting pattern, the spectator, far from being thrown into metaphysical crisis, may experience instead a pleasurable nostalgia (consider the value of chiaroscuro in such films as *Sin City 2: A Dame to Kill For* (2014)).

Acting

Lighting is crucially articulated with the final pro-filmic component: *acting* or *performance* (the repertoire of on-screen facial expression, body positioning, gesture, movement and speech). After all, an actor's facial arrangement that is perfectly adequate for romance in conditions of abundant, soft fill lighting becomes more suited to horror film if it is underlit instead. There have, in fact, been surprisingly few attempts to theorise acting in cinema (discounting those that collapse it into the phenomenon of 'the star' discussed in Chapter 7). Some pioneering statements on this topic position film performance against theatre acting and judge it to be impoverished by comparison. Edgar Morin writes of the film actor's 'borderline utility' in the face of cinema's array of visual and auditory effects (2005: 124). In his important essay, 'The Work of Art in the Age of Mechanical Reproduction' (1935–39), Walter Benjamin characterises the film actor as an almost ghostly figure, surviving minimally in his or her two-dimensional screen image but deprived of that vivid bodily presence – or 'aura', in Benjamin's language – which the theatre actor communicates to a live audience. It is only slight compensation that the film industry responds to this 'shrivelling of the aura with an artificial build-up of the "personality" outside the studio' (Benjamin, 1999: 224). Kracauer, an intellectual descendant of Benjamin, also evokes an existential crisis for the film performer, referring to the 'decomposition of the actor's wholeness', both by different camera positions that fragment the body and by the discontinuous way during shooting in which an actor plays a part (1997: 97).

However, there are dangers in assessing film acting by criteria developed for the evaluation of theatrical performance. Here a remark by the American actor Fredric March, who worked on both stage and screen from the 1930s, is instructive. Interrupted by his director during the shooting of one film scene, March apologised: 'Sorry, I did it again. I keep forgetting – this is a movie and I mustn't act' (Kracauer, 1997: 94). From one perspective, this may be evidence of a persistent hierarchy of cultural forms: there is a long history, in the United States and elsewhere, of actors noted for careers in theatre disparaging their work in the supposedly lesser domain of film. However, March's comment also hints that film acting has conventions which overlap only partially with those of theatrical performance. In his film version of *Coriolanus* (2012), for example, Ralph Fiennes utilises close-ups and thus draws on restrained gestures and reduced voice amplification compared with when he was trying to reach the dress circle during London stage performances of the same role in 2000. Variously magnified, distanced or distorted by the camera's positioning, and further modified during editing, the performance of film actors signifies not less than – but *differently from* – that of their theatrical counterparts.

Assessment of film acting also requires sensitivity to historically and geographically variant performance styles. When a woman in silent film evokes anguish by wringing her hands and violently throwing back her head, a contemporary temptation might be to identify overstated, even 'bad' acting (an 'Oscar Clip' of the sort lampooned in *Wayne's World* (1992)). But it is vital to leave behind such evaluative language and acknowledge instead how gestures of this sort belong to a well-established performance style of the period that was strongly influenced by conventions of melodrama. Film acting in later periods – including our own – is equally codified, even if its relative economy in the deployment of both body and voice may make it more difficult to perceive its conventions. Most recent performance in English-speaking cinema is broadly *naturalistic*, aiming to align itself not with the artifice of some theatrical modes but with observed human behaviour; nevertheless, actors in this tradition, from Marlon Brando in *A Streetcar Named Desire* (1951; see Figure 3) to Imelda Staunton in *Vera Drake* (2004) and Gary Oldman in *Tinker Tailor Soldier Spy* (2011), draw upon a systematised repertoire of expressions, gestures, movements and vocalisations in order to achieve the effect which we are now habituated to think of as 'truth to life'.

Acting in a non-naturalistic mode has not entirely disappeared even from Anglo–American cinema. Think, say, of the more manic performances of Jim Carrey. Or consider Jack Nicholson's work in *The Shining* (1980), a performance that disconcerted some critics – including Stephen King, author of the film's source-novel – by seeming histrionic, excessive, a violation of verisimilitude. Rather

3 Naturalistic acting: Marlon Brando in *A Streetcar Named Desire* (1951)

than condemning a lapse into implausibility, however, a more interesting option is to consider how Nicholson's performance style interacts with other elements of mise-en-scène in the film (the acting of Shelley Duvall, say, or the choice of setting, or director Stanley Kubrick's cinematographic decisions). Do Nicholson's heightened gestures and vivid facial tics undermine a prevailing naturalistic effect, or, rather, do they advance tendencies already in the film towards Gothic excess? While many general accounts of mise-en-scène assume that its various elements co-operate to produce a coherent and homogeneous work, it is important to recognise that, sometimes, these features may cut across each other, thereby disrupting the smooth, continuous surface of a film.

STOP and THINK

- Choose a sequence some two or three minutes long from any narrative film. Be as exhaustive as possible in listing the extract's notable pro-filmic features (leaving to one side for the moment its cinematographic choices). Be unafraid to be inventive, even provocative in suggesting the significances of these pro-filmic items. Although Jonathan Culler overstates the case when saying that 'interpretation is interesting only when it is extreme' (Eco et al., 1992: 110), 'over-reading' is certainly to be preferred to 'under-reading' – in film studies as in Culler's own discipline of literary criticism.
- Chapter 7 will consider the 'commutation test', a valuable exercise that assesses how the meaning of a particular film would be modified if a different star than the one actually cast played a particular role. In similar vein, replace each pro-filmic item in your selected film sequence with an equivalent (for example, substituting a futon for a four-poster bed or a hoodie for a cardigan). How do these revisions affect judgements you had previously made about character, narrative, genre classification, realism, ideology and so on?
- Mise-en-scène analysis often mimics literary critical modes such as American New Criticism in assuming harmony and continuity among all stylistic elements. Assess whether the pro-filmic components of your sequence are organically

interrelated in this way, thereby affirming the coherence of the film-world. Or do pro-filmic elements jar against each other? Instabilities of this sort may sometimes be attributed to the continuity person's doziness (Roman gladiators wearing watches; jet vapour trails hanging in the sky above nineteenth-century cowboys): consider, however, whether there may be *deliberate* disarray among pro-filmic features, and explore the effects of this.

Cinematography

The spectator has little choice but to witness the pro-filmic features itemised above. Unless we are watching through our fingers or from behind a cloth – the latter a viewing practice adopted, in pursuit of novel aesthetic experience, by the Surrealist Man Ray – our eyes cannot avoid falling upon all these components of a film's visual field. However, spectators vary considerably in the extent to which they also register the numerous cinematographic processes that endow props, costumes and so on – infinite in their possible implications prior to the camera's activity – with certain meanings rather than others.

Acknowledgement of the camera's material presence may initially be alien or disquieting. In mainstream cinema, evidence of the means of image capture itself is generally withheld from the spectator (other than in inadvertent sightings of, say, a camera operator's shadow). A moment in Mel Brooks's Hitchcock spoof *High Anxiety* (1977) is suggestive here. When the camera, prowling towards a window in thriller fashion, goes too far and crashes through the glass, the effect is to make visible technical operations that are usually unadvertised and, as it were, 'naturalised' in film. The demystification of the image-making process that this affords may, of course, have been forgotten the next time we encounter a thriller's tracking shots (given the power of such techniques to enthral). Yet the aim of this part of the chapter is to preserve the self-conscious, *High Anxiety* moment – though not in killjoy style – and to offer some essential terms for recognising and evaluating cinematographic strategies.

'Cinematography' describes the host of decisions taken during the recording and processing of the film image (whether that image is imprinted on celluloid or encrypted in digital videotape). Some of these technical options are relatively distinct from those bound up with the functioning of the camera itself. Filmmakers may, to begin with, choose between different types of film stock that generate images of strikingly contrasting kinds. The director and cinematographer of *Three Kings* (1999), set during the First Gulf War, selected a stock more customarily used in still cameras so as to yield bizarre, highly saturated colours for a sequence showing the protagonists' hallucinatory journey through alien Iraqi desert. However, another section of the film – where visual approximation of war documentary footage was wanted – exemplifies the many laboratory (or, latterly, computer) manipulations that are available during post-production. This time the effect was created by 'bleach bypass' (omitting bleach during developing so as to give an antique silver tint to the image).

Without discounting the creative importance of such decisions taken either side of filming, we concentrate in this section on major properties and operations of the camera itself. As Aldous Huxley, English novelist and occasional Hollywood screenwriter, remarked in 1926: 'A good subject to talk about, cinematography' (Clark, 1987: 17).

Distance

With exceptions such as wildlife documentaries and abstract experiments, film tends to be a human-centred medium; it is unsurprising, therefore, that camera distances are generally tabulated according to the relative smallness or largeness of the human figure as it appears on screen. The most distant perspective – common in westerns, say, but rare in romcoms – is afforded by the *extreme long shot*, in which the figure is barely visible in an overpowering setting (hence the industry's alternative term, 'the geography shot'). Background is still significant in the *long shot* (or *full shot*), also, although here the figure is close enough to allow the spectator to make confident judgements about its identity. From this point on, however, shots do not disclose the entire human body, but cut it instead into successively smaller portions: the *medium long shot* frames the subject from below the knee upwards; the *medium shot* from the waist up;

the *medium close-up* from roughly chest height; while the *close-up* isolates the head and perhaps neck. Finally, the camera is most intimate (or intrusive) in the *extreme close-up*, which breaks up the unity of the face by showing only particular features such as the eyes or mouth.

This terminology has been subject to historical adjustment. David Bordwell notes that 'close-up' – a term entering English around 1912 – originally referred to a shot which included a significant amount of background, rather than, as now, one tending to focus upon the human face in isolation (1997: 122–4). To point this out is not, for Bordwell, mere semantic quibbling, since grasping the precise definition of shot-types in particular periods allows the scholar to make more informed assessments of the evolution of film style. It is also important that we offer specific and nuanced – rather than absolute – judgements on the significance of various shot distances. Here brief discussion of a single example – the extreme close-up – may be helpful.

One practical guide to cinematography asserts that this shot 'lacks dignity'; it 'makes nearly any subject sinister, aggressive and nasty', and therefore should not be used in narrative film but restricted instead to such specialised forms as medical documentary (Thompson, 1998: 84). Leaving to one side the dubious proposition that cinema should always aim to confer 'dignity' upon its subjects – what about satirical or polemical films? – Thompson also unduly narrows here the semantic range of the extreme close-up. A shot of a character's eyes may evoke grief or love or religious fervour as easily as it does brutishness. Even where the extreme close-up is used on morally questionable figures, its effects can vary. When the film noir *Force of Evil* (1948) cuts from a close-up of a telephone now understood as bugged by the police to an extreme close-up of the criminal protagonist's eyes, the result is a more striking representation of panic than would be achieved by a more discreet camera distance. Yet when eyes appear in extreme close-up in the climactic gunfight of Leone's 'spaghetti' western, *The Good, the Bad and the Ugly* (1966), the shot is no longer principally informative about character (though it does disclose the relative coolness of the three protagonists); rather, as shown in Figure 4, the extreme close-up has become playful, even exuberant, one of many tactics utilised

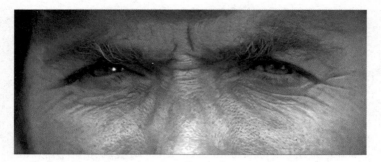

4 Extreme close-up: Clint Eastwood's eyes in *The Good, the Bad and the Ugly* (1966)

by the director in his reworking of the scenic choreography of the western. Similar shot distances may thus signify very differently according to the particular contexts in which they are utilised.

Height, angle and level

The first of these categories refers to the degree of elevation in the camera's positioning. As with disparate meanings of the same shot distance, variable effects can be generated by a seemingly identical choice of camera height. In Tim Burton's *Edward Scissorhands* (1990), for example, placing the camera strikingly low during one early interior scene amounts to a critique of postwar American suburbia by suggesting, depressingly, that a dull-coloured carpet stretches to infinity. In the Henry James adaptation *What Maisie Knew* (2013), however, the camera's low positioning is more sustained and functions to approximate the perspective on the world of its child protagonist (this option sometimes results in adults' heads being cropped, further emphasising the partiality of Maisie's knowledge of events occurring around her).

With respect to camera angle, three basic options are available: *high angle*, *straight-on angle* and *low angle*. If the straight-on angle is presented as neutral and devoid of emphasis, the other two permutations have often been correlated with specific meanings: broadly speaking, the high angle shot from above is taken to diminish the power of its subject, and the low angle shot from below, conversely, to enhance it. Yet, as with camera distances, such claims about the fixed significance of types of camera angle are suspect. Again, our reading of particular film sequences needs to be contextually sensitive: after all, low angle shots of a baby held up in the air by its parent scarcely impress as an image of power. Barthes argues similarly that 'the analogical relationship between "high angle shot" and "domination" strikes us as naïve' (Hillier, 1986: 279). Evidence for the greater semantic range of high angles can be found in the credits sequence of the Blaxploitation film *Shaft* (1971). When the camera zooms out from above its African American protagonist as he crosses a busy Manhattan street, he might be expected to appear ever more vulnerable, an insignificant figure in the metropolis; however, the use of high angle allows us better to recognise the cool with which he weaves through traffic – an early judgement about his mastery of urban space that is quickly confirmed as the film cuts to a straight-on, much closer shot of him giving an irate white motorist the finger.

As with angle, the spectator tends to become aware of level in cinematic framing only when there is significant variation from the norm. While the frame is generally balanced in mainstream cinema, filmmakers can alter it from the horizontal so as to produce a *canted shot* (sometimes referred to as an 'oblique shot' or 'Dutch angle'). A signature use of this technique occurs in *The Third Man* (1949), where a gathering sense of crisis in a noirish postwar Vienna is visually marked by canted shots that increase in obliqueness during the film (see Figure 5). However, the device survives into contemporary cinema, not least for its economy in evoking a world out of joint. In *The Constant Gardener* (2005), concerned with shady pharmaceutical testing in Africa, the lopsidedness of the frame in one sequence fulfils initially the low-grade function of showing the view from a truck that has crashed; more profoundly, however, the framing also hints at the region's unbalancing by dark forces.

Masking

While the canted shot skews the film image, other cinematographic practices offer alternatives to the image's rectangular format itself. In masked shots, variously shaped attachments to the camera lens block out some of the available light, leaving portions of the frame black or obscured. This device is most frequently used to mimic the

5 Canted angle in *The Third Man* (1949). Note also the scene's use of low-key lighting

effect of other optical devices such as a telescope or microscope or, as in countless war films, binoculars: very common is the cut from one army's general raising a pair of binoculars to an extreme long shot of the opposing forces, masked in the shape of the binocular lenses. Another variation in masking is the *iris shot*, whereby the usual rectangular image either contracts towards or opens out from a small circular point on the screen (respectively, *irising-out* and *irising-in*). Given that the heyday of the iris was in silent cinema and immediately afterwards, its use in contemporary film tends to be nostalgic or stylised (as with Michael Winterbottom's irising to advance the sense of self-conscious performance in *A Cock and Bull Story* (2005)).

Movement
None of the many cinematographic options discussed above implies or requires that the camera is *moving*. Yet cinema is a dynamic art not only because the projection of a series of discrete celluloid or digital images generates a sense of motion, but because the apparatus involved in recording them is itself often mobile. An accurate

account of the camera's movement, however, should distinguish between practices involving shifts in its entire body and those where there is only modification of a peripheral component. In this latter category would be placed, first of all, the *pan* and the *tilt shot* (respectively, rotations of the camera in the horizontal and the vertical planes, achieved not by its bodily relocation but by activation of a pivoting device attached to it). It is striking that some textbooks in professional cinematography argue against the use – or, at least, overuse – of pans and tilts. For Bruce Mamer, the pan is actually 'unnatural' since its systematic lateral movement falsifies the rapid, impressionistic, often reversible scanning of the visual field which is carried out during our extra-cinematic lives (2014: 11). Dangerously proffering certain techniques as the essence of cinema, while discounting others, this argument binds film aesthetics too closely to the properties of the human eye. Such biologically based reasoning has sometimes been used to counter another common way of achieving on-screen mobility without repositioning the camera itself: namely, the *zoom* (utilising a lens of variable focal length so as to produce a sensation of progressively moving towards or away from the subject – respectively, *zooming-in* and *zooming-out*). For Roy Thompson, wedded like Mamer to a realist approach that would effectively outlaw much distinctive filmmaking, the zoom is alien because it is 'a highly artificial way of recording a picture' (1998: 54).

Categorically distinct from zooms and pans and tilts are those techniques that *do* involve moving the camera itself. A basic distinction should be made here between horizontal and vertical manoeuvres. Horizontal camera motions commonly take the form of *tracking shots* (this term, deriving from tracks laid down to enable the movement of bulky film cameras, is still current, even though the balanced, lightweight equipment available now may not require such infrastructural support). A tracking shot can be varied in speed, rhythm and direction so as to generate diverse effects: if a slow, stalking motion of the camera is apt for enhancing the suspense of a horror film or thriller, it would be undesirably eerie in a costume drama, where tracking shots might instead trace nimble, circular patterns around participants in a formal dance. Movements in the vertical plane – the camera rising or descending on a mechanically operated mount of variable length – are referred to as *crane shots*. While horizontal and vertical camera motions are typically kept separate in shot design, they may sometimes be combined to striking effect. Here a bravura example is the three-minute opening shot of Orson Welles's film noir *Touch of Evil* (1958). After beginning at ground level, in a Mexican border town, the camera cranes upwards and then moves laterally for a rooftop perspective before descending and resuming a tracking motion along several streets. The same unbroken shot is extended so as to incorporate most conceivable directions of camera movement (up, down, left, right, forwards, backwards), as well as multiple rhythms (rapid approaches, slower advances, stately aerial sweeps) and variable distances (from the extreme close-up of a bomb attached to a car to extreme long shots of the cityscape). Besides advertising itself as a grand stylistic flourish, the shot also encompasses multiple individuals whose labyrinthine relationships will be disclosed as the film unfolds.

When a cut finally occurs in *Touch of Evil*, it signals a switch of cinematographic style. The measured movements of the camera give way, for a while, to a jerky motion as people run towards the site of the bomb explosion. This hectic, staccato effect is achieved by use of *handheld* equipment – quite innovatory at the time of Welles's work, but widespread, even institutionalised since in genres such as war and disaster films (*Cloverfield* (2008), set on a panicky night when New York is under monstrous attack, is a notably sustained venture in the handheld aesthetic). One hugely important piece of portable apparatus in this respect is the *Steadicam*, invented in the early 1970s by US cinematographer Garrett Brown. This incorporates a stabilising mount for the camera that is attached to the operator, thus reproducing the handheld camera's intimacy and extensive territorial range but without repeating its unsteady, even queasy locomotion. Discussion in Chapter 2 of Aleksandr Sokurov's film *Russian Ark* (2002) will consider how the Steadicam has modified not only mise-en-scène but also editing.

Focus

All of those camera movements so far described potentially affect one further property of the film image: its quality of focus. Here the filmmaker's selection from lenses that range from wide-angle through medium focal lengths to the telephoto will also be significant. Options include *shallow focus*, where the foremost plane of the image is sharply outlined in contrast to fuzzier middle and rear portions; *deep focus*, where all of the planes are defined clearly; and *racking* or *pulling focus*, where focal sharpness is redistributed in the course of a shot from foreground to background, or vice versa. As with all other cinematographic choices, these are more than merely technical matters. Deep focus, for example, first prominent in such geographically dispersed films as Erich von Stroheim's *Greed* (1924), Kenji Mizoguchi's *Osaka Elegy* (1936) and Jean Renoir's *The Rules of the Game* (1939), has figured in film studies as a topic of ideological and philosophical debate. Bazin argues in *What Is Cinema?* that, mimicking our natural habits of vision, deep focus is the most humane of film modes. 'Every technique relates to a metaphysic', he writes elsewhere (Hillier, 1985: 78); and, for Bazin, the philosophical significance of deep focus consists in its implying the unbrokenness of space and time, since such shot composition presents with perfect clarity multiple events that are occurring simultaneously on different planes. Yet it has been a key argument of this chapter that it is dangerous to derive fixed meanings from a particular technical choice. If deep focus in some films seems indeed to have harmonious, humane connotations, its occurrence elsewhere may be more ambiguous (as, for example, where it is combined with a canted camera angle). As with all other aspects of mise-en-scène, then, locally sensitive interpretation is necessary in order to assess the meaning or value of deep focus in a given context.

STOP and THINK

- Returning to the film sequence that you surveyed earlier for pro-filmic elements, unpack now its cinematography. Identify precisely choices of camera distance; heights, angles and levels of the camera; uses, if any, of masking the lens; varieties of camera movement; and focal selections. What meanings are produced, singly and collectively, by the cinematographic options taken in the sequence? Is there coherence – or perhaps dissonance – among the techniques used?
- Narrowing your focus still further, select just a few shots from the sequence (remembering that a shot is a segment of

continuous filming before a cut or some other transition). In each of these shots, alter at least one cinematographic variable. For example, the extreme long shot of Julie Andrews singing exultantly with her arms outstretched on an Austrian mountain at the start of *The Sound of Music* (1964) might remain but be masked now by binocular lenses, or might occur with the camera lowered in height from the sky to edelweiss level. How do the adjustments that you make transform the meaning of your chosen shots?

• Broadening your range of reference, select one or two of the cinematographic practices outlined above – the close-up, perhaps, or the pan, or the canted shot – and review their use in films with which you are familiar. Test one of this chapter's arguments by assessing whether the meanings generated by these techniques are relatively stable and uniform or, on the contrary, variable and context-specific.

Colour and its meanings

When the Russian writer Maxim Gorky attended an early programme of Lumière films in 1896, the new medium struck him not so much as freshly stimulating the senses as causing two kinds of sensory deficit. Chapter 3 will turn to Gorky's remarks on the soundlessness of film compared with everyday noise; here, however, we draw attention to his observations on film's disquieting lack of colour: 'Everything there – the earth, the trees, the people, the water and the air – is dipped in monotonous grey. Grey rays of the sun across the grey sky, grey eyes in grey faces, and the leaves of the trees are ashen grey' (Leyda, 1960: 407).

Gorky was, of course, writing during that earliest cinematic moment when monochrome images – their monochrome also quite undifferentiated tonally – were all that were possible. A little later, hand-painting of some film frames would begin, followed first by artificial colouring of sequences through stencilling, toning and tinting, then by capture of the entire colour spectrum on film's photographic medium itself, most vividly in the Technicolor process that was pioneered in 1917. Yet it is striking that in his very early contribution to commentary on cinema, Gorky should give the question of colour an

importance which it has occupied only occasionally in later film studies. While such a lack has been partly rectified by Bristol University's
recent programme of research in this field and by publication of a
number of important books (see this chapter's 'Selected reading'), film
studies has often been marked by what David Batchelor calls *chromophobia*: a tendency, seen by Batchelor as extending beyond coverage of
cinema to that of painting too, for colour as an object of interest to be
'systematically marginalized' and 'diminished' (2000: 22). There have
been only a few instances, in fact, when colour has been paramount
in thinking about film. Its growing availability to Hollywood before
World War II, for example, occasioned fierce debate between on the
one hand those welcoming it just as they had sound as an enhance-
ment of cinema's capacity to document the world fully, and on the
other hand anti-realists like the German-born critic Rudolf Arnheim
who deplored colour – as in his 1935 essay, 'Remarks on Colour Film'
– for threatening the aesthetics of cinema that had developed during
the monochrome era. More typically, however, film studies has either
treated colour cursorily or omitted it altogether. The topic's historic
lack of status is fairly reflected by the fact that it occupies only a few
pages even in the encyclopaedic account given of mise-en-scène by
Bordwell and Thompson in *Film Art*.

Bordwell and Thompson place colour within the pro-filmic elements of mise-en-scène, notably as a sub-class of 'setting'. This
makes some sense: colour signifies powerfully in cinematic locations ranging from the beige hospital spaces of *Dallas Buyers Club*
(2013) to the variously red, green and white portions of the baroque
restaurant in Peter Greenaway's *The Cook, the Thief, His Wife and
Her Lover* (1989). It is also to be found elsewhere in the pro-filmic
range, especially as a key attribute of costume. However, besides
dwelling, as it were, on the surface of objects scanned by the camera,
colour is also liable to be augmented, altered, even invented at the
cinematographic level. As in the case of *Three Kings*, filmmakers
working with celluloid may begin by choosing a stock that produces
unexpected colour relations. During filming itself they might select
from a number of filtering media that moderate or even exclude certain colours while promoting others (Steven Soderbergh's *Traffic*
(2000) systematically uses colour filters to achieve three distinct
looks of bleached-out yellow, steely blue and vibrant primaries,

each corresponding to one of the film's several narrative strands). Colour may also be chemically modified after filming via manipulations of the developing process. All of these adjustments to colour are feasible even without taking into account the multiple creative possibilities that have been opened up by the decision of many current filmmakers to shoot on digital videotape rather than traditional stock.

However it is achieved, colour performs a number of functions in film. Besides serving as a device for historical and geographical authentication (black for Victorian England, say), or as a means of genre specification (few dull browns crop up in 1950s American musicals, few pinks in Ken Loach's radical political dramas), colour may, as in *Traffic*, contribute towards narrative organisation. Exemplary here is the Chinese martial arts film *Hero* (2002), which has a tripartite colour scheme: red and gold, white and green, and blue. But whereas in Soderbergh's film these colour motifs are distributed spatially, in *Hero* they are segmented temporally, with one replacing the other to mark the shift to another version of key events that are in dispute. The example of *Hero* also alerts us to colour's symbolic and thematic potentialities. Consider briefly some work by one of contemporary Hollywood's more distinctive colourists, Tim Burton. In *Edward Scissorhands*, the vivid primaries used for the suburb's houses would seem to connote optimism and well-being; however, the excessive saturation of these colours, coupled with the fact that no darker or mixed shades are visible, alerts the spectator to a critique of suburban blandness and conformity. By contrast, black in the clothing worn by Johnny Depp as Edward carries suggestions of rebelliously Gothic, romantic, even punk sensibility (as well as hinting at a racial diversity repressed by the all-white suburb). While maintaining a thematic approach to colouring, however, Burton reverses the value of particular hues in the animated *Tim Burton's Corpse Bride* (2005). Bright primary colours signify positively now, suggesting the vibrancy of the film's underworld as against the oppressive society above ground that subsists in a grey as monotonous and desolate as that observed by Gorky.

Variations of this kind across the work of a single director indicate the need for us to be sensitive to film colour's multiple interpretative possibilities. Film studies requires alertness to the many possible forms of what the art critic John Gage calls 'colour-thinking' (1993: 8). Experimental British director Derek Jarman, who worked with colour in painting and gardening as well as in cinema, evokes a state virtually of chromatic chaos when he refers to 'the bordello of the spectrum': one person's 'green of birth' might be another's 'colour of pus' (1995: 52, 70). While Jarman makes a fair point about people's differing chromatic sensibilities, it would be unsatisfactory for study of film colour to consist simply in inventorying a mass of subjective impressions. One way to move beyond discussion of individual tastes, then, is to explore the cultural determinations of colour on screen. Chromatic effects in film have, to begin with, a history: the Technicolor sequences of *The Wizard of Oz* carried a greater utopian charge in Depression-era America than they can do in the colour-saturated consumer economy of the United States today. Chromatic effects also have a geography: the 'colour world of England', for instance, 'is not the same as that of Berlin' (Batchelor, 2000: 37). In similar vein, the Soviet film director and theorist Sergei Eisenstein acknowledges that 'different countries have different notions of colour. For example, white here is not associated with grief, whereas for the Chinese it is the colour of mourning' (1996: 323). Finally, we should also register and explore 'the gendering of colour' (Gage, 1993: 208). Without endorsing a crudely classificatory approach that looks out for 'masculine' earth tones and 'feminine' lavenders and lilacs, sensitivity to the relations in particular film contexts between colour coding and sexual politics is important.

The history of colour in cinema is one of its *normalisation*. From patchy beginnings in only the most commercially advantaged cinematic cultures, it has come to be globally adopted: part, indeed, of the common sense of film now. This naturalisation of colour, however, means that in our period heightened significance may be accrued by work that is variously shot or processed in monochrome (or, using less technically precise terminology, 'black-and-white'). Recently, colour has been renounced not only by avant-gardists but by some directors still aiming for mass audiences: Michael Hazanavicius's Oscar-winning *The Artist* (2011), for instance, or Alexander Payne's *Nebraska* (2013), or Ben Wheatley's English Civil War drama, *A Field in England* (2013), or Pawel Pawlikowski's

Ida (2013), set in a bleak Poland of the early 1960s. If each of these films aptly utilises monochrome to advance a sense of 'pastness', that is not to say that this stylistic choice conduces only to nostalgia or elegy. Colour's expunging from film may, in fact, be as semiotically rich and varied as its exploitation.

Case study: *12 Years a Slave* (2013)

For Steve McQueen, the British director of *12 Years a Slave*, fashioning his film's visual dimension was charged with ethical and political seriousness. 'All I wanted to do was see those images', he says in an interview, referring to the many shots he includes of African American slaves being abused, punished, even killed: 'That has always been the power for me. Seeing those images' (McQueen and Gates, 2013: 1). Mise-en-scène, then, he conceives as a principal means of political intervention, intended to counter sanitised, sentimental imagery of slavery in the United States that extends back through other films such as *Gone with the Wind* (1939) to the photographs and paintings of their slave 'families' that paternalistic slaveholders commissioned during the nineteenth century. However, if there is great promise in McQueen's attempt to transform slavery's visual repertoire by his framing of scenes of violence, there are dangers too. Scholars remind us that making a spectacle of punishment was central to how slavery functioned as a system. As Jasmine Nichole Cobb writes, 'an entire visual culture' was designed around 'displays of violence and the promotion of surveillance': 'Slavery depended upon racialized notions of visibility and objective observation [...] making visual culture the central location for the sedimentation of slavery's faulty racial logics' (2014: 340).

This sense of the visual as crucial both to slavery's institutional reproduction and to its possible undoing makes *12 Years a Slave* an apt choice for studying mise-en-scène. Here, therefore, we consider a short sequence of the film that starts some forty-seven minutes in and concludes three minutes later. The episode begins with Chapin, overseer of the first plantation on which Solomon Northup is enslaved following his kidnapping, exiting the frame after he has saved Northup from lynching by the vengeful Tibeats but otherwise done nothing to alleviate his desperate situation (tied by the neck to an overhanging tree branch with only the fact that his feet just reach the ground preventing him from being strangled). The sequence concludes, after a change in the natural lighting that indicates that Northup's punishment extends into the evening, with his being being cut free by the plantation owner Ford. How should we evaluate mise-en-scène here, in particular the elements of shot distance, focus and setting?

Careful consideration is needed of how, exactly, the viewer is positioned with regard to this spectacle of Northup's punishment almost to the point of death. A few moments before this scene, challenging Tibeats's provocative assertion that the carpentry he is doing on a new plantation building is not square, Northup has said: 'It's all a matter of perspective.' Perspective, now rendered an issue of great ethical moment, is vital to consider in the sequence under discussion. McQueen's shot selection here potentially elicits identification between us as viewers and Northup's persecutors who wish to look upon his punishment. Responding in particular to a long shot of this site of violence that lasts significantly more than a minute, Valerie Smith speaks of an 'unbearably long take' that 'requires viewers to watch the scene of Northup's torment and to be aware of our status as spectators' (2014: 363). At the same time, however, the ethical problem of gazing indifferently upon Northup's suffering is self-consciously posed by McQueen's shot design, raising the possibility of the film viewer's moral adjustment. Choices of camera positioning and focal depth are especially important in this regard. Chapin the overseer, for example, is clearly seen in the background of one shot, gazing towards Northup; while not absolutely sharing Northup's viewing position, the camera's placement close to him at this point evokes in the film's spectator identification with the suffering figure rather than complacent occupation of the oppressor's perspective. Something similar occurs a bit later in the sequence, when, with the camera placed just behind the suspended Northup, Ford's wife appears on the balcony of the plantation house. McQueen allows us to register in the same composition both the luxurious mansion and – out of focus, but still clearly decipherable – the noose around Northup's neck, subtly unveiling how slaveholders' privilege was enabled and sustained by punishment of others. The shot bears out a fact about slavery noted by Brian Jarvis: 'Punishment was not an unfortunate by-product of a means of production; economic and punitive imperatives were irrevocably integrated' (2004: 81).

There may be risks in the sheer vividness with which Northup's individual suffering is realised in this sequence. From his first work in video art through to his direction of the earlier feature films *Hunger* (2008) and *Shame* (2011), McQueen has been fascinated by the particularities of bodies put into heightened situations; unsurprisingly, then, in this scene from *12 Years a Slave* his camera is attentive to the distortions of Northup's body as he struggles to avoid hanging himself. While some shots show the totality of his awkwardly aligned figure, others venture closer, registering graphically his harrowed face and even his feet and lower legs as they slither in the mud. The spectator may be drawn by these vivid details to perceive individualised suffering, rather than any allusion to slavery's institutional violence. This would make the sequence vulnerable to comments made by the Slovenian political and cultural theorist Slavoj Žižek against undue emphasis on what he terms 'subjective' violence. By subjective violence, Žižek means visible aggressions 'performed by a clearly identifiable agent' (2008: 1); as a category, it is to be contrasted with the less immediately visible 'systemic' violence, that is to say 'the often catastrophic consequences of the smooth functioning of our economic and political systems' (1). The problem with visual representations of subjective violence, for Žižek, is precisely their powerful, direct effect upon the spectator: 'the overpowering horror of violent acts and empathy with the victims inexorably function as a lure which prevents us from thinking' (3). Applied to the sequence from *12 Years a Slave*, this argument would have it that the horror of Northup's near-strangulation and the procuring of audience empathy with him inhibit thinking about the systemic violence of slavery (of which the appalling cruelty directed against Northup constitutes only a fragment).

Evidence can be gathered from McQueen's film, however, to counter such reasoning and to suggest that in fact subjective and systemic violences may be recognised simultaneously here. Certainly, images from elsewhere in *12 Years a Slave* place Northup's suffering in the context of collective trauma: the film's opening shot, for example, shows him standing amidst fellow slaves. Yet even within the sequence under discussion, aspects of mise-en-scène serve to dramatise slavery's systemic functioning, Again, here, questions of framing and focus are crucial. As the suspended Northup is seen in the painfully drawn-out long shot, for instance, other slaves are shown going unobtrusively about their labours in the background (Figure 6). The effect is not one of their callous indifference to his plight, but, rather, of their recognition of its unexceptional quality, powerfully evoking for the spectator the routinisation of cruelty during slavery. In another shot from this sequence, Northup's head, positioned close to the camera, is blurred, while sharply focused in the background are slave children continuing to play. As with the previous shot, the viewer is prompted by this image to co-ordinate investment in Northup's suffering with larger reflection on slavery's normalisation of violence.

It is important also to consider the setting of this episode. *12 Years a Slave* is, unexpectedly perhaps, a beautiful film, replete with well-crafted images of lush vegetation, silvery-blue bayous and beguiling sunsets. In the scene under review, the tree from which Northup is hanging is covered picturesquely by Spanish moss; behind, the plantation mansion, painted a pleasingly pure white, is overspread by foliage. To enhance the aesthetic effect of this setting, McQueen also designs his frames with formal sensitivity: the long shot of Northup hanging, for example, observes *the rule of thirds*, situating his figure harmoniously against both vertical and horizontal axes (again as shown in Figure 6). While there is the danger that some spectators will succumb to moral amnesia in gazing upon this attractively composed scene, a more likely reaction, however, is shock at the juxtaposition between formal beauty and symmetry on the one hand and moral ugliness and distortion on the other. There are parallels here with the landscape of violence mapped by Toni Morrison in her novel of African American slavery, *Beloved* (1987): 'Fire and brimstone all right, but hidden in lacy groves. Boys hanging from the most beautiful sycamores in the world' (1988: 6).

The protagonist of *Beloved* experiences a terrifying moment of being distracted by this beauty from the suffering of fellow slaves:

6 The spectacle of punishment: Chiwetel Ejiofor as Solomon Northup in *12 Years a Slave* (2013)

'It shamed her – remembering the wonderful soughing trees rather than the boys' (6). If such moral diversion is also possible during this episode of *12 Years a Slave*, it is nevertheless guarded against by McQueen's formal choices. Variable shot distances and focal depths, as discussed above, combine to register the disruptiveness in this alluring setting of the violence aimed at Northup. The disturbing effect of actor performance should be noted, too, given Chiwetel Ejiofor's embodiment of his suffering as he hangs from the tree. However, while this discussion has tried to show the usefulness of mise-en-scène analysis, the partiality of such an approach should also be acknowledged. The meaning of this episode, after all, inheres not in a single image but in the articulation of several shots (for example, cuts from more distanced, potentially more distracted shots of Northup to tighter framing of his pain). Hence the importance of moving beyond individual shot analysis to a concern with editing, the subject of this book's next chapter. Similarly, this episode's meanings are not generated by visual components alone but by sound design also. As the sequence plays out, the noise of cicadas buzzing – evocative of a sleepy afternoon in the American South – is violated by sounds of Solomon's choking and of his boots squelching in the mud. Suggestively, just a few moments before, Northup has said to Tibeats, 'I simply ask you use all your senses before rendering judgement' – advice we will heed in Chapter 3 by extending consideration of film's formal qualities from the visual to the aural.

Selected reading

General

Bordwell, David and Kristin Thompson (2012), *Film Art: An Introduction*, 10th ed. (New York: McGraw-Hill).
An indispensable text: lucid, compendious and sumptuously illustrated; at times, however, risks sealing off stylistic topics from film studies' ideological and cultural concerns.

Corrigan, Timothy and Patricia White (2012), *The Film Experience: An Introduction*, 3rd ed. (Boston: Bedford / St Martin's).
Covers a broader range of film topics than Bordwell and Thompson, but still treats mise-en-scène in great detail and with plentiful visual illustration.

Gibbs, John (2002), *Mise-en-scène: Film Style and Interpretation* (London: Wallflower).
Short, helpful text which, enlighteningly, includes coverage of fierce postwar debates over the place of mise-en-scène in film studies.

Gibbs, John and Douglas Pye (eds) (2005), *Style and Meaning: Studies in the Detailed Analysis of Film* (Manchester: Manchester University Press).
Engaging, wide-ranging collection; like this chapter, the editors take it as axiomatic that sensitivity to film style provides 'a foundation for the full range of approaches to and interests in the products of cinema'.

Acting

Taylor, Aaron (ed.) (2012), *Theorizing Film Acting* (New York: Routledge).
Timely, stimulating collection that approaches film acting from a range of critical positions; case studies include Heath Ledger's work in *The Dark Knight* (2008).

Wojcik, Pamela Robertson (ed.) (2004), *Movie Acting: The Film Reader* (New York: Routledge).
Generous sampling of materials on theories and practices of screen acting, including reflections by early as well as contemporary critics.

Cinematography

Goodridge, Mike and Tim Grierson (2012), *Cinematography* (Lewes: ILEX).
Brings together revealing interviews with a global cast of directors of photography, and thus makes an excellent, practically oriented counterpart to academic studies of cinematography.

Colour

Coates, Paul (2010), *Cinema and Colour: The Saturated Image* (London: BFI / Palgrave Macmillan).

Combines theoretical sophistication and formal sensitivity in studying colour in many films, principally from art cinema and the older Hollywood.

Peacock, Steven (2010), *Colour* (Manchester: Manchester University Press).

Astute, eloquent studies of colour symbolism in six films, mainly from European art cinema; despite this narrow range of reference, an excellent prompt to thinking about colour's central place in what Peacock calls 'the plastics of cinema'.

Watkins, Elizabeth (2015), *Film Theories and Philosophies of Colour: The Residual Image* (Abingdon: Routledge).

Breaks new ground by developing a sophisticated psychoanalysis of film colour, exploring its place in the construction of the spectator's subjectivity and sexual identity.

Costume

McDonald, Tamar Jeffers (2010), *Hollywood Catwalk: Costume and Transformation in American Film* (London: I. B. Tauris).

Enjoyable and clearly written study, albeit with a narrower geographical and generic remit than other studies of costume listed here.

Munich, Adrienne (ed.) (2011), *Fashion in Film* (Bloomington: Indiana University Press).

Excellent collection, attentive to costume's varieties and meanings in many film cultures besides the US. Who could resist a book that includes an essay entitled 'What to Wear in a Vampire Film'?

Street, Sarah (2001), *Costume and Cinema: Dress Codes in Popular Film* (London: Wallflower).

Good, succinct introduction to this element of film stylistics.

Lighting

Thompson, Lara (2015), *Film Light: Meaning and Emotion* (Manchester: Manchester University Press).

Pioneering study of this neglected aspect of film aesthetics, venturing beyond technical description of lighting regimes in sensitive analyses of their cognitive and emotional effects upon spectators.

Online resources

'Film Terms Glossary', www.filmsite.org/filmterms.html.

This glossary is the strongest strand of an otherwise intellectually variable website (filmsite.org): a comprehensive, accessible lexicon (covering other areas of film studies besides stylistics).

'Observations on Film Art', www.davidbordwell.net/blog/.

Part of David Bordwell's 'website on cinema', this regularly updated blog by Bordwell and Kristin Thompson, authors of *Film Art: An Introduction*, addresses film stylistics in engaging essays (some in video form).

'The American Widescreen Museum', www.widescreenmuseum.com.

Awkwardly jokey in tone at times, but a well-illustrated resource on early developments in, among other things, film colour.

2
Film editing:
theories and histories

The Last Tycoon (1976), adapted for the screen by Harold Pinter from F. Scott Fitzgerald's unfinished last novel, offers a waspish insight into the status of the film editor. While Fitzgerald already subjects to corrosive critique the Hollywood movie world in which his book is set, Pinter adds a plot twist of his own that is revealing about the industry's uneven distribution of power to those it employs. As the lights come up after a trial screening in a studio's projection room, it is discovered that the chief editor, or 'cutter', has quietly died of a heart attack. Not once during this traumatic episode did he draw attention to his plight. An assistant speculates that the editor did not want to disturb the omnipotent and terrifying studio head, also present at the screening.

This unfortunate character's fate is irresistible as an allegory of the invisibility of the editor – and of editing practice generally – in much of our thinking about film. Such human and conceptual neglect has a long history. Where they have been recognised at all, editors have often been regarded more as technicians or assembly-line operatives than as figures engaged in highly creative work. Historically, their status has also been shaped by a certain gendering of professional roles within filmmaking. It is noticeable that while openings as directors or screenwriters have often failed to materialise for women, including in Hollywood, opportunities have existed for them to develop careers in editing. A long tradition of female American editors descends from Dorothy Spencer and Margaret Booth in mid-century through still-active older figures like Thelma Schoonmaker and Susan E. Morse to a younger generation exemplified by Maryann Brandon and Mary Jo Markey, both collaborators with J. J. Abrams on the *Star Trek* projects.

Women's early entry into editing in Hollywood, according to editor Walter Murch, was eased by its association with stereotypically feminised labour such as sewing and librarianship. In his dialogues on film editing with Murch, Michael Ondaatje suggests that a gendered opposition of 'masculine' director/cinematographer and 'feminine' editor may still be stubbornly in place: 'the man is the hunter-gatherer, coming back with stuff for her to cook!' (2002: 25–6). This sexist hierarchy can also be observed in film contexts other than Hollywood. In his pioneering silent documentary *Man with a Movie Camera* (1929), the Soviet director Dziga Vertov restores the editor to visibility by including shots of a woman seated at a table inspecting, cutting and splicing footage. Yet while her editing miraculously animates what a moment earlier had seemed simply still images, it still, as an activity, lacks charisma or bravura when set against the heroism of the film's male cinematographer, who risks incineration in a metal smelting works or suspends himself perilously above a dam in order to obtain material.

This chapter, however, is not intended as an exposé of the film editor's vulnerability to prejudices of gender and class (important though such concerns are). Instead, more broadly, it aims to address Ondaatje's complaint that editing is often 'unimagined' or 'overlooked' in film criticism (2002: xi). As reparation, we will explore the history and value of several editing practices. Film editing will be presented here as not merely supplementary to or confirmatory of the real work that has already been done in production itself, but, rather, as a form of creativity and invention. In this respect the chapter follows the lead of the postwar French director Robert Bresson, who describes the careful articulation of pictures and sounds that is achieved during editing as a film's third 'birth', generating something qualitatively distinct from the work's two earlier embodiments in the scriptwriting and shooting phases. Or as Eric Rohmer, a central figure in the New Wave in France, puts it: 'In an extreme case, I could absent myself from the shooting, but I'd have to be there at the editing' (Hillier, 1986: 89).

Beyond the shot

Attempts have sometimes been made, in a scientific spirit, to understand film as a system of communication based on clearly identifiable
and tabulable rules. The Soviet director-theorist Sergei Eisenstein,
for example, experimented with analysing cinematic sequences
according to principles of musical notation. Several later theorists
were influenced more by the postwar 'linguistic turn' in the human
sciences and sought therefore a 'grammar' of film that might be
compared with models of the structuring and functioning of language itself (most ambitious in this regard was Christian Metz, in
studies including *Film Language*, translated into English in 1974).
Whether underpinned by musicology, by linguistics or by other
intellectual traditions, all systematic approaches to cinema of this
kind face the problem of identifying film's fundamental building
block, its irreducible unit of sense-making. What, in this medium,
is structurally analogous to the note in music or the phoneme in
language?

The most frequently proposed candidate for this role in film is
the shot: that is to say, an unbroken sequence of action recorded
by one camera. As Noël Carroll summarises, 'the moving picture
shot is the basic element of cinematic communication' (2008: 112).
While generally put into combination with many others in the finished work, the shot seems already a bearer of meaning in itself,
tempting us to compare it to a word in language. The shot is of
course highly variable in length: given film's normal running speed
of twenty-four frames per second, a shot may occupy any number
of frames from one to several thousand. At the extreme of minia-
turisation, Robert Breer's experimental short animation work *Fist
Fight* (1964) consists of shots each lasting only a single frame, the
result being flickering speed well in excess even of MTV tempo.
More common in film history, however, are examples of the contrary impulse to extend or elasticate the shot, seeking, so to speak,
to endow a humble word with the semantic scope and richness
of a sentence. Chapter 1 described the sustained opening shot of
Welles's *Touch of Evil*. A more ambitious elongation still of the
minimal unit of the shot occurs in Hitchcock's thriller *Rope* (1948).
Each reel of film Hitchcock was using yielded only ten minutes of

footage, preventing him from attempting a single-shot work; nevertheless, *Rope* includes only ten shots in its seventy-five-minute running time, and represses the evidence even of such minimal cutting by typically ending one sequence with a freeze frame and starting the next with the reloaded camera in the same position.

Nearer to our own time, an extremely inventive stretching of the shot occurs in a film mentioned in Chapter 1: *Russian Ark*, directed by Aleksandr Sokurov. In an accompanying documentary, Sokurov speaks of his aim 'to make a film in one breath'. During the ninety minutes of *Russian Ark*, then, a specially adapted Steadicam using digital videotape rather than 35mm film noses without interruption through the ballrooms, galleries, lobbies and backstairs of St Petersburg's Winter Palace. This spatial fluidity is matched historically, as episodes from three centuries of Russia's past are enacted in the various rooms. Sokurov's decision to avoid cutting is not merely a case of technical adventurism. On the contrary, the extreme duration of his shot is thematically motivated, seeking to evoke the palace's unbroken significance in Russian history. The regimes of Peter the Great, Catherine the Great, Nicholas II and Stalin are understood here as comparable in their attempts to consolidate Russian power, thereby lending themselves to unification by the camera's breathlessly sustained movement rather than to artificial separation by cuts or any other transitional device.

It would be incorrect, however, to regard *Russian Ark* as entirely free from protocols of editing. While the pictures may have been captured in one unbroken motion, the film's soundtrack was incorporated discontinuously during post-production. At the level of image, too, editorial interventions are still discernible, albeit faintly. There can be no escaping what Murch describes as a film editor's obligation 'to carry, like a sacred vessel, the focus of attention of the audience and move it in interesting ways around the surface of the screen' (Ondaatje, 2002: 277). Rather than redirecting the spectator's interest by overt transitions, *Russian Ark* achieves this by a kind of *in-camera editing*: that is to say, moving into and out of close-up within the same camera deployment, or passing out of one location and into another. As Sam Rohdie reminds us: 'all films are edited and a *mise en scène* is already a choice of relations, editing by other means' (2006: 21). Like those very brief, single-shot

'actualities' of trains or crowds or other kinds of everyday movement with which commercial film history began in the late nineteenth century, *Russian Ark* is already – if minimally – edited in the
very choices of action on which to open and close.

Nevertheless, Sokurov's film does represent a strain of cinema in
which the shot, in itself, prevails at the expense of editing patterns.
Despite the thematic grounding of its unbroken compositional mode,
Russian Ark may thus be vulnerable to the onslaught which Eisenstein
launched in an article of 1926 against the Hungarian film theorist Béla
Balázs. In Balázs's thesis that film's artistic distinctiveness lies in the
'poetic' or 'figurative' quality of the photographically derived shot,
Eisenstein detected a strain of bourgeois individualism, or what he
called 'starism': manifested on this occasion not by any flesh-and-
blood figure involved in film production, but by the single shot itself,
separated in the critic's mind from relations with other shots and
consequently exalted or aggrandised. The resulting baleful situation,
as Eisenstein sees it, is *'The shot itself as "star"'* (2010a: 79). Such
absolutising of the shot to the detriment of combinations achieved
in editing is anathema to Eisenstein, who asserts in the same article
that *'The expressive effect of cinema is the result of juxtapositions'* (80).
Where Balázs's key piece of filmmaking apparatus is the camera that
generates evocative photographic images in the first place, Eisenstein
emphasises instead the scissors that cuts them up (his essay, indeed,
is sardonically entitled 'Béla Forgets the Scissors').

Reserving until later in this chapter a detailed discussion of
Eisenstein's preferred mode of splicing and juxtaposing sequences,
we should note here the general importance of his claim that film's
identity as a medium inheres in editing. It is not necessary to sign up
to his political programme for cinema to be persuaded by his assertion that the single shot is less the commanding structure imagined
by Balázs than 'a detached house, as it were, in "Montage Street"'
(Eisenstein, 2010b: 11). Aiming always to go 'beyond the shot' – as
the title of another article, published in 1929, puts it – Eisenstein
forcefully redefines the minimal unit of cinematic composition, so
that it is understood now as an articulated series of images rather
than any image in solitude. Here he not only puts the practice and
theory of film on a radically new footing, but, in passing, offers
retrospective rationalisation of the first film exhibition practices.

Those late nineteenth- and early twentieth-century suppliers of programmes of single-shot films to vaudeville theatres and fairground booths were, in effect, the earliest cinematic editors, their choice of a particular running order suggesting they had already grasped the importance of shot combination and juxtaposition.

An equally forceful dethroning of the single shot was carried out by Eisenstein's collaborator in early Soviet cinema, Lev Kuleshov. Witnesses to experiments Kuleshov conducted in his Moscow film workshop vary considerably in their recollection of details, but all testify to experiencing a sudden revelation of the power of editing. According to the most authoritative first-hand report, Kuleshov took fairly neutral close-ups of the actor Ivan Mosjukhin from an existing film and spliced them together with, successively, single shots of a bowl of soup on a table, a woman's body lying in a coffin and a little girl playing with a toy bear. Although Mosjukhin's facial expression was constant across the three sequences, spectators recorded admiration for his chameleon-like ability to evoke hunger, or grief, or fatherly love. Limited perhaps in their individual eloquence, shots of the actor's face accrued significance by virtue of their interrelation with other images. Unpersuaded, Don Fairservice objects that there would have been spatial and logical incongruities between Mosjukhin's material and the new footage, or that the actor's expression must already have been articulate enough to permit spectators to infer particular emotional states (2001: 180–3). Yet even allowing for such empirical uncertainties, Kuleshov's experiment retains its power to unsettle the shot's autonomy and to question its foundational status in the study of film.

Summing up the theoretical advances achieved by Kuleshov, Eisenstein and other cinematic pioneers, Robert Stam writes that 'The shot gained meaning, in other words, only relationally, as part of a larger system' (2000: 38). While a crucial insight, however, this may still seem somewhat abstract and obscure. What is important now is to go beyond mere acknowledgement of film's juxtaposition of one shot with others in 'a larger system', and to outline and evaluate the precise forms that such shot combination may take. Rather than a singular editing pattern in film, there are several competing modes, all with their distinct histories, processes and – arguably – ideological dispositions.

Principles and practices of continuity editing

As a term for a particular kind of editing, 'continuity' appears quite late in film history. Citations given in the *Oxford English Dictionary* for the word used in a cinematic context indicate that, at first, it functioned simply as a synonym for a screenplay. One entry from 1926 states that it is 'the correct name for the working script'; another, from 1940, has Scott Fitzgerald claiming during his Hollywood scriptwriting days that he has 'written a really brilliant continuity'. The *OED* includes no reference before this time to 'continuity' as a distinctive form of editing that puts a premium on narrative smoothness and coherence. There is thus a pronounced lexicographical lag behind the facts of actually existing film production. Many scholars – most exhaustively David Bordwell, Janet Staiger and Kristin Thompson in *The Classical Hollywood Cinema* (1985) – have shown that, in mainstream American cinema at least, the principles of what came to be called continuity editing were largely formulated and institutionalised as early as the end of World War I.

This accurate dating of continuity editing's codification still leaves out of account some twenty years of filmmaking after the Lumière brothers' first public display of their cinematograph in 1895. First-wave directors of films longer than a single shot often combined sequences quite discontinuously so as to maximise spectacle rather than fashion a coherent narrative line (a topic for further discussion in Chapter 4); as Bordwell, Staiger and Thompson write: 'Time, space, and logic did not fit together unproblematically at this early point' (1985: 251). As the overwhelming mass of spectators around the world is now most familiar with films made broadly on continuity principles, this reminder of alternative editing logics is salutary. If continuity editing has come to dominate global production, it has done so for its effective contribution towards highly profitable narrative cinema, not because it is intrinsically superior to other forms of editing or is somehow encrypted in film's DNA. Rival practices not only predated continuity editing, but have continued to exist alongside it (if sometimes in obscure or peripheral contexts). The story of film editing, then, is best understood not by any linear or teleological schema but, rather, as one of historical and geographical variations, incorporating the perhaps temporary success of one particular mutation.

Positioning continuity editing as just one option among a number of possibilities, we can now attempt to describe its principles and protocols. There is irony in being so explicit since, unlike other forms of editing discussed below that flamboyantly advertise themselves, the continuity mode often aims at self-effacement to the point of invisibility. The Hollywood editor Tom Rolf, whose credits include *Taxi Driver* and Michael Mann's *Heat* (1995), speaks for many practitioners within this tradition when he says that 'the unseen cut is the way it should be. You don't want to remind people they're looking at a movie' (Oldham, 2012a: 128). This language, however, is not merely normative, according a particular cinematic practice the status of unarguable common sense (as, in Chapter 1, we saw industry professionals doing with specific choices of lighting and cinematography); it is also lacking in historical perspective. While often unobserved by us now because of our long habituation to it, cinematic cutting between shots *was* noticed by early audiences to the point, at times, of puzzlement or disorientation. The 'invisibility' of continuity editing, then, was not a given from the start, but is an effect of its long subsequent history.

Before turning in detail to the cut itself, reference should be made to three other of continuity editing's transitions from shot to shot. Early films in this mode make especially heavy use of the *dissolve* (or *lap-dissolve*), in which the incoming image is superimposed on the outgoing one and gradually replaces it; the *wipe*, whereby a line travelling either horizontally or vertically across the screen pushes away one image to clear a space for the next; and the *fade*, a slower manoeuvre during which the screen either becomes progressively darker so that an image disappears (*fade-out*) or progressively lighter so that a new one can emerge (*fade-in*). These bridging devices enable a range of expressive effects. A dissolve from one sequence to another, for example, might suggest a shorter interval between these events than a fade would, or it could imply greater closeness between two characters or spaces shown in outgoing and incoming shots respectively than would a cut from one to the other. As the independent American director John Sayles says to explain his use of transitions other than cuts in *Lone Star* (1996), a film set among entangled racial communities on the modern US/Mexico border: 'A cut is very much a tear. You use a cut to say there's a separation between this thing and that thing' (Sayles and Smith, 1998: 230).

While the dissolve, the wipe and the fade were routinised by such cinemas as classical Hollywood, they are liable to seem too conspicuously artificial for most current needs. Still with many exceptions, of course, these transitional devices thus tend to occur now where a nostalgic or parodic or artfully self-aware effect is required. Testament to this is given by Mark Livolsi, reflecting on his incorporation of wipes in editing the Owen Wilson and Vince Vaughn vehicle, *Wedding Crashers* (2005): 'wipes can live in a comedy environment because they're whimsical, like a page turning' (Oldham, 2012b: 20). Generally speaking, however, the dominant form of punctuation between shots in modern continuity editing is *the straight cut*, where one shot instantaneously replaces another but without causing the viewer significant spatial or temporal disorientation. Patterned relationships of various kinds between the first shot and its replacement serve to make the transition more navigable still. As well as consistencies of character or location across the cut, there may be pronounced visual harmonies or antitheses. In a lakeside scene in Ang Lee's *Brokeback Mountain* (2005), for instance, a shot showing one of the male lovers positioned towards the right edge of the frame is balanced by the next shot of his partner in the frame's left half, evoking the emotional separation of the two men while still affirming the continuity of time and space. Besides matching graphically in such a way, continuity editing can also *match on action*. Exemplary of this is when a cut is made between two phases of a sustained event. From ground level, a woman is shown, say, starting to climb a flight of stairs; the next shot is a high-angle view of her reaching the top. This avoids the potential tedium of seeing every step negotiated, while still having sufficient continuity of action to render unproblematic the time and space that have been edited out (of course, an art film intent on registering each minimal increment of time, or a documentary exposing hardship in high-rise housing, might find it opportune to restore what has been elided).

As these examples of continuity practice suggest, this type of editing seeks generally to render spaces on screen comprehensible to and negotiable by the spectator. One of the key strategies here is *découpage* (a term borrowed by cinema from the French for 'cutting up or out'). Whereas early in film history events tended to be staged relatively far from a fixed camera position, *découpage* aims to cut up the space of action so that audiences may grasp it in both its totality and its significant, intimate details. Often, in the construction of a mainstream sequence, an initial long-distance, or *establishing*, shot of a key locus of action – a particular building, say, or landscape – gives way to a series of closer shots of protagonists or objects that require our attention. Paul Greengrass's *Captain Phillips* (2013), for instance, opens with a long shot of an affluent New England home, before cutting to closer interior shots that introduce us to the title character (played by Tom Hanks). The next sequence initiates the dialogical or comparative structure of the film, but follows a similar rhythm: a long shot of an impoverished Somali settlement gives way to closer views of the particular villagers about to go to sea as pirates.

Continuity editing is fluid in its interweaving of expansive and restricted shots of the narrative space. However, spatial prescriptions also apply in this editing mode. Among the most familiar of its protocols is *the 180-degree rule*, which presumes that a horizontal *axis of action* divides the visual field into two semicircles. Labelled AB, this imaginary line can be seen in Figure 7. Proponents of continuity editing suggest that, broadly speaking, any cut from a first to a second shot of the same scene should respect and reinforce the axis of action, rather than transgress it by inclusion instead of a shot originating from a camera position on the other side of the line. This editing convention aims to preserve the comprehensibility and coherence of spatial relations in a film: when it is not followed, some confusion may be experienced by the spectator. To demonstrate this, it is helpful to refer again to Figure 7. In the first of two shots illustrated here (camera position 1), a couple is shown talking, with the man on the right, the woman on the left. Consider, though, the effect of cutting next to a medium shot of the woman only, framed from the other side of the axis of action (camera position 2). Now she appears on the right of the frame, with the direction of her gaze reversed, which suggests unhelpfully that her (out-of-shot) male companion no longer holds her interest.

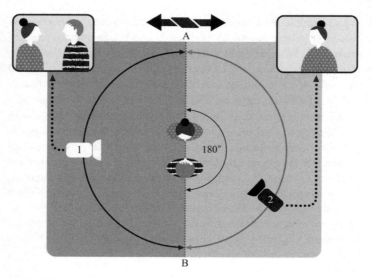

7 The 180-degree rule in continuity editing

Despite the rigour implied by its name, however, the 180-degree rule is not fixed or binding. To begin with, unbroken movement by the camera to-and-fro across the line during a particular sequence demonstrates that the axis of action may shift ceaselessly without this necessarily becoming problematical for the viewer. Second, even filmmakers working broadly within the continuity tradition may seek on occasion to complicate spatial relations and develop narrative intrigue by including at least some *cross-line edits* (or *reverse cuts*). Nevertheless, the convention usually holds in mainstream cinema and serves to reassure the spectator of the stability of his or her viewing position. The rule's authority is evident in a familiar pattern of edits used during dialogue scenes in particular: *shot/reverse-shot* (also known as *shot/reverse-angle shot* or *shot/counter-shot*), whereby first one character, then the next, is seen from a position close to or actually replicating the other's perspective. Should the two lovers above re-establish contact and begin to talk, continuity editing is most likely to alternate shots of each of them from camera angles that do not trespass beyond that imaginary line drawn between their bodies.

Continuity editing also seeks to stabilise filmic space by the practice of *eyeline matching*. Here a shot of someone looking towards something off-screen is followed by a shot which discloses that object of interest. The narrative world thus seems complete, with any uncertainty the spectator may feel about what is not immediately visible dispelled (though a horror movie, say, will often delay eyeline matching so as not to reveal too early the source of a character's panic). Eyeline matches provide further proof of the artifice of continuity editing, since the shot that unveils what is being looked at does not always tally with the realities of the onlooker's perspective: thus a cut to a previously off-screen building a character is looking towards may show the building magnified to a degree not optically justified by the character's position. Even less grounded in the biology of the human perceptual system are those daring eyeline matches pioneered by such figures in early cinema history as the Hollywood director D. W. Griffith. In Griffith's *Intolerance* (1916), a guilt-stricken woman looks off-screen; rather than cutting to something in her vicinity, however, the next shot is of a faraway prison cell and the innocent man whom she has helped incarcerate. But while this transition is for psychological rather than strictly optical reasons, the fact that it is to a figure already introduced in *Intolerance* means that it still serves the eyeline match's customary functions of tidily connecting spaces and advancing narrative.

Griffith's inventive eyeline matching here is also an instance of *cross-cutting* – that procedure in film editing which intercuts two or more sequences that are occurring simultaneously but in different locations. Early cinema struggled to find a grammar to express simultaneous occurrence, sometimes, as in the first version of Edwin S. Porter's *Life of an American Fireman* (1902), resorting to showing consecutively two sequences of action that narrative evidence indicates were happening at the same time. Griffith, on the other hand, was noted for what he called his 'switchbacks', cutting dynamically between someone in peril and others rushing to his or her rescue (one such switchback occurs at the climax of *Intolerance*, alternating between the falsely incriminated man approaching the scaffold and the party racing to prove his innocence). Crucially, however, such practice often supports rather than compromises continuity editing's project to maintain narrative clarity. Cross–cutting in the kind of narrative cinema with which we are most familiar tends, after all, to occur between characters or locations whose relationship is already clear (or will shortly be made so). By indicating simultaneity, cross–cutting may also function to stabilise rather than problematise a film's representation of time. Nevertheless, *parallel editing*, as it is also called, can be appropriated by filmmakers for more enigmatic or provocative purposes. A very striking venture of this sort is Alain Resnais's *Hiroshima mon amour* (1959), where cross–cuts between two entwined lovers and footage of the damaged Japanese city, or between postwar Hiroshima and wartime France, have the effects of radically complicating time and space and of prompting the spectator to reflect on what these juxtapositions mean.

STOP and THINK

- Using a short sequence from a mainstream film, make visible what often goes unnoticed by analysing its continuity editing. How many shots are there? What is the average shot length (or ASL)? Is the duration of shot fairly constant or subject to variation? What transitional devices are used between shots – straight cuts, fade-outs and so on – and what are the consequences of these editing choices? Consider the effect of possible alterations to the type of bridge between any two shots in your sequence: how would meaning be modified if, say, a dissolve was substituted for a straight cut?

- Explore how editing choices in your chosen sequence serve to organise *space*. Is space articulated according to the logic of *découpage*, whereby long or extreme long shots of a scene are dissected into closer views? Is there fidelity to such conventions as shot/reverse-shot and eyeline matching? Or perhaps the sequence resists some or all of these protocols, violating the 180-degree rule by cross-line edits, for example, or substituting deep-focus editing for *découpage*? Whatever the specific editing choices made, assess whether they produce a sense of stable, coherent space or, rather, trigger spatial disorientation in the spectator.

- Consider, too, how editing decisions in the sequence contribute to the conceptualisation of *time*. Does the editing function to establish a sense of coherent temporality? If so, how? Or, on the other hand, is there something about the sequencing of shots that problematises time? As in judging the editing's production of space, assess the meanings and effects of its temporal schema.

Reviews and revisions of continuity editing

Prioritising the achievement of fluency, coherence and clarity in the organisation of shots, continuity editing has contributed vitally to the success of that narrative cinema which began to develop, in the United States and elsewhere, early in the twentieth century. The practices that have been outlined above serve to maintain the momentum of storytelling and to minimise any sense of spatial or temporal anomalies. The spectator seemingly enjoys command of an intelligible cinematic world and is carried seamlessly from shot to shot by a now largely invisible editing system. As a result, he or she may be considered entirely absorbed by – or into – the film's narrative order (an effect known ominously in film studies as *suture*, after the medical term for a type of stitching). But while this binding of the viewer is integral to narrative cinema's commercial prospects, it has also been the focus of fierce critique by figures ranging from Soviet montage theorists of the 1920s and 1930s to writers affiliated in the 1970s and 1980s with the radical British journal *Screen*. Continuity editing is understood from these positions to be the vehicle of a reactionary politics.

While fuller engagement with criticism of the ideology of mainstream cinema will be deferred until Chapter 8, it should be acknowledged here that these militant scholars and filmmakers have done important work in bringing the devices of continuity editing into visibility and evaluating their potential absorptive power with respect to the spectator. Nevertheless, to propose that the continuity system is always and everywhere complicit with political conservatism is open to counter-arguments. For a start, this thesis risks abstraction of editing from the broad ensemble of cinematic practices, thereby denying the potential ideological effects of, say, a film's colour palette or its set of actor performances. Second, the anti-continuity argument is prone to inattentiveness to other questions such as genre and period. Does a horror film from 2010, for example, have the same political implications as a musical made in 1950 simply by virtue of sharing an editing pattern? Continuity rejectionists also have a tendency to model the film spectator as a rather abstract, colourless figure who is, in effect, rendered immobile by the editing devices that have been described here. This inappropriately homogenises a host of actually existing viewing situations, including forms of spectatorship that are more active or resistant with regard to the screen than is allowed for by the suture theory.

Negative assessments of continuity editing are also liable to present it as an undifferentiated system, thereby overlooking its internal variations. Two such permutations may briefly be considered here. The first of these is *deep-focus editing*. Films made according to this logic downgrade *découpage* as a method of composing a scene in favour of a sustained shot that shows action or dialogue occurring across the various planes of an image that is uniformly in sharp focus. Rather than being directed towards key events or motifs by successive cuts, the spectator himself or herself is assigned responsibility for scanning the image for centres of significance. William Wyler, the mid-twentieth-century American director who was a significant exponent of deep focus, argued that this sort of construction of a sequence 'lets the spectator look from one to the other character at his own will, do his own cutting' (1947: 10). Interactivity with the screen was stressed, too, by André Bazin, cited in Chapter 1 as the chief philosopher of deep focus. In his important essay, 'The Evolution of the Language of Cinema' (1950–55), Bazin goes so far as to claim that, unlike editing styles that employ frequent cuts, deep-focus editing respects the wholeness of the spatio-temporal continuum we inhabit and offers the best cinematic approximation of how we scan the world off-screen (2005a: 23–40).

There is no need here to expand upon Chapter 1's suggestion that Bazin risks inflating his sensitive response to deep focus in a particular cluster of films into a questionable manifesto for cinema itself. More to the point for the present discussion is to ask whether, with its strictly limited cutting, deep-focus editing represents a variant of the continuity system or constitutes an entirely distinct practice. Bazin's choice of metaphors hints in fact at an *adaptation* of continuity editing, rather than its revolutionary overthrow. As well as the reference to evolution in his essay's title, he compares the effect of deep-focus editing to a major geological event's deepening and widening of an already existing river (2005a: 31). While caution should be exercised in applying the language of natural change to a culturally situated practice like filmmaking, Bazin's argument is useful nevertheless in prompting us to recognise irregularities and alternatives *within* continuity editing itself. For all the greater spectatorial freedom it promises, deep-focus editing in narrative films such as Welles's *Citizen Kane* (1941) or Wyler's *The Best Years of Our Lives* (1946) is still affiliated to continuity principles by smooth transitions between scenes and by orderly configuration of time and space. Typically, too, in these films, deep focus is not the only editing option taken, but is combined with instances of *découpage*.

At the other extreme to the long takes characteristic of deep-focus editing is a recent development that David Bordwell has termed 'intensified continuity' (2006: 119–38). Compared with earlier film, contemporary narrative cinema is for Bordwell characterised by radically increased pace of cutting, enhanced camera mobility, greater variety in choice of camera lens and tighter framing of characters engaged in dialogue. Making no pretence of adequate scientific sampling, a case study of our own in average shot length (ASL) offers some support for this claim. Whereas the fatal shooting of the gangster played by James Cagney near the end of *The Public Enemy* (1931) incorporates a stately eighteen shots in a sequence lasting two minutes twenty seconds (giving an ASL of 7.7 seconds), the killing of the gangster played by Johnny Depp near the end of Michael Mann's *Public Enemies* (2009) includes forty shots in an identically timed but much more hectic scene, producing an ASL of 3.7 seconds and adding to the body of evidence Bordwell can draw upon regarding changed editing protocols. Bordwell is careful, however, not to overstate the novelty of what is happening now, or to argue for a cinematic paradigm shift; on the contrary, he writes that 'the new style amounts to an *intensification* of established techniques. Intensified continuity is traditional continuity amped up, raised to a higher pitch of emphasis' (2006: 120). Just as Bordwell sought in his earlier work with Staiger and Thompson on classical Hollywood

cinema to co-opt apparently non-continuity practices into a hegemonic continuity system, here, too, he might be said to be expanding
unduly the scope of the dominant editing regime. Even dizzyingly
rapid cuts, it seems, can be assimilated into it. Whether or not one
shares Bordwell's views on the elasticity of the continuity system,
however, his thinking valuably allows for the possibility of its historical variation in a way that the thoroughgoing critiques do not.

Montage(s)

Montage is one of the most unstable, plural terms in film studies.
Its definition slides back and forth between the particular and the
universal, referring both to highly specific editing options and to the
very process of film editing itself. For some people, it is a word of
flavourless technical description; for others, a term of provocation
and controversy, focusing intense struggles over the aesthetics and
politics of cinema. Here we briefly discuss some of the geographically and historically dispersed understandings of montage, before
turning in more detail to the influential form that emerged in early
Soviet cinema.

The first definition the *OED* gives of 'montage' is sufficiently
neutral as to contain no hint of highly charged formal and ideological disputes: 'The process or technique of selecting, editing,
and piecing together separate sections of film to form a continuous whole; a sequence or picture resulting from such a process.'
In everyday English usage, however, 'montage' is likely to signify
not so much editing itself as, rather, a particular editing practice
that developed as a means of marking economically the passage
of time. Montage of this sort in classical Hollywood cinema condenses days and months – years, even – by such devices as a series
of spinning newspaper headlines or the peeling-off of pages from a
calendar. More recent narrative cinema may still choose to abridge
the representation of time by montages showing in rapid succes-
sion a number of chronologically distinct events, woven together
sonically by voiceover or music. The practice can serve dramatic
or lyrical purposes: John Sayles's *Matewan* (1987), a film discussed
later in this chapter, incorporates a montage that movingly, as well
as efficiently, evokes the spread of radical labour activism in early

twentieth-century America. At our point in film history, however, montage of this kind risks seeming clichéd. The Hollywood montage, in fact, may not have fully recovered from its parodying in the police spoof *The Naked Gun* (1988), where two lovers engage during an improbably action-packed day in activities that include rodeo-riding, beach-going and visiting a tattoo parlour. Even more damage to the convention – wickedly laying bare its motive of condensing narrative – was done by the 'Montage' song in *Team America: World Police* (2004): 'In anything, if you want to go/From just a beginner to a pro/You'll need a montage (Montage)/Even Rocky had a montage (Montage).'

Both flamboyant and sober instances of this specialised montage-type have the effect of accelerating cinematic storytelling. The desire to advance narrative also figured in intense debates over the nature and potential of montage which took place in the post-Revolutionary Soviet Union. Where Kuleshov refers enthusiastically to 'American montage', however, he has something broader in mind than the highly specific editing option just discussed. He understands by montage, in fact, the dynamic breaking-up of time and space by shot combination that promises to liberate film from more static, theatre-based forms of presentation. For Kuleshov, indeed, montage in this expanded sense represents 'the essence of cinema' (Taylor and Christie, 1994: 46). Writing in 1918 of its fundamental creative role, he proposed that 'Montage is to cinema what colour composition is to painting or a harmonic sequence of sounds is to music' (Taylor and Christie, 1994: 73).

If Kuleshov pioneered thinking about montage in the Soviet Union, however, he was soon overpowered intellectually by Eisenstein. By 1929 he was, in Eisenstein's damning verdict, 'theoretically quite outmoded' (Eisenstein, 2010a: 163). Eisenstein conceded that Kuleshov understood cinema's distinctiveness to lie not in the discrete image – otherwise it would only be a variant of photography – but in the articulation of multiple shots. Where he erred, however, was in drastically misconceiving the mode of relationship between them. Eisenstein's satirical brio led him to assert that, in Kuleshov's benighted film theory, one shot was viewed as harmoniously connected to the next like links in a chain or bricks in a wall (2010a: 143–4). For Eisenstein, this simply serial accumulation

of shots reduces cinema to a medium of efficient storytelling; it falsifies film's project, since 'montage is conflict' (2010a: 144).

To read Eisenstein's cinematic polemics is an exhilarating intellectual and rhetorical adventure. However, any search for his considered, conclusive views on montage is liable to be frustrated.
Although, in one critic's phrase, 'Eisenstein equals montage'
(Aumont, 1987: 145), his theory of what it consists of is expressed
not in an elegantly finished position-paper but in tumultuous life-
long reflections, full of leaps and contradictions. The reader is faced
by the task of tracking conceptual modulations across his volumi-
nous writings, as well as correlating these with the realities of composition in the films he directed from the 1920s onwards. At his
most expansive, the polymathic Eisenstein dislodges montage from
film narrowly considered and theorises it instead as a compositional
principle that may be identified in numerous other art forms. Thus
the 'montage family tree' that he designs (2010c: 216) is less a tidily
pruned specimen than a crazily branched thing which reaches even
to Greek architecture, Indian sculpture and Japanese poetry – also to
Dickens, whose multi-centred narratives and scene dissections are
taken by Eisenstein to comprise an early and bookish 'cinema'. At his
most miniaturising, however, Eisenstein is dissatisfied with having
to wait for one shot to be juxtaposed with another before conflictual
montage can occur: he conceives therefore of a form of *intra*-shot
montage, whereby the single shot no longer disposes its elements
harmoniously but is torn by graphic or volumetric or kinetic clashes.

There are dangers, given these many conceptual turns, in
attempting to present a systematic Eisensteinian theory of montage. Nevertheless, key aspects can be identified of that particular,
strategic form of shot combination which he termed 'intellectual
montage'. Eisenstein argues that each new shot must represent
not simply a quantitative addition to the one that precedes it,
but *a qualitative leap*. Images should not smoothly succeed each
other – for purposes only of narrative fluency – but be conflictively
juxtaposed. Such juxtaposition differs, however, from the provocative combination of random images – prompted by unconscious
association – that is familiar from Surrealist filmmaking (and from
Surrealist aesthetics more generally). 'The montage phrase' must,
in Eisenstein's stern words, comprise 'not just any two fragments

and not in random proportions. But precisely and solely those which, when combined, will evoke the image, concept or idea that I shall determine in advance and that I wish to make' (2010a: 267). Only this systematic, self-conscious arrangement of images will suffice, since 'the collision of marmalade and ground shinbone will not produce an explosion' (2010a: 268).

It is important to note Eisenstein's incendiary metaphor here for filmmaking. If continuity editing is taken by its critics to enfold the viewer comfortably in the film experience, such spectatorial inertia could not be further from Eisenstein's model of montage's effects. The spectator should, on the contrary, expect to be assaulted and scourged: an appropriately composed film 'ploughs' his or her sensibility, or 'cuts through' to the skull, or amounts to a 'fist' delivering a black eye. In a more scientific variant of this language of forceful, even violent reshaping of the audience, Eisenstein draws on the contemporaneous researches of the Soviet physiologist Pavlov to describe how reflexes might be reconditioned by the presentation on screen of carefully considered shot juxtapositions. While these metaphors of physical transformation seem to imply a filmmaking practice chiefly intended to operate on the spectator's body, Eisenstein speaks nevertheless of *intellectual* montage. Images are combined in his version of cinema in order to disrupt habitual patterns of thought in the viewer and yield higher-level theoretical reflection.

Like any theory, Eisenstein's reflections on film emerge not from a pure realm of ideas but from a specific historical conjuncture. His thinking took shape in the immediate aftermath of the Russian Revolution of 1917, a period of intense agitation for a society transformed not only in its material base but in its cultural forms as well. If inconsistently or idiosyncratically so, Eisenstein's concept of montage is *dialectical*, taking its shape and projected effect from the Marxist schema of thesis, antithesis and synthesis whereby an initial clash of opposing terms is subsequently resolved or unified in a third term that promises greater social emancipation. The point can be made concrete by considering a famous 'montage phrase' in *October 1917: Ten Days that Shook the World* (1928), which Eisenstein directed with the assistance of Grigori Aleksandrov. This film narrates the course of political events in the Soviet Union in 1917, from

8 Part of a 'montage phrase' in *October 1917: Ten Days that Shook the World* (1928), directed by Grigori Aleksandrov and Sergei Eisenstein

the time of Alexander Kerensky's Provisional Government until the October triumph of the Bolsheviks led by Lenin. Unexpectedly, at one point, shots of Kerensky and his associates relishing their quasi-Tsarist power in St Petersburg's Winter Palace are inter-cut with material having no obvious narrative connection: namely, shots of a mechanical peacock spreading its feathers (see Figure 8). A protocol for understanding the relationship of these seemingly discrete strands of imagery, however, is provided by Rohdie: 'It is not an editing of likenesses (naturally generated and linked) but an assembly or construction of differential realities that have no natural similarity in time or place, instead a connection that is conceptual (unnatural)' (2006: 80). The 'thesis' of the seemingly authoritative and dignified leader is juxtaposed with the 'antithesis' of the showy peacock, prompting the spectator to an intellectual 'synthesis' that recognises Kerensky's posturing, counter-revolutionary tenden-cies. The Soviet spectator of the period is mobilised thereby to repudiate incomplete versions of social change – as exemplified by Kerensky – and to embrace Bolshevik radicalism instead.

There is a long history of dissent within film studies to this type of polemical montage. Among those deploring what they see as montage's simple-mindedness are Balázs, Bazin and Kracauer, as well as the much later Soviet filmmaker Andrei Tarkovsky, given in his own work to a lyrical, extended compositional form rather than to rapid Eisensteinian juxtapositions. Balázs says that Eisenstein was fatally drawn towards 'film-hieroglyphics', designing shot combinations that yield blatant, easily decipherable meanings. For Kracauer, who values above all else in cinema its capacity for photographic revelation of the world in all its circumstantiality, the problem with Eisenstein's montages is that 'They stand for something outside them; any peacock would do, indeed'. More impoverished even than hieroglyphs, they are 'rebuses which, once solved, lose all their magic' (Kracauer, 1997: 208). Despite landing some wounding blows, however, these critiques are tempered when we recognise that they are based not on unimprovable criteria of film assessment but, more vulnerably, on alternative models of cinema that may themselves be challenged. To reject Eisenstein's montage because of its readily comprehensible meanings risks overvaluing ambiguity as an aesthetic goal. Such a view also takes no account of the fact that his films emerged at a time still of political crisis in the Soviet Union, and were primarily designed not to cultivate nuance but to foster or reinforce revolutionary consciousness in their audiences. Kracauer's complaint regarding the scene from *October 1917* that 'any peacock would do' seems what philosophers call a category mistake. The sequence is, after all, more intent on satirising counter-revolutionary traitors than observing ornithological niceties.

More damaging to Eisenstein's theory and practice is the argument that there is no *necessary* correlation between montage as he understands it and a radical politics. While his own films derive politically oppositional effects from the montage phrase, this combinatory form may in itself be ideologically neutral, capable of being filled by material of quite different value. That this may be the case is glimpsed in Eisenstein's own restless inquiries into artistic fields besides cinema. If montage, as a compositional practice given over to conflictive juxtapositions, can be seen everywhere from primitive sculpture to nineteenth-century American poetry, then it seems open to appropriation for diverse political and cultural purposes rather than inevitably aligned with the cause of revolution. Stam points out that, depressingly, there is even the possibility of naked commercial exploitation of Eisenstein's schema: 'shorn of its dialectical basis [...] Eisensteinian "associationist" montage could easily be transformed into the commodified ideograms of advertising, where the whole is more than the sum of its parts: Catherine Deneuve plus Chanel No. 5 signifies charm, glamour, and erotic appeal' (2000: 41). As with features of mise-en-scène discussed in Chapter 1, then, the effects of particular editing practices cannot be unequivocally assumed in advance of their use in a given context.

The jump cut and its meanings

The ideological promiscuity of editing protocols may be further illustrated by brief study of *the jump cut*. Unlike the sense of smooth progression achieved by straight cutting, the jump cut, unsurprisingly, produces a jerky or staccato transition from one shot to the next. It often registers as an uncanny jolt, functioning similarly to an ellipsis in a written passage that erases connective materials and potentially problematises understanding. Thus a film might cut abruptly from one sequence to a second, incongruent one, without any attempt to ease the transition by employing those matches of eyeline or action or graphic property that are central to the continuity mode. Or, within a scene set in a single space, the film may violate another principle of continuity editing's geometry: *the 30-degree rule*. This convention states that where a new shot has the same subject as the preceding one, the cut from the first to the second should justify its existence by producing a change of angle of not less than 30 degrees (as illustrated in Figure 9). Without such significant variation, the new shot risks appearing awkward or puzzling, a malfunction in the editing mechanism.

Given that the term 'jump cut' was adopted in 1974 as the title of an important, left-leaning journal in film studies, it might be assumed that the practice invariably has progressive intent. The history of its use, however, discloses a plurality of motivations and consequences. It first appears in cinema, in fact, because of technological limitations rather than to advance any radical political agenda. When early makers of 'actualities' shot an event from a

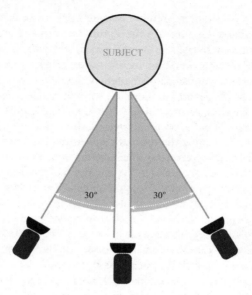

9 The 30-degree rule in continuity editing

fixed camera position, their only way of including just the most engaging moments on the relatively short reel of film was to stop the camera at some point and then restart it, the identical angle of the second shot registering as a jump cut. Other filmmakers saw creative possibilities in this otherwise pragmatic cutting-out of time. The French pioneer Georges Méliès, who figures as a character in Scorsese's *Hugo* (2011), realised that a jump cut could have magical or comic effects if the appearance of a subject filmed from a single vantage point was altered between shots (as with particular daring in *The Temptation of St. Anthony* in 1898, where the crucified Christ transmutes across the cut into a seductive woman). While this anticipates radical filmmaking by disclosing the artifice rather than 'naturalness' of film composition, the manoeuvre is nevertheless more playful than politically earnest.

Modern use of the jump cut is more associated with ideologically committed filmmaking, in particular, perhaps, the work of Jean-Luc Godard. Beginning with his first full-length feature, *Breathless*

(1959), and continuing through a body of films spanning fifty years, Godard utilises the jump cut for disruptive purposes. At the start, the technique functions as a minor variation within still largely familiar scenic choreography: in *Breathless*, for example, successive shots from the same angle of the female protagonist in a speeding car mark a slippage in time and space without radically compromising narrative comprehensibility. Later in Godard's work, however, jump cuts are liable to occur between entire sequences, interfering with and interrogating the spectator's pleasurable immersion in the film experience. Nevertheless, the jump cut is only one among many devices that Godard utilises in the attempt to dismantle continuity cinema. His films may also disturb soundtrack, or include intertitles that signal a pedagogic or satirical intent, or incorporate characters aware, in Brechtian fashion, of their own constructed status.

Godard's recourse to an array of anti-continuity strategies suggests that there can be no guarantee that the jump cut, in and of itself, transmits political radicalism. Where it is deprived of support by a larger revisionary apparatus, it may serve less ideologically challenging purposes. Consider, say, the several transgressions of the 30-degree rule that occur as Heather, the female protagonist, apologises tearfully to camera in *The Blair Witch Project* (1999). Jump cuts here introduce formal variety into a gruelling two-minute sequence shot from a fixed position; yet because they intensify a sense of the character's terrifying predicament, they actually share continuity editing's aim of suturing the spectator ever more tightly into the narrative order (rather than, as with Godard's practice, interrupting and provoking questions about this). Emma E. Hickox, another in that long line of prominent female editors mentioned earlier, actually connects jump-cutting to effective storytelling when she describes her work on the Hollywood historical romance, *Becoming Jane* (2007): 'The trick is to jump-cut so that nobody really notices, but they get the feeling of what is going on in the scene and move forward with the story' (Oldham, 2012b: 187). Like Eisenstein's montage that was originally designed to advance the cause of revolution, then, the jump cut risks becoming part of mainstream filmmaking's extended formal repertoire – and, potentially, as invisible to us in the future as straight cuts have already become.

STOP and THINK

- This chapter has suggested it may not be possible to align particular editing practices with fixed ideological meanings. Test this thesis with examples from different film traditions. Consider initially whether it is possible to reach a decision on the politics of continuity editing. As noted above, radical critiques of continuity indict it for its manufacture of the passive spectator who is tied into cinematic illusion and carried from shot to shot as smoothly as a piece of (pre-digital) film itself advancing over its sprockets. Do you have sympathy for this argument? Or does the thesis strike you as too dogmatic and despairing an assessment of the effects of continuity editing?
- By way of contrast, explore the politics of anti-continuity cinema: examples might include Eisenstein's intellectual montages in *Strike*, *October 1917* or *Battleship Potemkin* (1925) or Godard's use of the jump cut in his 1960s work. Consider the positioning of the spectator by such editing practices. Assess whether they still carry an oppositional charge that may be activated by filmmakers, or whether there is a danger of their routinisation now as part of mainstream cinema's stylistic array.

Case study: *Strike* (1925), *Matewan* (1987), *Made in Dagenham* (2010)

These three films are brought together by shared subject matter. Set respectively in a Russian factory town before the Revolution, the West Virginia coalfields in 1920 and the Ford car plant in Dagenham, Essex, in 1968, they all narrate instances of labour struggle culminating in the taking of militant strike action. In other ways, however, these are radically distinct works. They emerge, to begin with, from very different production contexts. While *Strike* is Eisenstein's first feature, it is less an individual experimentalist's vision than a contribution to collectively designed cinematic output in the early Soviet Union. The film was envisaged not as a self-contained project, but as one component of *Towards the*

Dictatorship, an ultimately uncompleted seven-film sequence that would narrate the course of the Russian Revolution. *Matewan*, by contrast, lacks such powerful institutional backing and is the fifth feature of John Sayles, an American director and screenwriter who works independently of the mainstream. It was enabled by 'this pastiche of money' (Sayles and Smith, 1998: 121), drawing its finances from private investors, from a small production company and from Sayles himself (utilising the proceeds of pieces of Hollywood hackwork). The origins of *Made in Dagenham* differ again: Nigel Cole's film is a relatively low-budget British feature, but guaranteed quite high visibility by having the BBC among its funders.

Unsurprisingly, in light of these varying sites of production, the three films differ markedly in form. *Strike* and *Made in Dagenham* represent both ends of a cinematic spectrum, with the former Eisenstein's first experiment with montage and the latter a fairly conventional instance of work made according to continuity principles; in between, *Matewan* presents a modified version of continuity editing. Their shared thematic material, however, offers a good opportunity to consider the politics of distinct editing practices. Since all of the films intend to show labour activism in a sympathetic light, setting them against each other raises the question of whether different ideological effects may be generated by differences in editing itself.

Compared with the brisk rhythm of both *Strike* and *Made in Dagenham*, *Matewan* is, in its director's own words, 'very dissolve-y and slow' (Sayles and Smith, 1998: 188). At least until its climax, the film tends to resist contemporary continuity editing's preference for the straight cut and utilises instead dissolves and lingering fades. Rather than the instantaneous replacement of one image by the next, shots overlap or succeed each other lyrically. This editing mode works to counter suggestions by the film's narrative itself of disruptiveness: hints of social change as the West Virginia miners struggle for union recognition risk being compromised by the emphasis in the editing upon recurrence and harmony. Indeed, Sayles has written about 'a mood and rhythm' in this part of the United States that is flatly non-revolutionary: 'There is a cyclical sense of time there' (Sayles, 2003: 10).

The evidence of this case study's other two films, however, is that more rapid cutting than that practised in *Matewan* is variable in its ideological implications. In *Made in Dagenham*, the crisis generated at the narrative level by the female machinists' campaign for equal pay may be contained by editing choices that, ironically enough, favour *continuity*. A case in point is a series of shots of the women on indefinite strike, where any sense of disruption is managed both by the smooth straight cuts and by overlaying on the soundtrack the Small Faces' song, 'All or Nothing'. In *Strike*, by contrast, shots relate to one another clashingly rather than harmoniously, seeking to evoke a dynamic, conflictive political situation. Where Eisenstein does use a dissolve, it carries a polemical force, not the lyricism achieved by Sayles. Early on, the faces of three agents-provocateurs employed by an oppressive factory manager dissolve into the features of, respectively, a monkey, an owl and a bulldog (there was to have been a frog, too, but Eisenstein rejected as not ugly enough the specimens his crew obtained from a freezing lake). In these dissolves, Eisenstein constructs a rudimentary 'montage phrase'. The juxtaposition of shots of a human face and of three animals is intended to foster spectator awareness of the 'bestial' nature of the managerial class in pre-Soviet Russia. Such a sequence comprises a cinematic hieroglyph or rebus of the kind disliked by Balázs and Kracauer. So, too, does the most vivid of *Strike*'s montages, from very near the end. Here shots of strikers and their families being brutally cut down by mounted troops are intercut with images – originating from outside the film's narrative – of a bull being slaughtered for meat. Eisenstein writes that, whereas footage of an abattoir used by his Soviet contemporary Dziga Vertov was of merely documentary interest, his own incorporation of such scenes is '*gorily effective*' (2010a: 63). This instance of montage forces spectators to acknowledge an equation between two sorts of slaughter – not so as to advance vegetarian sentiment, of course, but to consolidate rage against owners prepared to regard their own workforce as so many carcasses for disposal.

There is no such radicalising conclusion to either *Made in Dagenham* or *Matewan*. In the finale of Cole's film, the continuity editing serves to underwrite a message of measured labour relations: the striking women win their battle, yet Ford is able to resume production and the larger inequities of capitalism go unchallenged. Similarly, while *Matewan*'s generally slow rhythm is varied near the end by an increased pace of cutting, this is not in order to produce a searing sense of difference between classes. Indeed, Sayles recalls trying to edit the film's final shoot-out sequence so as 'to really make it flow' (Sayles and Smith, 1998: 136). Fluidity, of course, is precisely what Eisenstein does *not* want at the climactic moment of *Strike*; instead, he seeks an editing style which maximises awareness of the jarring and the discontinuous. Sayles's alternative emphasis in *Matewan* upon flowing rhythms does not exactly function to reunite boss and worker, but it nevertheless moderates any sense of fracture and evokes instead a continuous, eternal time within which political differences may be absorbed as merely transient phenomena.

However, caution is needed before reaching the conclusion that it is entirely because of montage that *Strike* serves revolutionary praxis and, conversely, that *Matewan* and *Made in Dagenham* tend towards political quiescence because of their continuity-based editing. Rather than isolating the analysis of editing strategies in this way, it is important also to consider the impact upon the three films' politics of variant conditions of production and spectatorship. Here we follow Eisenstein himself, who acknowledges that in the absence of appropriately sensitised audiences even the most militantly intended montage phrases may remain empty or inert. While his film theory often presumes a somewhat monolithic spectator always responding as the director intends, he nevertheless recognises the possibility that viewers of the climactic montage in *Strike* may react in different ways. A 'peasant' in the Soviet Union, say, used to slaughtering his or her own animals, might not be incited to reflection by this juxtaposition of bovine and human fatalities (Eisenstein, 2010a: 65–6). This montage, then, risks remaining purely virtual, in need of activation by an ideal audience that will make the necessary metaphoric leap between shots of a bull and of striking workers and generate the concept of a 'human slaughterhouse' that should be destroyed in favour of a new political settlement.

The discussion above suggests that, while certain editing strategies may be more plausibly correlated with particular political tendencies than with others, it is possible to overstate their potency. The efficacy of *Strike* is traceable not only to Eisenstein's editing brilliance but to the fact that the film emerged at a time of ideological ferment and was watched by audiences already primed to respond to narratives of oppressive bosses and martyred workers. *Matewan* and *Made in Dagenham*, on the other hand, were both released in contexts much less conducive to militant activism. Their moments of production coincided with phases of transatlantic neoliberal advance when the labour cause – indeed, the cause of the US and British left more generally – was in a state of crisis. Certainly, the films' editing modes – evoking continuity rather than fracture – may already reflect and reinforce that mood of political retrenchment. At the same time, however, the lack of revolutionary impetus in *Matewan* and *Made in Dagenham* cannot be attributed solely to their ways of combining shots. After all, it is possible to imagine other spectatorial conditions – times of increased labour militancy, say – in which even the former's dissolves and fades and the latter's straight cuts will not prevent their narratives of, respectively, heartless mine owners and exploitative car manufacturers from galvanising their audiences politically.

Selected reading

Besides the specialist studies listed below, see also extensive coverage of editing in the books by Bordwell and Thompson, and Corrigan and White, cited in Chapter 1's 'Selected reading'.

Crittenden, Roger (2006), *Fine Cuts: The Art of European Film Editing* (Oxford: Focal Press).
    Valuable counterpart to Oldham's volumes below, comprising interviews with European editors from the French New Wave onwards.
Dancyger, Ken (2013), *The Technique of Film and Video Editing: History, Theory, and Practice*, 5th ed. (Burlington, MA: Focal Press).
    A substantial text, full of information for aspiring industry professionals but also attentive to editing's shifting histories, theories and aesthetics.
Eisenstein, S. M. (2010a, 2010b, 2010c), *Selected Works*, 3 vols, trans. Michael Glenny, William Powell and Richard Taylor, ed. Michael Glenny and Richard Taylor (London: I. B. Tauris).
    Indispensable, expertly annotated writings by cinema's foremost philosopher-practitioner. Eisenstein theorises all aspects of film with prodigious energy and erudition, but continually returns to the question of

montage; while Vol. 2 is subtitled 'Towards a Theory of Montage', however, Vols 1 and 3 actually include more systematic statements on editing.

Fairservice, Don (2001), *Film Editing: History, Theory and Practice*
(Manchester: Manchester University Press).
Theoretically underdeveloped in places and needs updating to discuss digital practice more fully, but accessible, well-researched and
wide-ranging.

Nesbet, Anne (2003), *Savage Junctures: Sergei Eisenstein and the Shape of
Thinking* (London: I. B. Tauris).
Helpful companion to Eisenstein's own writings, ranging across the
totality of his film theory and practice; includes detailed discussion of
Strike.

Oldham, Gabriella (2012a, 2012b), *First Cut: Conversations with Film
Editors* (Berkeley: University of California Press) and *First Cut 2: More
Conversations with Film Editors* (Berkeley: University of California
Press).
Less intellectually searching than, say, the dialogues of Ondaatje and
Murch, but engaging, enlightening volumes that collect interviews with
two generations of US film editors.

Ondaatje, Michael (2002), *The Conversations: Walter Murch and the Art of
Editing Film* (New York: Knopf).
Wonderfully eloquent, learned and suggestive dialogues. Drawing upon
his work on such films as *Apocalypse Now* (1979) and *The English Patient*
(1996), Murch, prompted subtly by Ondaatje, teases out the aesthetics of
picture and sound editing.

Orpen, Valerie (2002), *Film Editing: The Art of the Expressive* (London:
Wallflower).
Good starting point: lacks Fairservice's substantial historical detail, but
clear, concise and featuring helpful case studies.

Rohdie, Sam (2006), *Montage* (Manchester: Manchester University Press).
Stylistically strained at times, but reflects richly on editing's varieties and
meanings in work by Eisenstein, Griffith, Hitchcock and other directors;
the book itself, in its inventive, non-linear sequence of short chapters,
takes the form of montage.

Online resources

'The History of Cutting – The Birth of Cinema and Continuity Editing',
http://vimeo.com/84542388.
Relatively brief, yet helpful and engaging video lecture on the origins of
continuity editing in the United States.

'Video: The History of Editing, Eisenstein, and the Soviet Montage',
http://nofilmschool.com/2014/02/video-the-history-of-editing-
eisenstein-the-soviet-montage-explained.
Belongs to the same series as the video lecture on continuity editing cited
above, and has similar virtues.

3
Hearing film: sound and music

For the distinguished pianist and conductor Daniel Barenboim, hearing, as a sense, lacks prestige. In a world of multiple, heterogeneous visual stimuli, we tend, he says, to 'neglect the ear' (2009: 39). Given his own area of expertise, Barenboim is especially vexed by inattention to music even as it achieves 'a cacophonous omnipresence in restaurants, aeroplanes and the like' (3). However, his thesis of inequality between the senses can be productively extended to film, where, historically, the ear has been outranked by the eye. The very names popularly bestowed upon the medium evoke the visual's pre-eminence: if *movies* and *the flicks* already hint at stimulation for the eye rather than a multisensory experience, *the pictures* is more ocularcentric still. This bias in everyday discourse has often been replicated in film studies itself. Beginning her pioneering book on music in cinema, Claudia Gorbman laments the discipline's tendency towards 'visual chauvinism' (1987: 2). Even Michel Chion – the French critic who has done as much as any scholar to promote and conceptualise film's neglected auditory dimension – says gloomily that 'The sound-camel continues to pass through the eye of the visual needle' (1994: 143).

This privileging of sight over hearing, however, runs counter to what human biology tells us about development of the two senses. While the infant in the womb keeps its eyes closed until approximately twenty-six weeks old, it is already attentive to a soundscape as complex as in one of David Lynch's films, its ears sufficiently developed from eighteen weeks onwards to register the mother's voice, her intestinal gurgling and the thrumming of her heart and blood vessels. If not the originary sense – the infant's responsiveness to touch, for example, begins still earlier, at eight weeks – sound still has, biologically speaking, a suggestive temporal priority over vision. This insistence on hearing's crucial, constitutive place in the array of senses is salutary for film studies. From its beginnings, after all, cinema has been a mixed sensory form, quite as aural as it is visual; indeed, Chion proposes that the convention of speaking of a film's 'viewer' be dropped in favour of referring to an 'audio–spectator' who is engaged in 'audio–viewing' (1994: xxv). Less directly, Christian Metz also contests the hegemony of the eye when he identifies the five 'tracks', or 'matters of expression', that generate meaning in film. There is, it emerges, an auditory majority here: while two of the tracks are visual in their address (the photographic image; text that appears on screen), the remaining three – dialogue, sound effects, music – solicit the ear (Stam, Burgoyne and Flitterman-Lewis, 1992: 38).

For Chion, provocatively, 'there is no soundtrack' (1994: 39). To separate out and assess discretely a film's aural elements is, he argues, an unsatisfactory exercise, since in actuality sounds are not autonomous but are intimately bound up with the images they accompany. While taking Chion's point, however, this chapter on sound, like that earlier on mise-en-scène, still assumes the usefulness for analytical purposes of temporarily isolating the element of cinematic form under review. Later, we will introduce and evaluate theories and terminologies that have been proposed for film's aural realm, including music. First, however, it is important to relive key moments in the history of film sound, beginning with the unexpected noisiness of 'silent' cinema.

Deafening silents

From Chapter 1, the reader will recall Maxim Gorky's anxiety, while watching very early films in Nizhny-Novgorod in Russia in 1896, that all the colour in the world had leached away. If Gorky found the film experience to be saturated in 'monotonous grey', however, it struck him with no less force as eerily silent. On screen, carriages were to be observed rolling along a busy Paris street; yet no rumble of the wheels is heard, no sound of footsteps or of speech. Nothing. Not a single note of the intricate symphony that always accompanies the movements of people. Noiselessly, the ashen-grey foliage of the trees sways in the wind, and the grey silhouettes of the people, as though condemned to eternal silence and cruelly punished by being deprived of all the colours of life, glide noiselessly along the grey ground. (Leyda, 1960: 407)

Clearly spooked, Gorky writes that the screen conveys 'not motion, but its soundless spectre' (407). Other writers, too, have mobilised metaphors of spectrality in the attempt to evoke early cinema's uncanny combination of movement and silence, the animated and the deathly. Siegfried Kracauer suggests that the images presented by silent film 'affect us as a ghost-like replica of the world we live in – the limbo through which the deaf are moving' (1997: 135). While Kracauer saw in cinema a thrilling potential to render the world in all its vivid circumstantiality, this was compromised by noiselessness; thus he welcomed the addition of sound as correcting film's ghostly atmospherics and advancing its realist project. For Kracauer's German contemporaries Theodor Adorno and Hanns Eisler, on the other hand, it was not so much film sound in general as the incorporation of music in particular that rescued the early spectator from 'the unpleasantness involved in seeing effigies of living, acting, and even speaking persons, who were at the same time silent' (2007: 50).

While such expressions of spectatorial anxiety are striking, they actually overstate the silence of 'silent' cinema. If the film that unfolded in front of Gorky was mute, the same could not be said of the café in which he watched; indeed, he was rescued from his impression of the medium's terrifying noiselessness by awareness of ambient sounds: 'suddenly, alongside of you, a gay chatter and a provoking laughter of a woman is heard … and you remember that you are at Aumont's' (Leyda, 1960: 408). Gorky's account gives few details, though, of other, less appealing aural phenomena that would undoubtedly have been part of this early film experience. His description of the mechanics of screening is limited to 'something clicks', making no direct reference to the whirring of the projector itself (a machine that, before the invention of sound-proof projection booths, was located in the auditorium – not only noisily but sometimes catastrophically, given the combustibility of nitrate film stock). Itemising such incidental laughs and clicks may seem trifling, far removed from any serious attempt to delineate and evaluate film sound; it accords nevertheless with film studies' recent interest in the materiality of the moment of exhibition, including auditory stimuli regardless of their sources.

The viewer of silent film, in any case, rarely required contingent phenomena such as the chatter of audiences or the humming of machines to relieve a potentially desolating sense of noiselessness. If a number of early works were indeed shown without any form of acoustic accompaniment, the great majority were enmeshed in programmed soundscapes. While several decades would pass before the material integration of sound and vision – an optical soundtrack carrying recorded audio content was first incorporated in the filmstrip itself around 1930 – exhibitors from the first days of cinema devised and implemented many aural accompaniments for the image. Rick Altman speaks, in fact, of the 'extraordinary variety of sounds associated with early cinema exhibition' (2004: 22). The groundbreaking research of Altman and other scholars has encouraged us to reconceive silent cinema as already a multisensory experience, characterised not by on-screen spectacle in isolation but by interaction between the image on the one hand and diverse sound practices on the other. The phonograph, invented some two decades before the cinematograph, was utilised in exhibition spaces to play recorded music. More frequently still, silent films were accompanied by live musical performances of varying kinds and scales: depending on the venue, music was supplied by a solitary pianist or organist, or by a larger ensemble, even at times a full-scale orchestra. However, it is important to acknowledge the incorporation of many sounds other than music in the acoustic environment of early cinema. Images were, for example, sometimes accompanied by the interpretative words of a lecturer stationed near the screen (a practice soon discontinued in the West as cues for understanding came to be integrated into films themselves – including on-screen caption cards, or *intertitles* – but surviving longer elsewhere, including in Japan, where lecturers, or *benshi*, were prominent until the mid-1930s). On other occasions, performers or phonographs usually positioned behind the screen provided sound effects – from church bells to gunshots, train whistles to horses' hooves – that synchronised with on-screen action.

Within these diverse exhibition contexts, the relations of image and sound were fluid and negotiable rather than stable and hierarchical. For every spectator drawn to film by its promise of visual magic, there was another who attended chiefly in anticipation of hearing phonograph music or the virtuoso playing of a favourite pianist. If silent cinema's audio content was often cued by and responsive to particulars on screen, it was on many other occasions digressive or unanchored, producing what Altman calls an 'aesthetics of discontinuity' (2004: 44). Significant in this context is the early practice of *funning* a film, whereby the authority, even the dignity, of the image on screen was compromised by parodic musical accompaniment in the exhibition space. A staple of early film programmes – *the illustrated song* – reconfigured more radically still the power relations between sound and image, hinting at the former's privilege and the latter's secondary, belated quality. During the illustrated song, performance first by a soloist, then by the audience, of a romantic ballad or comic number would be accompanied by a series of slides, the relatively functional visual matter seeming as though it had been conjured into being by sound itself. While this musical phenomenon belongs to cinema's earliest period (it had died out in the US by 1913), its readjustment of the hierarchy of image and sound set a precedent for a number of later film practices. Sequences in Sergio Leone's 'spaghetti' western, *Once Upon a Time in the West* (1968), say, might be regarded as 'illustrations' of Ennio Morricone's music, which had already been composed by the time shooting began. Kathryn Kalinak reminds us, too, that 'picturisation', as this matching of images to a pre-existing soundtrack is called, has a long history in popular Hindi cinema, or Bollywood: 'Film songs were so important [...] that they came first in the production process: the job of the screenwriter was to provide a narrative framework upon which to hang these songs' (2010: 55).

Sound and fury

The introduction and diffusion of synchronised sound from the late 1920s onwards was a matter of more than merely technological interest. In adding to the stock of film's formal options, integrated sound also prompted arguments about the nature and purpose of the medium itself. When the Vitaphone discs offering partial matching of the image track, as with *Don Juan* (1926) and *The Jazz Singer* (1927), gave way to the imprinting of full acoustic accompaniment on the filmstrip, some voices could be heard pronouncing the end of film as a significant art form. Rudolf Arnheim, whose despondency about colour was cited in Chapter 1, was just as gloomy when reflecting on integrated sound. Writing in 1928, he conceded that it might enhance films given over to 'instruction and journalism', but that, otherwise, it posed a grave threat to cinema's distinctive aesthetic (Arnheim, 1997: 30). In another essay written a few years into the regime of sound film, Arnheim acknowledged some artistically promising instances of 'asynchronism' between sound and image tracks (164); on the whole, however, he found a mechanical, literalist synchronisation of picture and sound that betrayed cinema's formal adventurism. For the French screenwriter and critic Alexandre Arnoux, integrated sound was, quite simply, a 'savage invention' (Bickerton, 2009: 4). Yet while Arnheim and Arnoux deplored the effects of integrated sound, other figures, including the Surrealist Salvador Dalí, welcomed them as liberating. Cinema had become, in Dalí's view, increasingly corseted by formalism and abstraction, and so the addition of a synchronised soundtrack renewed the medium's contact with the material world: 'Sound cinema brings with it a marvellous impurity ... the reestablishment of certain notions of the concrete' (Hammond, 2000: 65).

These debates about the coming of integrated sound took on the character, at times, of intense theological dispute. If Arnheim had something like the loss of Eden in mind when writing despairingly of silent cinema's passing, the French Surrealist Marcel Mariën actually evoked Good Friday in his description of how he wept over 'the tomb of silent pictures' (Hammond, 2000: 141). From the other side of the argument, however, André Bazin mobilised tropes of resurrection. Given its great contribution to film's realist endeavours, Bazin wrote, 'sound has given proof that it came not to destroy but to fulfil the Old Testament of the cinema' (2005a: 23).

In thinking about this contentious transition from silent to sound film, two things are advisable. First, as argued above, it is crucial to inventory silent film's multiple soundscapes and to recognise that it was already an aesthetic experience by no means organised exclusively around the image. Second, we should resist the extremist rhetoric utilised by both sides in this debate. As the important British critic V. F. Perkins pointed out over four decades ago, film has 'no essence which we can usefully invoke [...] we can evolve useful criteria only for specific types of film, not for the cinema' (1972: 59). Thus the coming of synchronised sound neither betrayed nor fulfilled cinema; instead, more modestly, it added to film's stylistic stock, but without being assessable by reference to some ideal cinematic form. Such caution with regard to heightened narratives variously of the medium's regression or realisation in the face of changing sound practices is important, given the allure they continue to have for some commentators. Invited to call the post-1970 Dolby era of noise reduction and multi-channel audio the 'second coming of sound', Bruce Stambler, a Hollywood sound editor whose credits include three entries in the *Fast & Furious* franchise (2001–9), replied that he would rather describe this time as 'the coming of sound, period! ... because we didn't really have sound. We pretty much had dialogue and had a centre speaker and that was it' (Sergi, 2004: 134). For an industry professional, the era of Vitaphone discs reproducing only snatches of a film's dialogue and music must indeed seem impoverished when set against current conditions of digital recording and speakers positioned all around a cinema so as to deliver an acoustic experience Chion terms the '*superfield*' (1994: 150). However, it is possible to register technological changes of this sort – and to explore their effects on us as audio-spectators – without incorporating them in a story of cinema's fulfilment (or, conversely, of its death).

Analysing film sound

Definitions of film sound have sometimes, as already indicated, been very expansive. Rick Altman is among a number of recent scholars wishing to include in the reckoning *all* of the acoustic matter produced by the film experience. From this standpoint, the analyst would attend not only to particular films' syntheses of dialogue, sound effects and music but to the manifold ambient noises of situations in which audio-viewing occurs: 'the kids in the front rows, the air conditioner hum, the lobby cash register, the competing sound track in the adjacent multiplex theater, passing traffic' (Altman ed., 1992: 6). Altman's list can, of course, be infinitely extended: the rustling of popcorn, say, or the ringtones of mobile phones or the chatter of family and friends when viewing takes place at home. Such reconfiguration of 'soundtrack' has greatly enriched our knowledge of diverse cultures of film consumption. An exemplary contribution here is made by Annette Kuhn in *An Everyday Magic: Cinema and Cultural Memory* (2002), which recalls the tumultuous soundscapes of prewar matinées in Britain when, in addition to noises emanating from the screen, the watching children would crack open peanuts or stamp clog-covered feet on bare wooden floors. Besides movingly retrieving the detail of ordinary lives often ignored by scholarship, Kuhn's account also remodels film reception so that it is understood less as passive textual absorption and more as an interactive experience that involves, among other things, the making of noise.

There are, however, costs as well as benefits in such an inclusive approach to film sound. To begin with, listing all of the noises made during screenings may generate data of such abundance, eclecticism and even triviality as to resist theorisation. Legitimate curiosity with regard to ambient sound may be taken so such an extent that it overpowers or even displaces interest in the films' own sound designs. Research into the acoustics of, say, slurping milkshakes in the American multiplex might thus carry as much conceptual weight as study of the carefully calibrated soundtracks of those Quentin Tarantino films the drinkers are watching. Kuhn, to be sure, avoids this pitfall, since her book juxtaposes the noisy audience with the variously terrifying and alluring soundscapes of 1930s horror films and Astaire/Rogers musicals. However, it is because of these dangers of overdoing contextual description that the remainder of this section seeks to restore the film text itself to centre-stage and, at least provisionally, to detach its own soundtrack from more incidental noises that accrue around it.

Film studies has actually found it difficult to fashion a single, universally shared terminology for the analysis of soundtrack. There is, however, initial agreement that it comprises four basic elements:

speech (including voiceover besides dialogue), *music*, *sound effects* and *silence*. These elements may not be equal in power, but, rather, subject to hierarchical ordering. For Chion, the narrative cinema to which we are most accustomed is 'verbocentric' (2009: 74), in that it places its highest premium upon the intelligibility and vividness of dialogue. As Walter Murch puts it, noting how Hollywood's prevailing sound practices tend to occlude or diminish sorts of acoustic material in which he is interested: 'Dialogue is the moon, and stars are the sound effects' (Ondaatje, 2002: 175). Some audience discomfort, then, may be caused by films like Robert Altman's *Nashville* (1975), with its overlapping and muffled voices – or by newer works from the US such as *127 Hours* (2010) and *All Is Lost* (2013), in which each protagonist's extreme isolation serves to deprivilege dialogue and promote other acoustic matter instead. Both of these recent films, in fact, experiment in dialogue's absence not only with sound effects and music, but with silence also (the fourth component of any soundtrack). Paradoxically, silence as a conscious choice of filmmakers only became available in the sound era: where it occurred in pre-talkies cinema, it may simply have been an accidental outcome, as with the pianist's resting of tired fingers.

Beyond this identification of the basic elements of film sound, however, concepts and terminologies have tended to multiply, sometimes confusingly. As an aspect of cinematic form, in fact, sound has proved much more resistant to theorisation than image. There is, to begin with, no agreement on what constitutes the auditory equivalent of the image track's minimal unit, the shot. If demarcating one shot from another is a relatively straightforward exercise, the continuity across these visual transitions of dialogue or music or sound effects, or of all three polyphonically combined, is evidence that soundtrack does not lend itself so easily to segmentation. In addition, whereas image analysis is devoted to the space of the screen itself, discussions of film sound have to be more spatially inquisitive, finding ways of describing also its emanation from significant *off-screen* places. Further complications arise when critics propose terms for assessing the overall effects of a film's soundtrack: Bordwell and Thompson suggest in *Film Art* that it has attributes of *rhythm*, *fidelity*, *space* and *time*, whereas Gianluca Sergi's own quadripartite model in *The Dolby Era* favours *orchestration*, *contrast*, *focus* and *definition*. The effect is thus one of conceptual promiscuity, rather than the coherence and consensus that characterise analysis of film's image track.

Different vocabularies exist, too, for describing the fundamental relationship between what is visible on screen and what is audible on the soundtrack. Influentially, Karel Reisz and Gavin Millar's *The Technique of Film Editing* (1968) proposed that, in this respect, film sounds be divided into two broad types: *actual* and *commentative*. Actual sounds are those that can be ascribed to a visible or implied on-screen source, as when a character speaks or plays a guitar or turns on a car's engine. Commentative sounds, on the other hand, are acoustic phenomena which have no point of origin on screen: principally, voiceover and musical score. While Reisz and Millar's basic typology of film sounds has survived into work by later scholars, their original terms have been superseded because of the potential for confusion (an 'actual' sound may prove to be a film technician's ingenious construction, for example, or it may also have a commentative function, as when the guitar player's choice of piece to play reveals something of his or her state of mind). Instead of 'actual' and 'commentative', therefore, most critics now prefer the more technical alternatives of *diegetic* and *non-diegetic*, respectively (these being adjectival forms deriving from *diegesis*, the Greek word for 'narration' or 'recital').

'Diegetic' and 'non-diegetic' thus designate two distinct categories fundamental to the analysis of film sound. Nevertheless, sounds may still migrate in particular works from one realm to the other, and back again. A playful illustration of the permeability of these categories occurs in the Wallace and Gromit film *The Curse of the Were-Rabbit* (2005), as a character's blood-curdling announcement about the power of the monstrous creature is followed by a series of crashing organ chords. The music's instrumentation, pitch and volume recall a horror movie's score and tempt the viewer to identify it confidently as non-diegetic sound; mischievously, however, the next shot proves it to be *diegetic* after all, generated by an overexcited organist who was initially off-screen (see Figure 10). If this snatch of music crosses from non-diegetic sound to diegetic while still leaving each category intact, other experiments by filmmakers

10 Non-diegetic into diegetic sound in *The Curse of the Were-Rabbit*
(2005)

have the effect of making unstable this seemingly straightforward
distinction. Whether a preference is expressed for Bordwell and
Thompson's *internal diegetic sound* or for Christian Metz's *semi-
diegetic sound*, then, critics are conscious of needing another term
to characterise acoustic matter that emerges from the narrative
space without quite being *of* it. Examples of such sound range from
low-level, paranoia-inducing industrial hums in David Lynch's
work to unlocalisable noises, including voices, in Tarkovsky's films
that hint at the suffusion of the visible world on screen by religious
presences.

   Regardless of whether film sounds are characterised as diegetic,
non-diegetic or something in-between, they relate in a number of
different ways to the images they accompany. Although filmmakers sometimes refer to the unification of vision and sound that is
achieved during editing as 'the married print', the harmonious
matching this term evokes is actually only one possible relationship
between these two tracks: tensions, separations, even divorces are
also feasible. In *Theory of Film* Kracauer proposes that the terms
parallelism and *counterpoint* be used to describe the two basic alternatives of agreement and discordance between sound and vision
(1997: 113). Despite its broad usefulness, however, 'parallelism'
is insufficiently sensitive to the many different ways in which

soundtrack may clarify and intensify the contents of the image. 'Counterpoint' is problematical, too, even as it hints productively at antagonism between the two tracks. To begin with, Chion has shown that the musical analogy intended by Kracauer is inexact: if counterpoint in music is an extended playing against each other of two or more voices or instruments, film's more momentary mismatching of image and sound is better described as *dissonant harmony* (1994: 37). There is also a danger of hierarchism here, since, with its distinguished musical provenance, 'counterpoint' seems to promise something aesthetically superior to the less ambitious 'parallelism'. Indeed, from the 1920s onwards, avant-garde circles fastened upon counterpointed sound for its potential to save cinema from the literalism they feared would result from the new audio technology. Eisenstein, Pudovkin and Alexandrov made precisely this case in the Soviet Union in their 'Statement on Sound' (1928), as did the French Surrealist Georges Hugnet in 1929 when proposing colourfully that all cinematic sounds should be 'mistranslations', with a kiss accompanied by the rolling of a drum and seduction by a banging door (Hammond, 2000: 19). However, like the jump cut considered in Chapter 2, acoustic counterpoint carries no predetermined meaning and, according to context, is available for light-hearted as well as transgressive use. Here a moment from *Singin' in the Rain* (1952) comes to mind. As Gene Kelly's character recalls in voiceover his vaudeville past before he broke into films, the claim that these performances always had 'dignity' plays across shots of buffoonish costumes and unfortunate pratfalls.

All soundtracks are of course constructions, even fictions. If the relationship between sound and picture is often conventionalised to the point where such invention goes unnoticed, it is still in an important sense *arbitrary*. As the third of four-and-a-half fallacies that he suggests undermine study of film soundtrack, Altman refers therefore to 'the reproductive fallacy': 'Recordings do not reproduce sound, they represent sound' (1992: 40). The most apparently 'faithful' or 'literal' on-location recording is not, innocently, a slice of raw acoustic life but is already mediated by numerous decisions such as microphone placement. Elsewhere, during post-production, dialogue may be rerecorded, location noise modified and extra auditory effects incorporated from sound libraries or digital archives. Far from applying a dead weight of realism to cinema, sound proves to be mutable and playful. Noises that seem unproblematically attached to objects on screen often turn out to be acoustic artifice. Stambler recalls trying to render a lion's roar for African scenes in *The Ghost and the Darkness* (1996). Since the lion's own efforts were considered insufficiently leonine, the effect used in the end was a composite of a bear, a tiger and a drag-racing car (Sergi, 2004: 129).

Sustained insights into the fictiveness of soundtrack are offered also by Peter Strickland in his darkly comic film *Berberian Sound Studio* (2012). Here a gentle English sound engineer, accustomed to recording birdsong and church bells for documentaries on the English countryside, finds himself in an Italian studio working on a horror movie. Required, against his better judgement, to generate the sounds of women being tortured, he stabs watermelons, rips cabbage leaves and twists the tops off radishes (see Figure 11). With his ability to conjure a sense of acoustic verisimilitude from an array of everyday objects, this protagonist is a gifted example of that film technician known as a *Foley artist* (named after the early Hollywood sound engineer, Jack Foley). Like contemporary work in film studies itself, however, *Berberian Sound Studio* valuably discloses that,

11 The fictiveness of film sound: *Berberian Sound Studio* (2012). Toby Jones as a sound engineer with the vegetables from which the sounds of a woman's torture will be conjured

in a sense, *all* film sound is Foley art: representation, not reproduction (to utilise again Altman's pivotal distinction).

STOP and THINK

- As in Chapters 1 and 2, begin by taking a manageably short segment of any film. Explore, this time, its acoustic properties, shaking off what remains of the ear's 'indolence, dreaminess, and dullness' (Adorno and Eisler, 2007: 14). Consider initially how, and with what consequences, the sequence distributes – and perhaps hierarchises – the four acoustic elements of speech (dialogue and/or voiceover), sound effects, music and silence. Arrange the components of this bit of soundtrack also into diegetic and non-diegetic phenomena, assessing their respective power and value.

- To explore further sound's role in the production of meaning, undertake the exercise that Chion calls *masking* (1994: 187–8). This involves running your chosen sequence several times, but in different ways: first with both image and sound intact, then with sound muted, and then, most counter-intuitively, with the image concealed and your attention only upon sound. How does your evaluation of the image alter when sound is withdrawn? What do you learn about film sound by listening to it in its pure state, momentarily freed from its condition as the image's conjoined twin? Does such heightened acoustic sensitivity survive once sound and vision are reunited in a final viewing of the sequence?

- These exercises require a listening environment that, if not quite hermetically sealed, is protected from many incidental noises. Scholars including Altman and Sergi, however, resist as artificial and falsifying any approach that detaches film soundtrack from the ambient noises that occur in all actual audio-viewing situations (from crowded multiplex to family living-room). Are they right to argue that the composed soundtrack should be inserted into this larger acoustic context?

Film music

Edward Bast, an earnest young composer in William Gaddis's novel *J R* (1975), finds himself having to undertake some commercial projects in order to keep body and soul together. He is particularly dismayed, however, when one film producer requests from him 'some nothing music', which, so as to leave intact the sovereignty of dialogue, 'couldn't have any real form, anything distinctive about it any sound anything that would distract' (Gaddis, 1985: 112). This fictional character's horror at such a peculiar commission echoes the responses of several concert-hall composers when asked to write music for films. Most stridently, Igor Stravinsky declared in 1946 that 'I cannot accept it as music' (5). Unlike complete and organic musical forms such as the symphony, even the fullest film score is discontinuous, existing only in bursts and seemingly never able to achieve autonomy as aesthetic statement because of its adhesion to the image on screen.

Film music is most subservient with respect to the visual track when it takes the form known as *mickey-mousing*: 'illustrative musical effects synchronized with specific events in a film's physical action' (Cooke, 2008: 29). As the term indicates, this practice is strongly associated with animation: recall, for example, pizzicato playing of the violin as the cartoon mouse tiptoes past a cat. The unfortunate Bast in *J R* suffers here, too, asked to supply 'zebra music' for a wildlife documentary (Gaddis, 1985: 202). But if mickey-mousing represents the score at its least artistically ambitious, some critics argue that film music even of a less literal-minded sort similarly tends towards banality. According to Adorno and Eisler, the classical Hollywood score 'converts a kiss into a magazine cover, an outburst of unmitigated pain into a melodrama, a scene from nature into an oleograph' (2007: 21). From this perspective, film music is not simply reproductive (finding an equivalent in another artistic language for the image's contents), but also *reductive* (simplifying the import of those images and inciting spurious emotionalism, rather than rational engagement, in the audio–viewer). Music is thus central to mainstream cinema's conservative functioning. Adorno and Eisler write, to be sure, in a specific conjuncture, as not only adherents of musical modernism but as German Marxists unhappily exiled in capitalist America just after World War II. Caution should be exercised, then, in extending their critique to the totality of classical Hollywood scoring, let alone to the varied film musics of later times and other places. Nevertheless, their observations retain piquancy. What is achieved by John Barry's swooning 'prairie music' in *Dances with Wolves* (1990), say, if not the conversion of 'a scene from nature' into a decorative tableau, 'an oleograph' indeed?

If film's sound practices tend to be conservative in selecting only certain acoustic materials from a near-infinite array to accompany particular images, this tendency is especially marked in the case of musical scoring. Shots denotative of specific times and places, or of specific racial and ethnic communities, often have, almost as a second skin, a familiar type of musical accompaniment. No image of Native Americans massing for attack in the classic Hollywood western was complete without scoring by the beating of tom-toms. More recently, too, such musical reductionism and stereotyping can be detected in cinema. The shock of hearing Aaron Copland's orchestral music over shots of an African American urban neighbourhood in *He Got Game* (1998), for example, comes precisely from recognition that the director, Spike Lee, is not succumbing here to the expectation of hip hop accompaniment. Scenes of rural Ireland, also, may continue to be sonically fitted out with bodhrán, fiddle and uilleann pipes. At one level, film scores of this kind play a relatively harmless role of narrative cueing: hearing a bodhrán tells us economically that the unidentified landscape on screen is in Ireland, not Wales. There is still, however, the risk in such instances of film music flattening out complexities as Adorno and Eisler allege. Choosing, in this Irish example, a traditional musical arrangement rather than an electric guitar solo or an acid jazz performance threatens to render the nation in terms of an antique postcard.

The gravitational pull that particular film images exert upon certain kinds of music is acknowledged by Quincy Jones even as he whimsically floats alternatives: 'I've always wanted to see a juxtaposition of a Victorian setting with modern soul music. It would really crack me up to find, in the middle of a scene out of Dickens, James Brown screaming away as the town crier' (Gorbman, 1987: 83). It was never likely, of course, that Elizabethan lute-plucking would accompany a Roman epic such as *Gladiator* (2000), or that the protagonist of Spielberg's *Lincoln* (2012) would abolish slavery in the United States to the beat of drum and bass. Yet the problem with such alternative soundtracks is precisely *not* one of their historical inauthenticity. For it is not as if the scores of *Gladiator* and *Lincoln* seek to replicate the musical forms and instrumentations of ancient Rome and mid-nineteenth-century America respectively: lute-playing and drum and bass would actually be no more alien to these films' historical settings than are the orchestral modes actually chosen. But the tradition of scoring established in the classic Hollywood era means that romantic symphonic-style music has been naturalised, as it were, and does not register as troublingly asynchronous with respect to the period a film represents in the way that electronic breakbeats would in *Lincoln*. Conventions restricting what type of music may permissibly accompany an image are still powerful in mainstream Western cinema, despite examples of dissonant, counter-intuitive scoring that range from Brian Eno's electronic compositions for Jarman's *Sebastiane* (1976), set in an outpost of the Roman Empire in AD 300, to the disturbing drones and pitches composed by Radiohead's Jonny Greenwood for *There Will Be Blood* (2007), which is set in the US at the turn of the twentieth century. The hip hop, rock and pop inclusions in Baz Luhrmann's *The Great Gatsby* (2013), discussed below in this chapter's case study, are also instances of bold, period-inappropriate music.

These experiments in disparity between image and music have the effect of making us aware of the strangeness, in general, of film's musical accompaniment. Given that mainstream Western cinema's intent has usually been to naturalise its storytelling, to remove all traces of cinematic construction itself, the inclusion of something as obviously artificial as a musical soundtrack would seem self-defeating. As Gorbman asks pointedly: '*why music ...* why is it permitted into the narrative regime of the sound film at all?' (1987: 4). The answers that she and other critics have given to this question vary. From one perspective, cinema may be following earlier expressive modes such as Greek tragedy and Victorian melodrama that sought to maximise the impact of new kinds of narrative and spectacle through the addition of music; indeed, early in the twentieth century, the composer Arnold Schoenberg and painter Wassily Kandinsky expressed a belief that because of its technological powers film was equipped to become the supreme musiconarrative art. Another suggestion by scholars is that a musical score provides continuity across disparate shots and thereby serves to distract from the artifice of the editing process. Considered in this light, film music does not expose the cinematic illusion, as might have been presumed, but actually *conceals* it.

There is another cluster of possible reasons for film music's existence which Gorbman terms *psychological/anthropological*. She argues that film music, not least the classic Hollywood score, offers the audio-viewer the kind of gratification associated with infancy. It supplies a 'bath or gel of affect' into which audiences sink; it 'relaxes the censor, drawing the spectator further into the fantasy-illusion suggested by filmic narration'; it mimics a 'hypnotist's voice' in both its soothing, melodic quality and its invitation to submit to a process of regression (Gorbman, 1987: 5–6). Not just any regression either, but, extremely, regression to the point of immersion once more in the primal space of the womb. Fashioning an all-around soundscape, the film score replicates what the French psychoanalyst Guy Rosolato calls the 'sonorous envelope': that is to say, the seamless acoustic environment – pulsing, bubbling, murmuring – by which the infant is enfolded while still within its mother's body.

The psychoanalysis of film music pioneered by Gorbman valuably uncovers the regressiveness of much of our audio-viewing. A musical score, permeating the cinema (or other spectatorial venue), may indeed join with the space's darkness to conjure up an approximation of the uterine condition. For all its insights, however, this approach is also vulnerable to serious critique. To begin with, the psychoanalytic construction of the audio-viewer is achieved at the cost of drastically neglecting his or her cultural positioning. Like all music, after all, film music is implicated in what Edward Said calls 'an ensemble of political and social involvements, affiliations, transgressions' (1991: 71). Rather than simply promising the audio-viewer a return to some primal state of being, then, the forms and contents of any score also induce in us a variety of real-world responses. To hear tom-toms in a classic western is thus not necessarily to become immersed in blissful regression: another possible reaction, now at a *conscious* rather than unconscious level, is to reflect angrily on the past and present condition of Native Americans.

Restoration to centre-stage of analysis of the audio-viewer's conscious activity is precisely what is proposed by theorists who approach film music from a *cognitivist* rather than psychoanalytic standpoint. Jeff Smith, in an important essay, writes that 'if film music is to play any part in the text's construction of meaning through its cuing functions, it could not only act on the unconscious, but would need to be perceived and cognized by film spectators' (1996: 235). Helpfully, Smith goes on to say that a cognitive account of film music seeks to address 'the spectator's mental activities in utilizing cues that musically convey setting, character and point of view' (240). The audio-viewer, in this light, is ceaselessly engaged in processes of information-gathering, deduction and interpretation as he or she listens to a score. Settings, then, may be identified by musical cues, and characters can be judged, at least provisionally, according to their acoustic accompaniment (put crudely, a figure who appears with dissonant scoring on the soundtrack is unlikely to prove the romantic hero). Conscious recognition may take place also of a score's use of *leitmotif* – a musical phrase attached to a particular character or location which will recur during a film, each new use cueing the cognitively engaged listener.

If the film score offers, in Gorbman's terms, a gel of affect, it is, to say the least, spread unevenly. As Smith states wittily, 'the intermittent nature of film music suggests that it is at best partial and fragmentary, a slatted playpen rather than a womb, a topical solution rather than an enveloping bath' (1996: 237). Even the fullest scores are supplanted for long periods by other acoustic matter. But while a case might still be made for an all-absorbing music with respect, say, to some of classical Hollywood's extended, single-authored scores, it is less convincing as a thesis when applied to recent film's compositional practices. Musical soundtracks conceived as heterogeneous, discontinuous sampling of already existing materials are now an important adjunct of – or even alternative to – the commissioned work of a composer. Stanley Kubrick was innovatory here, notoriously rejecting the music that had been specifically written for *2001: A Space Odyssey* (1968) and substituting an eclectic score comprising work by such classical composers as Johann Strauss, Richard Strauss and György Ligeti. But where Kubrick is interested here in counterpointing music and image – what happens to our sense of a spacecraft when, counter-intuitively, it is accompanied by a Viennese waltz? – other, later filmmakers appear absorbed by possibilities of sampling to the point where music's interaction with image and its role in advancing or intensifying narrative become less important and the soundtrack almost stands alone as a source of pleasure. This transition can be loosely measured by juxtaposing Kubrick's earnest practice in *2001* (and his subsequent films) with the use of music by Tarantino. The soundtracks for the two *Kill Bill* films (2003–4), for instance, are a musical bazaar, heaping together earlier movie scores by Bernard Herrmann and Ennio Morricone, songs by Nancy Sinatra and Johnny Cash, the theme tune from the US TV series *Ironside*, musical fragments from Japan and Latin America, and much more. While certainly not indiscriminately chosen, these eclectic musics have a greater potential than in Kubrick for detaching themselves from each film's visual field and becoming objects of investment in their own right (a delight then extended by purchase of the musical soundtrack).

Tarantino may be quite thoroughgoing in his prioritising of musical pleasure, but he is far from unique here. Consider other recent works like the two *Bridget Jones* films (2001–4), *Marie Antoinette* (2005), *Kick-Ass* (2010) and *The Wolf of Wall Street* (2013) that take on additional post-cinematic lives in the spin-off CDs and downloads of the rock and pop music sampled in each case. There is nothing new, of course, about such slippage between film and music industries. Such 'synergistic marketing' or 'cross-promotion' (Cooke, 2008: 415, 416) was evident as early as the silent era, when consumers would buy sheet music of songs or instrumental pieces they had previously heard accompanying a film. Nevertheless, some film music now appears semi-autonomous, only temporarily and imperfectly anchored to the film image before it finds its true home in an iPod's playlist. The logical next step would be full separation itself – 'soundtracks without films', as Kevin Donnelly terms them (2005: 150). A pioneering venture of this kind is the Austrian composer Arnold Schoenberg's 'Accompaniment to a Film Scene' (1929–30), an orchestral piece written without any specific movie sequence in mind. More recently, Brian Eno's *Music for Films* album (1978) includes tracks with such cinematically suggestive titles as 'Events in Dense Fog', 'Patrolling Wire Borders' and 'Final Sunset'. Film music in these instances is freed from subordination to vision and finally, in a kind of answer to Stravinsky's objections with which this section began, able to realise itself as autonomous artistic expression.

STOP and THINK

As another exercise to help sharpen analysis of soundtrack, Chion proposes a *forced marriage* of sound and vision (1994: 188–9). Of course *any* matching of these two tracks involves a measure of coercion: even the bark that straightforwardly accompanies the on-screen dog is the outcome of technical operations that range from microphone positioning on set to the bark's modification or even fabrication during editing. Chion has particularly in mind, however, an activity to develop awareness of how non-diegetic music interacts with the film image. Follow his lead, then, by choosing a sequence that is already musically scored. With a wide selection of musical alternatives to hand, substitute each of these in turn for the original choice. You might, for example, replace Celine Dion singing 'My Heart Will Go On' at the lachrymose conclusion of *Titanic* (1997) with a Chopin piano prelude, then a traditional military march, then Beyoncé's 'Crazy In Love'. Assess how understanding of the image mutates during each of these musical substitutions. What general conclusions might be drawn about the functions and powers of film music?

Case study: *The Great Gatsby* (2013)

The Great Gatsby (1925), by F. Scott Fitzgerald, is a *noisy* novel, fully as attentive to the acoustic particularities of the world it describes as to visual details such as Gatsby's yellow Rolls-Royce, or his shirts of 'coral and apple–green and lavender and faint orange' (1990: 89). From the very beginning of his recapitulation of events, Nick Carraway, the book's narrator, documents significant sounds, registering, for example, Tom Buchanan's 'gruff husky tenor'

(12), the 'murmuring' and 'whispering' that by contrast are Daisy Buchanan's vocal modes (14, 15), and the 'boom' as Tom abruptly shuts a window in a characteristic display of masculine force (13). Later, of course, *Gatsby* becomes a notably *musical* novel, with Nick's narration discriminating between musics that range from a 'notorious contralto' publicly performing a jazz song (48) to, more intimately, Klipspringer playing a romantic ballad on the piano to mark the visit Daisy makes to Gatsby's mansion.

Baz Luhrmann's adaptation of *The Great Gatsby* replicates this acoustic sensitivity. If some commentators on the film foreground its visual specificities, such as the computer-generated replicas of 1920s Manhattan or the vertiginous zooms from the tops of skyscrapers, others, in moods variously of exhilaration or distaste, have been quick to fasten upon its sound design. The film's soundtrack is ceaselessly busy, layering multiple musics (both diegetic and non-diegetic), sound effects, voiceover and – rarely, though suggestively – silence. A comment made in interview by Luhrmann brings out this complexity even as it addresses only the musical accompaniment to one sequence, without considering the role played in the scene by other acoustic materials: 'we go in a very short time from Jay Z rapping over a contemporary track, "100$ Dolla Bill", into a jazz version of that contemporary track, into a piece of score, back to the contemporary track, back into traditional jazz by the Bryan Ferry Orchestra, and then end the scene with a new contemporary track that is jazz influenced' (Luhrmann, 2013: n.p.). For hostile reviewers, the result of such hectic activity is auditory chaos, with this ceaseless intercutting between sounds mimicking the MTV rhythm by which the image track is edited and having a comparable effect of denying the audio-viewer an interval for reflection. Careful study, however, will uncover calculated motivations for and interesting consequences of *The Great Gatsby*'s sound design.

There are, certainly, risks in the scale and diversity of *The Great Gatsby*'s musical samplings. While the film incorporates a commissioned score by Craig Armstrong, frequently a collaborator with Luhrmann, this is dominated by lush romantic strings that hint at a sentimental take on Fitzgerald's novel. Much more striking is the pre-existing music of many provenances laid over Armstrong's work. Jay Z's hip hop contributions may have attracted the greatest critical attention, but there are also, for example, a rap by will.i.am, music by British indie acts The xx and Florence and the Machine, work by the Belgian-Australian indie musician Gotye and Bryan Ferry's song 'Love Is the Drug'. A jaundiced perspective would see here rather too naked an attempt to synergise with multiple musical demographics, Luhrmann's film functioning, in this respect, not as a critique of excess consumption but as an active abettor of it. The audio-viewer of *The Great Gatsby* may at times be uncomfortably close to the devotee of 'world music', sampling a wide range of musics deprived of their cultural and political co-ordinates and rendered equivalent now as sources of listening pleasure. There is another danger, too, with this kind of *compilation score* made up of already existing music; as Kathryn Kalinak points out, such songs may 'trail with them personal histories and trigger memories, experiences, and emotions, which may be at odds with [a] film's dramatic needs' (2010: 87). A case in point is Amy Winehouse's 'Back to Black', featured non-diegetically in *The Great Gatsby* (albeit as performed by Beyoncé and André 3000). Rather than responding to this musical cue for the narrative clarification and thematic underlining it might offer, the audio-viewer will possibly be distracted by poignant thoughts about Winehouse, who died in 2011.

For the literary critic T. Austin Graham, the eclectic musical sampling undertaken by Luhrmann seems initially to disclose a lack of seriousness or edge in the film. Everything, acoustically as well as visually, gets sucked into 'a pop cultural vortex': 'This is the Jazz Age in a remix and mash-up culture' (Graham et al., 2013: n.p.). The language, however, is kindly intended, evoking what is for Graham a salutary sense of disunity or discomposure in Luhrmann's film (not least in its soundscape). Paul Giles, another literary scholar, follows a similar line, identifying this adaptation's governing principles as 'jarring displacement' and 'strategic dislocation' (2013: 13). While the examples Giles gives of such radical, troubling juxtapositions are visual rather than auditory, his argument is more conducive still with respect to *The Great Gatsby*'s heterogeneous sound design. Many previous film representations of the American 1920s, not least the last cinematic adaptation of Fitzgerald's novel in 1974, have turned the period into an object of nostalgia, as predictable acoustically with its jazz pieces as it is visually with its flappers and cocktails. However, as the audio-viewer of Luhrmann's film is jolted abruptly between musical genres, or forced to process the meshing of contemporary pop and hip hop on the non-diegetic soundtrack with shots of people dancing the Charleston, the ear as well as the eye is prevented from slipping into complacency.

It is important to consider who performs the interpolated songs in *The Great Gatsby*. From early in Fitzgerald's novel, there are suggestions that traditional white hegemony in the US is facing challenges: Tom is reading *The Rise of the Colored Empires* and expresses a fear that 'if we don't look out the white race will be – will be utterly submerged' (1990: 18). If Luhrmann's film is attentive visually to an assertive African American presence (prominent shots, for example, of a black trumpeter in Manhattan), it carries out much of its most racially progressive work at the level of the non-diegetic soundtrack, with the incorporation of music not only by Jay Z but by other hip hop and jazz artists. Similar arguments might be made for the film's acoustic treatment of women. In Fitzgerald's novel Daisy is something of a cipher, less an agent in her own right than a projection by Gatsby; the same might largely be said of Luhrmann's adaptation, despite Carey Mulligan's affecting performance. On the non-diegetic soundtrack, however, female voices are potent. Particularly notable here is Lana Del Rey, performing the song 'Young and Beautiful', which is first heard as Gatsby shows Daisy around his mansion and then recurs – more faintly – when Gatsby retreats with her to the garden during one of his lavish parties. The song, performed by an artist with a persona fashioned partly in the lineage of strong female musicians such as Janis Joplin and Courtney Love, actually functions in counterpoint to the images. Whereas the visual track is co-ordinated at this point with Gatsby's desire, Del Rey's track articulates instead a sardonic female perspective ('And will you still love me/When I'm no longer young and beautiful?').

While female voices are important in the musical part of *The Great Gatsby*'s non-diegetic soundtrack, they are much less prominent in the voiceover portion. At one point, it is true, Jordan Baker's voice passes from the diegetic to the non-diegetic register as she recalls the earlier relationship of Gatsby and Daisy; elsewhere,

Daisy begins to read aloud on screen one of her old love letters to
Gatsby, before her voice is relocated to the non-diegetic soundtrack
(albeit to be abruptly silenced by the shrill ringing of a telephone).
Female voiceover in mainstream film, Britta Sjogren argues, is 'a
particularly powerful formal feature that produces an awareness
of heterogeneous consciousness, plural point of view' (2006: 197).
Precisely, however, because of this radical potential, it remains a
rarity in the Hollywood tradition; and so it is unsurprising that in
The Great Gatsby, too, voiceover is predominantly male property.
Nick's voice is heard frequently on the non-diegetic soundtrack,
offering the audio-viewer cues to the interpretation of events and
characters (in particular, of course, seeking to cue a positive evaluation of Gatsby). The authority of this narrator is enhanced by his
implicit identification with Fitzgerald himself (the book that we
see him writing about Gatsby and that he reads aloud from non-
diegetically is exactly the text that Luhrmann is adapting here).
Nevertheless, another critical commentary on voiceover in cinema
cautions us against endowing it with too much narrative power.
Kaja Silverman acknowledges that 'the embodied voice-over desig-
nates not only psychological but diegetic interiority [...] it emanates
from the center of the story, rather than from some radically other
time and place' (1988: 53). She goes on, however, to argue that
'Hollywood dictates that the closer a voice is to the "inside" of the
narrative, the more remote it is from the "outside" [...] In other
words, it equates diegetic interiority with discursive impotence and
lack of control' (53–4). Nick, in Luhrmann's film, is 'inside' because
of his closeness to events and the privileged access he has to the
space of the voiceover in which he can describe and evaluate them;
he is 'outside', however, in that his rule over the narrative extends
only so far. Besides being unable to command the film's visual track
(there is relatively little use of subjective cinematography to imply
his vision of things), he cannot exert authority over the totality
of non-diegetic sound. Here, his narrative voice frequently has to
give way to those of female and African American singers, evoking
indeed that sense of 'heterogeneous consciousness' and 'plural point
of view' to which Sjogren refers.

   Not surprisingly, critical commentary on *The Great Gatsby*'s
soundtrack has dwelt on its more startling features, in particular

the anachronistic use of hip hop. Significantly less attention has been paid to the utilisation of humbler sound effects. Before concluding, however, it is important to itemise and evaluate a series of jarring diegetic noises in Luhrmann's film. Recall, for example, the crunching of the workmen's spades in the valley of ashes that hints at the exploited labour underlying conspicuous wealth here; or a glass smashing, an ice-pick stabbing at ice and the roaring of car engines that collectively evoke the destructiveness of the privileged class. Above all, perhaps, is the loud ringing – several times – of telephones, suggesting imperatives from elsewhere that in the end will not be denied. At times, these everyday sounds register more loudly than might be expected. The clearest instance of this occurs when Gatsby is awaiting the arrival of Daisy in Nick's cottage and the ominous ticking of the clock next to him becomes magnified. Here is an experiment in *subjective sound*, the relocation of what film studies terms *point of audition* from a relatively neutral, unmarked place in the scene to Gatsby's own hearing. Despite the further evidence such moments give of film sound's fabricated nature, the diegetic soundtrack in *The Great Gatsby* has the salutary effect of evoking the pressures of *the real*. If the world on screen seems amenable to Gatsby's desires, all of these abrasive noises suggest that, in the end, it is not. To borrow a distinction used by Nick in Fitzgerald's novel, the image track of Luhrmann's film often seems 'enchanted' by this moneyed milieu (its architecture, décor, costumes), yet the soundtrack is 'repelled' (37).

Selected reading

Besides the specialist studies listed below, see also extensive coverage of film sound in the books by Bordwell and Thompson, and Corrigan and White cited in Chapter 1's 'Selected reading'.

Altman, Rick (2004), *Silent Film Sound* (New York: Columbia University Press).
The definitive work on silent cinema's varied, evolving soundscapes: convincingly theorised, prodigiously researched and accessibly written – handsomely illustrated, too.
Beck, Jay and Tony Grajeda (eds) (2008), *Lowering the Boom: Critical Studies in Film Sound* (Champaign: University of Illinois Press).

Stimulating, varied investigations into cinematic uses of sound and music (of silence, too); case studies range from Jonathan Demme's *The Silence of the Lambs* (1991) to the soundscapes of documentary and avant-garde film.

Chion, Michel (1994), *Audio-Vision: Sound on Screen*, ed. and trans. Claudia Gorbman (New York: Columbia University Press).

The most sustained attempt yet to raise the conceptualisation of film sound to the level of studies of the image; occasionally too easily tempted by neologisms, but an indispensable work.

Chion, Michel (2009), *Film, a Sound Art*, trans. Claudia Gorbman (New York: Columbia University Press).

Longer and less systematically organised than *Audio-Vision*, but an invaluable companion text, offering reflection on sound practices in films of many periods and traditions.

Cooke, Mervyn (2008), *A History of Film Music* (Cambridge: Cambridge University Press).

An immensely useful text, prioritising 'factual information above theoretical abstraction' and covering its subject engagingly, in compendious detail and with pleasing attention to film music's geographical variants.

Kalinak, Kathryn (2010), *Film Music: A Very Short Introduction* (New York: Oxford University Press).

Excellent starting point on this subject, prior to tackling studies empirically fuller like Cooke's or theoretically more elaborated like Gorbman's.

Lastra, James (2000), *Sound Technology and the American Cinema: Perception, Representation, Modernity* (New York: Columbia University Press).

Conceptually and empirically rich, this book explores industrial, aesthetic, ideological, even philosophical disturbances caused by US film's conversion to sound.

Sergi, Gianluca (2004), *The Dolby Era: Film Sound in Contemporary Hollywood* (Manchester: Manchester University Press).

Valuable consideration of aesthetic, technological and economic questions posed by sound reproduction in recent American cinema; also features interviews with key innovators and practitioners of film sound, including Ray Dolby.

Wierzbicki, James (ed.) (2012), *Music, Sound and Filmmakers: Sonic Style in Cinema* (New York: Routledge).

Engaging, varied essays on a multiplicity of film soundscapes, extending from classical Hollywood through European art cinema to recent US work by Tarantino, Gus Van Sant and the Coen brothers.

Online resources

'Film Sound', http://filmsound.org/.

Seemingly moribund since 2008, but still a valuable resource, collecting a mass of materials on the history, theory, practice and terminology of film soundtrack.

'How Film and TV Music Communicate', www.brianmorrell.co.uk/film-books.html.

Features the texts of two online books by composer and musicologist Brian Morrell: full of specific analyses, deploying more specialist terminology than most other studies of music in film.

'Silent Era', www.silentera.com.

Enthusiastically maintained resource on silent cinema, which includes both contemporaneous and new materials on the period's sound practices.

4
Film and narrative

Narrative film and its others

'N, there's no doubt about it, has to be for Narrative', writes Peter Wollen in 'An Alphabet of Cinema' (2002: 12). Wollen fashions here a miniature narrative of his own, delineating the history of cinema from its beginnings as 'the history of the development of a "film language" that would facilitate storytelling' (12). Certainly, the telling of stories has been fundamental to both the aesthetics and the economics of film, reaching far back into the medium's history and extending globally also. It did not take long following its emergence late in the nineteenth century for film to become principally or predominantly a storytelling medium, and it remains one today, with cinema heavily implicated in what one critic describes as 'the immense demand for narrative material by modern media systems' (Thompson, 2003: 83). Acknowledging the importance of this subject, then, this chapter will mainly be concerned to introduce and assess a number of critical approaches to film's narrativity. But before doing so, it is vital to recognise significant *non-* or even *anti*-narrative traditions in cinema. Despite Wollen's confident storytelling above, the history of film is not, after all, to be emplotted straightforwardly as one of narrative's inevitable and absolute hegemony.

Research by Tom Gunning, André Gaudreault and others has established that, for much of its first decade, film was more concerned to demonstrate its powers of visual representation than to tell stories. This early *cinema of attractions*, in Gunning's enduring phrase, was an 'exhibitionist cinema' rather than one dedicated to

absorbing the spectator narratively (2006: 382). Pioneering filmmakers such as the Lumière brothers in France, Robert W. Paul
and G. A. Smith in England and the innovators at the Edison
Manufacturing Company in the United States attempted the 'har-
nessing of visibility', in order to present 'a series of views to an
audience' (Gunning, 2006: 382). Seemingly mundane, everyday
occurrences might be rendered engaging by the sheer novelty of
their presentation as spectacles of movement. Hence, for example,
the Lumières' *Arrival of a Train at La Ciotat* (1895) and *Children
Playing Marbles* (1896), or Paul's *Rough Sea at Dover* (1895). As
critics have shown, however, other very early films sought to shock
or astound, rather than simply to satisfy a basic desire to see something previously uncaptured by a medium able to record motion.
What Gunning terms 'an aesthetic of astonishment', a non-narrative
'cinema of instants, rather than developing situations' (2004: 870),
was supplied by films of multiple sorts, ranging from Méliès's short
trick movies (one of which, utilising the magical properties of the
jump cut, was referenced in Chapter 2) through variously documentary or restaged battle scenes to the so-called *phantom rides* in
which cameras placed on trains or trams communicated an exhilarating sense of speed. Typical of this mode of presentation was
Edison's *Electrocuting an Elephant* (1903), in which the unfortunate
animal was decontextualised from any kind of story and made an
occasion instead for vivid, shocking spectacle.

In the wake of the scholarship by Gunning, Gaudreault and their
colleagues, early films have been significantly reframed. No longer
judged simply in the light of subsequent narrative cinema, with their
makers found to lack the conceptual acumen and technical nous to
compose stories, they emerge instead as contributions to an alternative film aesthetic. Although it is true that from the first decade
of the twentieth century onwards narrative film became dominant
in the United States, England and elsewhere, this should not lead
to the conclusion that the cinema of attractions or the aesthetic of
astonishment was simply superseded; rather, as Gunning writes,
it 'goes underground, both into certain avant-garde practices and
as a component of narrative films, more evident in some genres
(e.g. the musical) than in others' (2006: 382). 'Attractions' can be
found co-ordinated with storytelling in many films, not least the

films of our own moment. What is the lengthy first shot of *Gravity*, for instance, but an astonishing, updated phantom ride, whirling the spectator through interstellar voids rather than over the East Anglian cobblestones that were traversed in *Norwich – Tramway Ride through Principal Streets* (1902)? If this episode is bound into storytelling by its initiation of the crisis faced by Sandra Bullock's and George Clooney's characters, it nevertheless offers the audience a distinct capsule or module of visual and aural gratification: to borrow a final time from Gunning's work on early cinema, we recognise here 'this primal power of the attraction running beneath the armature of narrative regulation' (2006: 387). Equally, while some audiences for Michael Bay's *Transformers: Age of Extinction* (2014) might have been chiefly exercised by its plot of global peril, it is likely far more were engaged by the visual and sonic array of chases, explosions and robot retoolings (especially when the film was experienced in 3D and on IMAX scale). In instances such as these, then, it is possible to see recurrences of that non-narrative aesthetic that critics have uncovered in the earliest filmmaking. Recurrences but not direct replications, however: Wanda Strauven reminds us that the old cinema of attractions may take on different values when it is 're-used, re-mastered, re-loaded' in contemporary conditions (2006: 25).

As Gunning's work in particular has shown, the earliest film spectacles should be aligned not only with a popular visual economy represented also by vaudeville, fairgrounds and the newly established amusement parks, but with avant-garde artistic experiment. Even as late as the 1920s, a time when advanced storytelling had achieved dominance in the cinemas of the United States and Western Europe, significant figures associated with innovation in the arts could be seen challenging the idea that film was a medium predestined towards narrative. Expression of such anti-narrative sentiment was especially vehement in French avant-garde circles. In 1921 the director and critic Jean Epstein, given in his own practice to an Impressionist aesthetic, went so far as to call narrative in film 'a lie'; six years later, Germaine Dulac, an important pioneer of Surrealist as well as Impressionist cinema, was outspoken enough to convict of 'a criminal error' those of her fellow filmmakers who neglected to exploit the rich potentialities of the image simply so that they could tell stories instead (Kracauer, 1997: 179). In the very ways in which they consumed cinema, besides through the films they made and the critical writings they produced, members of artistic vanguards fought against the rule of narrative. Here the strange spectatorial habit of André Breton, author of the Surrealist Manifestos, is instructive. Breton recalled how, as a young man in Nantes, he moved rapidly from cinema to cinema, watching only a fragment of film in each and trying thereby to configure the medium as a source of local, discontinuous sensations rather than as a machine merely for storytelling (Hammond, 2000: 73).

Frenetic cinema-hopping of this sort testifies, by its very existence, to film narrative's power and to the inventive strategies required to outwit or challenge this. More substantial resistance from the same period before World War II is evident in Luis Buñuel and Salvador Dalí's two Surrealist films, *Un chien andalou* (1928) and *L'Âge d'or* (1930). Here images are juxtaposed in such a way as to disrupt spatio-temporal continuity and block the emergence of stable characters: the opening shots of the first of these works, for example, feature among other things a woman's eyeball apparently being sliced, a man cycling and a severed hand. In both films the image tracks are not reducible to customary narrative order (though interpreters have tried to bind them to alternative logics, notably to dreamwork as Freud theorises it).

The Surrealism of Buñuel and Dalí can be joined to all those other avant-garde and experimental ventures in cinema that eschew the medium's facility for storytelling and explore instead its imagistic or material properties. Several of those alternative practices may briefly be cited here. Surrealist juxtaposition itself maintains a vestigial life in contemporary filmmaking, as in the work of the US director David Lynch that culminates in *Inland Empire* (2006). At other times, the overbearing narrative tradition has been challenged so as to invest cinema instead with the properties of religious or metaphysical vision. To the work of the Soviet director Andrei Tarkovsky, alluded to glancingly in Chapters 2 and 3, might be added a film such as Terrence Malick's *To the Wonder* (2012). Certainly, a plot can be discerned in the Malick film, focused upon the personal crises of a character played by Ben Affleck; it is likely, however, that in watching the film audiences are engaged less by the turn of events or the psychology of character than by the rapturous charge carried by Malick's images of cornfields or Mont Saint-Michel. While Malick fashions a series of striking shots, other film-makers of an experimental, non-narrative kind have been interested in exploring the hypnotic power of a single image (echoing, inter-estingly, those one-shot 'actualities' with which cinema begins). A striking venture in this respect is Andy Warhol's eight-hour *Empire* (1964), in which the camera gazes on New York's Empire State Building as night falls. If narrative remains at all here, it has been drastically downscaled to the drama of lights going on or off.

For all their richness and variety, however, cinematic inter-ventions of the sort just described may appear marginal or aber-rant phenomena. The twentieth century witnessed, after all, the emergence, consolidation and globalisation of narrative cinema. Narrative's gravitational pull is even such that, as in this chapter so far, attempts to uncover and describe alternative practices are liable to have storytelling at their backs. Given this centrality, it becomes still more imperative to develop instruments for the analysis of film narrative. To identify and categorise the protocols of those cin-ematic stories by which we are often absorbed, however, is not nec-essarily an easy matter. In film as in other media, narrative does not usually draw attention to its own operations; it is, as Roland Barthes says, 'simply there, like life itself' (1977: 79). Bringing to the surface something as deeply embedded as this thus requires approaches and vocabularies that may seem alien or abstract. Nevertheless, these resources are helpful in developing our critical self-consciousness and in enabling us to recognise – and perhaps to resist – the designs which film's stories have upon us.

Two approaches to character in film

'People who make fiction films', writes Paisley Livingston, 'typi-cally devote a great deal of effort to the invention and portrayal of characters. Making sense of these characters is, in turn, a central part of most filmgoers' experiences' (1996: 149). In view of the importance of character to both the realisation and the reception of films, then, it is surprising that as a topic it has not always been cen-tral to film studies. Murray Smith, author of one of the key books in this part of the field (*Engaging Characters: Fiction, Emotion, and the Cinema*, first published in 1995), has recalled that when he began his work 'the subject of character seemed irredeemably unfashionable' (2010: 232). We can speculate on why the subject has often struggled to gain traction. In the first place, perhaps, discussion of film characters threatens to be no more rigorous than an exchange of personal likes and dislikes, with contributor X expressing enthusiasm for Ron Weasley and contributor Y loathing of Hermione Granger. Second, the sheer human stuff of characters on screen may seem to put obstacles in the way of that critical abstraction on which academic work depends. However, in the first of two approaches to this topic considered below, we see a properly cold and distancing discourse. By contrast, the second approach is closer to the fleshiness, so to speak, of film characters; nevertheless, as will be disclosed, reckoning with them as substantial figures that inspire our sympathy or our distaste need not be at the expense of conceptual rigour.

We begin, though, by bringing across to film studies work on character produced during the moment of Russian Formalism. Flourishing in the post-Revolutionary Soviet Union, until falling foul of Stalinist orthodoxy, the Russian Formalists were, as their name indicates, relatively unconcerned with artistic *contents* and dedicated instead to uncovering the formal or structuring principles of aesthetic production (not least the operations of narrative). While much of the movement's output specialised in literature, several key scholars also took a keen interest in cinema, their enthusiasm galvanised by the contemporaneous wave of innovative filmmaking in the Soviet Union by Eisenstein, Vertov, Kuleshov and others. In one of the earliest phases of film theory, articles on the semantics and stylistics of the medium poured forth. Of particular concern to us here, however, is a critical text by a Formalist who was less obviously engaged by cinema. Far from affiliating himself with such a modern artistic practice, Vladimir Propp actually took as his object of study the archaic form of the Russian fairytale. His pioneering *Morphology of the Folktale* (1928) emphasises the 'two-fold quality' of these traditional tales (1968: 20). On the one hand is their 'amazing multiformity, picturesqueness, and color', all of those vivid local details that differentiate one story from another (21). But on the other is the stories' 'no less striking uniformity', the 'repetition' uncovered by the reader in moving from one to the next (21). Once the underlying compositional logic of the fairytale has been identified, in fact, surface variations among particular instances of the genre become conceptually unimportant.

Propp's analysis of the story-form's deep structure has a forbidding mathematical exactitude. He subdivides the Russian folktale into thirty-one *functions*, defining a function as a major narrative event placed in a linear sequence that begins with the crisis-inducing 'One of the members of a family absents himself from home' (26) and culminates happily in 'The hero is married and ascends the throne' (64). Suggestive for our purpose is that these functions are enacted by seven key dramatis personae or, in Propp's stoutly non-humanistic terminology, *spheres of action*: the villain, the donor, the helper, the princess, the dispatcher, the hero and the false hero. Few potential adapters of this schema to film will want to transpose it wholesale (though in 1976, in his article '*North by Northwest*: A Morphological Analysis', Peter Wollen had a good go). Given its provenance in the study of verbal culture, the very applicability of Propp's model to the materially different medium of cinema has also been questioned, most trenchantly by David Bordwell in his 1988 essay 'ApProppriations and ImProprieties: Problems in the Morphology of Film Narrative'. Nevertheless, allowing for its flexible deployment, Propp's narratology has much to offer to analysis of film storytelling, not least to the study of character. With regard to films of a given genre, say, it prompts us to set aside their myriad local differences and search instead for group resemblances, including recurrent character-types. *Pretty Woman* (1990), *Bridget Jones's Diary* (2001) and *Begin Again* (2014), for example, differ markedly in setting and tone; application of a Proppian analysis to these three romcoms, however, is likely to find them having a set of characters in common, with most 'spheres of action' occupied. More ambitiously, the model encourages us to consider the possibility of consistent characterisation *across* as well as within genres. For all their obvious differences, John Ford's western *The Searchers* (1956) and Russell Crowe's post-World War I drama *The Water Diviner* (2014) both find slots in their narrative structures for the villain, the helper, the hero and so on.

Questions can certainly be asked about this model's sensitivity with respect to film narratives, produced of course in very different conditions from those that generated Russia's traditional verbal culture. Nevertheless, even if the princess Propp speaks of is now close to extinction, structurally equivalent female quest objects continue to appear in cinematic storytelling: Broomhilda in Tarantino's *Django Unchained* (2012), say, or Cheryl in Ben Stiller's *The Secret Life of Walter Mitty* (2013). Similarly, villains in film may look rather different and yet, in what they do, be analogous to the character-type identified by Propp. Even where the spheres of action enumerated in *Morphology of the Folktale* are complicated or even disavowed by film narratives, such negative information may be revealing. In *The Searchers*, for example, the hero does not exactly 'ascend the throne' by way of conclusion. At the end, instead, the protagonist played by John Wayne exits through the homestead's doorway, heading into the desert rather than staying to participate in a scene of family reunion and celebration. The shift towards social disintegration is vividly disclosed by placing Wayne's character against Propp's idealised hero, derived as the latter figure is from a storytelling tradition that worked to reproduce established communal roles.

One further use of Propp is to inspire us to a higher degree of abstraction in our thinking about character in film. Practitioners of other art forms have sometimes sought to block audiences' interest in characters as if they were figures of flesh-and-blood: E. M. Forster, for instance, writes coldly that the novelist 'makes up a number of word-masses [...] These word-masses are his characters' (2005: 55). Intuitively it seems hard to dismiss characters in film as, by analogy, mere image-masses. The actor's stubbornly corporeal presence – albeit flattened on screen to two dimensions – may serve to distract spectators from the artifice of cinematic character. Attempts to challenge an anthropomorphic understanding of characterisation and reveal its constructedness have been mistrusted as weakening that sense of *identification* on which narrative cinema depends and so have, by and large, been confined to avant-garde or experimental filmmaking. Exemplary here would be Godard's Brechtian work, where characters are liable to be subject to a distancing external commentary. Note, also, a number of films in which, adventurously, several actors play the same role, thereby inhibiting any sense of character's 'naturalness'. Instances include the Brazilian director Glauber Rocha's *The Age of the Earth* (1980) – featuring Christ in variously 'Indian', 'black', 'revolutionary' and 'military' incarnations – and Todd Haynes's *I'm Not There* (2007), where Bob Dylan is played by six actors of varying age, sex and race.

Were we to take Propp's schema into film studies, however, we would be equipped to interrogate the category of character without quite resorting to these directors' idiosyncratic techniques. Recall that this narrative model understands figures in folktales for their capacity to be designated as one or more of the spheres of action. It is of no consequence if the 'donor' in one story is a toothless crone and in another a magically speaking frog; the differences between these two figures are analytically trivial, since what matters is their identical role within story structure. By analogy, it is open to us to liberate ourselves from thraldom to the flesh-and-blood dimensions of characters on screen and to become mindful instead of their narrative functions.

As Noël Carroll writes, however, 'We are emotionally tied to movies in large measure through our relationship with characters, especially the protagonists' (2008: 177). In accord with this insight, then, a second approach to film character has emerged that avoids Proppian abstraction and aims instead to offer nuanced description and evaluation of this intense spectator/character dynamic. Work done in this regard belongs broadly to *cognitive film studies*, a form of scholarship that has developed in the last three decades and challenges the paradigms previously dominant in the discipline by drawing upon resources that extend, across a scientific spectrum, from cognitive psychology to neurophysiology. In Chapter 3, we saw a cognitivist account of film music, emphasising the audio-viewer's conscious response to cues rather than those unconscious associations generated by the music which would interest a psychoanalytic critic. Much cognitive work in film, however, has been directed towards analysing how we process narratives. Later in this chapter we will consider Bordwell's application of a computational theory of mind to the activities carried out by the receiver of film narrative. Here, though, we briefly take stock of cognitivists' study of the richly emotional investments made by audiences in characters on screen. The opening-up of this topic reflects cognitive science's recent shift from 'a focus on "cold" cognition (information-driven mental processes described in terms of inferential and computational models) to "hot cognition" (affect-driven mental processes)' (Nannicelli and Taberham, 2014: 5).

Everyday discourse about the spectator/character relationship often revolves around questions of identification. Indeed, viewers may gauge the success or failure of a film on, respectively, its facilitating or obstructing identification with the protagonist ('I really identified with/couldn't identify with Bilbo Baggins'). One of the achievements of a cognitivist approach to character, however, has been to demonstrate that the concept of identification lacks refinement. By way of substitution, scholars have devised a spectrum of finely graded interactions between film audiences and characters. Carroll, perhaps the most influential of current cognitively minded critics, argues that there are degrees of separation between spectator and character, rather than any simple immersion of the first in the second. Distance as well as affinity is implicit in his suggestion that these two figures may be in 'vectorially converging emotive states' (2008: 169), or might occupy 'a state of roughly the same emotive valence' (170). If this language is not quite as far removed as Propp's from immediate, sensuous encounter with a text, it is still characterised by intellectual precision. So, too, is 'asymmetry of affect' (164), a term that Carroll uses to describe occasions when films might cue emotional dissonances rather than continuities between spectator and character.

In *The Philosophy of Motion Pictures*, Carroll questions something of a received idea in film discussion by asking whether the sense of affinity a spectator often experiences towards characters on screen is best described as *empathy*. It is more accurate, he suggests, to think of this response as one of *sympathy*, which he goes on to construe as 'non-fleeting care, concern, or, more widely, a non-passing pro-attitude toward another person (or fictional character, including anthropomophized beings of all sorts)' (2008: 177). Not every writer on the arts, of course, casts sympathy in such a good light. The literary scholar Terry Eagleton, for instance, argues in another context that 'in passively possessing its object [sympathy] is powerless to affect it. Sympathy doesn't get you anywhere' (1983:

12 The striking women in *Made in Dagenham* (2010): what is the nature
of spectator engagement with these characters?

54). However, where Eagleton writes of sympathy as 'possessive',
Carroll is careful to incorporate within it a measure of distance or
detachment from its object that allows for the possibility of critical
reflection. It remains, though, in his account a *transitive* emotion,
'a supportive response [...] an impulse toward benevolent action
with respect to those to whom it is directed' (2008: 177). While the
film experience itself offers no immediate occasion for acting upon
such well-meaning impulses – the sympathetic viewer of *Made in
Dagenham*, discussed in Chapter 3, can find no picket line after the
screening on which to join the striking women (see Figure 12) –
Carroll and other cognitive critics nevertheless take this spectator/
character dynamic as a potential model for interaction with others
in the world beyond the screen. Here it is possible to see that
cognitive approaches to character are not aimed solely at refining
accounts of our absorption by film narratives. Rather, scholarship
of this sort is also charged with ethical and political implications,
since screen characters activate our social concerns as well as supplying escapist pleasures.

STOP and THINK

- Assess how productive are the two approaches to film character outlined above, beginning with Propp's narratological
  model. You might take a small number of narrative films
  and consider to what extent figures in the story of each

can be aligned with the seven character-types, or spheres of action, identified by Propp in his analysis of the Russian folktale. What can be learned from such an exercise? Does Propp's schema provide a helpful interpretative template even when it lies awkwardly or inexactly over particular film narratives? Or, stepping back a bit, should we be suspicious about applying to film a model such as Propp's that can have nothing to say about the medium's material specificity?

- Drawing upon the same selection of films, offer finely calibrated accounts of your responses to their characters (the aim here is to outwit a merely impressionistic criticism and to do rigorous cognitivist work). How, exactly, would you describe your affective or emotional dispositions towards them? What is it in the films' composition, not least in their shaping of narrative, that activates these responses? Consider, too, the real-world consequences, if any, of the emotional repertoires you try out with respect to film characters.

- The narratological and cognitivist approaches to character introduced here differ markedly in their conceptual frameworks and methodologies. Do we have to choose between them? Or can you imagine ways in which they might be productively entwined?

Film and time

In *Morphology of the Folktale* Propp is adamant about the linearity of the narratives he discusses. While he allows that not all folktales include all thirty-one of the functions he has identified, he insists that functions appearing in any particular story do so in strictly chronological sequence. There is no wacky Russian tale that begins with the hero ascending the throne and then works backwards. Such linearity has, of course, also been the norm in cinematic storytelling; as Bordwell writes, relatively few films engage in significant 'temporal reshufflings' (1985: 33). Nevertheless, the folktale's invariant observance of a progressively unfolding chronology is clearly at odds with how at least some films have attempted to represent time. In this part of the chapter we introduce a number of frameworks and terminologies for the analysis of film temporality, including the non-linear as well as the chronologically orthodox.

Viktor Shklovsky, one of Propp's Formalist colleagues in the Soviet Union, provides important resources towards the discussion of time in narrative. Employing Russian terms that have passed into the Anglo-American critical lexicon, he differentiates between two narrative orders that may be identified in any work. The first of these is the *fabula*, translatable as 'story' and referring to a narrative's events in their linear sequence that begins with the chronologically earliest and concludes with the latest. On the other hand is the *syuzhet*, translatable as 'plot' or 'discourse', which defines a story's events in the order in which they are actually presented to us. Bordwell puts the distinction succinctly: '"Syuzhet" names the architectonics of the film's presentation of the fabula' (1985: 50). Fabula and syuzhet are, of course, identical in those film narratives constructed according to linear principles. Perhaps more striking, however, are cases where differences or discontinuities occur between these two narrative orders. A filmmaker may choose to present events not in chronological sequence but according to a more unruly time scheme, oscillating backwards or forwards around the narrative present and thereby observing what the French narratologist Gérard Genette calls *anachrony*. At the risk of piling more Greek terminology on Russian, these temporal disruptions in film can be broken down into two basic types: *analepsis* (flashback) and *prolepsis* (flashforward or foreshadowing).

Flashbacks were utilised as early as silent film: in the modern quadrant of Griffith's *Intolerance*, for example, a brief flashback to the hero's handing over his gun confirms to the spectator that he is not guilty of the murder of which he has been accused. However, in American cinema at least, analepsis became more common from the 1940s. Just as classic film noir has its stylistic signatures of low-key lighting and canted camera angles, so it is marked narratively by the flashback: works such as *Double Indemnity* (1944), *Mildred Pierce* (1945) and *The Killers* (1946) begin in the narrative present, with the protagonist defeated or desperate, and then revert to the past to reconstruct his or her fall into criminality or dangerous passion. In these instances, analepsis has a clarifying effect, remorselessly filling in any narrative blanks. Elsewhere, however, the flashback may have less conservative applications, serving to 'ambiguate' storytelling, so to speak, rather than to tidy it up. This is the case in *Citizen Kane*, where each new segment of the narrated past fails to explain Kane convincingly because it generates evidence that runs counter to other flashbacks. Similarly, *Catch-22* (1970) follows Joseph Heller's source novel by several times flashing back cryptically to an airman moaning that he is cold; the disorienting effect is intensified by bleached colour and muffled sound, and only towards the end of the film is there a confirmatory flashback of the man's mortal injuries.

Some films seek to go beyond a relatively modest use of flashback and attempt a more thoroughgoing reversal of temporality. In his novel *Slaughterhouse-Five* (1969), Kurt Vonnegut imagines what a film genuinely running backwards would be like. His hero, 'unstuck in time', watches a war movie in this fashion and finds it turned from bellicosity into something utopian: 'bullets and shell fragments' are miraculously withdrawn from airmen's wounds, while the bombs that had ravaged a city are lifted from the ground into 'the bellies of the planes' (Vonnegut, 2000: 53). But even if this high degree of reversibility is available only in fantasy, or through projectionist error, instances exist of films oriented significantly towards the narrative past. Most sensationally in recent English-language cinema there is Christopher Nolan's *Memento* (2000), which braids a forward-moving strand in monochrome with a series of receding flashbacks in colour. A less baroque example of sequenced flashbacks, each further from the narrative present than the previous one, occurs in François Ozon's *5 × 2* (2004). Owing some debts to Harold Pinter's 1978 play *Betrayal* (itself adapted for cinema in 1983), the film is organised as five lengthy scenes between a married couple. Since the first segment shows the couple about to divorce and the last features their first meeting, this structure produces a sense of desolation greater than more linear emplotment of the crisis in their relationship would have done.

The flashback is by now a familiar piece of the grammar of cinematic storytelling. In its simpler forms, visibly marked off from a film's narrative present, it has been normalised to the point of causing spectators little discomfort. The structurally antithetical device of the flashforward, however, is used much less often and remains potentially disorienting. Whereas the flashback is often motivated by routine processes of memory, prolepsis has connotations of weirder mental operations such as prophecy and premonition, and thus appears uncanny. Unsurprisingly, then, it has sometimes been utilised by art cinema. In France, famously, prolepsis occurs in Chris Marker's sci-fi short *La Jetée* (1962), where the protagonist time-travels to the future as well as to the past. In England, Nicolas Roeg uses the device on both macro- and micro-scales in *Don't Look Now* (1973): substantially so as to show premonitions that Donald Sutherland's character has of his death, but also locally, as during a long lovemaking scene where intercut flashforwards to the couple's subsequent dressing have the effect of short-circuiting the viewer's voyeuristic pleasure. Such arthouse precedents, however, do not mean that the flashforward is entirely foreign to the narration of mainstream film. Playfully, during Ron Howard's comedy *Parenthood* (1989), a father experiences flashforwards to two wildly contrasting possible fates for his son. In Sydney Pollack's drama of the American Depression, *They Shoot Horses, Don't They?* (1969), by contrast, anticipatory shots of the hero's arrest empty the narrative present itself of many of its pleasures.

A film's syuzhet may modify not only the order of events as set out in the fabula, but also their *duration* (or *speed*) and *frequency*. Here brief exposition of these terms will be helpful before returning to cinematic examples. In his classic study *Narrative Discourse* (1980), Genette considers these two elements of narrative organisation. Drawing his examples from literary fiction rather than cinema, he suggests in the first instance that several ratios are possible between the set of narrative events on the one hand and the speed of their narration on the other (1980: 86–112). At one extreme, narration may be greatly abbreviated by use of ellipsis or summary, passing over some events entirely and sketching others only in insubstantial outline; at the other, it may be considerably expanded by description, with a text lingering over details rather than immediately discharging its obligation of storytelling. In between these opposing possibilities is a kind of narrational degree zero, a normative narrating rhythm that is neither too hectic nor too dilatory. Genette calls this a narrative's 'constant speed' and makes it a standard by which to measure any variations in the speed of storytelling.

The cinematic equivalent of Genette's constant speed is a film in *real time*, where the duration of events corresponds exactly to their duration on screen. This strategy is generally employed to maximise a sense of tension within claustrophobic locations, from the clock-filled western frontier town of *High Noon* (1952) through the eponymous setting of *Phone Booth* (2002) to the doomed aircraft of *United 93* (2006). The makers of *The Silent House* (2010), a Uruguayan horror film that enjoyed some global success, drew attention to the relationship between presentational mode and spectator response by promoting their work with the tagline 'Real Fear in Real Time'. In other contexts, however, real-time filmmaking may serve to intensify meditative rather than terrified attention to the particulars of the present moment, as in the Iranian work *The White Balloon* (1995), which is centred upon a seven-year-old girl's interactions with the adult world.

The real-time film is still, of course, a rare cinematic venture; much more usual are films which variously accelerate or retard the speed of narration. At one end of the spectrum, filmmakers may condense time by employing the type of Hollywood montage considered in Chapter 2; they may also literally quicken action by use of fast-motion photography. Fast-motion is plastic in its effects: while it generates comedy during a wild sledge chase in *The Grand Budapest Hotel*, it supports social critique when nauseously speeded-up footage of city traffic is incorporated in Godfrey Reggio's documentary, *Koyaanisqatsi* (1983). On the other hand, time in cinema may be slowed down, even stilled. This tendency is taken to its furthest extent in the freeze frame (a topic for discussion later in this chapter). Without arresting time to quite that degree, filmmakers may employ slow-motion photography, again for a variety of reasons: contrast slow motion's elegiac resonance as a soldier falls at the end of Oliver Stone's *Platoon* (1986) with the technique's utilisation in Vertov's *Man with a Movie Camera* to restore to visibility the often neglected gestures and textures of everyday life. Nolan's *Inception* (2010), this chapter's case study below, makes bravura use of slow motion of varying rates of slowness. Alternatively, a film may linger upon the details of a scene, impeding narrative momentum. Malick's *The Thin Red Line* (1998), for example, ostensibly a war film, is driven to register the visual and aural plenitude of particular moments, as in long takes of grasses blowing in the wind.

Finally in this section, we should consider the question of frequency: how often do films narrate the events of which their stories are comprised? Genette suggests that in this respect the maker of a narrative may adopt one of three protocols: *singulative* (that is to say, narrating once something that happened once), *iterative* (narrating once something that happened many times) and *repeating* (narrating many times something that happened once) (1980: 113–16). Despite its origins in the study of literary fiction, his model is again suggestive with respect to cinema. Most films can be seen to practise singulative narrative, transiting from one unique event to the next. Other movies, however, modulate narrative frequency in variously iterative or repeating directions. Iterative storytelling is attractive not least for reasons of economy. At the other extreme, a film's repeated return to the same event, as in *Source Code* (2011), may mark a site of crisis (albeit sometimes simply to maximise suspense rather than to advance moral or political or philosophical investigation). Narrative recurrence of this kind may also be to evoke the complexity of an event, its openness to multiple interpretations. The classic film in this vein is Akira Kurosawa's *Rashomon* (1950), where a dead samurai (speaking through a medium), his wife, a bandit and a woodcutter variously and incompatibly frame the circumstances of the samurai's death. Storytelling itself is put in crisis; as one character says: 'The more I hear, the more confused I am.' Such problematising of narrative reliability is ultimately averted in the First Gulf War film *Courage Under Fire* (1996), a Hollywood product that nevertheless for the earlier part of its duration models itself upon *Rashomon*. Meg Ryan, implausibly, stands in here for the dead samurai.

STOP and THINK

- Assess the modes of narration in several films. Consider, in the first instance, how they stage the relationship between fabula and syuzhet: does the syuzhet in each case respect the fabula's chronological laying-out of events, or does it significantly disorder this by use of flashback and flashforward? Second, is storytelling in your films either accelerated (as by ellipsis, Hollywood-style montage and fast-motion photography) or retarded (as by freeze framing, slow-motion photography, a shot's dwelling upon scenic details)? Third, are narrative events shown singly in each case, or is there evidence also of those narrative modes Genette terms iterative and repeating? Explore the consequences and implications of the temporal strategies pursued by your sample of films.

- Art cinema has a long tradition of fragmenting or otherwise complicating narrative. Recently, however, narrative experimentation has migrated from earnest arthouse practice to become part also of the repertoire of mainstream cinemas. In Hollywood itself, the linearly plotted work is still dominant, yet co-exists now with temporally (and spatially) disarranged movies put under such rubrics as 'puzzle films', 'mind-game films' and 'forking path narratives'. If this trend is often seen as inaugurated by Tarantino's *Pulp Fiction* (1994), later examples include *Being John Malkovich* (1999), *Donnie Darko* (2001), *The Hours* (2002), *21 Grams* (2003), *Eternal Sunshine of the Spotless Mind* (2004), *Babel* (2006), *Synecdoche, New York* (2008), *Shutter Island* (2010), *Source Code* and, of course, *Inception*. Evaluate your responses to this body of complex film narratives, calculating the ratio of curiosity to boredom, engagement to withdrawal.

- Why *has* popular US cinema recently made a home for complex storytelling of this sort? You might, hard-headedly, stress commercial imperatives: the 'difficult' narrative's profitability as a niche commodity, not only in cinemas but in homes where its DVD and downloaded versions may be repeatedly viewed. Or you might consider the ambitions of scientifically and technologically literate filmmakers, their desire to inflect storytelling by insights about time or identity gained from contemporary physics and neuroscience. Or you may seek socio-cultural reasons, linking the crisis or, at least, the complicating of linearity and coherence in these films to such developments as the radical reconfiguring of time and space produced by globalisation. At what level of explanation do you find *your* answers?

The sense of an ending

Just as in literary scholarship, thinking in film studies about narrative form has tended to neglect beginnings and middles and to focus instead upon *endings*. Where discussion can be found of earlier stages in cinematic narratives, it is more likely to appear in manuals for aspiring screenwriters than in academic study. Nevertheless, it is unsurprising that critical attention has been directed chiefly towards the end, given expectations that it is at this point that still-unresolved issues will be settled and a narrative's design completed. As Noël Carroll writes: 'The end of a motion picture narrative has an aura of consummation about it; it yields a quite definite impression of completeness' (2008: 134). Or, to quote Edgar, the filmmaker protagonist of Godard's *In Praise of Love* (2001): 'It's strange how things take on meaning when the story ends.'

This film by Godard is actually careful, in its own ending, *not* to yield unambiguous meanings. A corrosively satirical work, it bundles the drive to closure together with other practices of mainstream cinematic storytelling as signs of an Americanisation that should be resisted. The neatest, most conclusive type of film ending has indeed been ascribed most often to Hollywood, particularly in its classical period; as Robert Stam writes about this cinema's characteristic story arc: 'Everything becomes subordinated to a teleology as relentlessly purposeful as the Fate of classical tragedy' (2005: 43). To point out Hollywood film's end-directedness, however, is not in itself to deliver a knock-out blow. Stam's own reference here to tragic drama is suggestive: the spectator of Sophocles's *Oedipus Rex* or Shakespeare's *Hamlet*, after all, is also agog from the beginning to see how things will turn out, without this orientation towards the ending prompting critics to draw dark conclusions about artistic impoverishment. Where the Hollywood ending suffers is in the suspicion that it is too pat, too anally compelled to resolve lingering questions, too concerned to offer certitudes to its audiences. Such tendencies are subjected to scrutiny not only by critics but by Woody Allen in his film *Hollywood Ending* (2002), revealingly, perhaps, a failure at the box office.

Storytelling in mainstream film often follows the simplified, tripartite model sketched by the French narrative theorist Tzvetan

Todorov. Here an initial state of *equilibrium* is provoked into *disequilibrium* by some complication or crisis – the crime film's unsolved murder, say, or the musical's temporary separation of two people destined for each other – before this unsatisfactory situation yields to the phase of *equilibrium-restored*. For the moment, we can set aside the problem that a film's final equilibrium will differ from the settled state shown at the beginning, thereby representing something other than simple 'restoration'. More to the purpose is to note the long history of trouble – not least in popular US cinema – for film narratives that do not sufficiently repair the crises they include. As early as 1928, MGM added a hastily made optimistic coda to *The Wind*, a prairie drama ending in the heroine's desolation that had been directed by the Swedish émigré Victor Sjöström. In 1982, following audience unease at preview screenings of *Blade Runner*, aerial panoramas of a romantic, mountainous landscape – actually, unused second-unit photography from Kubrick's *The Shining* – were unenthusiastically bolted on to the original film's dystopian ending by director Ridley Scott (an enormity corrected only by release of the Director's Cut ten years later). Even as late as 2005, the version of *Pride & Prejudice* released in the United States included a final moonlit kiss between Darcy and Lizzie that had not featured in the UK print. The British DVD edition includes this maudlin scene as an extra, so that the film, albeit quite clunkily, begins to resemble a computer game with the possibility of multiple narrative trajectories.

In certain cinematic traditions, pessimistic endings are as conventionalised as Hollywood's affirmative dénouement. Russia's taste for melancholy early in the twentieth century was so pronounced that Danish director August Blom felt it prudent, for that particular market, to add a tragic ending to *Atlantis* (1913); conversely, the endings of some Russian films had to have their misery deactivated before being exported. Overt pessimism of this sort tallies with what is already regarded by some critics as the deathliness of film endings. This thesis that cinematic narratives tend towards a state of termination identical with death itself has been argued most eloquently by Laura Mulvey (a scholar whose work in another context we will encounter in Chapter 8). The triumph of what Freud theorised as the death drive is, for Mulvey, discernible in cinema, given that films end by literally arresting speed and by immobilising previously animated figures. As she writes, uncovering a deathly quality in an art form that is supposedly defined by movement: 'at the end, the aesthetics of stillness returns to both narrative and the cinema' (2006: 70).

For Mulvey, film's terminal aspect is most apparent in the freeze frame: 'As stillness intrudes into movement, the image freezes into the "stop of death"' (2006: 32). While provocative, however, this thesis is overly generalised and risks detaching each instance of the freeze frame from its specific filmic context. It is unlikely that spectators of *The Full Monty* (1997), which ends by freezing the joyous male striptease, left the cinema muttering darkly about the triumph of the death drive. Similarly, morbid reflection may not have been common among patrons of *The Curse of the Were-Rabbit*, concluding as it does with one of the cartoon rabbits fixed in mid-air. To end a film on a freeze frame may actually be *more* rather than less resistant to a dismal sense of termination. After all, the device leaves a narrative open and undecided, rather than resolving it in a single direction. Things are still 'up in the air' – literally so in the Wallace and Gromit film, and also in *Thelma and Louise* (1991), where the frozen final shot of the car flying into the Grand Canyon defers, at least momentarily, the protagonists' destruction. In Truffaut's *The 400 Blows* (1959), a key film of the French New Wave, the concluding shot freezes the delinquent young protagonist, Antoine Doinel, as he stands in shallow waters off a beach and looks towards the camera (Figure 13); the moment is suspended between several narrative possibilities, some alarming certainly yet none definitive. The film's diegetic world is still – just about – up for grabs and open to reinvention.

STOP and THINK

• Return to the films that you assessed earlier for their temporal schemas, and consider the implications of their endings. To borrow a phrase used by the literary critic Frank Kermode, what 'sense of an ending' does each film provide? Do you find closure or openness, clarity or ambiguity, reassurance or unease? What consequences follow?

13 Freeze frame ending: Jean-Pierre Léaud as Antoine Doinel in *The 400 Blows* (1959)

- Review the endings of some films from different eras. The conclusion of an early gangster movie like Howard Hawks's *Scarface* (1932) might be set against Scorsese's *Goodfellas* (1990); or the ending of a classic American musical like *Meet Me in St. Louis* (1944) compared with that of *Les Misérables* (2012). Are there continuities, in this respect, across film history? Or can we speak of a distinctively modern, or postmodern, film ending? If you do detect a shift in cinematic endgames, explore the reasons – economic, cultural, ideological – for this.

Narrative and power

Fabula, *syuzhet*, *function*, *singulative*: the terminology rehearsed so far in this chapter appears at times to evoke a rarefied narrative science, conducted by white-coated practitioners plotting grids and drawing graphs with respect to their objects of study. Yet as suggested by references above to the ethics of the spectator/character dynamic and to the variable politics of endings, film narrative is worldly through and through. Suzanne Keen reminds us that, from its introduction, the term *narrative* had socially charged rather than merely formalist connotations: first entering common English usage in the mid-eighteenth century, it referred to a statement lodged in court during legal disputes (2003: 1). Even when detached from such explicitly contestatory situations as cases in law, stories are necessarily implicated in questions of power. This section addresses a number of these issues in film narrative, beginning with assessment of how authority is distributed *within* films, before moving outwards to review how film studies has modelled the spectator's own authority with respect to stories told by cinema.

It is imperative to put to film two questions that Genette says are advisable to ask about literary narrative: 'Who sees?' and 'Who speaks?' (1980: 186). Because of cinema's ocular foundation, the question of seeing, or *perspective* or *focalisation*, is urgent here. In many films, certainly those produced within mainstream traditions, *point of view* tends not to be explicitly marked. The camera frames the action in such instances without any suggestion that the resultant view is the product of a situated, bodily presence. Francesco Casetti proposes that this be called 'nobody's shot' (Gaudreault and Jost, 1999: 60), a term which is open to question but nevertheless captures the sense of an impersonal or disembodied perspective. More usually, unmarked cinematic vision of this sort is called an *objective shot* – again dubiously, since it emerges nevertheless from a specific location in a film's narrative world. While this is not the place to consider in detail the ideology of mainstream cinema, it should be briefly noted that the pretence to objectivity and realism implicit in such camerawork has occasioned fierce political critiques.

There is an alternative to the objective regime in the so-called *subjective* or *point-of-view (POV) shot* which aims to mimic the optical situation of an embodied figure within the narrative itself. Very early cinema sometimes put such a shot to playful uses: witness the English filmmaker G. A. Smith's *Grandma's Reading Glasses* and *As Seen Through a Telescope* (both 1900), which advertise their perspectival experimentalism in their titles. On the whole, the subjective shot is a relatively lightly used variation in cinema, as if respecting Bernard F. Dick's sternly normative judgement that it 'should be restricted to specific scenes or sequences' and 'should never dominate a film' (2002: 59). A striking early attempt to organise an entire feature around subjective shots is Robert Montgomery's crime film *The Lady in the Lake* (1946), in which, even in a kissing scene, the camera continues to stand in for the private eye Philip Marlowe. Yet this film remains an eccentric venture, rather than one which inaugurated a large-scale subjectivisation of cinematography. It also exemplifies how the subjective shot may often be utilised simply to vary the spectator's pleasure, rather than to rethink the politics of film narrative by ceding optical authority to characters usually fixed by the camera's objectifying gaze. In the thriller or horror film, in particular, point-of-view camerawork brings excitingly close the spectator and the menaced protagonist (an effect that perhaps reaches its apotheosis in the sustained, handheld subjectivity of *The Blair Witch Project*). Here, however, we might note the claim by William Seeley and Noël Carroll that this technique serves the needs of narrative clarification without entirely conflating audience and character: 'to the degree that we simulate perspectival seeing in our engagement with [point-of-view] shots, we do so in order to collect information salient for understanding the depicted visual experiences of characters. However, we do not, in so doing, put ourselves into the narrative' (2014: 247).

If the power to see within film narratives is only seldom delegated to characters themselves, might we say the same, turning now to Genette's second question, about the power to speak or narrate? Immediately, films come to mind where some of the storytelling is done through voiceover, usually – though not always – spoken by someone from within the narrative itself. While the device is not universally favoured, it has been institutionalised in some times and places, as in classic film noir or traditional documentary. Despite claims by a number of critics that it represents film narration at its most clunky, an uninspired recourse to *telling* of events or feelings rather than *showing* them by non-verbal cinematic means, the voiceover retains some currency. Consider, for example, David O. Russell's *American Hustle* (2013), in which it is pluralised, being shared by no fewer than three of the film's characters (including a woman, countering Hollywood's traditional masculinisation of voiceover which was noted in Chapter 3). However, any suggestion that voiceover in general signifies a narrative revolt, a blow for freedom by characters against the impersonal narrating agency that oppresses them, should immediately be tempered. As we showed above when discussing *The Great Gatsby*, voiceover confers upon its speaker only temporary and partial powers, rather than command over the totality of a film's storytelling operation. Seymour

Chatman's theorisation of what he calls 'the multiplexity of the cinematic narrator' makes clear that voiceover co-exists with dialogue, sound effects and music and thus cannot dominate even the auditory output, let alone direct the image track (1990: 134–5).

The question of exactly *who* or *what* narrates a film has periodically been a concern of the discipline. In *Logique du cinéma* (1964), Albert Laffay argues that narration is the product of a colossal apparatus he personalises as '*le grand imagier*' (the master of images). Writing a little later from within French film theory, André Gaudreault presumes a similarly potent storyteller when he refers to 'the mega-narrator' (a figure communicating by sound as well as through the visual channel prioritised by Laffay). For David Bordwell, however, theories of this sort are mistaken in tracing film narration to some sort of shadowy originating force, a Wizard of Oz equivalent. In his important book *Narration in the Fiction Film* (1985), he counter-argues that film studies should forsake the quest for the narrator's identity; a three-post model that had been devised for filmic storytelling – narrator/narrative/narratee (or receiver) – should be simplified to include only the latter two terms. Nevertheless, in further twists of the theoretical spiral, Bordwell's provocative proposal to eliminate the figure of the narrator has been resisted by some other scholars, including Chatman and Edward Branigan.

This debate might look like film studies' equivalent of those disputes in medieval theology concerning how many angels could dance on the head of a pin. Certainly, discussions of the source of filmic narration have not been free of hair-splitting and airless formalism. Yet the conversation is also a worldly one, since in arguing their corners the disputants draw, explicitly or implicitly, upon different models of the respective powers of the cinematic apparatus itself and the spectator. In rejecting Laffay's and Gaudreault's hypothesis of an omnipotent narrator, Bordwell deploys similar objections to those he has towards that strain of film theory, emerging in the early 1970s, which characterises the spectator as tightly sutured into mainstream cinema and therefore vulnerable to its reactionary effects. This strand of ideology-critique will be considered in detail in Chapter 8. Here we just note how Bordwell challenges such work for its implication of the spectator's passivity, or occupation of a fixed 'position', in the face of film narrative. His counter-proposal is that 'A film [...]

does not "position" anybody. A film cues the spectator to execute a definable variety of *operations*' (1985: 29). Achieving precise definitions of these 'operations' of inference-making, hypothesis-building and problem-solving preoccupies Bordwell both in this book and in some of his later work, as he seeks to develop what he calls a 'perceptual-cognitive' model of film spectatorship.

Bordwell's cognitivist account of the film narratee's relationship to narrative is not, however, without significant problems. While he properly challenges film theory's more morbid exponents and attempts to restore a sense of the viewer's conscious generation of meaning, he risks underestimating the more insidious effects upon us of cinematic storytelling. In addition, his description of the spectator's deductive and problem-solving activities is well suited to modelling our response to the detective film, but perhaps lacking in emotional generosity as an account of how we watch a melodrama. Hence critics following in his tradition have sometimes sought to co-ordinate his computational model of mental processing with cognitive film theory's newer interest in the emotional engagements of the spectator. Like other cognitivists, though, Bordwell generalises spectator response, hypothesising that film narratives activate in us a universally shared mental functioning. Variations in spectatorship – how audiences in different times and places interact dynamically with the same narrative – are not a major concern here. Finally, it should be said that work by Bordwell and others on narrative comprehension has valuably generated granular accounts of spectator activity, but has come at the cost of neglecting interest in other, less respectful things that might be done with film stories, such as taking them apart politically.

Case study: *Inception* (2010)

'It's designed as a labyrinth', says Ariadne (Ellen Page), the dream-architect in *Inception*, about one of the structures she has fashioned: the snowbound fortress that the inception team raids on the third of four levels of dreaming mapped by the film. Frustrated by complexity of this degree, however, Cobb (Leonardo DiCaprio) retorts that 'There must be access routes that cut through the maze.' This exchange is one of many self-referential moments in *Inception*,

when remarks that characters make about their movement through
the nested dreamscapes mimic or anticipate spectators' reactions to
the 'labyrinth' or 'maze' that is Nolan's film. What 'access routes',
critically speaking, might we follow to find our way into and out
of this intricately structured, designedly baffling work? Below we
consider ways in which *Inception* rewards some of those approaches
to film narrative considered above, while also acknowledging several
respects in which it may ask for deployment of different interpretative resources.

It is helpful, to begin with, to test the applicability to *Inception* of
Shklovsky's model of fabula and syuzhet. Clearly, the film's events
as laid out chronologically in the fabula undergo some significant
reordering at the level of the syuzhet. The film opens not at what
is, temporally speaking, its earliest point, but *in media res* (that is to
say, in the middle of things). Rather than beginning at the beginning, with the attempt by the Japanese businessman Saito to recruit
Cobb and his team for the purpose of carrying out an inception, it
starts with Cobb waking up on a beach and briefly seeing two young
children playing nearby before he is taken to the hideaway of an
older Japanese man. When the moment is revisited near the end,
it proves to be situated temporally in the inception's latter stages
and spatially in Limbo, the lowest of the dream levels (shown in
Figure 14). To open the film in the midst of action like this, however, intrigues (even if the viewer experienced in Hollywood cinema

14 Narrative intricacy in *Inception* (2010): Cobb (Leonardo DiCaprio)
and Mal (Marion Cotillard) in Limbo, the lowest of four nested dream
levels

still assumes with confidence that enigmas regarding the identity of these characters and the nature of their relationship will ultimately be resolved). From this sequence onwards, however, *Inception* proceeds in broadly linear fashion, deriving its trajectory like that of any heist film from the conceiving, planning and executing of a criminal operation. The suspenseful forward movement is broken only by momentary temporal variations, including some flashbacks to Cobb with his troubled late wife Mal (other scenes involving the couple, however, are read by Ariadne as Cobb's 'projections', thereby complicating their temporal status).

The terminology of fabula and syuzhet is, however, insufficiently elastic with respect to elements of *Inception*'s narrative. Strictly speaking, it is correct to observe of the actions contributing to the inception itself that here the syuzhet tends to observe the fabula's chronological order. To say this, however, is also radically to falsify the film's narrative structure, in the process downplaying the cognitive demands this makes upon the viewer. For while Shklovsky's theory presumes discrete narrative events that may be plotted in variously linear or non-linear sequences, *Inception* is also interested in actions that occur *simultaneously*, or near-simultaneously, and thus cannot so readily be thought of in terms of a chain or series. Events in much of Nolan's film should be understood according to principles not only of temporal unfolding but of spatial distribution, since each new happening on one level of dream generates happenings on other levels. Cause and effect, then, are to be grasped here as not just extending horizontally in time but travelling vertically up and down the several dream spaces. To take one example, the car chase in which Yusuf is involved in the noir-like city of the first dream level unspools temporally, yet also, spatially speaking, ramifies to a level down so as to disorient Arthur. The film's characters again offer a helpful guide for its spectator when they observe that navigation of this complex world calls for movement in several planes or dimensions; as Cobb says in a moment of crisis: 'Downwards is the only way forwards.'

Inception belongs to a wave of non-linear, spatially diffuse, highly reflexive films recently produced by Hollywood that has prompted some critics to query the usefulness still of the narratological tools employed earlier in this chapter. Warren Buckland asks: 'Can we continue discussing puzzle films in narratological terms, or do we need to move beyond narratology to other theoretical frameworks such as new media theory, complex systems theory, network theory, or game theory?' (2014: 7). Nolan's film, in particular, suggests there is no easy or unequivocal answer to the inquiry that Buckland makes. Certainly, elements can be found in *Inception* that seem predisposed towards analysis by paradigms other than those, like narratology, which are particularly concerned with questions of time. As noted above, events are not exclusively plottable as horizontal series but also ramify through the film's 'complex system'. Where time *is* at issue in *Inception*, it often appears multiple rather than singular: recall that different temporalities apply across the dream levels, so that tiny increments of time on the first one as the van plunges in slow motion towards the river house longer and longer durations when the dreamers descend further. The 'problem-solving' that *Inception*'s characters collectively undertake while trying to implant an idea in the businessman Fischer is also of a complexity that far exceeds the goal-setting that has always underpinned Hollywood narrative, and it echoes, thereby, network theory's concern with optimisation of shared tasks.

Nevertheless, it is unwise with regard to a film such as *Inception* to forsake familiar narrative approaches entirely in favour of other conceptual frameworks. Here a helpful way forward is proposed by Henriette Heidbrink. For Heidbrink, a *mix* of interpretative resources is called for by *Inception* since it articulates traditional Hollywood storytelling with modes of organisation more associated with new media, particularly the video game: '*story-logic*' is braided with '*game-logic*' (Heidbrink, 2013: 152). The latter can rapidly be uncovered in Nolan's film, this feature of the work in fact making almost superfluous the release of an accompanying video game that has sometimes been mooted. Consider, for instance, the spectator's gratification in witnessing the design of a labyrinthine space, characterised by 'levels' on which the figures have to problem-solve before progressing. These characters, too, are stripped down to their operational functionality: so thoroughly are Ariadne, Arthur and the others defined by their roles in the inception that it is literally impossible to imagine them doing something else like booking a holiday or going for a woodland walk.

Heidbrink argues, however, that in *Inception* and some other films a reciprocal relationship obtains between the gaming and the storytelling elements, so that each donates particular features to the other. If gaming in Nolan's film adds to the story what she calls '*modular qualities*' (blocks of action and spectacle), storytelling imports into the game '*dramaturgical qualities*' (the sense of humanly involving characters, caught in personal crises) (2013: 153). This point about *Inception*'s dramatic appeal is perhaps hard to see in the case of Cobb's assistants, since they are totally stripped of subjectivity. It is very apparent, however, with regard to Cobb himself, who registers here not simply as an adept problem-solver but as a grieving widower and yearning father. While other characters are little more than avatars to whom the spectator has, at best, a purely functional relationship, Cobb is bound to us by an affective dynamic: what is felt to be at stake is not whether he will succeed in the mental challenge of the inception but whether he will get to see his children again. Here the imprint of traditional Hollywood narrative, engaging audiences emotionally, can quite clearly be seen on *Inception*. Albeit on a grander scale, the effect is similar to in *Memento*, where the doubled temporality is not a stand-alone intellectual marvel but is induced by protagonist anxiety as the amnesiac Leonard Shelby struggles to find out what has happened to his wife.

Inception's narrative appeal is evident in the nature and volume of commentary the film has generated from critics, reviewers and fans. Bordwell finds a compulsive element in all this interpretation and reinterpretation, writing that 'Recidivism, thy name is *Inception*' (Bordwell and Thompson, 2010: n.p.). Much of the discourse about cruxes in the film's storytelling revolves, of course, around the ending. As is very well known, *Inception* finishes with Cobb, now back in the United States, entering the garden where his two children are playing; he leaves behind him, spinning on a table, the totemic top whose continuing or stopping he has used to tell whether he is either dreaming or back in the real world. The top is still in motion when there is a cut to black, followed by the closing credits. A good deal of critical ingenuity has been expended on these final moments: some interpreters have measured the top's rate of oscillation or the children's height compared with their earlier appearances in flashback, while others, eagle-eared, have claimed to hear over the black screen the noise of the top coming to rest on the table, which would confirm that Cobb is indeed back in reality. For the moment, however, we can duck any responsibility to choose one of the many interpretations over another and simply say that in their sheer number they testify to *Inception*'s ongoing narrative productivity. It should also be acknowledged that the openness of this finale runs counter to 'the Hollywood ending' as it was delineated above. Nevertheless, that narrative tradition can still be discerned here, even in this final deviation that Nolan's film takes in its own storytelling.

Selected reading

Altman, Rick (2008), *A Theory of Narrative* (New York: Columbia University Press).
  Best-known for his work on film, particularly film sound, Altman is here concerned to a greater extent with literature; however, cinematic references are never far away, and this is a cogent volume of great interest to film studies.
Bordwell, David (1985), *Narration in the Fiction Film* (London: Methuen).
  Boldly develops a 'perceptual-cognitive' account of the viewer's processing of film narrative: open to dispute, but suggestive, eloquent and displaying Bordwell's customary multi-disciplinary erudition.
Branigan, Edward (1992), *Narrative Comprehension and Film* (London: Routledge).
  Sophisticated, challenging study which enters into debate with Bordwell's model of film narration, and should also be read alongside Chatman.
Buckland, Warren (ed.) (2014), *Hollywood Puzzle Films* (New York: Routledge).
  Timely and stimulating collection, with particularly extensive coverage of *Inception*; interestingly, several contributors wonder about the attention given to the contemporary Hollywood puzzle film at the expense of interest in other forms of cinematic narration.
Cameron, Allan (2008), *Modular Narratives in Contemporary Cinema* (Basingstoke: Palgrave Macmillan).
  Tracks a 'database aesthetic' across an international range of post-1990 films, demonstrating how their narrative experiments go well beyond conservative uses of flashback.
Currie, Gregory (2010), *Narratives and Narrators: A Philosophy of Stories* (Oxford: Oxford University Press).

Lucidly revisits key questions in narrative, including character and point-of-view; of considerable interest to the film student (as well as the literary scholar).

Mulvey, Laura (2006), *Death 24× a Second: Stillness and the Moving Image* (London: Reaktion).

Original, provocative reflections – shaped by Freud's theory of the death drive – on cinematic endings: both the deathlike closures of the medium's narratives and, in the context of new digital technologies, the possible ending of film itself.

Powell, Helen (2012), *Stop the Clocks!: Time and Narrative in Cinema* (London: I. B. Tauris).

Helpful, accessible consideration of the problematic of time in film from its beginnings to the present digital age.

Shimamura, Arthur P. (ed.) (2013), *Psychocinematics: Exploring Cognition at the Movies* (New York: Oxford University Press).

While contributors to this collection have wide-ranging cognitivist interests with respect to film, many essays bear suggestively on the spectator's mental operations and emotional responses as activated by narrative.

Smith, Murray (1995), *Engaging Characters: Fiction, Emotion, and the Cinema* (Oxford: Clarendon Press).

Pioneering volume that brought film characters, and the emotionality of our engagements with them, into the purview of film studies.

Strauven, Wanda (ed.) (2006), *The Cinema of Attractions Reloaded* (Amsterdam: University of Amsterdam Press).

Ample collection of essays, bringing together the early work of Gunning, Gaudreault and others on 'the cinema of attractions' with more recent pieces by critics on the productivity and applicability of this concept.

Online resources

'Narratology and Narration in Film and Transmedia Storytelling', Film Studies for Free, 7 September 2010, http://filmstudiesforfree.blogspot.co.uk/2010/09/narratology-and-narration-in-film-and.html. Substantial collection of scholarly articles on aspects of film narration, gathered by this unfailingly excellent website.

'Understanding Film Narrative: The Trailer', Observations on Film Art, 12 January 2014, www.davidbordwell.net/blog/2014/01/12/understanding-film-narrative-the-trailer/. Another posting from Kristin Thompson's and David Bordwell's film studies blog, with Bordwell exploring the narrative design of *The Wolf of Wall Street*.

5
Film and genre

Somewhere you come across a film that has already been running for some time. On screen is a gaunt, middle-aged man in baseball cap and overalls, who is walking slowly through a cavernous, sparsely lit space. Chains hang from the ceiling, and water is trickling down too. Evidently, the man is searching for a cat. Other than his calls to the animal, no voices are heard. On the soundtrack, however, is an initially muffled yet progressively loud thrumming, which might be the diegetic noise of an engine, but could equally be non-diegetic in origin and evoke the protagonist's agitation.

How do you begin to make sense of, or *place*, this film? What *kind* of film is it? Rather than defining it minutely, you might choose to assign it to one of three broader categories proposed by Alan Williams in an influential article, 'Is a Radical Genre Criticism Possible?' (1984: 121–5). Having to select from Williams's classes of narrative film, experimental or avant-garde film, and documentary, you might cautiously judge the sequence playing out on screen to belong to the first of these. There is no evidence in this scene of such signatures of experimental work as the problematising of time and space or the self-conscious advertising of filmic construction itself. Nor does the film appear to have the documentary's mode of audience address (though perhaps the option should be kept open a while longer that you are watching a non-fictional piece on former pets that now live wild in abandoned factories).

These classifications are, however, too unrefined and insensitive to offer you more than minimal help in categorising this film. While Williams aims for conceptual economy in devising a system of cinematic *genres* that has only three members, you should instead aim in your interpretation to mobilise knowledge of many more, treating each one as a schema or set of expectations to be placed against the sequence and then either ratified or disconfirmed. This finer-grained approach should eventually yield success, since, as Jacques Derrida says, 'there is no genreless text' (1992: 230). But to which genre from this broader classificatory array might the film you are watching be assigned? Certain options would seem to rule themselves out quickly. If the western, for example, is capable of historical elasticity – extending beyond frontier gunfights to machine-gunning in *The Wild Bunch* (1969), even to attack by interplanetary craft in *Cowboys & Aliens* (2011) – it tends to be geographically quite rigid, associated with spaces which seem far removed from your film's location. Similarly, it is unlikely the movie you are watching is a musical. While it is not inconceivable for musicals to be set and lit unglamorously – Lars von Trier's *Dancer in the Dark* (2000) being a case in point – the demeanour of the man on screen does not suggest someone about to burst into song and dance. Perhaps, too, the nature of his activity here enables you safely to conclude that you have not stumbled across porn? Yet even here it is advisable not to discard a particular classificatory schema or template too hastily. Umberto Eco observes that a porn film consisting exclusively of sexual couplings would be intolerable and that therefore there is a structural requirement for scenes of mundane, non-erotic action, such as people driving or travelling in lifts: 'Go into a movie theater. If, to go from A to B, the characters take longer than you would like, then the film you are seeing is pornographic' (Eco, 1995: 225). Where the protagonist dawdles in the sequence under discussion, then, he might actually be providing one of porn's necessary breathing spaces.

Nevertheless, the film's technical assurance and obvious expense may encourage you to continue ranging the system of cinematic genres for more convincing paradigms. A war movie, perhaps, given that the interior space on screen might be a bomb-damaged building in which the man is searching for a much-loved pet? Or maybe film noir, given evidence here of this genre's stylistic repertoire in the low-key lighting and tight close-ups of a seedy protagonist? However, there are more persuasive options still. In particular, the camera's creeping motion in this murky space and the slow accumulation of tension may cause you to apply to the film, with some expectation of success, the schema of the horror film. This tentative judgement is confirmed shortly afterwards: first by horror's familiar false climax – the missing cat suddenly appears, startling you – then by the pay-off, as a monstrous figure descends from above and kills the man.

This account of a scene from Ridley Scott's *Alien* (1979) indicates that consideration of genre when discussing films is both indispensable and problematical. Genre very helpfully breaks up generalised cinematic *stuff* into a manageable number of categories differentiated according to distinctive formal and thematic tendencies. Such classification is supple and informative compared with many other film cataloguing systems, not least that early practice of grouping simply by various running lengths the works offered to exhibitors. Organising films by genre is also more broadly revealing than organising them by particular directors or stars (approaches discussed below in Chapters 6 and 7). Less promisingly, however, criticism of film genres has often struggled to achieve scientific rigour in its definition of the categories with which it works. It is also not always responsive to hybrid or multi-generic films, which is a matter of consequence to *Alien*, itself a fusion of horror and sci-fi. Genre study's available classes can seem equally unwieldy in the face of *sub*-genres. Finally, such an approach is tainted by its traditionally narrow geographical remit, or what Robert Stam calls its '*Hollywoodcentrism*' (2000: 129). Although a substantial scholarly literature exists on the US western or the musical, the Anglophone reader will struggle to find studies of such distinctive non-American genres as the Italian *giallo* (merging horror, crime and sex), the German *Heimatfilm* (dating from the 1950s and sentimentally depicting rural life) and the Indian *mythological* (spectacularly rendering the figures and events of Hindu epic).

Despite identifying several deficiencies in the study of film genre, Stam still insists upon its value as an 'explanatory cognitive instrument' (2000: 129). As this chapter tries to demonstrate, genre is, in fact, an interestingly many-stranded thing for film studies to attend to. It requires sensitivity to cinema's aesthetics, politics and economics, since, depending upon the critical position adopted, a genre is a collection of formal devices, an indicator of socio-cultural conditions and a hook exploited by film producers in the marketing of their output. The topic is still highly productive for the discipline, despite pronouncements by some critics that we are currently witnessing 'the end of genre' (a proposition assessed later in this chapter). Far from being moribund, study of genres is actually undergoing a revival, even an expansion, as evidenced by the launch of several academic book series dedicated to defining and delineating various kinds of films (Bloomsbury's 'Film Genres', Wiley-Blackwell's 'New Approaches to Film Genre' and Routledge's 'Film Guidebook' strand). Such enduring interest in this subject should not, in the end, come as a surprise. For while genre is of course a property that film shares with other arts (think of the war comic, the novelistic western, the radio–play romance), it exerts a particularly compelling force on cinema. Michael Wood puts it well: 'film probably *likes* genre more than any other form or medium does now. It's as if the pleasures of repetition, recognition, variation, renewal were an essential part of what film does and what filmgoers like to see' (2012: 91).

Taxonomies of film genre

To a greater extent than most areas of film studies, work on genre has seemed to invite the application of scientific principles and methods. Shortly, we will consider the merits of modelling a genre's development according to the protocols of evolutionary theory. The fact that *genre* shares an etymological root with *genus* has also encouraged some writers to believe that the film genre system can be set out with the precision of botanical and zoological tabulations (even if the discipline is still awaiting its Linnaeus, the Swedish scientist who originated the modern classification of species). Yet although such approaches are tempting as a way of endowing this strand of film studies with a systematic rationale, they immediately confront the sheer slipperiness of genres themselves.

One major difficulty is the lack of consensus in identifying some core element that, acted upon differently by the various genres, would enable stable distinctions to be made between them. Candidates of varying degrees of plausibility have been proposed

for this unit of comparison. In his article 'On the Iconography of
the Movies' (published by the journal *Movie* in 1963), the art critic
and curator Lawrence Alloway suggested that film studies might
take a lead from the study of painting, specifically from Erwin
Panofsky's concept of *iconography*. Applied to paintings, an iconographic approach observes that certain meaning-bearing objects or
figures recur in particular sorts of work, while being consistently
absent from other kinds: a lamb, for example, is familiar in religious
pictures, but unlikely to feature in seascapes. If Alloway's analogy is
persuasive, significant things – cinema's own icons – can similarly
be found lodged in the visual contents of the different film genres.
And it is soon apparent that this method works well with respect to
certain types of movie. What is a western, after all, but a collection
of icons ranging from Stetsons and six-shooters to blowing tumble-
weed and swinging saloon doors? Witness some of these things on
screen and it is likely you are watching a western, or, at least, a film
that intends some parodic or allusive relation to westerns. Other
genres also marshal significant objects in this way. A bare-chested
or lightly armoured man wearing a skirt-like garment and carrying
a shield and short sword tends, on the whole, to make us feel we
are viewing epic rather than sci-fi (see Figure 15); similarly, a sub-
marine is part of the visual array of a war film but rarer in the high
school movie. However, while iconographic analysis is intermittently effective in this context, it breaks down when confronted by
genres that are less strongly marked by distinctive visual features.
What are the key icons of comedy, say, or romance? In addition,
icons that may appear securely assigned to one genre can easily
migrate to another: a man in a sharp suit might have conjured up the
gangster film in the 1930s, but the musical in the 1950s (and recall
also the polysemic top hat mentioned in Chapter 1).

The iconographic method does not, in the end, have sufficient
range and precision to underpin a total theory of genres. Rather
dismally, as was apparent above when considering varying grounds
for generic assignment of the scene from *Alien*, film genres have in
fact tended to be assessed according to inconsistent criteria rather
than by their different instantiations of something they all have
in common. Thus some genres are defined by narrative content
(the war film). Others are defined by setting (the western, the road

15 Iconography of the epic: Russell Crowe and Sven-Ole Thorsen in *Gladiator* (2000)

movie). Still others are categorised by centring on a type of protagonist (the gangster film, the biopic). Genres may also be differentiated by performance style (the musical, most obviously). Nor does this exhaust the set of distinguishing features, since several other genres are spoken of most frequently in terms of their vivid, even visceral effects upon the spectator: horror comes quickly to mind, but so too does the kind of cinematic melodrama sometimes called the 'weepie' or 'tearjerker'. In *Moving Pictures* (1997), an important early contribution to cognitivist film criticism, Torben Grodal attempted to go beyond these latter, special cases and to classify *all* genres – now reduced by his system to eight – according to the different emotional and sensory responses they generate in the spectator. Awkwardly, however, Grodal retains some familiar generic descriptors such as 'horror', at the same time that he sketches out new, not always persuasive categories that include 'lyricism' and 'schizoid fictions'. For all its boldness, then, this cognitivist intervention remains somewhat aside from the main drift of film genre criticism. We are left with the present, conceptually unsatisfying state of affairs in which, as crazily as comparing a carrot to a python, one sort of film distinguished by its emotional effect is placed in the same genre system as another defined by its presentational mode.

This is not the basis for an orderly, overarching classificatory regime, or *taxonomy*, which would pass muster with a zoologist or botanist. Facing defeat at the level of system-building, then, genre critics have sometimes retreated to individual categories of film and attempted to provide rich descriptions of these. Some of the earliest film genre criticism, by André Bazin and Robert Warshow, takes this form. In the first of his two pioneering essays on the western, Bazin conceptualises the genre's autonomy, or near-autonomy, when he refers to its 'essence' and suggests it has the robustness to ward off influences by other kinds of film (for instance, the detective story) (2005b: 140). Fusion of that sort is described by Bazin as 'contamination' of the western's purity (140), rather than as a way of revitalising westerns. While Bazin's second essay *does* allow for the possibility of transformation in the western (as signalled by the metaphor in its title, 'The Evolution of the Western'), this is still presented as a fall from the 'definitive stage of perfection' already achieved by the genre in John Ford's *Stagecoach* (1939) (2005b: 149). This tendency to construct and protect an idealised conception of a particular genre is also evident in Warshow's important essay on the gangster film, first published in 1948.

At its worst, such an approach seems the work of genre police, vigilantly patrolling a given film category for traces of deviant or illicit forms (revealingly, Derrida's essay on the subject is called 'The Law of Genre'). The prescriptive tendency that has been apparent in genre theory since the classical literary criticism of Aristotle and Horace is extended here into film studies. But the work of Bazin and Warshow is also suspect on evidential grounds. In modelling the western and the gangster movie, respectively, they succumb to that debilitating weakness in film genre study which Barry Langford calls 'endemic critical selectivity' (2005: 135). Warshow's understanding of the gangster film derives from a troublingly small sample of three works, two made in the early 1930s, the other in 1947; he thus passes over a host of other work that might have unsettled or modified his genre description. It is as if, from our present moment, we tried to devise an account of the comedy film after viewing only *Big Momma's House* (2000), Woody Allen's *The Curse of the Jade Scorpion* (2001) and *Alan Partridge: Alpha Papa* (2013). While Bazin casts his net more widely over the western, he too deduces generic shape from a limited archive (notwithstanding practical difficulties he faced in postwar France in obtaining works for viewing). These critical pieces indicate that, although genre criticism holds out the promise of greater hospitality to the *mass* of cinema than a director-based approach to which it is often opposed, it runs the same risk of casting many films into oblivion.

We should not, though, feel snootily superior to these early genre critics. With its focus upon genre, their work valuably opened up popular film to serious study at a time when it was generally disparaged. In addition, selectivity in genre criticism is not safely a thing of the past, but an ongoing problem (for further comment, see this chapter's case study on the superhero film). Nevertheless, it is clear that attempts in the lineage of Bazin and Warshow to distil the inviolable essence of any single genre are likely to fail. Even genres that seem notably self-contained prove to be quite leaky. Although on the face of it the western is coherent in its iconic repertoire, character-types and plot structures, it too is open to mutation and hybridisation. Besides hosting a number of sub-generic variants that extend from parodic westerns like *Blazing Saddles* (1974) to horror westerns like *Ravenous* (1999), this genre's icons and plots undergo reconfiguration when they travel into productions outside the United States – the Italian 'spaghetti' westerns most famously, but also films including *Tears of the Black Tiger* (Thailand, 2000) and *The Proposition* (Australia, 2005). And this still says nothing about traces of the western that may be uncovered in films that carry other generic labels: consider how the western's key tropes of the lawless frontier and the revenge plot have relocated to sci-fi with *Star Wars* (1977) or the war film with *The Deer Hunter* (1978), and even to the British independent drama with Shane Meadows's *Dead Man's Shoes* (2004).

Only in the most shoddily run zoo can a llama mate with a penguin; in cinema, however, interbreeding occurs between species very far apart, as when Michael Winterbottom fuses drama, hard core porn and the rock concert documentary in *9 Songs* (2004). Zoological law cautions against the lamb lying down with the lion, yet there is no cinematic edict to prevent seemingly the most ill-suited genres from combining, a particularly striking example being Roberto Benigni's hybridising of comedy and Holocaust drama in *Life Is Beautiful* (1997; see Figure 16). In case such combinations seem a tendency only of our postmodern moment, it should be pointed out that as long ago as 1935 *The Phantom Empire*'s story of a cowboy singing in outer space blended sci-fi, the western and the musical. Taxonomists of film genre have thus long had to face

16 Generic fusion: comedy meets Holocaust drama in *Life Is Beautiful* (1997)

the bad news that an elegant classificatory system is impossible. The genres that would comprise it can only ever be provisionally defined, since they are always liable to combination with and modification by other filmic kinds. As Rick Altman wittily describes this irrepressible tendency towards mutation: 'In the genre world [...] every day is Jurassic Park day' (1999: 70).

STOP and THINK

- Draw up your own list of film genres, making it as exhaustive as possible. Many studies of film genre, including those by Barry Langford and Steve Neale, settle on somewhere between twelve and fifteen categories. Other attempts, however, to do the arithmetic of genres arrive at a much higher figure. What is your own total? Might any of your nominations be subsumed into a broader category – as variants of the action-adventure film, say – or would such compression be misleading? This inventorying of kinds of film is best carried out with others, so that there are several mappings of the genre system to compare. From this experience, assess whether genre definition is amenable to scholarly consensus or seems more likely to be a matter of ongoing critical dispute.

- Choose one genre from your list. Aiming again at exhaustive-ness, catalogue everything you would expect to find in this category of film. You might consider features from across the textual range, identifying conventions in plotting, char-acterisation and iconography as well as marked tendencies in mise-en-scène (horror's point-of-view tracking shots) and sound design (romance's dreamy saxophone for love scenes). Do these attributes suggest it is possible to speak of your chosen genre as a fixed and stable thing? Or is it liable to historical change and to infiltration by other categories, and thus taxonomically unstable?

- Stick with this genre and analyse your own expectations as a spectator. Do you require the conventions you have identified – however provisional they may be – always to be observed? Or do you hope to see in new films in this category evidence of generic reinvention, even sabotage? Consider how particular examples of the genre negotiate between predictability and novelty.

Who creates film genres?

Discussion so far has focused upon two particular problems in the study of film genres: first, the difficulty of finding some unifying ground for the categories of film that are taken to comprise the genre system; second, the difficulty of realising secure and pre-cise definitions even of single genres. This still takes for granted, though, the existence and accreditation as categorising terms of 'the western', 'the musical', 'the biopic' and all the others. Yet where do these generic descriptors come from? Who, or what, gets to create film genres? If it seems uncontentious to place *Titanic* in the categories of 'drama' and 'romance', that is not something irrevoca-bly determined by the work itself but because these ways of group-ing movies have greater prestige and circulation than conceivable alternatives such as 'the shipping film' or 'the female memory film'. Generic designation here and in all other cases is thus a matter of *interpretative construction*, rather than mere discovery by the viewer. As Gary Saul Morson reminds us, his italics justified by the point's importance, '*genre does not belong to texts alone, but to the interaction between texts and a classifier*' (1981: x). In this section, therefore, we consider how genres have been created in interactions between film texts themselves and several constituencies of 'classifier'.

Writers have chosen quite different metaphors by which to make the point that various interest groups have an investment in film genre. For Paul Watson, 'genre resembles a golden thread that knits the concerns of the film industry together with the desires of its audiences' (2012: 189). Although helpful in presenting film genre as a concern of both producers and receivers, this figure of the thread gives a misleading impression of genre creation as something tidy and unifying. Watson's alternative image of genre as a 'conceptual prism' (189) is more successful, indicating how the particular situations of those engaged with film will materially affect how they look at specific genres and at the genre system as a whole. Even so, the metaphor still does not quite capture these constituencies' ceaseless, *competitive* efforts at genre construction. For this, we should turn to Rick Altman, whose contribution to the study of film genre has been as notable as that which, in Chapter 3, we saw him making to the theorisation of soundtrack. 'The process of genre creation', he writes, 'offers us not a single synchronic chart, but an always incomplete series of superimposed generic maps' (1999: 70). At first glance, the figure of the map, with its hint of something static, might seem as analytically suspect as those of the thread and the prism. Altman's metaphor, however, has two advantages: first, geographers have long demonstrated that cartography is not a neutral practice but a grab at power or control that issues from particular social locations; second, Altman speaks not of a single map, but of discontinuous, competing generic cartographies variously produced by the film industry, critics and spectators (including fan communities).

According to critics such as Steve Neale, study of genre construction should be centred upon the industry's own promotion and dissemination of categorising terms. Done well, this is no easy task, requiring the researcher to track references to genre not only through the archives of studios but across the masses of publicity material they send into the world to accompany film releases. In Neale's view, however, an adequate genre criticism is not possible until this thorough documentation of the production side has been achieved: 'it is only on the basis of this testimony that the history of any one genre and an analysis of its social functions and social significance can begin to be produced' (2000: 43). Other scholars, though, argue that a strong industrial emphasis of this kind risks aggrandising just one of the several forces involved in genre construction. Echoing Altman, Christine Gledhill suggests that critics, spectators and fans, as well as production moguls and studio publicists, contribute to the '*intertextual relay*' in which any film is embedded and through which its generic status is established (2000: 224). This concept of the 'intertextual relay' derives from a still very useful essay by Gregory Lukow and Steven Ricci (1984: 28–36), which argues that a given film's genre is not immanent in or entirely predetermined by its textual elements themselves but is arrived at during the interplay of numerous discourses produced by multiple parties both before and after the film's release.

While it is important to extend the conversation about genre to include the interlocutors identified by Altman, Gledhill and others, this should not be taken to the point of denying that the film industry itself still speaks with the loudest voice. As the duration and dispersal of its marketing efforts increase, so, proportionately, the genre-creating potential of other constituencies diminishes. Who or what can compete on equal terms with film producers' discursive arsenal of cinema trailers, TV and radio commercials, newspaper and magazine previews, posters in public spaces, and dedicated websites and social media interventions? To gauge this power, consider simply a tiny, though important part of the intertextual relay surrounding *The Equalizer*: its official Facebook page just before the film's release in the autumn of 2014. Even a cursory glance at this site quickly disclosed the producers' attempt to shape the generic image of the film and hence the terms of its reception (an effort evidently of some longevity, since the page had opened in July 2012). Much of the movie's target audience was likely to have little or no recollection of its progenitor US TV series (1985–89). However, the nature of the publicity material displayed on the Facebook page gave clear generic leads about *The Equalizer* the film, without ever needing to use words like 'action', 'crime' or 'thriller'. A prominently placed image of the film's hero in the distance in intriguing silhouette was accompanied by identification of its director as Antoine Fuqua, contextualised as 'Director of *Training Day* and *Olympus Has Fallen*' ('*The Equalizer*, Film', 2014: n.p.). Immediately, generic prompts were being given to the likely audience, since Fuqua was not credited here with his direction of the decidedly *non*-crime film, *King Arthur* (2004). The Facebook page also identified Denzel Washington as the film's star, though without including any of his former credits: such a move may have been felt superfluous by the producers, however, since much of the target demographic would have seen Washington in *Training Day* and would therefore have been able to make the necessary generic correlation with *The Equalizer*. Elsewhere, the page featured a trailer heavy with percussive music and vivid action scenes, and a series of single images of Washington that included him brandishing guns in noirish settings, again clearly encouraging viewers to place the film in particular generic contexts. Although the Facebook page gave spectators a right of rapid response not permitted anyone seeing a street poster for *The Equalizer* (other than graffitists), posts on the site prior to the film's release were of a uniformly excited and adulatory nature. Such evidence of one strand of the producers' publicity effort does not, of course, preclude audiences and critics from positioning *The Equalizer* in categories other than those officially favoured ('the African American film', perhaps). Even if alternative generic mappings of this sort are theoretically possible, however, they are decidedly lacking in institutional force.

Nevertheless, the concept of the intertextual relay is helpful in enabling us to move beyond a deterministic understanding of the film industry's power to shape generic definitions. Notwithstanding the implications of this brief case study of *The Equalizer*, compelling discourses about the genre identities of films may be developed and circulated by groups other than producers themselves. There are, to begin with, the interventions of film reviewers, not merely confirming a studio's preferred label ('the best comedy this year'), but potentially generating new terminology and assessment criteria of their own ('gross-out comedy'). And while academic film critics might seem very low down the intertextual food chain, they too have had successes in struggles over genre. A case in point is the category of 'the woman's film', this genre originated not by the industry itself but by feminist scholars from the 1970s onwards who gathered together and reinterpreted a body of female-centred movies from classical Hollywood in order to find ruptures in their seemingly conservative gender politics. The flow of genre definitions is not irremediably from industry to academia, but may sometimes be reversible. In the 1940s and early 1950s, for example, Hollywood thought it was making 'crime' or 'detective' pictures when it inserted seedy private eyes and dangerous blondes into mean urban streets where it was always raining. Yet critical activity over subsequent decades gradually reassigned these works to a category called 'film noir'. Then another phase in the intertextual relay saw this categorising term reappropriated by the industry itself and used to add allure and commodity value in the publicity for such neo-noir works as *Sin City 2: A Dame to Kill For*.

In discussing the role played in genre creation by producers, reviewers and academic critics, nothing has yet been said about the contribution of audiences. Spectators may turn in relatively disorganised and uncommitted fashion to social media and other communicational outlets to reflect on films, including those films' generic identities. We should, though, consider at greater length the activities of *fans*, since, as Henry Jenkins argues, 'Fandom generates its own genres' (2013: 279). Altman has written interestingly about what he calls 'generic communities' (1999: 156–64), understood as bodies of fans that cohere around enthusiasm for a particular kind of film (as well as, on occasion, for *individual* films, such as *The Lord of the Rings* franchise). The conversations that such a group has are not only interpretatively valuable in saying something about the genre in question, but socially enriching in affirming its members' sense of well-being and unity. A little sentimentally, perhaps, Altman goes so far as to argue that in the contemporary West 'it is possible for genre to stand in for an absent community' (187).

To see one generic community at work, consider the case of 'bicycle films'. While retailers and reviewers have tended to place films into a relatively small number of film categories, other genre classifiers need not be so parsimonious. A precedent for enthusiastic multiplication of genres exists, for instance, in the American Film Institute's index for the 1930s, which lists no fewer than sixty-one varieties of movie, including 'boxing', 'jungle' and 'newspaper' films (Neale, 2000: 241–2, 255–6). Although some of the AFI's categories are transport-related – 'automobile racing' and 'aviation' films – no mention is made in that historical moment of the existence of the cycling film. But that this genre has since been created, by fans if not by the film industry itself, can be discerned through research into online activities on both sides of the Atlantic.

Two outputs by the generic community drawn together by the bicycle film can be mentioned here. The first of these is a list of the 'Top Ten Bicycling Movies', hosted by the website of *Momentum Mag*, a US-based online magazine devoted to cycling. The selection 'span[s] the genres and styles', a comment that suggests initial hesitancy in claiming generic status for the bicycle film itself. If it is unsurprising to see the inclusion here of *Pedal* (2001), described as a documentary about 'the fast-paced daily activities of bicycle messengers in New York City', it is startling that also listed is *E.T. the Extra-Terrestrial* (1982) (Korcheva, 2011: 1). To take a few charming scenes in Spielberg's adventure-fantasy-sci-fi-children's film as the basis for its redesignation as a 'bicycling movie' seems a piece of criticism akin to calling *Othello* a 'handkerchief play' or Jane Austen's *Emma* a 'picnic novel'. Nevertheless, the move is characteristic of those generic communities devoted not to pre-existing categories but seeking to devise new ones and to assemble new canons by overriding the descriptors previously applied to the films in which they are interested. Similar reconstructive practices underlie the composition of another list to be found online, headed 'Some Bicycle Films'. Compared with the first selection, this one is more globally inclusive in its canon suggestions, extending beyond North America to cite, for example, Iran's *The Cyclist* (1987), Vietnam's *Cyclo* (1995) and the Chinese *Beijing Bicycle* (2001) ('Some Bicycle Films', 2011: n.p.). Once more, however, assertive generic recoding can be observed, notably in the list's inclusion of Vittorio De Sica's *Bicycle Thieves* (1948). Normally, this film, in which bikes appear to do no more than advance the plot, would be refracted through the prisms of Italian neo-realism and humanist cinema; it becomes a very different thing, however, when approached with the eye of the bicycle movie fan for handlebar and saddle design (Figure 17).

17 Neo-realist classic or masterpiece of humanist cinema – or 'bicycling movie'? Vittorio de Sica's *Bicycle Thieves* (1948)

In both of these online lists there is evidence of properly *communal* engagement, as theorised by Altman, rather than the idiosyncratic endeavours of one or two people. The first selection appears, as noted, in an online cycling magazine, so that formation of this new genre of film can be seen as part of a wide range of cycle-related activities. The second list suggests a more sustained attempt to establish and consolidate the bicycle film, since it incorporates links both to others' lists (enabling the new genre's canon to be argued over as intensely as would be that of the horror movie) and to bicycle film festivals (again international in scope, with events in venues including Helsinki, Moscow and New York). These latter occasions demonstrate that a generic community's instantiation may occur in face-to-face exchanges, rather than exclusively online. Of course none of this intertextual activity should be taken to imply that generic reassignment of *Bicycle Thieves* and *E.T.* will occur any time soon; nevertheless, it does suggest that even in the face of the film industry's discursive power fans themselves may, as Jenkins states, be productive genre critics.

STOP and THINK

• Reconstruct as thoroughly as possible the 'intertextual relay' of any current film. This will entail research across multiple domains, from newspapers and magazines to street posters and websites. Assess the strength of the industry's own genre signalling in this instance: do publicity materials tend to mark emphatically or, on the contrary, minimise the film's generic identity? In either case, why? Bearing in mind the various user-groups that make up the intertextual relay – producers, reviewers, spectators and so on – assess whether consensual definition of this film's category, or categories, is achieved. Or is there evidence of *dissension*, with the film the object of alternative generic mappings? One possibility is that online communities may jam the film industry's powerful discursive machinery and generate new perspectives on the work.

Genres and history

The iconoclastic literary scholar Franco Moretti offers another suggestive metaphor for genres. They are, he says with reference to the Roman god of doorways, 'Janus-like creatures, with one face turned to history and the other to form' (2005: 14). Yet even to phrase the matter like this is to introduce a false dichotomy between form and history, since seemingly 'formal' or 'internal' aspects of a genre are not isolated from historical processes but, on the contrary, saturated by them. As Moretti has written more recently, in outlining his preferred analytical mode of 'sociological formalism': 'Forms are the abstract of social relationships: so, formal analysis is in its own modest way an analysis of power' (2013: 59). To take a particularly clear example from cinema: the western's familiar formal features – recurrent plot trajectories and character-types, frontier settings, frequently used props and costumes, extreme long shots of landscapes, and so on – are significantly shaped by dynamics of race, gender and nation-building in the United States. And, as we have seen, these repertoires of the western are not permanently fixed but subject to modifications over time through which socio-cultural shifts might be discerned. Film genre criticism, then, should be historicist through and through, attending both to the development of particular genres and to the broader cultural resonances of this.

Several commentators on film genres, however, have pointed out the difficulty of composing their histories. Altman criticises a tendency to employ biological models when writing about changes to such cultural constructs as genres. Two explanatory schemas are dubiously utilised, he points out: first, a developmental language that likens a film genre's history to the natural arc of a human life; second, more grandly, though quite loosely, an evolutionary paradigm that traces a genre's course from life-generating novelty to predictability, stasis and ultimate extinction (1999: 21–2). It is striking, in fact, how often film critics have adopted a tripartite plot-structure with respect to generic history. For Thomas Schatz, in *Hollywood Genres*, a genre's three stages can be labelled 'experimental' (before it has a recognisable identity of its own), 'classical' (when its conventions have stabilised and are at their most coherent) and 'formalist' (when its conventions are no longer straightforwardly reproduced, but, rather, are advertised, even parodied) (1981: 38). Writing initially at the same time, Richard Dyer proposed a comparable trajectory, with only the names he gave to its three phases differing: 'primitive' (exhibiting the genre, as Dyer says, 'in embryonic form'), 'mature' (demonstrating 'the full realization of its expressive potential') and 'decadent' (marked by 'a reflective self-consciousness about the genre itself') (2002: 60). If the sequence is comparable to that devised by Schatz, however, this nomenclature can be seen to add a note of moralistic judgement.

No one should deny the partial usefulness of schemas of this sort. At the very least, the sense of development which they incorporate encourages genre criticism to move beyond taxonomic stasis. At the same time, however, a fixed trajectory is flawed as a model of a genre's history. Dyer, Schatz and others sketch out a single line of development for film genres without sufficiently considering how this might be complicated by the discontinuous fates of *sub*-generic categories. The narrative they propose of successive phases also struggles to account for deviant films that, to use Dyer's language, are 'decadent' before their genre's time or, alternatively, still formally 'mature' at a point when the genre's death has been

pronounced. In addition, how is this developmental model to cope
with films in which the putatively separate generic stages may be
seen to co-exist? Consider, for instance, Spielberg's *Saving Private
Ryan* (1998). With its virtuous American hero and its drive towards
a consoling ending (morally regenerative, if not exactly 'happy'),
the film erases any trace of counter-cultural anti-militarism and
thus still resembles the works belonging to the war movie's 'classical' or 'mature' moment (to draw again upon Schatz's and Dyer's
terminologies). However, in its visceral footage of the Normandy
landings *Saving Private Ryan* also seems a self-consciously *late*
or 'post-classical' war film, antagonistic towards earlier representations of painless combat in work like *The Longest Day* (1962).
Things become more complex still when we deduce from subsequent films such as Ridley Scott's *Black Hawk Down* (2001) and
Kathryn Bigelow's *The Hurt Locker* (2008) that the handheld camerawork and rapid editing of *Saving Private Ryan* are not actually
the war genre's dying breath but already stabilised as among its new
'classical' or 'mature' conventions. Paradoxes of this sort, or loop-
ings back and forth between generic pasts and futures, throw into
crisis unilinear emplotment of any film category.

Whether it draws upon evolutionary biology or some other conceptual resource, the history of any film genre, or sub-genre, cannot
be written without regard to broader historical processes. Even as
a category of film seems to observe its own dynamics, these are
already socially overwritten. To cite one example: works ranging
from *Saving Private Ryan* to *The Monuments Men* (2014) and *Fury*
(2014) that reinvigorate the sub-genre of the World War II movie
at a time when it seemed to have been extinguished are readable
as part of the cultural work of post-Vietnam recuperation in the
US (perhaps in the more recent cases post-Iraq rehabilitation, too,
with imagery of America's 'good war' displacing thoughts of the
debacle in the Middle East). Generalising from this example, we
can interpret the waxing and waning of particular genres and sub-
genres as socio-cultural symptoms (an analytical exercise that will
be repeated in Chapter 7 with reference to the rise and fall of particular film stars). Like the canary once taken down a coal mine, a
genre is an unusually sensitive instrument for measuring changes in
the atmosphere.

At the same time, however, care is needed in correlating shifts in the course of a film genre with specific social conditions. It is possible to be crude and over-emphatic in asserting a genre's capacity for historical revelation. The emergence of film noir in the 1940s, for example, has been traced retrospectively to social developments such as the beginnings of Cold War paranoia and a crisis in American masculinity following women's unprecedented opportunities for work and sexual liberation during World War II. In Darwinian terms, the genre might be understood as 'selected' because of its particular facility in registering cultural anxieties at that historical juncture. Yet the case for the genre's diagnostic power with respect to postwar America should be made cautiously: after all, at the same time as a mass of dark crime films of this sort was released, comedies and musicals continued to appear (though of course *those* genres, too, are open to historicist interpretation). Finally, to recall an important point from above, the ideological status of any genre, including film noir, is not given in advance or universally agreed; rather, this is the stuff of ongoing dispute between different generic communities.

STOP and THINK

- Moretti argues that 'a genre exhausts its potentialities – and the time comes to give a competitor a chance – when its inner form is no longer capable of representing the most significant aspects of contemporary reality' (2005: 17n.). Do you agree with this thesis that a genre's fate is tied to its capacity for engagement, however codedly or disguisedly, with 'contemporary reality'?
- Return to the list of genres you compiled earlier and consider which of them are particularly prominent now and, in a Darwinian sense, seem well-adapted to the present moment. Conversely, which genres appear weakened, no longer prolific, perhaps about to vanish (if only temporarily)? Speculate on reasons for this generic promotion or relegation.
- Can film genres ever *die*? Since even categories of film that appear moribund can unexpectedly revive (not too many

people were predicting the recovery of epic before *Gladiator* emerged in 2000), it may be advisable not to be too terminal in your thinking here. Also: even if a genre does not actually re-enter production, it may still be sustained at the level of *reception*, through fan activity.

The end of genre?

For some two decades now, a number of critics have pronounced the death of genre, referring to the obsolescence not of any particular category of film but of this principle of film categorisation in itself. Particularly in Hollywood, they suggest, generic identity has ceased to be both a major criterion in production and a key concern in post-production promotional activities. Here we will briefly mention and respond to two of these obsequies for film genre. The first is voiced by Paul Watson, who argues that by contrast with its classical incarnation *contemporary* Hollywood is not bound to spectators by a kind of unofficial contractual arrangement requiring it to deliver films that can be securely placed in one of a number of well-defined categories, each providing audiences with particular satisfactions. Instead of discrete kinds of movie such as 'the western' and 'the sci-fi film', there is now a type of trans- or even post-generic cinema which Watson says is constituted by '"the blockbuster", "special-effects movies", "event cinema", "summer movie", even "action cinema", which tend to fall outside of, or in between, traditional generic groupings' (2012: 198). Features once distributed quite evenly among Hollywood's genres are now synthesised in complex ways that go well beyond an old-fashioned devising of relatively basic compounds (the comedy thriller, say, or the musical western).

The second critical source cited here predates Watson, which indicates that ideas about Hollywood's post-generic settlement have been in circulation since at least the mid-1990s. Briefly quoted in fact by Watson, Jim Collins argues that Hollywood cinema is increasingly characterised not by observance of discrete genres but by filmmakers' 'eclectic appropriation' of heterogeneous generic materials (1995: 135). A paradoxical outcome of these activities of multi-generic quoting, borrowing and assembling is that we

encounter films 'composed entirely of generic artifacts that con-
tradict, as an assemblage, the function of genre as coordinator of
narrative conventions and audience expectations' (148). In support
of his argument, Collins cites a host of US films from the late 1980s
and early 1990s, including Tim Burton's *Batman* (1989) and one of
Arnold Schwarzenegger's vehicles, *Last Action Hero* (1993). And
we can readily think of many subsequent Hollywood movies that
Collins might have called upon as further evidence: the *Lord of the
Rings* series, for instance, or the work of Quentin Tarantino, Baz
Luhrmann and, indeed, Christopher Nolan.

Watson, Collins and other critics undoubtedly pinpoint a significant tendency in contemporary Hollywood. The argument can, in
fact, be extended beyond the United States: Collins himself alludes
to the work of Hong Kong filmmaker John Woo, while reference
could also be made, say, to the delirious fusion of horror, sci-fi,
comedy and the stuff of other genres that occurs in *The Host*, a successful export from South Korea in 2006. Old genre classifications
can indeed seem as cumbersome as boxing gloves when attempting
to handle with precision something like the 'summer movie' or
'event cinema'. There is a problem, however, in that breathtaking
generalisation tends to follow from identification of this new wave
of blockbusters. Here the 'endemic critical selectivity' for which
Langford indicts earlier students of genre like Bazin and Warshow
returns with a vengeance to undermine the *post-generic* writers.
This latter group of scholars tends to privilege an equally small
corpus of titles. The sheer dazzle of this narrow selection of films
appears to blind critics to the relatively routine genre production
that continues prolifically in mainstream US cinema and indeed
elsewhere. For every ironically eclectic and multi-generic event
movie, after all, there is a new Judd Appatow comedy or Vin Diesel
action picture.

Attention still paid to film genre on the production side is
matched by ongoing critical activities such as the several series of
single-genre studies referred to earlier. Nevertheless, any reassertion of the usefulness of genre for film studies should not be taken
to indicate that this concept is beyond reproach. Rather, it is still
open to modification at both macroscopic and microscopic levels.
With regard to the first of these, Langford argues that critics might

make at least some use of *modes*: that is to say, diegetic and thematic dispositions, such as melodrama, whose presence can be detected across several, traditionally differentiated genres (2005: 29). This is an approach followed productively by Geoff King in a study of film comedy that does not restrict itself to a single genre officially labelled as such: 'Comedy is a *mode* – a manner of presentation – in which a variety of different materials can be approached, rather than any relatively more fixed or localised quantity. Any genre might be treated as a subject for comedy' (2002a: 2). At the other extreme, more work is certainly needed of a higher magnification, identifying multitudes of *sub*-genres and unfolding their histories.

Case study: the superhero film

For Dan Hassler-Forest, the superhero film 'has established itself as the dominant genre in 21st-century Hollywood cinema' (2012: 3). Such a claim is hard to dispute, given the commercial power and media ubiquity of, say, Christopher Nolan's *Dark Knight* trilogy (2005–12); Sam Raimi's *Spider-Man* series (2002–7) and its almost immediate rebooting by Marc Webb (2012 and 2014, with further instalments due); the highly prolific *X-Men* franchise (2000–), with successive additions exploiting every conceivable opportunity for rotation of the central characters; the trio of *Iron Man* films (2008–13); *Avengers Assemble* (2012) and its sequel (2015); and the two *Thor* episodes to date (2011, 2013). Movies with protagonists of this sort go back further, too, as evidenced by previous *Batman* films and multiple entries in the *Superman* canon. Neither the superhero movie's long appeal to producers, however, nor its current popularity with audiences appears to have won it universal academic accreditation as a genre; rarely is it endowed by critics with the same solidity as the western, for example, or the musical. Below, we address this conceptual deficit, evaluating the superhero movie's generic status, its identifiable conventions and its ideological resonances.

1. *'Genrification'*. In cinema, as in literature, genres do not emerge fully formed; instead, a cluster of films undergoes what Altman calls a 'process of genrification' (1999: 54), gradually recognised

as having narrative, stylistic and thematic commonalities. Altman describes how a previously *adjectival* variant of a larger category of film may become prolific enough to form a *substantive* category of its own (as happened in the early twentieth century when 'the western comedy' outgrew subordination to the comic genre, and 'the western' itself was established) (199). Something similar may be observed in the genesis of the superhero film. Registering adjectivally at first as an option within the broader categories of sci-fi, fantasy, action and adventure, it later achieved substantive status by a series of films that began with Richard Lester's two *Superman* movies (1978, 1980), continued through work such as Tim Burton's *Batman* instalments (1989, 1992), and has proliferated markedly in post-2000 US cinema.

If there is genrification, however, there can also be *de*genrification, whereby a category of film begins to lose its shape or definition, dissolving back into the larger cinematic system. While, a moment ago, we saw Hassler-Forest positing the superhero movie's current supremacy as a genre, in another passage he calls it '"post-genre", freely mixing and matching from established generic frameworks as diverse as horror, romantic comedy, action, epic, fantasy, and science fiction, often within a single film' (2012: 200). This list could, in fact, be considerably extended, given the superhero movie's incorporation of elements of the war film, the martial arts film, the spy thriller, noir, even the western. However, to go from proper acknowledgement of its jackdaw tendencies to disqualifying it entirely as a genre is an unwarranted move. If the superhero genre, like many others, includes multi-generic materials, it nevertheless refashions and repurposes these according to its own distinctive logic. It would be a pity to abandon it, generically speaking, before it has even been subjected to detailed investigation as a film category.

Like more universally recognised genres, the superhero film has now accumulated sufficient complexity to produce *subgeneric* variants. 'One has to adapt to survive', Curt Connors, later Lizard, remarks in *The Amazing Spider-Man* (2012); and, appropriately enough, the superhero movie has mutated and regenerated. To use a term from evolutionary biology (a field, as noted above, that has interested genre theorists), this category of film has an extensive *diversity spectrum*, ranging from the noir of the *Dark Knight* trilogy or the horror of Guillermo Del Toro's two *Hellboy* movies (2004, 2008) to the comedy, even slapstick, of *Iron Man* (2008) as Tony Stark is propelled chaotically around a laboratory by his superpowered invention. There is also evidence in the genre now of heightened self-consciousness, even self-parody, hinting that it might be approaching that phase characterised by Dyer as 'decadent'. The two *Kick-Ass* films (2010, 2013), for instance, are intertextually knowing, and muse sardonically on their own genre's conventions. Characteristic is the title character's remark in the first instalment: 'This is awesome; I look like fucking Wolverine!'

2. *Conventions.* While attempts to tabulate the icons, character-types and plot points of a given genre can exhibit a rather arid formalism, this work is also essential information-gathering before thinking about the genre's place in the cinema system and in the culture at large. Consideration, firstly, of the superhero movie's typical protagonist might dwell on his (rarely *her*) social dislocation: if you encounter a troubled young orphan on screen, you are even more likely to be watching a superhero film than a Dickens adaptation. Otherwise, however, there is variation among these central figures, with the source of their superpowers, for instance, ranging from the genetic mutations of Hulk or Spider-Man to the expensively engineered prosthetic enhancements of Iron Man. Elaborate transformation scenes – Bruce Wayne's accessorising as Batman, or Peter Parker's shift to adhesive, agile Spider-Man – are recurrent set-pieces in the genre; so, too, are superhero 'training montages', these sequences creatively recycled from the war and sports categories.

In a moment we will assess socio-cultural explanations for the superhero movie's selection as one especially well suited to our current moment. Its contemporary prominence, however, is technologically as well as ideologically determined, with the genre functioning as a profitable showcase of cinema's most spectacular effects. CGI (computer-generated imagery) is paramount here (frequently enhanced by 3D presentation), engineering kinetic fight sequences, space-bending chases and vertiginous swoops over city streets, the latter scenes giving the viewer an experience of liberated movement through space that contrasts with a sense of his or her *political immobility* often presumed by the genre at narrative level. Yet while spectacle is crucial to the genre, it operates in collusion with narrative, rather than as its substitute: a reimagined 'cinema of attractions', to recall that filmic mode discussed in Chapter 4, is fastened tightly here into orders of storytelling. Audiences for *The Dark Knight Rises* (2012), for example, are absorbed by the fraught psychodrama of Bruce Wayne besides being thrilled by the sight of bridges and stadia collapsing.

3. *Ideology.* Given its declining output, the western is no longer so well equipped to fulfil its historical role of contributing to the reproduction of white patriarchal masculinity; it may be, however, that this function has now substantially devolved to the superhero film. Beneath this genre's visual trappings of ultra-modernity subsists an ideological core of ultra-conservatism. Startlingly, even Hollywood's least reconstructed genres have practised affirmative action more vigorously than the superhero movie, since the latter only occasionally puts non-white figures centre-stage: rare examples would include Halle Berry as *Catwoman* (2004) and Will Smith as *Hancock* (2008). And, while powerful females certainly operate in the genre – Jennifer Lawrence as Mystique in three *X-Men* instalments (2011, 2014, 2016), for example, or Scarlett Johansson as Natasha Romanoff/ Black Widow in the *Avengers* films – narrative centrality itself is largely the preserve of males. As a rule, these male protagonists are also visibly engaged in the acquisition of patriarchal author-ity by overcoming real or substitute fathers in oedipal strug-gles. In times, then, when the Law of the Father is perceived to be under stress, the superhero film operates as an agent of *remasculinisation*.

Though variable in tone, as we have already seen, the super-hero film takes as axiomatic *a state of crisis* (here is an ideo-logical reason for its prominence compared with other genres that seem less closely aligned with our current moment). At times, these movies lend themselves quite obviously to inter-pretation as allegories of 9/11 and its aftermath: consider, for

18 The iconography of 9/11 in the superhero film? Three of the title
characters pictured with New York under attack in *Avengers Assemble*
(2012)

example, the airborne attack on Gotham in *The Dark Knight
Rises*, or the recapitulation of the iconography of September 11th
in the ground-level, hectic footage of urban collapse in *Avengers
Assemble* (see Figure 18). However, in its presentation of the
protagonists' enemies, the superhero film is generally careful
to evacuate itself of any allusion to oppositional forces and programmes recognisable from our globe now: thus the Joker in *The
Dark Knight* likes 'to see the world burn', and Loki in the *Thor*
franchise causes chaos, yet neither is exactly readable in terms of
Al-Qaeda or the Taliban. Contributions to this genre, then, tend
to evoke the anxious atmospherics of the contemporary West
without identifying its political causes. There is also something
troubling about the films' proposed solutions to perceived crisis.
The general population in superhero movies is usually cowed
and inert, even infantilised; it characteristically cedes agency to
the hyperbolised central figures. 'You're just one man!' exclaims
incredulous Gotham policeman Jim Gordon in *Batman Begins*
(2008). In the superhero film, however, one man – one *man* – is
sufficient more often than not.

     The genre is open, too, to accusations that it not only takes for
granted but also *glamorises* the contemporary capitalist order. In

a trenchant Marxist study, Hassler-Forest reads *Batman Begins*, which offers 'a corporate CEO as a new kind of capitalist super-hero' (2012: 149), as symptomatic of the genre's retrograde class politics. Here, again, the *Kick-Ass* series does some useful work in uncovering the superhero movie's ideological assumptions. As the loathsome young villain of the second instalment remarks: 'My super power is I'm rich as shit' – a remark applicable to Bruce Wayne, too, and to other protagonists in this genre such as Tony Stark of the *Iron Man* franchise. The superhero movie often effects, at the imaginary level, repairs to the neoliberal capitalism brought into crisis by twenty-first-century recession.

If genres can accommodate narrative variety, however, they may also deviate ideologically. Thus the superhero movie should be scanned for its progressive possibilities as well as read militantly for its reactionary value. In diagnostic mode, as noted above, the genre productively delineates a crisis of contemporary agency (even if its preferred solution of a super-powered individual, or even a superpowered collective as with the assembled 'avengers', is problematical). More positively, however, some of the franchises polemicise on behalf of *difference* (thereby disclosing the superhero movie's debts to sci-fi – always a privileged genre for investigating alternative or aberrant identities). Recall, for example, the declaration by Mystique in *X-Men: First Class* (2010) of 'Mutant – and proud', her statement asserting the value of races, sexualities and abilities other than those endowed in the West with hegemonic force. It is troubling, then, that mutants become 'weaponised' in this and some other superhero films, meaning that the radical alternative they have evoked may be forgotten in displays of spectacular violence.

Selected reading

The texts listed below are all concerned with the totality of film genres. However, many specialist studies of individual genres are also available: see, for example, particular volumes in Wiley-Blackwell's 'New Approaches to Film Genre' series.

Altman, Rick (1999), *Film/Genre* (London: BFI).
Engaging, sophisticated attempt to rethink film genres, developing a 'semantic/syntactic/pragmatic' approach adequate to their mutability and their status as objects of constant cultural contestation.

Cornea, Christine (ed.) (2010), *Genre and Performance: Film and Television* (Manchester: Manchester University Press).
Takes a distinctive approach to genres by exploring how they elicit particular performance styles: the book's cinematic sections include coverage of the biopic, Bollywood, film noir and sci-fi.

Friedman, Lester, David Desser, Sarah Kozloff, Martha Nochimson and Stephen Prince (2013), *An Introduction to Film Genres* (New York: Norton).
Further evidence of film genre's ongoing conceptual importance: a colossal yet highly accessible overview of thirteen genres.

Geraghty, Lincoln and Mark Jancovich (eds) (2008), *The Shifting Definitions of Genre: Essays on Labeling Films, Television Shows and Media* (Jefferson, NC: McFarland).
Casts its net wider than cinema, but includes fascinating, meticulously researched essays on attempts by interested parties of various kinds to frame the definitions of such genres as film noir, horror, the musical and the western.

Grant, Barry Keith (2006), *Film Genre: From Iconography to Ideology* (London: Wallflower).
A lucid, astute and economical overview of this topic.

Grant, Barry Keith (ed.) (2012), *Film Genre Reader IV* (Austin: University of Texas Press).
Generous collection, bringing together critical writings from a variety of periods and positions that address both overarching theoretical issues and specific genres.

Grodal, Torben (1997), *Moving Pictures: A New Theory of Film Genres, Feelings, and Cognition* (Oxford: Clarendon Press).
A sophisticated, cognitive approach to genre, seeking to counter historical and sociological approaches by aligning each film category with a specific emotional effect and mode of mental functioning.

Langford, Barry (2005), *Film Genre: Hollywood and Beyond* (Edinburgh: Edinburgh University Press).
Less internationalist than its subtitle promises, but a lively survey of the shifting, entangled histories of genres from the western and the musical to pornography and the Holocaust film.

Neale, Steve (2000), *Genre and Hollywood* (London: Routledge).
Slightly drier than Langford, but formidable in its scholarship and still

valuable on many counts, not least for proposing a programme of 'cross-generic and multi-cyclic' study.

Sanders, John (2009), *The Film Genre Book* (Leighton Buzzard: Auteur).
Compendious study of seven genres: less intellectually demanding than some other studies cited here, but has a pleasing textual and historical range.

Online resources

'Film Genres', www.filmsite.org/filmgenres.html.
Cheerfully populist in tone, and American in emphasis, yet gathering much useful material on the history of genres and sub-genres.

'Horror Film History – A Decade by Decade Guide to the Horror Movie Genre', www.horrorfilmhistory.com.
A good example of a resource dedicated to a single genre, tracking in abundant verbal and visual detail the horror film's mutations from the silent era into the twenty-first century.

6

Film and authorship

Genre criticism represents film studies at perhaps its least person-alised, dealing with substantial bodies of films (musicals, epics and so on) and tending in the process to suspend, or at least downplay, interest in the creative contributions made by individuals. Such concern, however, returns with a vengeance in debates over film authorship. Yet, as we will uncover in this chapter, identifying the authors of films is an area of inquiry that has proved both concep-tually challenging and historically mutable. Can a film even be said to *have* an author in the same way that we conventionally ascribe authorship of novels, plays and poems? If Shakespeare is usually nominated as the author of *Macbeth* and Dickens as the author of *Bleak House*, who, or what, is the author of *Fast & Furious 7* (2015)?

Some of the complexities of this chapter's subject can be adver-tised by brief reference to *Contempt* (1963), directed by Jean-Luc Godard. With its sunny Mediterranean locations and its casting of Brigitte Bardot at the height of her pin-up celebrity, this film is among Godard's most crowd-pleasing; nevertheless, for our pur-poses, it can be read as a searching exploration of questions of film authorship. Paul Javal, the protagonist, is hired for work on an American movie about Ulysses because of his writing talents, previously channelled into other forms but now to be applied in fashioning a screenplay. However, his own claim to authorship of the resulting film is merely partial, since he is seen cutting a very deferential figure next to its director (played, as a version of him-self, by the eminent Austro-German filmmaker Fritz Lang). Lang already has a clear vision of the film he wishes to make, irrespective of Paul's scripted suggestions; the final scene, when he orders shooting to begin, demonstrates that he combines this creative force with practical supervisory powers, the kind of 'foreman's' authority ascribed to the Swedish director Ingmar Bergman by an observer of the making of *Winter Light* (1962) (Livingston, 2006: 306).

However, any suggestion that *Contempt* is thus an allegory of the director's authorial potency is over-hasty. Lang, it turns out, is like Paul a hired hand on this project, one hatched in Hollywood and administered by the boorish US producer Jeremy Prokosch. There are uncomfortable biographical parallels here, since the real-life Lang's own career trajectory took him from German film in the 1920s to the much more tightly regulated Hollywood studio system in mid-century. In *Contempt* it is actually Prokosch, rather than Lang or Paul, who determines that in order to gain a larger audience share the adaptation of Homer's *Odyssey* on which they are all working should include more nudity and be marked by levity rather than epic seriousness. If the resulting film has an authorial signature, then, it appears to belong neither to director nor screenwriter but instead to the producer (or, more properly, to those institutions of commercial cinema that he represents). Here, however, further complications are apparent. After all, the project that Prokosch is attempting to control is, however crass and vulgar, an adaptation of a prior text and thus marked by another's authorial signature. For all his swaggering air of answering to no one, this producer is caught up in *an intertextual web*, unable therefore to make an absolute proprietary claim on his film's material.

Contempt neatly condenses several stages from the history of debate over film authorship. Initially, in Paul's hope that as a screenwriter he might exercise creative control, there are echoes of what François Truffaut, Godard's New Wave contemporary, referred to contemptuously as *'scenarists' films'* (2008: 10). By contrast, the model of a director-led cinema for which both Godard and Truffaut were vivid polemicists during the late 1950s and early 1960s is embodied in Lang's magisterial demeanour. Yet in its attention to the shaping force exerted by studio systems and market imperatives, *Contempt* also anticipates challenges within film studies from the late 1960s onwards to the concept of the director as an author endowed with near-omnipotent powers. With uncanny prescience, the film hints, too, at how theories of intertextuality will disrupt thinking about original or exclusive authorship. It achieves this not only through the sustained story of the characters' attempt to adapt Homer's pre-existing text, but, more fleetingly, by including a shot of a poster for Roberto Rossellini's *Journey to Italy* (1954), a film to which *Contempt* itself is intertextually bound. These shifts in conceptualisation of film authorship are discussed in detail in this chapter. While, periodically, film studies has sought to do without the figure of the author or the topic of authorship more generally, such moments have been short-lived. As one recent commentator puts it: 'The author, it seems, is a part of film that we simply cannot do without' (Sellors, 2010: 2).

Auteur theory

A poll to nominate the most influential journal in the history of film criticism is likely to have only one winner: *Cahiers du cinéma*, first produced in April 1951 by a group of Paris-based cineastes and still in existence. Its success, though, could not easily have been foretold. During its heyday in the 1950s and 1960s, its pre-eminence even in France was not guaranteed, since it had to compete with rivals that included the more politically engaged *Positif*. As a French-language magazine, it also seemed far removed from the film industry's major centres of power in the United States. Yet in the first two decades of publication, *Cahiers* not only transformed the study of film on both sides of the Atlantic but had an energising effect on cinematic production itself.

Cahiers was distinguished from other film journals in its early years by being largely the work of critic-practitioners. Other than André Bazin, the majority of its writers went on to comprise the New Wave of French filmmaking: Claude Chabrol, Jacques Rivette and Eric Rohmer, besides Godard and Truffaut themselves. Connections can clearly be traced between their critical and directorial practices: if their first films look like essays on cinema, their articles in the journal are implicitly outlines for future film projects. To read *Cahiers* from these early decades is to encounter some of the most exhilarating writing ever produced about cinema. Though

19 'Cinema is Nicholas Ray', exclaimed Godard. Shown here is an image from one of Ray's best films, *In a Lonely Place* (1950)

lacking an equivalent theoretical apparatus, the journal fizzes with the medium-specific enthusiasm shown also by that collective of Russian writer-filmmakers gathered around Eisenstein during the 1920s. Pieces in *Cahiers* are prone to suspect generalisations and lurid overstatements – 'cinema is Nicholas Ray', exclaimed Godard about a favourite American director (Hillier, 1985: 118; see Figure 19) – but running through the prose are an absolute commitment to film and a belief in its great possibilities as an art form. This sense of a serious vocation is sometimes overlooked by opponents. Thomas Schatz, for example, complains that the work done by the journal in its first decades is responsible for having kept film studies in 'a prolonged stage of adolescent romanticism' (1988: 5). While adopting some of Schatz's language, James Naremore intends a more generous evaluation when he says that these early contributors to *Cahiers* are, together with their devotees in Britain, the United States and elsewhere, 'surely among the last romantics' (1999: 16). The 'romanticism' at issue here expresses itself not only in feverish outbursts from which academic film studies should keep a safe distance, but in forms of engagement and sensitivity from which the discipline can still profit.

During the 1950s and early 1960s, the polemical vibrancy of writing in *Cahiers* was not accompanied by systematic conceptualisation. Nevertheless, several critical positions on film, not least on film authorship, can be extrapolated from the essays and reviews which featured in the journal. Broadly speaking, the *Cahiers* writers of this time sought to

- legitimise cinema as an art commensurate with traditional aesthetic forms such as literature, painting, sculpture and music
- locate film's artistic quality not so much in thematic contents as in formal elements, particularly shot composition and combination
- conceptualise the director, above all other figures, as a film's chief source of creativity, in a word its author
- make evaluative distinctions between functionally competent directors (*metteurs-en-scène*) and those whose films are unified by a strong artistic signature (*auteurs*, French for 'authors').

None of these positions is entirely original. For a start, snobbery against cinema had for some decades previously been countered by critical work in France, Russia and other countries that was designed to affirm film's high aesthetic status. In 1948, a few years before the founding of *Cahiers*, the French critic and director Alexandre Astruc argued that cinema had finally lost its connotations of fairground spectacle and vaudeville amusement, and was now legitimised as 'a form in which and by which an artist can express his thoughts, however abstract they may be, or translate his obsessions exactly as he does in the contemporary essay or novel' (1968: 18). Similarly, precedents exist for the *Cahiers* critics' valorisation of the figure of the director above all other film personnel. Besides Astruc's own metaphor of the 'camera-pen' ('*la caméra-stylo*') – an instrument that he saw as manipulated by the director rather than anyone else – the British filmmaker and critic Lindsay Anderson proposed a 'director's cinema' in the Autumn 1950 edition of the British journal *Sequence*. Anderson also anticipated here *Cahiers*' position that 'director's cinema' would be a party to which not all filmmakers are invited.

But if elements of the thinking that characterises *Cahiers* are visible earlier or elsewhere, this new group of French cineastes provided rhetorical verve and a certain critical mass. Their provocative reconceptualisation of film authorship is apparent as early as Truffaut's article 'A Certain Tendency of the French Cinema', published in the journal in 1954. Here the chief object of attack was the 'scenarists' films' briefly alluded to above – a body of mid-century French work in which, as Truffaut saw it, screenwriters played an overmighty role to the detriment of directors' creative freedom. Where Truffaut criticises these screenplays for their anti-clerical and anti-militaristic attitudes, or for their 'very marked taste for profanation and blasphemy' (2008: 12), he sounds like someone more ready to man a church pew than a revolutionist's barricade. More significantly for our purpose, however, his article also excoriates the cinema of screenwriters for its complete inattentiveness to the specific formal properties of film and to the new authorial possibilities these open up.

By way of corrective, *Cahiers* maintained in its first two decades a strong emphasis upon mise-en-scène, editing and sound, conceiving of these as the dimensions in which filmmakers demonstrate expressiveness and, in a word, authorship. For the first time in the history of cinema, a collective of writers subjected the use of tracking shots and close-ups to the degree of scrutiny which critics in other fields had long brought to a sonnet's metaphors or a painting's brushstrokes. Even some later theorists who distance themselves from the *Cahiers* project acknowledge the value of its rerouting of critical attention from the contents or subjects of films to the realm of *form* in which those contents are elaborated and transformed. John Caughie, writing in this vein, refers nicely to the journal's promotion of 'a certain historically necessary formalism' (1981: 13). At times, to be sure, heightened attention to mise-en-scène at the expense of other elements of a film's totality is pushed to excess or even self-parody. One *Cahiers* writer admits that *Party Girl* (1958), directed by Nicholas Ray (Godard's favourite, as cited above), 'has an idiotic story'; however – given its qualities of shot composition – 'So what?' (Hillier, 1986: 123). Throughout, of course, the *Cahiers* project is partisan and evaluative rather than coolly analytical: hence narrative absurdities in *Party Girl* are forgiven because of Ray's accreditation already as an auteur. While many directors were damned by the journal as mere technicians (*metteurs-en-scène*), knowledgeable in logics of film assembly but lacking artistic personality, select others were by contrast awarded auteur status on the basis of the distinctiveness and unity of cinematic form that could be detected across their work.

The identity of those directors *Cahiers* invited into its pantheon during the 1950s and 1960s is intriguing. Certainly, the *pro-Americanism* of these selections can be exaggerated: Rohmer, for instance, confessed that his 'dearest masters' were Dreyer (Danish), Eisenstein (Russian), Murnau (German), Renoir (French) and Rossellini (Italian) (Hillier, 1985: 93). Nevertheless, the journal's search for auteurs ranged much wider, and bestowed this status upon other filmmakers of the Hollywood system besides Ray, including Ford, Hitchcock, Welles, Sam Fuller and Howard Hawks. No longer perceived as mere functionaries within cinematic mass-production – Ford once complained to a studio mogul that he felt like 'a piece-goods worker in the Hollywood sweatshops' (Wexman, 2003: 8) – these directors were reimagined as artists able to transcend the constraints of formulaic filmmaking. Although Ford worked frequently in the western, Fuller in the war movie and so on, genre was not considered by the *Cahiers* critics to comprise non-negotiable limits or binding constraints upon filmmakers, given the auteur's creative power. Indeed, as Barry Langford neatly summarises auteurist thinking on this matter: 'Genre is thus in some measure the culture – like a petri dish – on which genius feeds, rather than meaningful material in its own right' (2005: 9).

The energy and iconoclasm of *Cahiers du cinéma* earned it an international audience. In the United States, Andrew Sarris's key article 'Notes on the Auteur Theory in 1962' was published by the East Coast journal *Film Culture*. While his title was an inaccurate translation of *Cahiers*' phrase, '*politique des auteurs*' – with the French term for 'policy' now gratuitously firmed-up as 'theory' – Sarris had a significant effect in disseminating auteurist thinking to America. Meanwhile, in Britain, auteurism took hold at the journal *Movie*, founded in 1962 by a group of Oxford contemporaries. These writers, too, advocated a new sensitivity to matters of cinematic form and a model of directorial authorship at the expense of narratively or sociologically framed responses to film. If their work seems unexceptionable now, that in itself is evidence of the subsequent universalisation of at least some auteurist assumptions. During the 1960s, however, intellectual combat was bloody, with *Movie*'s auteurist bias causing a feud with editors of the British Film Institute's house journal, *Sight and Sound*.

STOP and THINK

- At different moments in film history, the figure of the director seems especially powerful, even insistent. Not least because of the influence of *Cahiers du cinéma*, directorial recognition was notably strong in the case of European art cinema in the 1960s and 1970s: spectators would talk of seeing 'the new Fellini' or 'the latest Fassbinder', rather than organising the films they watched according to other criteria such as themes, genres or stars. Contemporary Hollywood, too, is adept in exploiting the branding potential of individual directors' names: 'a Steven Spielberg film' or 'a Martin Scorsese picture'. However, how aware are *you* of directors? How strong a factor, if at all, is the director's identity in your choice of what films to see? Subsequent to viewing, what place does the director have in your film criticism?

- Take any director with whose work you are familiar. Is it possible to detect underlying patterns across his or her films? As the *Cahiers* writers argue, these may well be stylistic or formal consistencies; however, they could equally be thematic continuities (potentially even stretching across different genres). If such repetitive features may be detected, can they confidently be taken as evidence of a film author at work?

- Finally, list as many directors as possible. Then, giving reasons for your decisions, try to divide them between *Cahiers*' categories of artistically distinctive auteurs and merely efficient *metteurs-en-scène*. You may find more and more director names crowding into the more favoured category, making auteurism a currency as hyperinflationary as the German *Papiermark* in the 1920s: horrified at the prospect of just such a booming market in critical reputations, Godard spoke in elitist – and revealingly masculinist – terms about the need still to distinguish between 'the big boys and the little ones' (Narboni and Milne, 1972: 231). Or does such a hierarchising project strike you as impossible, even undesirable?

Problems with auteurism

The success of auteurist thinking as promulgated by *Cahiers du cinéma* and other journals and books from the 1950s onwards can be measured institutionally. Film societies, film festivals and specialised exhibition venues sprang up, not least in order to showcase the work of the newly favoured directors. Auteurism played a significant part, too, in the establishment and consolidation of film studies itself, providing the discipline not only with protocols of close reading of the screen but with a set of core 'authors' and 'texts'. While the majority of directors designated as auteurs remained European or American, these credentials were sometimes extended to filmmakers from elsewhere, including India's Satyajit Ray and Japan's Akira Kurosawa, Kenji Mizoguchi and Yasujiro Ozu. However, even as evidences of auteurism's practical success accumulated, this way of thinking about film was increasingly subjected to challenge. From the late 1960s onwards, *Cahiers* itself interrogated the individualised, romantic notion of film authorship that had once been the journal's defining commitment. A snapshot of these drastic intellectual shifts is provided by the trajectory of Jacques Rivette. Previously a major influence at *Cahiers* in exalting the director as a film's dominant creative force, he wrote in the journal in 1968 of his utter rejection of 'the idea that there is an auteur of this film, expressing himself. The only thing we can do in France at the moment is to try to deny that a film is a personal creation' (Hillier, 1986: 319). What exactly caused this paradigm shift? In which ways did auteurism prove vulnerable to attack?

Playing parlour games

As we have seen, auteur critics tended to display powerful enthusiasms and equally strong antipathies. Positively, this zeal focused new attention on the work of certain directors, including some from Hollywood who had formerly been placed well below the salt. Less productively, however, whole bodies of work by other filmmakers were abruptly damned and thus excluded from serious consideration. Such blatantly *evaluative* criticism proved in the end an inadequate base on which to found a rigorous academic discipline. At its worst, auteur criticism descended into cinematic parlour games, struggling to operate at a conceptual level beyond the exchanging of value judgements. This tendency culminates in Sarris's book *The American Cinema: Directors and Directions 1929– 1968* (first published in 1968). In a veritable mania of evaluative categorisation, Sarris places two hundred mainly, but not exclusively US directors into eleven hierarchically arrayed classes of achievement. At the apex is the 'Pantheon', a sanctum into which only fourteen directors are admitted. The names given to other categories smack similarly of the vagaries of someone's personal taste, rather than contributing to the analytical advancement of film studies: for instance, 'The Far Side of Paradise', 'Less Than Meets the Eye' and 'Lightly Likable'.

It is not that Sarris does not have interesting things to say in passing about the directors he discusses – he does. However, his book also allows us to identify conceptual and methodological problems at the heart of auteurism's evaluative project. Assessing directors against eleven categories of relative distinction – or even against two, as in the founding separation of auteurs from *metteurs-en-scène* – looks more like after-hours diversion than a core task for serious film study. This is not, though, to rule out in some puritanical spirit the making of *all* statements about the relative value of films and their makers: it would be an enfeebled discipline indeed that left itself without the wherewithal and willingness to say something like 'Michael Haneke is a better director than Michael Bay'.

Film as a collaborative art

According to the Australian director Fred Schepisi, 'The term "auteur" just denigrates everyone else's job' (Gilbey, 2002: 12). Part of the riposte to auteurism, then, has involved restoring a sense of the *collaborative* – rather than individualistic – nature of most film production. The director is generally not alone on a project, but works alongside producers, designers, editors, cinematographers, composers, actors and perhaps screenwriters (to say nothing of all those technical specialists whose labour is apparent in the completed film). There are, of course, exceptional cinematic cases that more closely approximate the solitariness of the poet's garret or painter's studio: here the artisanal model of production developed by the American experimentalist Stan Brakhage comes to mind, its self-sufficiency enhanced by the way in which he functioned as his films' subject besides their director, cinematographer, scriptwriter and editor. In general, however, cinema is an extrovert rather than solipsistic art. As Michael Ondaatje observes in conversation with Walter Murch: 'a film set resembles a beehive, or daily life in Louis XIV's court – every kind of society is witnessed in action, and it seems every trade is busy at work' (Ondaatje, 2002: xi). Murch adds suggestively that a director is 'the immune system of the film', his or her activity safeguarding the effective functioning of everyone involved in its creation (28). To put it like this is to describe a key role, certainly, but one notably less romantic than auteurist figurations of the powerful director striving to render on film a distinctively personal vision.

Recognition of the many creative figures involved in filmmaking has, however, not always led to the abandonment of auteurism as a conceptual model. Instead, critics have sometimes followed their dethroning of overmighty directors by proposing alternative auteurs instead. There are occasional moments in *Cahiers* itself where auteurist powers are reallocated in this way, as when Rivette argues that the mid-century French star Jean Gabin's distinctive movement and speech make him 'almost more of a director' than those credited with that function in the films he made (Hillier, 1985: 37). Claims of creative pre-eminence have sometimes been made for film personnel other than actors. One instance is Mervyn Cooke's auteurist approach to the composer Bernard Herrmann, who insisted, against Hitchcock's objections, that the shower scene in *Psycho* (1960) should have musical accompaniment (Cooke, 2008: 208). Intriguingly, one writer on film colour also suggests that Natalie Kalmus, who was the consultant on films made using the Technicolor process from 1934 to 1949, be considered an auteur (Peacock, 2010: 61). Yet such strong readings of the creative role played by figures other than directors risk leaving auteurism intact, simply altering the auteur's identity rather than doing away altogether with this romantic model of creativity. A more productive option, therefore, is to think in terms of 'a collective authorship' of films (Sellors, 2010: 74). Thus the American critic Pauline Kael waged a fierce war with Sarris over her claim that co-screenwriter Herman Mankiewicz was as responsible as Welles for *Citizen Kane*. Co-authorial credits could also be given in specific instances to set designers (consider Ken Adam's iconic sets for the 1960s James Bond films), sound editors (not least Murch himself for *The Conversation* (1974)), choreographers (for example, Lester Wilson in *Saturday Night Fever* (1977)), martial arts arrangers (Yuen Wo Ping in *The Matrix* (1999)) and many others. More recently, the increasing digitisation of filmmaking might persuade some critics to identify CGI designers, too, as heavily involved in the authorship of the films on which they work. Lest this multiplying of candidates for critical attention get out of hand, however, C. Paul Sellors proposes a distinction between a film's 'authorial collective' and its 'production collective': 'It is important that we distinguish between authoring a work and manifesting the work materially' (2010: 124). Such differentiations are, of course, not always easy to preserve in practice. Sellors acknowledges as much, yet still believes this critical project to be achievable by a combination of archival research and close reading of films themselves.

Rather than tracing film authorship to a plurality of identifiable individuals, however, other critics have posited instead what might be termed *the corporate author*. To what extent were directors in classical Hollywood not so much free-spirited creators as conduits for the transmission of 'studio styles', adhering, for example, to the template for the Warner Bros gangster film of the 1930s or the MGM musical of the 1940s? Should authorial powers be bestowed too upon the Walt Disney Company, proprietors of a form of animation that is to be reproduced rather than modified by directors on specific projects? But while any reminder of the institutional constraints within which filmmakers always operate is salutary, it is important not to totalise these. Otherwise, film creation comes to look morbidly predetermined, allowing no possibility of decisive authorial acts by flesh-and-blood figures involved in the process.

The death of the author

Auteurism was also a casualty of critical investigations that aimed to uncover substantive rather than merely etymological linkages between *author* and *authority*, even *authoritarianism*. From the late 1960s onwards, the individualised, romantic model of authorship which had been appropriated for film by *Cahiers* writers and many others came under attack as an agency of oppressive power. The two most piercing anti-authorial critiques were produced in France. The political protest that would culminate in May 1968 when the French state was shaken to its foundations by the activism of students and industrial workers was already gathering force when Roland Barthes produced his 1967 essay, 'The Death of the Author'. A little later, in 1969, the Paris cobblestones thrown by rioters had barely been replaced when Michel Foucault wrote 'What Is an Author?' While principally intended as contributions to literary criticism, these two articles had a significant reconstructive effect upon film studies also.

Even now, the title and substance of Barthes's essay can still scandalise. In seven iconoclastic pages, he argues that attempts to frame reading by reference to 'the author' – what is discovered of his or her biography, what is surmised from the text about his or her intentions – are both conceptually flawed and politically restrictive. Critical attention should be redirected from the producer to *the receiver* – and no author can determine and regulate the meanings that a text will accrue from readers when it is out in the world. In addition, Barthes provocatively asserts that what the romantic critical tradition takes to be an author's original work is actually a weaving together of prior textual materials: 'a text is made of multiple writings, drawn from many cultures and entering into mutual relations of dialogue, parody, contestation' (1977: 148). As it turned out, Barthes himself did not apply to examples from cinema this model of the author's intertextual indebtedness rather than self-originating creation; his relatively few articles on film tend in fact towards auteurism, as when he writes on Eisenstein. Yet it is clear that this critical framework offers resources for a new, non-auteurist approach to cinematic authorship. If the idea of textual assemblage would seem to lend itself especially well to the hybrids and pastiches self-consciously fabricated by Tarantino and directors in his vein, it has the potential for extension to *all* cinema.

Foucault's essay is less verbally incendiary than Barthes's, but equally far-reaching in its implications. The article is concerned to historicise authorship itself, demonstrating that the notion of a solitary, visionary producer of literary work is not timeless and universal, but, on the contrary, temporally and geographically situated. Foucault argues that, displacing an earlier model of *communal* production, the figure of 'the author' emerges during the Renaissance and is closely aligned with a developing ideology of individualism. While certain types of cultural output remained relatively 'unauthored', privileged expressive forms such as literature subsequently carried authorial signatures. Relevantly for us as we review the operations of auteurism in film studies, Foucault also considers how an attribution of authorship works to unify what might otherwise appear a disparate group of texts bearing the same person's name. The 'author-function', as he calls it, posits three sorts of consistency in such cases: 'a standard level of quality', 'a certain field of conceptual or theoretical coherence' and 'a stylistic uniformity' (1977: 128).

Although Foucault does not venture into the topic of cinematic authorship, his essay has nevertheless had a significant impact on film studies. The assumption of authorial consistency which he uncovers allows us, for a start, to identify a key operating procedure of the early *Cahiers* writers and other auteurists. Recall from a few moments ago one critic's response to Nicholas Ray's *Party Girl*. Admittedly, a risible plotline causes momentary glitches in the film's critical processing; however, Ray's status as an auteur soon allows the work to be accommodated to a pre-established grid of conceptual and stylistic coherencies. The dangers that an auteurist approach might function in this way so as to constrain rather than enliven film interpretation did not entirely escape *Cahiers* itself. Bazin, who tended to adopt a temperate stance at the journal compared with more excitable colleagues, objected to evaluating each new movie by 'the aesthetic portrait of the filmmaker deduced from his previous films' (Hillier, 1985: 256). In a different way to Barthes's announcement of the author's death, then, but with equal pointedness, Foucault's demonstration of the limitations imposed by the author-figure challenges basic assumptions underlying auteurism in film studies.

STOP and THINK

- Return to the director whose work you considered earlier from an auteurist perspective and reassess his or her films in light of some of the anti-auteurist positions just discussed. Is it appropriate, in this instance, to speak of an individual's creative hegemony? Or is it more compelling to think in terms of *collaborative* authorship? If so, what are the key contributions made by figures besides the director, and how may these be identified and assessed?
- Much work on film authorship has sought to modify or complicate or collectivise it, rather than altering entirely the terms of discussion. However, consider applying to cinema the more radical anti-authorial critiques of Foucault and Barthes. For example, in the attempt to trace consistencies across the work of your chosen director, have you found the 'author-function' to operate as dogmatically and restrictively as Foucault suggests it does? Do his or her films also gain in interpretive richness once the figure of the author is relinquished, as Barthes urges? Barthes says that the death of the author is simultaneously 'the birth of the reader' (1977: 148) – a remark that prompts us, by analogy, to think of the enfranchised spectator who generates a film's meanings.
- Is the entire debate over whose authorial signature to affix to a film – director's? screenwriter's? star's? cinematographer's? producer's? studio's? – wearisome and unproductive? Are there better things we could be doing in film studies? Is it time to shelve the problematic of film authorship itself?

The rebirth of the author

In film as in literary studies, announcement of the death of the author proved to be premature. Since the discipline absorbed the implications of Barthes's memorialising essay, it is true that there have been only intermittent returns to the full-blown, romantic version of auteurism purveyed by *Cahiers du cinéma* and those influenced by the journal's early years. This is not to say, however, that the question of film authorship itself has been suspended. In this section we briefly consider three critical approaches that have, for good reason, kept it alive.

Analytic philosophy

Like literary criticism, film studies has been significantly shaped by conceptual traditions from continental Europe: the structural Marxism of Louis Althusser, for example, and the psychoanalysis of Jacques Lacan. More recently, however, writers positioning themselves within the alternative, Anglo–American lineage of *analytic philosophy* have revisited familiar questions in the study of film, including issues of representation, spectatorship, and the image. In a brief but helpful essay, Paisley Livingston brings to bear on film authorship itself this philosophical strand's commitment to clarity and its methodical, problem-solving approach. His aim is thus to persuade by arguments that are cautious and modest, rather than sweeping in their reach.

Livingston's opening gambit, in fact, is to acknowledge that there are many other worthwhile things to do with a film besides trying to fix upon it an authorial signature. He concedes, too, that accounts of the agency manifested by directors or other creative personnel involved in cinema are vulnerable, at least in part, to theoretical attacks on authorial *intentionality*. Given the complexity of film texts, with both image and sound tracks having multiple constituents, filmmakers cannot hope to govern audience interpretation to the extent they might intend. Having given this much ground, however, Livingston still activates a model of film authorship, albeit one that is now moderated in its claims:

> If one recognises that an utterance can be both intentionally produced by someone and have meanings that are not all and only those intended by that person, then it follows that strong intentionalism is not entailed by a broad conception of authorship. We can identify someone as the author of an utterance without having to say that that person has authored each and every meaning (or significance) that the utterance manifests. (2006: 302)

Whereas Barthes describes the author-figure he seeks to overthrow as a godlike force, overbearing in his or her attempt at textual control, Livingston utilises very different vocabulary. Instead of absolute authority, *partial* authority; instead of strong intentionalism, *weak* intentionalism, with the managerial effort of a given film's authors having only some success in shaping the response of spectators. Thus Livingston hopes to avoid the twin extremes of romantic auteurism and Barthesian rejectionism, preserving in between these a conception of film authors endowed with *relative* – rather than total – power.

Feminism

Whether by mere coincidence or by patriarchal ruse, the author's death was first pronounced at precisely the time that feminist scholarship across a range of fields was striving to identify and assess previously neglected female authorial traditions. In film studies, as in literary criticism, feminist critics have continued to foreground an interest in women authors, whether these are directors or other female creative personnel. This has certainly not entailed a naive return – now in the name of women, rather than men – to notions of unfettered auteurism. Nor, in unsophisticated and politically dangerous fashion, should we correlate sexual identity and gender position, thus straightforwardly reading off a feminist politics from films made by directors (and others) who lack the Y chromosome. Like their male counterparts, female film authors have to speak through pre-established cinematic conventions, negotiating formidable stylistic, generic and narrative codes. Working within such a deromanticised, scaled-down model of authorship, however, critics have done fascinating work in recovering and theorising female cinematic voices. Women's authorial imprint might be deciphered, for example, in moments of 'rupture' or 'excess' in what otherwise seem unexceptional films. Claire Johnston's consideration of the filmography of Dorothy Arzner, one of very few female directors in classical Hollywood, stands as pioneering research in this vein. However, the approach remains viable with respect to the scandalously small population of contemporary women filmmakers. Does it, for example, make sense to highlight the sex of the director whose films in the action genre include *Blue Steel* (1990), *Strange Days* (1995) and *K-19: The Widowmaker* (2002)? Barry Keith Grant asserts that it does, writing that 'Kathryn Bigelow uses the action

film to address fundamental issues of genre, gender and spectatorship, and to negotiate a place for women both in front of and behind
the camera within traditionally masculine discourses' (2008: 290).

A continuing lack of opportunities for female filmmakers makes
it premature to forsake interest in questions of author identity. In
Britain, for instance, resources are still unevenly distributed across
sexual lines, despite the presence of a group of innovative women
directors that features Andrea Arnold, Lynne Ramsay and now Clio
Barnard, whose work includes *The Arbor* (2010) and *The Selfish
Giant* (2013). Elsewhere, Sweden's National Film Agreement for
2013–15 seeks to address a dearth of female-led cinema by including
a commitment that funding offered by the Swedish Film Institute
will be divided equally between women and men 'in the key positions of director, screenwriter and producer' ('Gender Equality in
Swedish Film', 2013: n.p.). Here, quite clearly, film authorship
is considered not a subject of indifference but, potentially, a site
of gender inequality that, like other forms of sexism in Sweden,
requires redress. In other global instances, too, it would be politically irresponsible to suspend discussion of the sex of film authors.
Consider simply the case of *Wadjda* (2012), the first feature shot
entirely in Saudi Arabia and, coincidentally, another contribution to
the canon of 'bicycle films' discussed in Chapter 5. Given the patriarchal organisation of Saudi society that restricts women's voices
in other public forums, it is important to know that this film has a
female director, Haifaa Al Mansour.

In an overview of thinking on film authorship, Sellors acknowledges the gains resulting from radical anti-authorial critiques such
as Barthes's (not least the devolution to the spectator of responsibility for generating meaning). He goes on, however: 'The abandonment of authorship as expression exacted a political price [...]
these theories, in denying the author's conscious voice, also denied
expression to underrepresented groups struggling to make their
voices heard' (2010: 129). Hence, while certainly acknowledging the
need for remodelled ideas of creativity, feminist critics have sought
in the case of female filmmakers to restore interest in 'authorship
as expression'. Sellors's argument can also be extended to other
constituencies. For example, rather than considering *Bhaji on the
Beach* (1993), *Bend It Like Beckham* (2002) and *Bride & Prejudice*

20 British Asian cinematic authorship? *Bride & Prejudice* (2004), directed by Gurinder Chadha

(2004) as impersonally constructed machines for signification set in motion by the spectator, it might be more productive to place these films directed by Gurinder Chadha in a body of cinema by British Asians (see Figure 20). Similarly, discussion of *Smoke Signals* (1998) should reckon with the fact that this film about young, contemporary Native Americans is not white-authored, but, rather, has an all-Indian 'authorial collective'. Here is evidence, then, of an emergent Native American film authorship – even if, as noted above with respect to films made by women, this shift in author identity is not in itself guarantee of an alternative politics.

Legal studies

Film authorship is a matter not only for seminar room debate; it is disputed, too, in other venues, and sometimes with more directly material consequences. One of the most important of these alternative locations is legal discourse. It emerges that, rather than clarifying and settling the question of the authorship of films, the law further complicates it because of significant global variations. Schematically, for our purposes here, a broad distinction can be made between the copyright laws of the European Union and Anglo-America respectively.

Article 2 of Directive 2006/116/EC, issued by the European Parliament and the Council of the European Union, states boldly with respect to any 'cinematographic or audiovisual work' that the 'principal director […] shall be considered as its author or one of

its authors' ('Directive 2006/116/EC', 2006: 3). There is the hint
of a retreat from this near-auteurist position in the paragraph that
follows, which, specifying the time of expiry of a film's copyright,
says it will occur '70 years after the death of the last of the following persons to survive [...] the principal director, the author
of the screenplay, the author of the dialogue and the composer of
music' specifically for use in the movie (3). Even so, the secondary placement of this clause means that it does not significantly
weaken the directive's attribution of film authorship to the figure of
the director. The notion of his or her pre-eminent creative force is
upheld in a way that would have resonated with early *Cahiers* critics. Suggestively, too, when a later copyright directive issued by the
EU acknowledged that 'musical genres such as jazz, rock and pop'
support compositional processes which are 'collaborative in nature',
no extension was made from this to thinking of *film* authorship, too,
as collective ('Directive 2011/77/EU', 2011: 3).

Problematical, perhaps, in its exaltation of the director above
other personnel, EU copyright legislation is still notable for conceiving of film authorship as personal expression. By contrast, the
law of copyright as it pertains to film in both the United Kingdom
and the United States contests any such romantic model of creativity. UK law, it is true, begins by recognising the 'principal director's' authorial role. Even in this preliminary statement, however,
ominous shadows are gathering: 'In the case of films, the author
is the producer and the principal director' (Intellectual Property
Office, 2011: 8). Where there is pluralisation of film authorship
here, it is not to extend creative privileges to screenwriter or editor,
say, but to the representative of those commercial and institutional
apparatuses from within which the movie emerges. And things get
worse still in a subsequent clause that ratifies the latter's authorial
pre-eminence and downgrades the director from visionary originator to mere hired hand: if a film 'is made by an employee in the
course of their employment, the employer is the first owner of copyright in the work' (8). While this proviso might not capture self-
commissioned, artisanal forms of filmmaking, it certainly applies
to all those projects that in the current economic order are enabled
only by corporate financing. It can be observed, then, that UK film
copyright law exists principally to safeguard company investment

rather than to recognise individual expression. A similar situation obtains in the US. The graphic differences between this legislative model and that of the European Union indicate that in law, as elsewhere, film authorship must be considered a matter of ongoing debate, with multiple, conflicting theories in circulation rather than one that enjoys consensual support.

Digital authors

Disputes in law are a vivid reminder of the commercial ramifications of film authorship. The figure of the director, in particular, continues to command high economic value as well as aesthetic prestige. Directors' names are used, for example, to underpin the publication of academic book series: think only of Wallflower's internationally expansive 'Directors' Cuts' strand or Manchester University Press's series on 'British Film Makers' and 'French Film Directors'. Directorial signatures are also crucial in the marketing of films themselves, as we saw in Chapter 5 with advance publicity for *The Equalizer* prominently featuring the name and partial filmography of director Antoine Fuqua as well as identifying star and genre. Directors are frequently foregrounded, too, in the repackaging for DVD and Blu-ray formats of already exhibited films. A glance almost at random at *Sight and Sound*'s issue for September 2014 finds advertisements for the following choices of home viewing: *The Werner Herzog Collection*, bringing together eighteen films by this German feature film maker and documentarist; *Kurosawa: Samurai Collection*, which assembles five of the best-known films by this Japanese director who, as noted above, has long been accredited with auteur status; and four titles released separately but all contributing to *The François Truffaut Collection*. In each of these cases the director's name is the chosen branding device, functioning as a marker not only of artistic distinction but of niche commodity status.

Notwithstanding the multi-stranded critique of auteurism reviewed earlier in this chapter, other opportunities have opened up in recent decades for promotion of the director as a film's author. Video's emergence in the early 1980s helped to create the phenomenon of 'The Director's Cut'. This release of a longer (very occasionally shorter) or significantly modified version of a previously exhibited film evokes a return to auteurism's founding principles. Finally, a Director's Cut seems to promise, the author's vision can emerge in all its purity, freed from any marks of interference by the production company. The transition from VHS to more flexible and capacious home exhibition formats has offered additional ways of reinforcing the director's creative authority. The 'Director's Commentary', included in the special features of many DVD and Blu-ray releases, blocks out much of a film's original soundtrack in order to allow the director, in voiceover, to explain the manifold choices made during shooting. From one perspective, this addition of contextualising speech would seem to strip a film of its absorptive power over the spectator and to demystify the director's role by casting it as one merely of technical decision-making. In another light, however, a Director's Commentary represents the *consolidation* of auteurism, not only intervening strongly between spectator and screen but seeking to redirect spectator interpretation towards the author's preferred readings.

In contemporary conditions of film production and reception, however, care should again be taken not to overstate the authorial power of the director (or any other single figure). If phenomena such as the Director's Cut and Director's Commentary appear to rehabilitate an auteurist model of film creation, other developments indicate instead a *dispersal* of authorship. For, as Sellors helpfully reminds us, most films threaten a lone creator's control of their meanings and effects by existing in *many* versions, including dubbed releases, subtitled releases and copies adjusted variously for length, aspect ratio (proportioning of the image's height and width), profanity, violence or sexual content so as to permit TV screening. And, in Sellors's words: 'If we have a plurality of prints, then we must certainly have an increase in the number of individuals with some form of authorial input' (2010: 118). Similarly, digitisation has opened up creative possibilities not only for the director but for the spectator, too. During home viewing in DVD or Blu-ray formats, he or she may choose to disrupt the film's organisation by tactics that range from rewinding to fast-forwarding, and from rewatching favourite moments to moving discontinuously between scene selections. Such spectatorial reconfiguration of the text amounts indeed to a form of film authorship, albeit a modest or minor version.

Another authorial option that has been exercised by viewers in the digital age is worthy of comment. This is *fan fiction*, elicited of course not only by film but by other media forms such as comic books and TV series. In the deadening guise of the 'book-of-the-film', spin-off fictions from cinematic works are nothing new and constitute simply another merchandising venture. Fan fiction, however, represents a substantial and distinctive, if qualitatively uneven upsurge of amateur authorship. It is distinguished from the deferential book-of-the-film by placing characters from the films with which it engages in unusual, sometimes provocative or even obscene situations. The several thousand texts deriving from *Inception*, for example, that are housed on FanFiction's website comprise responses to the film of various unofficial sorts: counterfactual narratives, so to speak, that devise alternative fates for the characters to those originally given; stories filling in the after-inception emotional and sexual lives of such figures as Arthur and Ariadne (thus rectifying a narrative deficit that we observed in Chapter 4); and also pastiches and parodies, undoing the solemnity of Nolan's film. What is also important to observe is fan fiction's sociability as a medium. The stories themselves comprise only one item in a multi-authored discursive chain, accompanied by much reader review and feedback. While it is undeniable that all of this creativity has been precipitated by a film authored by others, there is at least some sense here of this 'original' undergoing displacement and modification.

As with the 'generic communities' discussed in Chapter 5, it is important not to exaggerate the potency of online fan authorship. Despite the universalising rhetoric of the internet, for example, digital inequalities persist. Fan fiction is also limited in its immediate, material effectiveness: a host of unofficial stories about *Inception* may transfigure the film, but such textual adjustment occurs almost at subterranean level and will not yet be causing Nolan sleepless nights. At the same time, though, this attempt by fans to claim some rights of film authorship is a striking development. It also goes some way towards affirming the accuracy of Barthes's model of textual production. *Inception* should no longer be seen as a self-sufficient or stand-alone work: besides taking into itself pre-authored elements like the motifs of film noir and the heist movie, it precipitates, in its turn, further authorial output.

Case study: Ang Lee

Anyone making a word cloud from critical writings on the director Ang Lee, born in Taiwan in 1954, is liable to find 'versatile' most prominently displayed. After beginning his career with *Pushing Hands* (1992), *The Wedding Banquet* (1993) and *Eat Drink Man Woman* (1994), which comprise the 'Father Knows Best' trilogy of domestic melodramas, and were made in China utilising mainly Mandarin in their dialogue, Lee has ranged widely in his work, both geographically and generically. Thus in Hollywood he has directed a Jane Austen adaptation in *Sense and Sensibility* (1995); a tragicomedy of 1970s American suburbia in *The Ice Storm* (1997); a drama of the US Civil War in *Ride with the Devil* (1999); a superhero movie in *Hulk* (2003); a western unusual in both its contemporary setting and its homosexual preoccupation in *Brokeback Mountain* (2005); a drama of American counter-culture of the late 1960s in *Taking Woodstock* (2009); and a film oscillating categorically between melodrama and fantasy in *Life of Pi* (2012). Away from Hollywood, the two Chinese films Lee has made since his inaugural trilogy exhibit further generic experimentation. *Crouching Tiger, Hidden Dragon* (2000) is a refined contribution to the native *wuxia*, or martial arts, genre; while *Lust, Caution* (2007) merges the erotic drama, the war film and the spy film in its exploration of tangled personal loyalties in Japanese-occupied Shanghai and Hong Kong during World War II. Given his smooth cinematic shifts from wife-swapping parties to superhero transformations, or from Chinese banquets to sexual repression in Wyoming cowboy culture, it is little wonder that one critic refers to 'Lee's chameleon-like adaptability' (Pidduck, 2006: 394).

This transiting through multiple genres might seem, in itself, to militate against an auteurist approach to Lee's work. However, from its early Parisian days onwards, auteurism has proved adept in identifying continuities across a chosen director's apparently diverse films (exemplary here would be studies in *Cahiers du cinéma* of the mid-century US director Howard Hawks, who was required by the Hollywood system in which he worked to follow a screwball comedy with a war film, or a film noir with a western). In this vein, generic variations across the work Lee has done might be temporarily bracketed, so as to bring into view a set of recurrent thematic preoccupations and stylistic tendencies. This section thus begins by applying to Lee's films the 'strong' model of authorship associated with the auteurist tradition, before complicating this in light of some of the anti-auteur criticism reviewed above.

Many writers on Lee, as it happens, take auteurist stances. Thematically, for example, his films are often seen as structured by shared concerns, whatever their surface inconsistency. One critic refers, quite baldly, to Lee's 'themes of nationalism, ethnicity, cultural identity, and social practice' (Dilley, 2009: 61). Reflecting in the first instance upon the 'Father Knows Best' trilogy, Julianne Pidduck identifies 'themes that have come to be associated with Lee's oeuvre as a whole: family and "coming-of-age" social dramas, inter-generational and cross-cultural conflicts, and tensions between cultural tradition and modernisation' (2006: 394). Certainly, one unifying strand in Lee's palpably varied films is the exploration of inter-cultural clashes, as, anxiously or with desire, residual traditions encounter emergent social forces. Thematic commonality, then, binds *Sense and Sensibility* to *The Ice Storm*, or links *Eat Drink Man Woman* to *Brokeback Mountain*: in these films, conservative formations that range from early nineteenth-century systems of property and propriety in England to normative sexual codes on the postwar American frontier are challenged by new models of economics, family and gender. Patriarchs, in Lee's work, suffer rebellions by younger generations: thus structural parallels emerge between, say, the widower Chu attempting to regulate his three adult daughters in *Eat Drink Man Woman* and the father confronting the precociously strong Bruce Banner in *Hulk*, or between the German-born Union supporter dismayed by his Confederate son in *Ride with the Devil* and the suburban father who finds his teenagers experimenting in their sexuality and their reading in *The Ice Storm*. Lee's conservative forces, however, not only face rebellion, but often *face it down*, successfully containing dissent and desire. 'You're repressed as a turtle', a character says in *Eat Drink Man Woman*; and signs of repression are visible more generally in these films. D. A. Miller takes this thematic, in fact, to define Lee as a filmmaker, referring in an article on *Brokeback Mountain* to 'Lee's auteurism, which projects a similarly broad-spectrum repression

21 The *craft* of Ang Lee: Ennis Del Mar (Heath Ledger) double-framed in a shot from *Brokeback Mountain* (2005)

onto Jane Austen heroines, comic book heroes, Taiwanese families, Connecticut WASPs [white Anglo–Saxon Protestants], and gay cowboys alike' (2007: 54).

Miller makes a suggestive connection between this theme of repression and Lee's stylistics in *Brokeback Mountain*. He writes of the film's formally composed, decorous mode, the 'spectacle of fine workmanship' it offers the audience (2007: 51): in a word, the film's *craft* (see Figure 21). Provocatively, he argues that 'Craft has become a covert figure for the Closet itself' (52), implying a degree of control at the formal level that contrasts with and actually serves to repress the transgressive energies apparent narratively here in the passion of Jack Twist and Ennis Del Mar. Might we detect a similarly closeting stylistics elsewhere in Lee's work? It is evident that he is a refined, classical formalist, drawn acoustically to harmonic musical orchestration and visually to measured framing and painterly detail. Even where emotions rage or the elements boil over in his stories, Lee's design of mise-en-scène, editing and soundtrack exerts a moderating effect. Examples of this tendency abound, including the muted colour palette through which wartime Shanghai is presented in *Lust, Caution* or the use of calming music even as a boy is fatally electrocuted in *The Ice Storm* or the protagonist is endangered by tumultuous waves in *Life of Pi*. Although

Pidduck writes that 'Lee's core strength as a director arises from an ability to handle the subtle emotional registers of melodrama' (2006: 401), it is striking how *un*-melodramatic he is as a stylist. Lee is, for example, parsimonious in the use of close-ups, let alone extreme close-ups; his shot composition observes symmetry and decorum; and editing in his films, whatever their agitations of plot, tends to be smooth. Only occasionally is this formal composure ruffled, with the most startling instance being *Hulk*. Here, perhaps because of the 'popular' rather than 'literary' origins of his source material (the comic books published by Marvel), Lee's formal repertoire is extended: rapid zooms disrupt his camera's usual poise, split screens violate his classical framing, and psychedelic colours saturate the screen. Unsurprisingly, perhaps, *Hulk* is Lee's biggest critical failure to date, reviewers evidently finding it hard to square the film's aesthetic with their predefined sense of his authorial identity.

Our recalibration of Lee's authorial power might begin in fact by thinking about *Hulk*'s status as *an adaptation*. With the exception of the early Chinese trilogy, Lee has invariably turned in his work to adapt pre-existing narrative properties. While *Sense and Sensibility* transposes to the screen Jane Austen's classic novel of 1811, the other films are grounded in more recent written materials. Usually, these sources are literary fiction: *Crouching Tiger, Hidden Dragon* is based on a Chinese novel published just before World War II, *Lust, Caution* on Eileen Chang's novella (1979), *Ride with the Devil* on a novel by Daniel Woodrell (1987), *The Ice Storm* on Rick Moody's novel (1994), *Brokeback Mountain* on Annie Proulx's short story (1997), *Life of Pi* on a novel by Yann Martel (2001) and *Billy Lynn's Long Halftime Walk*, Lee's latest project, on Ben Fountain's fictional exploration of post-Iraq America (2012). In another instance, however, the adapted text is non-fictional, with *Taking Woodstock* having its origins in a memoir published in 2007. To what extent should Lee's practice of adaptation moderate, or compromise, assessments of his auteurist stature? Or, as Dudley Andrew asks in a recent reinvestigation of auteurism, 'what then of adaptations where the film itself rides underneath the imposing authority of a commanding text' (2010: 126)? Andrew goes on to say that 'Even if few films today fade in on a stately volume, the title and author of significant adaptations spread an aura to envelop the other names listed in the credits, underwriting the production by association' (126). Of course, the mere fact of adaptation need not, in itself, cramp a filmmaker's distinctive creativity. *Rear Window* (1954), *Vertigo* (1958), *Psycho* and *Marnie* (1964), for example, are all adaptations, yet exist now principally as 'Hitchcock films', the literary originals scribbled over and all but forgotten in the face of their radical refashioning to meet the director's thematic and formal predispositions. Nevertheless, the frequency with which Lee has adapted texts already in existence places him in relationships of fili- ation and obligation to others, denying him uncontested paternity of his films.

If Lee is clearly indebted to the authors whose work he adapts, he should also be situated in other collaborative webs. To refer to 'an Ang Lee film' is actually to designate the output of an 'authorial collective', in Sellors's useful term, rather than that of an autono- mous creative genius. Across his career, in fact, Lee can be seen functioning as the co-ordinator of regular artistic partners. Chief among these, virtually to the point of authorial equivalence with Lee himself, is the US-born James Schamus, who has written or co- written nine of the films (beginning with the 'Father Knows Best' trilogy) and been involved in producing eleven of them. Equally bound up with Lee is the American editor Tim Squyres, beginning similarly with the early trio of Chinese films and going on to edit a further eight titles. While these two figures have developed the most durable collaborations with Lee, other filmmaking personnel have been significant at different points in his career. Early on, for example, the US-born Frederick Elmes worked as cinematogra- pher on three films; more recently, the Mexican Rodrigo Prieto was responsible for cinematography on *Brokeback Mountain* and *Lust, Caution*. Similarly, Danny Elfman composed the music for *Hulk* and *Taking Woodstock*; while the Canadian-born Mychael Danna, his country of origin offering further evidence of the international- ised authorship of Lee's films, has scored three, most recently *Life of Pi*. Recognition of these frequent collaborators is, of course, not intended to repress the sense of Lee's own creative involvement in the films that carry his name last, or first, among their credits. At the same time, however, awareness of how he has worked as a member of periodically renewed creative clusters reminds us once again that film authorship is not adequately grasped by the strong auteurist model.

Selected reading

Bickerton, Emilie (2009), *A Short History of Cahiers du cinéma* (London: Verso).
Positions this crucial magazine knowledgeably in postwar French cultural and political history, with full attention to its shifting theories of film authorship.

Gerstner, David A. and Janet Staiger (eds) (2003), *Authorship and Film* (New York and London: Routledge).
Lively and productive essays, exploring questions of authorship across a wide range of US cinema.

Grant, Barry Keith (ed.) (2008), *Auteurs and Authorship: A Film Reader* (Malden, MA: Blackwell).
Indispensable volume, bringing together older and newer pieces that, collectively, enable the reader to follow shifts in the theorisation of film authorship.

Hillier, Jim (ed.) (1985), *Cahiers du cinéma: The 1950s* (London: Routledge & Kegan Paul).
Exemplary collection of articles, interviews and roundtables, buzzing with early auteurist excitement; like Hillier's companion volume below, best read alongside Bickerton.

Hillier, Jim (ed.) (1986), *Cahiers du cinéma: 1960–1968* (London: Routledge & Kegan Paul).
Edited with the same scrupulousness as the earlier volume, and tracing auteurism's collapse in the face of major transformations in French intellectual and political life.

Sarris, Andrew (1986), *The American Cinema: Directors and Directions 1929–1968* (Chicago: University of Chicago Press).
Originally published in 1968 and a pinnacle of American auteur criticism, amplifying Sarris's belief in this approach to film as first expressed in his article, 'Notes on the Auteur Theory in 1962'.

Schatz, Thomas (1988), *The Genius of the System: Hollywood Filmmaking in the Studio Era* (New York: Pantheon Books).
Abidingly important as a highly detailed, anti-auteurist study of the institutional frameworks within which films were authored in classical Hollywood.

Sellors, C. Paul (2010), *Film Authorship: Auteurs and Other Myths* (London: Wallflower).

Excellent book: carefully but pointedly surveys developments in this field, and contributes to the debate by proposing a model of 'collective authorship' of film.

Wexman, Virginia Wright (ed.) (2003), *Film and Authorship* (New Brunswick, NJ: Rutgers University Press).

Stimulating collection of essays, tracing shifts in film authorship across a wide range of institutional and ideological contexts.

Wollen, Peter (1998), *Signs and Meaning in the Cinema*, 4th ed. (London: BFI).

Important contribution to work on film authorship (and to film studies more broadly): adjustments in Wollen's thinking on the subject can be tracked by placing 'The Auteur Theory' (1969) against both the 'Conclusion (1972)' and the much later 'Afterword (1997)'.

Online resources

'Great Directors', http://sensesofcinema.com/great-directors/.

Excellent, compendious resource, collecting essays, from an auteurist perspective, on hundreds of directors ranging alphabetically from the New York experimentalist Peggy Ahwesh to the postwar Hollywood liberal Fred Zinnemann.

'Women Film Pioneers Project', https://wfpp.cdrs.columbia.edu/.

Valuable resource, maintained by Columbia University, New York: catalogues the authorial roles occupied by hundreds of women as directors, producers, writers, cinematographers and costume designers in the silent era.

7
Star studies

On 24 August 2006, under the headline 'Mission Over for Mister Impossible', *The Guardian* ran a story that said much about contemporary film stardom. The report detailed a catastrophic breakdown in relations between star Tom Cruise and business mogul Sumner Redstone. Redstone, chairman of the US media conglomerate Viacom which owns Paramount Pictures, had become so exasperated by Cruise's off-screen behaviour that he was about to sever any connection between him and the studio. In particular, Viacom would be ending the arrangement that aimed to bind Cruise to Paramount by paying his production company $10 million annually and giving it office facilities in Los Angeles (Burkeman, 2006: n.p.).

This news story indicates a reconfiguration of Hollywood's industrial system, with formerly mighty studios now merely part of larger entertainment and media corporations (a topic for development in Chapter 9). It also hints at differences between contemporary film stardom and the version that prevailed in classical Hollywood. Mention of Cruise's own production company is evidence of a tendency in recent decades for US stars to develop and manage projects of their own, offering an alternative to the near-feudal working conditions of actors during the studio era. At the same time, however, the *Guardian* report showed the persistence of thinking that the star is a commercially exploitable asset, a resource indispensable to the film industry's profitability. While Cruise had delivered success for Paramount in the past – especially for the first two *Mission: Impossible* films (1996, 2000) – the Viacom chief had observed falling box office returns for his star vehicles: Cruise's 'brand' seemed to be waning in its appeal. Significantly, Redstone did not attribute this falling-off in popularity to what might be called textual factors: that is to say, changes in Cruise's performance mode or star projection in films themselves. Instead, controversial passages in the star's off-screen life were to blame, with Redstone declaring roundly that 'His recent conduct has not been acceptable to Paramount' (Burkeman, 2006: n.p.). The winsome persona that Cruise had developed had been badly damaged by a series of militant public interventions on behalf of Church of Scientology beliefs, most scandalously when he denied the value of medication in treating psychological conditions such as post-natal depression.

Despite its trivial news value, the episode is helpful as a way into many of this chapter's concerns. If only in implicit fashion, the *Guardian* piece indicates that, like the concept of film genre reviewed in Chapter 5, stardom is a phenomenon best investigated not through a single critical optic but by a multi-stranded approach that is sensitive to the several domains of industrial production, textual composition, ideological formation and audience response. As Paul McDonald argues, the star occupies a complex position as 'person, performer, sign and asset', forming 'a point of intersection between meaning and money' (2013: 1, 3). At the start of its discussion of stardom's multi-dimensionality, this chapter will place the star system in shifting industrial contexts from its beginnings in Hollywood and elsewhere to the looser articulations of today. It then considers the construction and implication of a star's persona – the set of meanings associated with a particular actor that Paramount believed had become unstable in Cruise's case. One element of stardom, however, actually understated in the *Guardian* article is our intense investment in people like Cruise, the emotional and psychic bonds which attach us to film stars. Thus the chapter will explore audiences' powerful involvement in the star system, assessing ways used to conceptualise this engagement that have ranged from psychoanalytic accounts of the spectator to ethnographic surveys of fans. Finally, a film star's presence on a newspaper's front page, as was the case in this instance, would seem to indicate the continuing cultural potency of this category of being; cinema, in Christine Gledhill's words, 'still provides the ultimate confirmation of stardom' (1991: xiii). Nevertheless, we will also examine recent shifts in the balance of power between film stars and stars in other domains, including sport.

The political economy of stardom

Writing about Prince as an example of crossover between the film and music industries, Lisa Taylor rejects two well-established approaches to star study. Both ethnographic surveys of fans' responses to film stars and semiotic analyses of what a film star's *persona* or *image* means are lacking, she suggests, because of their neglect of cinema's fundamental commercial imperative. For Taylor, these two conceptual frames give too much weight to the enthusiastic fan and the alert cultural interpreter, respectively, in determining the significance of stardom. As a corrective, she proposes that stars be embedded instead in a more industrially focused form of film studies that she terms *political economy*: 'political economy approaches, which find it unfeasible to isolate the film "text" from the rest of its multi-media production-line, offer the most useful perspectives' (Taylor, 2004: 158). McDonald is in agreement, stating that, for a thorough understanding, it is 'necessary to place stardom in a particular economic and industrial context' (2013: 3). This alternative analytic is not without problems: it may rub out discussion of the specificities of film texts in favour of documenting the 'institutional production of commodities' (Taylor, 2004: 160), thereby absolutising the industry's power in shaping stars rather than acknowledging the role also played in this process by critics, spectators and fans. Nevertheless, given film's implication in most times and places in a capitalist mode of production, emphasis upon the star as primarily a commercial construct is salutary and a good place to start.

There is nothing inevitable about the star's centrality in film. Just as with continuity editing in Chapter 2 and narrative in Chapter 4, the star system is historically and geographically contingent rather than something encoded in cinema's DNA. 'The star was – and is – only one of the possibilities of the movies', as French critic Edgar Morin writes in his pioneering study of this subject (2005: 135). Avowedly *non-star* or even *anti*-star cinema has been developed in many locations, with examples including Eisenstein's utilisation of amateur actors in the early Soviet Union and the collectively made, politically engaged films that emerged in Argentina during the 1960s from the Grupo Cine Liberación. The emergence of a star system is certainly not synchronous with film's beginnings as a medium. Instead, cinema's first period saw it promoted for its spectacular visual presentations; interest was provoked by the sheer novelty of figures moving on a screen rather than by wondering who exactly they were. While stardom already existed in adjacent fields such as theatre and music, film initially seemed less hospitable to charismatic personalities. However, the consolidation early in the twentieth century of narrative cinema gave greater scope for vir- tuoso performance and stimulated audience curiosity regarding the identity and, eventually, the off-screen life of the actors themselves.

Given Hollywood's dominance in our thinking about stars, it is striking that one critic calls French comic performer Max Linder 'the world's first film star' (Vincendeau, 2000: 42). While he would go on to work also in the United States, Linder's name initially appeared in film publicity in France as early as 1909. The first American star is often said to be Florence Lawrence, poached from the well-established Biograph Company by an independent pro- ducer and introduced to the public in a blaze of sensationalist adver- tising in March 1910. However, a number of scholars have shown that, although she was the most vividly promoted early star in the US, Lawrence was not historically the first: some months before her unveiling, other studios had not only disclosed the names of their previously anonymous actors but had begun to utilise them in publicity campaigns that included foyer display cards and press advertisements. Soon enough, these rudimentary attempts at star promotion were surpassed by the incorporation of actor credits in films, by slides of the actors shown between reels, and – off-screen – by the establishment of dedicated fan magazines and fan clubs.

Internationally, star systems in the first half of the twentieth century took different forms. The film industries of nations such as Britain and France lacked the depth of infrastructure and volume of output to tie actors into lengthy, exclusive contracts. As a result, performers were more liable than their US counterparts to move between assignments in film and theatre. The political economy of stardom in these countries was thus a cottage industry compared with the advanced corporate capitalism of its American counterpart. Typically, actors in Hollywood during its classical period from the 1920s to the early 1950s would be signed up by studios on tightly confining seven-year contracts and then deployed in a series of films for which they were deemed suitable according to facial appearance, body shape and personality type. Studio bosses would remodel stars just like other items of fixed capital at their disposal. An actor might lose the opportunity to develop a range of performance (as when MGM responded to fan suggestions by consistently placing Clark Gable in tough-talking heroic roles). Even actors' given names were liable to be changed in the pursuit of higher studio profits: the former Lucille Le Sueur became Joan Crawford following a magazine competition organised by her employers, while Marion Morrison was peremptorily renamed John Wayne by executives at Twentieth Century Fox without his 'even being a party to the meeting' (Roberts and Olson, 1997: 84). Despite their glamour and charisma – most effectively communicated by the cinematic close-up – stars actually found themselves inserted into a system of mass-production with resemblances to the Fordist regime that at this time was turning out standardised consumer goods like cars and refrigerators. Ominously, they were not only instrumental in com-modity output, but were themselves infected by the logic of com-modification. Walter Benjamin, whose strictures on the alienating aspects of film acting were cited in Chapter 1, also observed that 'The cult of the movie star, fostered by the money of the movie industry, preserves not the unique aura of the person but the "spell of the personality", the phony spell of a commodity' (1999: 224).

Barry King refers to a film star's 'persona work', the efforts made to establish, systematise and occasionally modify an image that is portable across a career (2003: 60). During the classical Hollywood era, the star largely relinquished persona production to his or her studio. Suitable public appearances were arranged and fan clubs instituted so as to reproduce a star image already vividly conveyed by a set of screen performances. The aim was always to minimise the sort of disruption to persona stability glimpsed above in the case of Tom Cruise. Such a coherent image functioned primarily as a form of *branding* for films themselves, going some way towards marking their genre status and likely mood or atmosphere and, in the process, serving to recruit particular audiences. The star's brand could also, however, extend beyond cinema, burnishing the appeal of other commodities. Although prospects for multimedia and cross-market synergies were relatively restricted during Hollywood's classical period, stars' allure was still appropriated for a variety of commercial tie-ins, including clothing, cosmetics and toiletries. Even with regard to this early time, then, star studies should free itself from an exclusive focus on film texts themselves so as to incorporate analysis of the star's extension across other elements of the commodity world.

The commercial exploitability of the star has increased exponentially in subsequent decades. From the 1950s onwards, however, Hollywood has also witnessed the star's *relative autonomy* compared with the cramped labour conditions of the classical era. The collapse of the studio system under economic and legislative pressures discussed in Chapter 9 has led to looser, more provisional arrangements between stars on the one hand and production companies on the other. 'Persona work', in King's phrase, has become less an employing studio's responsibility than the star's own labour (albeit delegated to specialists in promotion and publicity). At the level of production itself, the star is now not a fixed asset under single ownership so much as a package offered to a series of users for the duration of particular projects. Geoff King writes that stars have increasingly converted themselves into 'their own franchise properties', over which the forces of film production may exercise only intermittent and imperfect control (2003: 68). This is not, of course, to suggest that stars are now invulnerable to the kinds of corporate calculation that prevailed in the studio era. Seth Rogen, for example, has a freedom of manoeuvre unimaginable during the 1930s, yet, given his particular comic 'brand', would still struggle to interest makers of a Roman epic. Thus a political economy approach to contemporary stardom needs a sense of nuance and detail, rather than positing an absolute break from Hollywood's studio era.

Star personas (1)

While indispensable, an approach to stardom oriented towards economics should not be uncoupled from inquiries into stars' socio-cultural significances. The *meanings* of stars, after all, exceed their mere marketability. This is the thesis of Richard Dyer's still essential book, *Stars* (first published in 1979), which proposes that a star's image is constituted by four different types of 'media text', not all of them subject to the film industry's management: *promotion*, *publicity*, *films* and *criticism and commentaries* (1998: 60). Although Dyer goes on to say that inevitably 'the films have a distinct and privileged place in a star's image' (61), placing them third in the list of media texts would seem to indicate otherwise. Indeed, in Dyer's successor volume, *Heavenly Bodies* (first published in 1986), there is more explicit demotion of an actor's on-screen work in the process of star manufacture:

> A film star's image is not just his or her films, but the promotion of those films and of the star through pin-ups, public appearances, studio hand-outs and so on, as well as interviews, biographies and coverage in the press of the star's doings and 'private' life. Further, a star's image is also what people say or write about him or her, as critics or commentators, the way the image is used in other contexts such as advertisements, novels, pop songs, and finally the way the star can become part of the coinage of everyday speech. (2004: 2–3)

Even without taking into account the subsequent, colossal accumulation of star discourse on websites and social media platforms, it is clear from Dyer's catalogue just how heterogeneous and dispersed are the forces involved in shaping the images of stars. The process is still not, as Dyer himself is quick to acknowledge, 'an equal to-and-fro' (2004: 4). In determining the meanings of stars, as with the labelling of genres that was discussed in Chapter 5, some film interests have more definitional power than others (here, again, the industrial focus recommended above by Taylor and McDonald is important). Nevertheless, the world of film discourse is multiply centred, rather than singularly controlled, giving individual fans, or at least groups of fans, the sense that they too may have some say in fashioning a particular star's image. We will expand upon this discursive role of the spectator later in the chapter.

For the moment, questions of the relative influence of all those groups involved in constructing a star's image can be set aside so as to consider instead this image's implications for both the performer and the culture at large. Rather than critical consensus, there are differences of opinion on how to label the cluster of associations that gather around a particular film star. McDonald favours 'the star-as-brand', which certainly enables close attention to how stars 'operate in the film market' (2013: 41), yet has those cultural blind spots already alluded to. As evidenced above, Dyer tends to favour 'star image', while other critics express a preference for either 'star persona' or 'star text'. Although these latter three terms are not exactly synonyms, they are equivalent nevertheless in conceiving of the star as something that requires interpretation or decipherment. Star studies is indeed calculatedly *non-anthropomorphic*, being concerned not with the flesh–and–blood performer as such but with the array of meanings and significances that he or she generates across platforms that, as we have seen, extend from films themselves to Twitter accounts, and from advertisements to chat show interviews.

Is a particular star's image or persona fixed, or, on the contrary, elastic and open to modification? For some observers, the associations that stars accrue function as imprisoning grids. John Sayles is making this point when he observes wittily that 'A woman alone at night who answers the doorbell to find Peter Lorre on the front steps is in for a different evening than one who finds David Niven' (2003: 46). Lorre, a whey-faced, physically squat actor identified with macabre roles in both European and Hollywood cinemas (Figure 22), is positioned here as the antithesis of Niven, an elegant figure who epitomised mid-century, upper-class English suavity (Figure 23). By Sayles's account, these two very different stars are equally bound by invariant associations assembled across their bodies of screen work, as well as through multiple other media texts. From this perspective, the film star carries predetermined meanings like a second skin. Images or personas of this sort may indeed be solid enough to withstand many potential disturbances: for instance, Hugh Grant's brush with sexual transgression and arrest by the Los Angeles Police Department in 1995 did not radically destabilise his projection of endearingly caddish upper-class Englishness, but in fact proved capable of alignment with this image.

While a star persona of this kind endows an actor with a niche identity, a comparative advantage in pursuing certain roles, it may also restrict performative range. Film history is thus full of

22 Star persona: Peter Lorre in *I Was an Adventuress* (1940)

23 Star persona: David Niven in *Happy Go Lovely* (1951)

examples of stars trying to resist reductive accounts of what they might signify: a case in point would be Robin Williams's efforts to shatter his comic-sentimental persona by playing grimmer parts in *Insomnia* and *One Hour Photo* (both 2002). It would be an inert theoretical model, however, that did not allow for the possibility of at least *some* modifications to a star's image across his or her career. Indeed, Barry King writes that, rather than being simply deposited in each additional film, a star's 'persona is differentially activated in successive roles' (2003: 47). Armed with this insight, then, the critic might be empowered to detect fine differences between, say, Jennifer Aniston's instantiation of her romantic–comic image in *The Break-Up* (2006) and in *He's Just Not That Into You* (2009).

STOP and THINK

Some time ago, John O. Thompson suggested that film studies might profitably carry across from linguistics *the commutation test*, which involves making small changes to a sample of verbal material in order to assess what alterations thereby occur in meaning (1991: 183–97). In Thompson's version of this exercise, stars themselves are the elements to be substituted. If the star who appeared in a particular film is replaced by another, what would happen to the work?

Before attempting your own commutations of some stars by others, consider instances of recasting from film history itself. How different would *Speed* (1994) be with Halle Berry, the producers' first choice, in the Sandra Bullock role? Or *American Beauty* with the initially preferred Tom Hanks, not Kevin Spacey, playing the lead? Now try some star substitutions of your own. These could be seemingly minor adjustments: *Hercules* (2014), for example, with Vin Diesel, rather than Dwayne Johnson, in the title role. Or they might be more radical modifications: Jamie Foxx and Dame Judi Dench, say, as the cop duo of *22 Jump Street* (2014), rather than Jonah Hill and Channing Tatum.

While substitutions of these kinds may be amusing, they are not frivolously intended. With each commutation you perform, explore what it reveals about the relative rigidity or elasticity, the portability or otherwise across films, of particular stars' personas. Building upon Chapter 6's discussion of film authorship, this exercise should also allow you to evaluate the part a star plays in textual composition.

Star personas (2)

Star personas or images have an importance that goes well beyond their implications for actors' careers. We have already seen how a political economy approach inserts a star into the commodity system, tracking his or her 'brand' from movies themselves to a host of other goods and services. Another major tradition in star studies draws instead upon semiotics and ideology critique in the effort to uncover *the socio-cultural significances* of particular stars. For stars carry an ideological charge in their faces and bodies, their ways of speaking and moving, their trajectories both on-screen in the film plots with which they are most commonly associated and off-screen in domains varying from charity work to celebrity scandal. To begin to make this more concrete, consider again the two actors named above by Sayles. Lorre's ready expression of anxiety, paranoia, even madness made him a privileged figure in the cinematic evocation of deeply troubled times either side of World War II. By contrast, the brand of urbanity developed by Niven not only in film roles but in autobiographies and chat show spots evoked England's late-imperial situation, appearing unruffled even as it was about to be thrown into crisis by profound global changes.

Star 'readings' of this sort are interested in what their objects of study reveal about culturally dominant models of gender, race and class. From this perspective, the flourishing or the failure of a given star reveals nothing as mundane as actor ability, but, actually, shifting values and behaviours in the star's society. Striking work along these lines has been done by Yvonne Tasker, Susan Jeffords and others in correlating the rise of masculine 'hard bodies' like Arnold Schwarzenegger and Sylvester Stallone in the 1980s with the period's post-Vietnam anti-feminist backlash and President Reagan's reassertion of US power abroad. The later decline of this cinematic type thus occurred not because of any deficiency in the stars' performances, but because such a hypertrophic version of masculinity registered in a different historical conjuncture as strident, hysterical, even risible. Similar study can be done of shifting feminine types in US cinema. The relative waning of Demi Moore, for instance, from a high point of popularity in the 1990s certainly owes something to Hollywood's relentless favouring of younger women, but might also be attributed to the insecure cultural status of that version of self-reliant, even narcissistic femininity she projected in sites ranging from her performance in *Striptease* (1996) to her two nude cover portraits for *Vanity Fair* in 1991–92.

This type of ideologically oriented star studies also finds that, at various times, particular African American actors have been selected for stardom by Hollywood for reasons that extend beyond their dramatic skills. Consider, for example, the consolidation of Sidney Poitier during the mid-1960s as the first major black star in US cinema. Handsome, clean-cut, well-dressed, Poitier played such representatives of the professional middle class as a teacher in *To Sir, with Love*, a doctor in *Guess Who's Coming to Dinner* and a detective in *In the Heat of the Night* (all 1967). This rise to prominence coincided with the reconfiguration of American racial politics following the passage through Congress of important Civil Rights legislation. While Poitier's stardom should be regarded positively since it placed a black actor at the heart of popular US film and gave him roles beyond stereotypes of aggressive criminality and demeaning servitude, his unthreatening personality both on- and off-screen, and his representation of *individual* rather than collective progress, suggest that his preferment as a star at that time endorsed a reformist – not revolutionary – version of black struggle in the United States. One critic writes that 'in this integrationist age Poitier was the model integrationist hero', and observes that other black actors of the period, with edgier personas, struggled to emulate his success (Bogle, 2001: 175). This example also bears out Dyer's point with which we began the previous section: namely, that a star's meaning is liable to be a contentious rather than consensual matter. After all, the Black Panther activist of the late 1960s would have deciphered Poitier's star semiotic very differently from a liberal white constituency.

Martin Shingler expresses reservations about attempts of this kind to correlate particular stars with structures of gender, race and class. He complains of 'the heavy burden of representation that some stars have been made to carry, sometimes by the film industry, sometimes by their audiences and fans, but most often by film critics, historians and academics' (2012: 150). Shingler's point is well-made, since critics have certainly been guilty at times of endowing stars with an excess of ideological efficacy or cultural force. This is arguably true of Dyer's *Heavenly Bodies* itself, which argues that Marilyn Monroe magically resolved in her persona conservative and progressive constructions of female sexuality that divided late 1950s America. Shingler is right, too, to warn against 'reductionism' (174) and 'reflectionism' (175) in this kind of study, since there is a danger of simply situating a star against a particular historical conjuncture without thinking hard enough about how he or she was actually *used* at that time by various constituencies. Even at the height of their popularity, Schwarzenegger and Stallone were taken by some of their fans to be exponents of camp rather than effective tutors in an American machismo for employment both at home and abroad. Unjustifiably, however, Shingler then extrapolates from these suitably cautionary observations to reject *all* ideologically or culturally framed versions of star study: 'Stars exist primarily in the realm of representation and, as such, are divorced from reality' (177). It is precisely stars' occupation of this 'realm of representation', centred upon but not restricted to the lustrous cinema image, that bestows attractiveness, charisma and, potentially, power upon the images they have. Shingler's remark, in fact, makes *more* rather than less essential investigation of stars as ideological and cultural agents.

STOP and THINK

If you are persuaded by the case above for taking into account the socio-cultural implications of stars, rather than simply isolating their contribution to film industry economics, consider whether any particular stars are aligned especially closely with our current moment. If successive phases in American masculinity, for example, have been represented cinematically by Fred Astaire (the 1930s), or John Wayne (the 1950s), or more androgynous figures such as Johnny Depp and Brad Pitt (the 1990s onwards), can any younger star be said to model a normative Western masculinity now? Consider the same question with regard to femininity. And if Sidney Poitier was a model African American hero for the Civil Rights era, is there a black star who fulfils this role in the Age of Obama? If so, why?

The star and the spectator

On 23 August 1926 the Italian-born silent movie star Rudolph Valentino, celebrated for such exotic spectacles as *The Sheik* (1921) and *The Eagle* (1925), died of septicaemia, aged thirty-one. A week later, his funeral mass took place in New York. As the cortège moved towards the church, the sidewalk mise-en-scène was as lavishly charged as sequences from Valentino's own films. A crowd of a hundred thousand – many wearing black and weeping – lined the streets. Valentino's lover Pola Negri, who fainted several times during the funeral itself, had rivals in both quantity and quality of mourning among the star's fans; indeed, she was exceeded in grief by several of them. Although reports of a nationwide, even global pandemic of suicide attempts prompted by Valentino's premature death have been exaggerated, some fans undoubtedly took their devotion to him to the point of seeking to end their own lives in a kind of star suttee. In London, a twenty-seven-year-old actress, surrounded by photographs of him, committed suicide by poisoning just two days after he died; later in 1926, a young American mother attempted to shoot herself, similarly making her bid for oblivion amidst an informal shrine to the star. Given the androgyny of Valentino's features and movements, and the camera's frequent lingering upon his beauty, many gay men in the United States and beyond also reacted in heightened ways to his death.

This episode is worth recalling for a number of reasons. First, it is a salutary reminder that celebrity culture is not a recent invention: news of Valentino's death that was dispersed by print, telegraph and radio had similar impact to Robin Williams's suicide in August 2014 that was disseminated by internet, TV and mobile phone. Second, the unrestrained mourners of Valentino alert us to a possible puritanism in star studies. For all their value, both political economy and semiotic approaches are liable to operate at some distance from the spectator's encounter with stardom. Film stars, after all, are often the cause of our most intense engagement with the medium. While film engages us in multiple ways, it may still be the star's appearance on screen that stirs the profoundest response. Watching and thinking about particular stars, the spectator is traversed by powerful desires – as well as, sometimes, by equally strong antipathies. Without detaching all of this affective substance from the economic and ideological data already considered, an adequate star studies still needs to take it fully into account. In the process, we should also introduce something that has largely been missing from the discussion so far: namely, a sense of *the star's body*. References to commodities and personas do not quite capture the extent to which audience engagement with the star is a tumultuously corporeal, even carnal matter.

Various conceptual frameworks have been utilised in analysing the dynamic between spectator and star. One tradition draws upon psychoanalytic approaches that have been fruitful elsewhere in film studies. Critics have made particular use here of the concepts of *narcissism*, *voyeurism* and *fetishism*. Although some writers argue it is narrative cinema's *characters*, not stars, which provoke such psychosexual complexes in the audience, characters are of course powerfully embodied by stars themselves. So, for instance, the male spectator may be solicited by vivid screen presence into narcissistic identification with a film's male star: he rides wish-fulfillingly with Clint Eastwood, or drives with Ryan Gosling, possibly making problematic his post-film reimmersion in a more mundane identity. Theorists have suggested, however, that the heterosexual male viewer's watching of *female* stars may be more agitated, even fraught. Concealed, traditionally, in the dark, he has the advantage of voyeuristic scrutiny of them. However, this rather Gothic version of star studies also proposes that in the figure of the female star on screen the male subject faces the terror of his own prospective castration, and so, to ward off these anxieties, breaks up her body into fetishised objects. Film history is full of examples of female stars 'morselised' in this way: the legs of Betty Grable in the 1940s, the breasts of Jayne Mansfield in the 1950s and, more recently, the lips of Angelina Jolie or Julia Roberts ('Major lippage' as the central duo sums Roberts up in *Wayne's World*).

Psychoanalytic work on star spectatorship has tended to be less empowering of women as viewing subjects, often restricting them to such unattractive options as passive or even masochistic identi-fication with the female clotheshorses that have often featured in narrative cinema. So, while Jackie Stacey's important study *Star Gazing* (1994) is influenced by psychoanalysis, it also draws upon an alternative resource in star studies: namely, surveys of fans' responses. Stacey was not the first critic to approach actual film viewers and ask them what they made of stars, rather than relying upon abstract, homogenising models of spectatorship (in *Heavenly Bodies*, Dyer makes use of letters sent him by fans of Judy Garland to assess how her persona had been important to gay men in homo-phobic postwar Britain). Stacey's project, however, is both larger in scale and more developed in methodology than any precursors, set-ting out its rationale for using ethnographic surveys that are more common in social sciences than the humanities. The second half of her book catalogues and evaluates the several hundred responses she had after placing requests in two British women's magazines for readers to contact her with memories of their favourite Hollywood female stars of the 1940s and 1950s. To understand the behaviours of her respondents towards their chosen stars, Stacey devises two categories: 'cinematic identificatory fantasy' and 'extra-cinematic identificatory practices'. Each of these two basic ways of relating to stars has its own spectrum of intensities: for example, cinematic identificatory fantasy begins most restrainedly with 'devotion' to the star and passes through stages of 'adoration', 'worship' and 'transcendence' before concluding in a state of 'aspiration and inspiration' where the star's image induces in the fan a 'desire to transform the self and become more like the ideal' (Stacey, 1994: 138–59). Extra-cinematic identificatory practices, this term sug-gesting material, measurable responses to the star, start with 'pre-tending' and intensify into 'resembling', 'imitating' and finally 'copying' (159–75). These states involve progressive realignment of the spectator's face, hairstyle, body, voice, movement and whole way of being to accord with those of the emulated star.

Criticisms can certainly be made of *Star Gazing*. A thoroughgo-ing psychoanalytic approach would question the evidentiary value of the letters from which Stacey begins: self-consciously written-up for public consumption as they are, they may not capture all of the messiness of spectatorial engagement with stars. The book is also restricted in its sampling. First, it records only female responses, rather than including men as well (contrast the mixed-sex witnesses in Annette Kuhn's own ethnographic venture, *An Everyday Magic*, mentioned in Chapter 3). Second, Stacey also asks her respondents mainly about female stars, thereby allowing them to withhold potentially fascinating evidence of their interactions with male screen idols of the time. Finally, she chooses to omit British and other non-American stars from the discussion, a decision reinforcing the Hollywoodcentrism that, as with film genre criticism, is already an unfortunate aspect of star studies. These problems notwithstanding, *Star Gazing* offers a stimulating example of spectator-centred work on stars that subsequent critics have built on in their own qualitative and quantitative surveys of audience responses.

Stacey's respondents are all relatively genteel older women when they communicate with her, and the types of yearning which they recall having been activated by their favourite stars seem, on the whole, containable rather than transgressive or anti-social. In this sample of fans, there are no stalkers. Nor are there any star-struck self-harmers: Morin describes how a sixteen-year-old female fan sent the prewar Canadian star Norma Shearer pieces of her skin (2005: 69). However, analysts of film stardom, and especially of recent and contemporary stardoms, need to expand the array of relatively well-managed identificatory fantasies and practices that Stacey catalogues. At the extreme of pathological fantasy would be John Hinckley, who developed a morbid interest in Jodie Foster as a child star, pursued her relentlessly by letter and phone call, and eventually, as a deviant love-offering, attempted to assassinate President Reagan in March 1981. More generally, star studies should aim to restore the unruly erotic dimension of our engagement with stars that is often sublimated by Stacey's respondents. Chapter 6 touched on fan fiction with respect to its reconfiguring or extending of films' existing narratives; however, a subdivision of this unofficial textual production is devoted to casting Hollywood stars in alternative, even transgressive erotic scenarios. McDonald also draws attention to the emergence of salacious websites displaying either photographs grabbed of stars in states of off-screen undress or digitally manipulated images that make it appear the star is naked or even involved in reputation-damaging sexual acts. Though McDonald overstates the spectatorial power produced by these sites – 'Fake nudes are members of the audience using technology to take control over the stars' (2003: 38) – he usefully points here to the underside of officially promoted star images. Forums designed to regulate and commodify audience engagement with stars – red-carpet appearances, promotional chat show interviews, carefully selected commercial endorsements – are increasingly countered by others in which less deferential and hygienic constructions of the star circulate.

Finally, a word should be said here about star/spectator dynamics in the era of social media. Shingler writes that, recently, many stars have taken to 'creating online social networking sites (such as Facebook) or using Twitter as a means of providing audiences with personal information about their lives' (2012: 144). This is a qualitatively new development, presenting stars to us without evidence of the chat show hosts, reporters and publicists who are conspicuous elsewhere. There is the suggestion here of an immediacy and intimacy of communication between star and spectator that differs markedly from the form of distanced worship that prevailed with respect to the stars of classical Hollywood. Unfortunately, however, social networking sites are liable to repurposing by stars so that they function less as spaces of informal, democratic interaction than as additional platforms for commercial promotion. To glance at Tom Cruise's Twitter feed during the summer of 2014, for instance, is not to encounter a stream of frank personal reflections (the sort of unauthorised media content that alarmed his erstwhile bosses at Paramount); instead, it is to observe the star as publicist for his new film, *Edge of Tomorrow* (2014). In remorseless fashion, each image or piece of text tweeted or retweeted by Cruise contributes to this commercial activity: 'I'm excited to visit Japan for Edge of Tomorrow (released as All You Need Is Kill – based on the book that inspired the movie). Can't wait' (23 June) or, in a fan's retweeted words, 'Can't stop thinking about Edge of Tomorrow. It is everything summer movies should be. @Tom Cruise never disappoints' (12 June) ('Tom Cruise on Facebook and Twitter', 2014: n.p.).

STOP and THINK

- How, precisely, would you characterise your engagement with film stars? The rapture, or reverence, in the voices of respondents to classical Hollywood's stars is striking: 'Stars were fabulous creatures to be worshipped from afar' (Stacey, 1994: 143) or 'Joan Crawford is my lucky star. I feel she is near me, like a goddess, in my darkest hours' (Morin, 2005: 69). Although these spectators are recalling the impact of stars during quite different conditions of mid-twentieth-century austerity, can you recognise *yourself*, if only faintly or nervously, in their sentiments?

- You might use Stacey's graded categories of 'identificatory fantasy' and 'extra-cinematic identificatory practice' to chart the forms taken by your own 'star gazing'. If the responses you have seem private fantasies, not detectable by effects in the world, locate them somewhere on Stacey's scale of devotion, adoration, worship, transcendence and aspiration/inspiration. If, however, your responses to stars are better described as 'practices', place these, according to their intensity, on a spectrum that extends from pretending through resembling and imitating to copying. Whereas Stacey is concerned primarily with same-sex interactions between spectator and star, develop the analysis of your own relationships to stars so that it operates also across sexual boundaries.

- Finally, it is important that the several conceptual paradigms employed in star studies do not become estranged from one another. Stacey mediates between psychoanalytic and political economy approaches when she shows how her respondents' fantasies about classical Hollywood's stars were expressed materially by acts of consumption. Explore the relationship between your own feelings for stars on the one hand and your economic behaviour on the other (from choices of film to watch onwards).

National and transnational stardoms

Even as he introduces a collection of essays on British film stars, Bruce Babington finds himself compelled to acknowledge that Hollywood has 'unquestionable status as the paradigmatic site of stardom' (2001: 3). The hegemony of popular US cinema is such that its stars have achieved greater global celebrity than the leading figures of other national film industries. Nevertheless, a Hollywood-centred approach to stardom should be supplemented or even complicated, rather than uncritically reproduced. Sensitivity to diverse local cultures, together with awareness of shifting patterns of film production, distribution and exhibition that have globalised the appeal of many stars from beyond the United States, makes it more important than ever to reconfigure the geography of star studies.

Different nations, as briefly noted earlier, have devised different systems of film stardom. The British model is not merely much tinier than its US equivalent, but determinedly less bombastic; it exhibits what Babington calls 'an ideologically meaningful reserve' (2001: 20). In France, the star system has more patriotic connotations, with its icons sometimes enlisted in the struggle against an Anglophone culture represented most forcefully by Hollywood film; on the whole, however, the relatively low rate of productivity in French cinema means that its star system, too, is limited in potency. Elsewhere, however, some national stardoms have a brashness that rivals or even outstrips Hollywood. Here the case of Bollywood – popular Indian cinema based in Mumbai – is especially vivid. Vijay Mishra writes that, from the early 1950s onwards, Bollywood has sought to promote charismatic figures both on- and off-screen: 'Popular cinema in India, perhaps even more so than in Hollywood, became the cinema of the star rather than the cinema of the director or the studio' (2002: 126). The organisation of film form itself so as to foreground the star – Mishra speaks of frequent 'song and dialogic situations' (127), allowing the central performers to be exhibited – is matched by the star's colossal multi-media promotion that extends beyond India itself into the Indian diaspora. This vibrant equivalent to Hollywood stardom is still invisible to many people worldwide: readers of *The Guardian* on 4 August 2006, for instance, might have been surprised to see a lead-in referring to 'the world's biggest film star' followed by a profile not of Cruise or Pitt, but of one of Bollywood's current male icons, Shah Rukh Khan. The situation may change, though, in the face of increasing exchanges of personnel between Bollywood and Hollywood (one recent example of this being the casting of Amitabh Bachchan, India's biggest star of the past fifty years, in *The Great Gatsby*).

Besides familiarising itself at a basic level with the personnel of non-US, particularly non-Anglophone film stardoms, a newly internationalised star studies also needs to produce detailed comparative examination of these systems. In addition, star studies should now have on its agenda heightened attention to the figure of the charismatic *transnational* performer. The actor leaving an indigenous cinema in order to find success in Hollywood is a durable type: from the first half of the twentieth century, consider not only Max Linder and Peter Lorre, mentioned above, but Sweden's Greta Garbo or Germany's Marlene Dietrich. However, the increasing globalisation of popular entertainment has accelerated the trend for stars from outside the US to work in its popular cinema. And the itineraries followed by these migrant stars may now not be unilinear, but susceptible to reversals and crisscrossings. Take the case of Benedict Cumberbatch. Though a star of big-budget Hollywood productions – notably the three *Hobbit* films (2012–14) and *Star Trek Into Darkness* (2013) – he is not restricted to this identity as a performer; on the contrary, less well-financed British works like *Third Star* (2010) and *Wreckers* (2011), together with work on TV and stage, indicate his mobility across different versions and levels of stardom. Perhaps more interesting still are examples of actors who, when in Hollywood, are working outside their first language as well as their national cinema. One instance of this type of transnational star is Penélope Cruz, who has alternated between commercial American movies and art cinema in Spain; another is Marion Cotillard, with the flexibility to follow a US blockbuster like *The Dark Knight Rises* with a French-language art film such as *Two Days, One Night* (2014), directed by Belgium's uncompromising Dardenne brothers.

Given the present gaze of the US towards the potent economies of the Pacific Rim, it is unsurprising that major Asian and Australasian stars, too, have been incorporated in Hollywood. Again, however, it

24 The transnational star: Michelle Yeoh in *Crouching Tiger, Hidden Dragon* (2000)

is important to stress the potential reversibility of their trajectories. This capacity for reverse migration, or indeed for a whole series of relocations, can be glimpsed in the recent careers of several stars of Hong Kong cinema. Note, for example, Michelle Yeoh's filmography, which includes on the one hand Chinese martial arts pictures such as *Crouching Tiger, Hidden Dragon* (2000; see Figure 24) and *Reign of Assassins* (2010), and on the other such English-language projects as *Memoirs of a Geisha* (2005). This latter role in particular hints at the dangers of Hollywood Orientalism, with the repackaging of an East Asian star as an exotic commodity for Western consumption. Pointed questions might also be asked about the use by popular US cinema of other Chinese stars, including Jackie Chan, Chow Yun-Fat and Jet Li. In each of these cases, the incoming stars face not only potential simplification of their native cultures but also opportunistic casting so as to enhance the films' access to the very lucrative Asian markets. To leave the account of the transnational star there, however, would be overly pessimistic, neglecting the possibility that Hollywood, as the 'host' cinema here, might itself be modified positively by this increased contact with stars from outside the United States.

Film stars and other stardoms

At the start of the 1990s, Christine Gledhill acknowledged the allure of pop and sports stars, yet, as we saw above, still felt able to claim that cinema provides 'the ultimate confirmation of stardom' (1991: xiii). Writing a decade later, however, Christine Geraghty was not so sure: 'We need to look at stars in a context in which film stars may struggle for prominence' (2000: 183). She went on to observe that, in a production regime now far removed from the conveyor-belt of the studio era, Hollywood films, at least, take a long time to emerge and are thus 'a relatively inefficient way of delivering fame compared with some other formats' (188). It is undeniable that other vehicles of stardom can boast of greater speed and manoeuvrability now than their cinematic counterpart. The ceaseless spectacle provided by today's sports-industrial complex, say, keeps its stars like Cristiano Ronaldo, Usain Bolt, Kobe Bryant and Rory McIlroy continuously in public discourse. The ubiquity of such figures in media texts and their ultra-attractiveness to advertisers suggest that the ratio of power between sports and film stardoms may indeed have changed from a time like the 1960s, when Paul Newman's charisma and beauty on screen easily saw off the challenge posed by the sensible sweaters of champion US golfer Arnold Palmer.

Just as the political economy of sports stardom increasingly rivals in magnitude its cinematic equivalent, so, too, there has been a rise in the sports star's ideological power. Earlier, we reviewed the argument that film stars exhibit in vivid, attractive ways socially favoured identities of gender, race and class; it is at least argu-able that this role in ideological reproduction has now substantially devolved upon sports stars, as well as stars from music. In Britain recently, no male film star – indigenous or otherwise – has negoti-ated masculinity in as complex a way and with as many effects, liberating besides commodifying, as David Beckham. Tabloid newspaper reports of university courses in 'Beckham Studies' were always mischievously intended and anti-intellectual; nevertheless, it says much about the status now of sports stardom that the images of Beckham and other contemporary stars in sport have been explored by cultural semioticians with a diligence not brought, say, to inter-preting Matt Damon. Consider, too, the relative significance of film and sports stars in constructions of race in the United States. Black movie performers have often been strongly implicated in these: not only Poitier, but earlier figures like Stepin Fetchit and Dorothy Dandridge, and later stars like Eddie Murphy, Denzel Washington,

Samuel L. Jackson and Whoopi Goldberg. However, it is debatable whether contemporary African American film stars are as central to negotiations of black identity as are Bryant, LeBron James and other basketball players, Tiger Woods in golf and the Williams sisters in tennis. And, as well as calibrating its relative force against sports stardom, analysts of film's star system should compare it with that in music now. Both economically and culturally, is Jamie Foxx equivalent in power to Jay Z, or Halle Berry to Beyoncé?

Case study: Jennifer Lawrence

Discussion of the stardom of Jennifer Lawrence, and its cultural, ideological and economic significances, might begin by considering some suggestive moments from *The Hunger Games*. Early in the film, Katniss Everdeen, played by Lawrence, faces threats not only to her physical survival but to the very sense she has of herself. Arriving in the Capitol in order to represent District 12 during the brutal Hunger Games, she refuses to fashion an image to suit the expectations of the cheering crowds; instead, safeguarding her integrity, she merely stares back at them (Figure 25). Later on, during and after the Games themselves, she disables rather than oils the system's publicity machine by resisting its attempts to position her as a 'star-crossed lover' or as 'the survivor who found romance'. These proffered identities strike her as artifices and contrivances, not corresponding to how she understands herself. There is similar

25 Jennifer Lawrence resisting attempts to fabricate and constrain her in *The Hunger Games* (2012)

unease later in the series, in *The Hunger Games: Mockingjay, Part 1* (2014), when she expresses awkwardness at simplified, manipulative constructions of her by the forces of rebellion.

Such episodes have implications for our evaluation not only of Katniss as a character but of Lawrence as a star. Like the figure she plays in this highly successful franchise, Lawrence is defined by resistance to fabrications, falsifications and masquerades of all kinds. 'Naturalness', 'authenticity' and 'sincerity' are taken by fans and film critics alike to underlie her spectacular trajectory that, even before she was twenty-four, had seen her star in both big-budget and independent hits, winning one Oscar and earning two further nominations. The appealing impression of 'the real' given by Lawrence in this body of film performances is reinforced by widely circulated reports and images of her off-screen. It is well known, for example, that she has received no formal training in acting, thereby furthering a sense that her screen work has a directness not replicated by most of her peers, bound as they are to actorly protocols and conventions. Similarly, both in falling over at successive Academy Awards ceremonies (2013, 2014) and in responding each time with good humour and a lack of embarrassment, Lawrence, like Katniss Everdeen, registers as straightforward and untutored, not restricted by the usual rules of celebrity image management.

Nevertheless, assumptions of Lawrence's naturalness should be examined carefully rather than endorsed uncritically. For, as Masha Tupitsyn puts it in a blog on Lawrence, quoting the French director Robert Bresson, actors 'can't go back' to some realm unmarked by performance once they begin their careers: 'Can't be natural. They just can't' (Tupitsyn, 2013: n.p.). While admiring Lawrence for her capacity for 'going off script, poking holes in some of the veils and mores of stardom', Tupitsyn also asks whether a rejection of contrivance and performance amounts nevertheless to a performative mode in its own right, 'another way of masking and maintaining the mask' (2013: n.p.). This is certainly not to allege any kind of deliberate fakery or simulation on Lawrence's part; it *is*, however, to acknowledge that naturalness itself registers as an image in the dense media world she inhabits, both on- and off-screen. In this section, then, we explore Lawrence's image or persona, assessing it as a repository of ideological values, a source of aspiration for fans and, not least, as a lucrative brand in Hollywood's current economy of stardom.

What version of femininity, to begin with, is embodied by Lawrence in her screen work and in an array of off-screen appearances? 'You seem like a tough girl', Pat (Bradley Cooper) says to Tiffany, Lawrence's character, in *Silver Linings Playbook*; and this remark might be freed from its particular occasion and taken to apply more generally to Lawrence across her career. One component of this toughness is verbal fortitude: consider, for example, the spirited, witty talk of her characters to overbearing males in *Silver Linings Playbook* or *American Hustle*, and how this is replicated in Lawrence's frank and sassy turns in numerous interviews. Her image also incorporates physical assertiveness and resilience. Particularly compelling evidence here is provided by her incarnation as an action heroine in the *Hunger Games* series, where she runs and swims and engages in stunning feats of archery. Unusually for a female star in Hollywood, Lawrence can also be seen chopping wood in not one but two films: *Winter's Bone* (2010) and the Depression era melodrama *Serena* (2014). If her face and body already deviate from norms of femininity in contemporary American cinema – contrast Lawrence with, say, the waif-like, alabaster Anne Hathaway – they are further estranged from the ideal by being subject in a number of films to injury and disfigurement. Thus in *Winter's Bone*, Ree, Lawrence's character, is badly beaten and speaks through broken teeth, a swollen, bloodied cheek and matted hair, with any glamour that might still be attached to the star stripped away by the film's muted colour palette and low-key lighting. Reference should also be made in this context to Lawrence's performances as Mystique in the *X-Men* series, where her character is yellow-eyed and exists under a carapace of stippled blue paint. 'Mutant – and proud', as Mystique declares in *X-Men: First Class* – a remark quoted above in Chapter 5's study of the superhero genre, but which is suggestive here as an expression of Lawrence's own deviations from stereotypical Hollywood femininity.

We should be careful, nevertheless, not to overstate the extent to which Lawrence recalibrates Hollywood's gender norms. At times, it is true, resilience and assertiveness in her persona amount almost to a stance of female self-determination. One of Ree's neighbours in *Winter's Bone* asks her, 'Ain't you got no man can do this?', astonished that Lawrence's character is not only raising two younger siblings in arduous circumstances but searching for her father through the dangerous backwoods of Missouri. Elsewhere in Lawrence's film work, too, as in the *Hunger Games* series or *House at the End of the Street* (2012), fathers, or other embodiments of masculine authority, are intriguingly absent. However, there are limitations upon the toughness she portrays. If in the first *Hunger Games* film her character survives largely by individual strength and initiative, in the second she succeeds as part of a network of collaborators; similarly, Ree in *Winter's Bone* has to be rescued from the community's violence by the male Teardrop, while Tiffany in *Silver Linings Playbook* migrates from an edgy isolation into first a dance couple and then a romantic relationship with Pat. Just as Marilyn Monroe, in Dyer's reading cited above, mediates between conventional and liberated models of female sexuality in postwar America, so Lawrence might be said to bridge a series of oppositions in order to generate a version of femininity apt for a post-feminist epoch. Thus her persona is self-willed without being narcissistic, assertive without being offputtingly abrasive, action-oriented without being unsettlingly masculinised; she projects an image that is robust yet caring, driven yet warm, forceful yet vulnerable. So, for example, despite feats of physical and mental hardiness, she also cries in a number of screen performances, including in *Winter's Bone* and *The Hunger Games: Catching Fire* (2013). Or she combines self-preserving actions with instances of sisterly or quasi-maternal solicitude, as when Katniss tries to protect the young African American girl Rue in *The Hunger Games*. This navigation of opposites can be discerned, too, in Lawrence's off-screen activity, where, for example, attention to her individual career is synthesised with involvement in national and global charities that include Feeding America, The Thirst Project and the World Food Programme ('Jennifer Lawrence Charity Work, Events and Causes', 2014: n.p.). Some glossing is needed, then, with regard to Lawrence's comment that 'I'm not very feminine anyway', made when explaining that the influences on her portrayal of Katniss Everdeen were mainly male rather than female (Weisz, 2014: 33). For, as the evidence above suggests, the image that Lawrence has developed in her career certainly extends to attributes of caring, emotion, even at times submissiveness, that are conventionally coded as feminine.

The elasticity of Lawrence's star persona is such that it is readable in different ways by various constituencies of fans. Young female spectators, particularly hooked by the *Hunger Games* franchise, see in her a model of empowerment. Typical of this heightened form of 'cinematic identificatory fantasy', to utilise Stacey's term from above, is the posting of one contributor to Lawrence's official Facebook page on 18 October 2014: 'hey Jennifer Lawrence I am a 14 year old girl and you are my inspiration you gave me hope to stand up for what girls believe in and not to underestimate a girl!!!' ('Jennifer Lawrence Actor/Director', 2014: n.p.). It is this particular cluster of fans, presumably, that serves as the principal market for T-shirts with such inspirational slogans as 'Jennifer Lawrence is My Spirit Animal' and 'In Jennifer We Trust'. However, other T-shirts on offer – including one that defines its wearer's relationship status not as 'Single' or 'Taken', but as 'Mentally Dating Jennifer Lawrence' – are aimed primarily at heterosexual male spectators. Thus while Lawrence undoubtedly galvanises a significant female fan base, this does not restrict a wider circulation of her star image.

Unusually in a period when stars are liable to provoke not only intense allegiances but visceral dislikes (a hatred that has been curiously neglected by film studies), Lawrence's negotiation of contrary qualities comes close to endowing her with universal popularity. Where resistance has been expressed to her stardom by some spectators, the terms of their dissent are revealing. Take, for example, an online post by 'Lindy', in response to advertisements Lawrence has done for Dior: 'This girl can wear how many fancy clothes she wants, but she still will look like a poor waitress smelling [of] hamburgers' ('Jennifer Lawrence Says', 2014: 2). The class hostility of this observation is readily apparent. Lawrence comes not from New England's upper echelons or California's media royalty, but from relatively unprivileged Louisville, Kentucky, where her father's small construction company specialised in concrete work (an attachment to concreteness perhaps passed on to his daughter, similarly suspicious of abstraction and pretension?). Notwithstanding occasional ascents of the class hierarchy during her screen performances (as when playing an heiress to timber holdings in *Serena*), Lawrence has fashioned a star image in which elements of everyday, democratic Middle-Americanness are important. It is unsurprising, then, given its suggestiveness as a model of her own career trajectory, that in *Joy* (2015) she plays an American woman of modest means who achieves great commercial success by turning ordinary products such as clothes hangers and a mop into highly desirable items.

While these ideological and cultural dimensions of Lawrence's stardom should not be neglected, it may be noted by way of conclusion that her naturalness and authenticity also operate as highly successful brands in contemporary Hollywood. The effect of her star presence in boosting the profitability of the films she makes is not to be underestimated. *The Hunger Games*, for example, made at a cost of $78 million, earned $408 million at the US box office alone ('*The Hunger Games*', 2014: n.p.); its first sequel was almost as lucrative, while Lawrence's continuing involvement was indispensable to production of the further, two-part follow-up, *The Hunger Games: Mockingjay* (2014, 2015). Unsurprisingly, Lawrence has also proved very attractive to advertisers wishing to endow their products with her connotations of the real. A thorough analysis of her star image will extend beyond film performance itself into such off-screen appearances as the series of Dior ads which she began making in 2013. If the Dior handbag she holds in these images is a niche product available only to elite consumers, it is here humanised, or stripped of some of its ostentation, by alliance with Lawrence. Contrarily, while her association in the ads with this luxury item discloses her own current class status, it nevertheless does so without harming the popular mandate she has been given by spectators. The power of Lawrence's image, at present, is such as to be able to withstand easily any small fluctuations or minor crises.

Selected reading

Dyer, Richard, *Stars* (1998), 2nd ed., with supplementary chapter by Paul McDonald (London: BFI).
    The foundational text of modern star studies (first published in 1979): still highly valuable, despite subsequent challenges to its combination of semiotics, cultural studies and ideology critique.

Dyer, Richard (2004), *Heavenly Bodies: Film Stars and Society*, 2nd ed. (London: Routledge).

Practical companion to Dyer's *Stars*, testing its insights in extended studies of Judy Garland, Marilyn Monroe and the mid-century African American film, theatre and musical star Paul Robeson.

Gledhill, Christine (ed.) (1991), *Stardom: Industry of Desire* (London: Routledge).

Pioneering collection, gathering important work on stars by critics including Barry King and John O. Thompson: productive still, though needs supplementing by newer materials.

Leung, Wing-Fai and Andy Willis (eds) (2014), *East Asian Film Stars* (Basingstoke: Palgrave Macmillan).

An excellent, timely contribution towards the geographical reconfiguration of star studies.

McDonald, Paul (2000), *The Star System: Hollywood and the Production of Popular Identities* (London: Wallflower).

Lucid, informed account of the US star system from its beginnings to its mutations in contemporary digital and celebrity cultures: a valuable prequel to McDonald's other book here.

McDonald, Paul (2013), *Hollywood Stardom* (Chichester: Wiley-Blackwell).

Well-researched study of Hollywood's contemporary star system: sharper, however, on the commercial than the symbolic side of what McDonald suggestively calls '*the symbolic commerce of stardom*'.

Meeuf, Russell and Raphael Raphael (eds) (2013), *Transnational Stardom: International Celebrity in Film and Popular Culture* (New York: Palgrave Macmillan).

Collects work on border-crossing stars from John Wayne to Javier Bardem: uneven in its coverage, yet a helpful contribution to the developing study of transnational film star stars.

Pomerance, Murray (ed.) (2012), *Shining in Shadows: Movie Stars of the 2000s* (New Brunswick, NJ: Rutgers University Press).

The most up-to-date contribution to this publisher's engaging, Hollywood-focused 'Star Decades' series.

Shingler, Martin (2012), *Star Studies: A Critical Guide* (London: BFI / Palgrave Macmillan).

Very helpful overview of key areas of star studies; pleasingly international in its coverage.

Stacey, Jackie (1994), *Star Gazing: Hollywood Cinema and Female Spectatorship* (London: Routledge).

Groundbreaking study of British women's responses to female American

stars during the 1940s and 1950s: conceptually rich and challenging –
moving, too, in its recovery of these neglected spectators' voices.

Willis, Andy (ed.) (2004), *Film Stars: Hollywood and Beyond* (Manchester:
Manchester University Press).
Still largely Hollywood-centred – lively pieces on such non-US stars as
Kenneth Branagh and Jackie Chan notwithstanding – but nevertheless a
set of vivid, accessible essays.

Online resources

'On Stardom/Celebrity and Film Acting/Performance', Film Studies
for Free, 2 September 2009, http://filmstudiesforfree.blogspot.
co.uk/2009/09/on-stardomcelebrity-and-film.html.
Eclectic, globally and historically diffuse collection of scholarly articles
on stars.

8

Film and ideology

In an essay on the African American film *Boyz N the Hood* (1991), Robyn Wiegman alludes to a 'now clichéd, polysyllabic referent "genderraceclass"' (1993: 174–5). Wiegman acknowledges that this portmanteau term may be valuably corrective for feminist critics: the reference to 'gender', for example, initiates concern with questions of masculinity besides those of femininity, while the other parts of this coinage serve to correct an earlier feminism's tendency to neglect racial and class differences that fissure female experience. Nevertheless, as Wiegman indicates, there are also problems with this conceptual formation. In the first instance, despite ritual invocations of the term 'genderraceclass', attempts to maintain a productive sense of the intertwining of these three dimensions of our subjectivity may sometimes deteriorate into hierarchical thinking, with one of them pushed forward and given a privileged shaping role. Or, worse still, the agglomerated word might prove unstable, with the result that each of the categories of gender, race and class becomes detached from the others, thereby forfeiting some sense of the complexity of our construction as social subjects. There are still further difficulties when it is appreciated that even such a capacious formulation as 'genderraceclass' is insufficient to express the full range of ideological realms in which we are implicated. At the very least, the critic should also consider sexuality and thus speak, more inelegantly still, of *gendersexualityraceclass*.

This chapter aims to introduce and evaluate a number of approaches to gendersexualityraceclass in film studies. Before turning to these, however, it is important to point out that the categories of gender, sexuality, race and class have already been operational throughout this book. Recall such topics as the framing of the suffering African American's body in *12 Years a Slave* (Chapter 1); the implications for class politics of editing protocols in three films about labour activism (Chapter 2); the gender and racial politics of diegetic and non-diegetic soundtracks in *The Great Gatsby* (Chapter 3); the ideological resonances of open-ended as against closed film narratives (Chapter 4); the ways in which the superhero film has provoked ideological debate, not least arguments that this genre ratifies both patriarchal and neoliberal regimes (Chapter 5); the importance of recognising female authorship of film, even in the face of theoretical scepticism about authorial signatures (Chapter 6); and stars' embodiment of culturally normative – or sometimes socially dissenting – forms of gender, sexual, racial and class identity (Chapter 7). Other areas of film study already discussed are also strongly marked by ideological questions: one example would be classical Hollywood's tendency towards the gendering of its genres, whereby a supposedly male-oriented repertoire of westerns and war movies was positioned against a generic set for women of musicals, romances and melodramas.

Film studies and questions of class

'The history of all hitherto existing societies', according to Marx and Engels at the start of *The Communist Manifesto* (1848), 'is the history of class struggles' (1967: 79). Given that an alternative, classless society has not been enduringly realised since these words were first written, the insight of Marx and Engels and their successors into structural inequalities and antagonisms has continued to motivate the political activism of generations of men and women. In addition, of course, this form of social analysis has oriented intellectual work across a host of disciplines. Yet the presence of class as an analytical category within film studies itself has been tenuous and intermittent. It is relatively rare for students in the field to encounter critical texts that put class nakedly and unabashedly centre-stage: prominent instances of this direct engagement of the topic might extend from Fredric Jameson's essay, 'Class and Allegory in Contemporary Mass Culture: *Dog Day Afternoon* as a Political

Film' (1977) to the chapters entitled 'Classical Hollywood Cinema and Class' and 'Cinematic Class Struggle After the Depression' in Harry M. Benshoff and Sean Griffin's *America on Film: Representing Race, Class, Gender and Sexuality at the Movies* (second edition, 2009). Elsewhere, as we will discuss below, film studies has often marginalised or occluded attention to particular class struggles in favour of more abstract, generalised analyses of the part played by cinema in ideological reproduction. Class has also been effaced at times as, quite properly, film studies has placed greater emphasis on concerns of gender, sexuality and race. Given these conceptual developments, then, it is unsurprising that, at the turn of the twenty-first century, David E. James entitled an essay 'Is There Class in this Text?: The Repression of Class in Film and Cultural Studies' (1999).

Even before it turns to the particularities of movies themselves, however, film studies should have the issue of class at its centre. Questions of where and how we watch films will be considered in detail in Chapter 10; for the moment, we can just note that the class status of film spectatorship has been contentious since the beginnings of this art form. At the level of production, too, unequal access to educational, financial and technological capital powerfully shapes who gets to make films in the first place. Thus even sympathetic portrayals of a disadvantaged class quite often come not from its own representatives but from filmmakers who originate from outside that social fraction (a case in point would be Clio Barnard's formally innovative explorations of life on Bradford's housing estates). This structural imbalance is replicated at a global level. Proletarianised within the world system, many nations in Africa, Asia and Latin America still lack the economic and cultural resources necessary to support significant film industries (or, sometimes, any film industry at all), and so are more liable to be objects than producers of cinematic representation. It remains to be seen to what extent lower-priced, digital filming and editing equipment and access to new, online forms of distribution will help to counteract such inequalities in cinema's domestic and international class systems.

Critics have long been concerned with the part that film may play in reproducing a conservative politics. Even as figures ranging from the Soviet montage theorists to the Franco–Spanish Surrealists welcomed cinema for its radical liberation from the constraints of time and space that characterised older art forms, others suspected it of an underlying social conformity. The mid-European novelist Franz Kafka (1883–1924), for example, declared himself by inclination 'an Eye-man', yet in a striking passage went on to say that in film 'Sight does not master the pictures, it is the pictures which master one's sight. They flood one's consciousness. The cinema involves putting the eye into uniform, where before it was naked' (Janouch, 1971: 160). Several decades later, as part of a systematic critique of popular cultural forms, the German Marxist theorist Theodor Adorno was also drawn to a military and disciplinary metaphor as he sought to evoke film's effects: 'The movements which the film presents are mimetic impulses which, prior to all content and meaning, incite the viewers and listeners to fall into step as if in a parade' (2001: 183). Building upon such arguments, Marxism was a major contributor to the conceptual paradigm that came to dominate film studies by the 1970s. Yet to reread critical work from this period now is not usually to find the explicit engagements with class that might be expected; instead, writers frequently produce a discourse that floats away from the sufferings of specific groups without social power. This abstraction occurred as theorists aimed to develop an ever more elaborate and total account of film's ideological operations.

Critics in this vein associated with the newly radicalised *Cahiers du cinéma* in France and the journal *Screen* in Britain drew much conceptual nourishment from the French structural Marxist Louis Althusser. For Althusser, the reproduction of capitalist normality is achieved not only at the point of a soldier's gun or policeman's baton, but, more subtly, by the work of a wide range of institutions he calls Ideological State Apparatuses (ISAs), such as the church, the media and the arts (including cinema). The dominated subject within a class-structured society thereby misrecognises, *Matrix*-style, his or her actual place in it, and consents imaginatively to the terms of oppression. Althusser's work on ideology leans, in turn, upon the psychoanalytic theory of his French contemporary Jacques Lacan. In particular, Lacan's theory of *the mirror stage* – that moment when an infant derives an illusory sense of wholeness and self-sufficiency by gazing at its reflection in a mirror – was taken up by Althusser as a suggestive way of thinking about the adult subject's ideological formation. The tropes of mirrors, images and gazes which it mobilised made Althusser's ideology theory especially attractive to film studies.

In borrowing and applying these terms and concepts, however, writers on film in the late 1960s and 1970s often also imported higher French theory's tendency towards political pessimism. Thus some of the canonical texts of Marxist film studies from this period present cinema as a machine ideally designed for the reproduction of conservative ideology and, by extension, of a class-divided society. In 'Cinema/Ideology/Criticism', a 1969 editorial for *Cahiers du cinéma*, Jean-Luc Comolli and Jean Narboni admittedly allow for the possibility of filmmaking that disrupts the spectator's usual ideological quietude. Any radicalising effects of this kind, however, occur against the grain of film's predisposition towards conservatism: 'the classic theory of cinema that the camera is an impartial instrument which grasps, or rather is impregnated by, the world in its "concrete reality" is an eminently reactionary one. What the camera in fact registers is the vague, unformulated, untheorised, unthought-out world of the dominant ideology' (Comolli and Narboni, 2004: 815). Still more fatalistic, perhaps, is Jean-Louis Baudry in a much-anthologised essay, 'Ideological Effects of the Basic Cinematographic Apparatus' (1970). According to Baudry, the specific properties of different films – 'the forms of narrative adopted, the "contents" of the image' (2004: 364) – should be set aside as having little analytical significance. Rather, film's ideological function is fulfilled by the optics of the cinematic situation itself: the spectating subject represses awareness of the machinery of image capture and projection that has delivered this experience to him or her and thus remains in a quiescent condition whereby the world on screen appears as natural, intelligible and unified. A misleading coherence and inevitability is bestowed by the spectator upon 'the discontinuous fragments of phenomena' (364) experienced during film viewing.

Baudry's argument that film carries the virus of conservative ideology in the optical regimes of projection and spectatorship puts major obstacles in the way of devising and delivering a politically oppositional cinema. Only in those instances where 'the

instrumentation itself [ceases to] be hidden or repressed' (364) –
that is to say, where spectators are cued to recognise the technological artifice that enables the film experience – does Baudry see
any progressive possibilities. Though his essay is in the service of a
militantly intended criticism, it often has an unworldly quality. To
a lesser extent, the same is true of the Comolli/Narboni article and
other writings from this significant wave of Marxist film theory.
Along with a worrying inattention to significant differences in situations of film spectatorship, there is a danger that such studies are
hasty in setting to one side the contents of highly divergent film
texts so as to articulate instead a unitary, abstract account of cinema
as a conservative ideological practice.

It is not quite the case that anti-cinematic critique of such scope
has disappeared from Marxist film scholarship since this highpoint
of the 1970s. Jonathan Beller's *The Cinematic Mode of Production*
(2006) represents an especially bold, provocative addition in recent
times to this lineage, articulating a Marxist suspicion of cinema not
only with regard to earlier film history but in the context of our
current, postmodern moment. There are echoes – intensifications,
even – of Kafka's and Adorno's military and disciplinary metaphors
when Beller writes of cinema's status as 'something like a command-
central of consciousness': 'Its penetration of the human organism is
increasingly total and totalitarian' (2006: 250). Beller's complex,
detailed analysis of how remorselessly the imperatives of capitalism's unjust system reach into the manufacture and consumption of
the film image takes on, at times, a Gothic quality – as in a remark
that this way of considering cinema 'radically alters the question of
visual pleasure by contaminating it with the question of murder' (8).
While working at a high level of abstraction, however, Beller does
not neglect the specificities of film texts themselves. Movies such as
the Coen brothers' *Barton Fink* (1991), the Oliver Stone-directed
Natural Born Killers (1994) and the Jodie Foster vehicle *Contact*
(1997) are all valued for disclosing the outlines of the prison in
which we live – even if they cannot yet show the way out.

Contemporary Marxist work in film studies tends to take more
modest forms than Beller's systemic critique of cinema. Debates
take place, for example, over the adequacy or otherwise of narrative film for expression of a radical class politics. While some leftist

filmmakers from the early Soviet era onwards have been suspicious of the mainstream's pleasures of story and image because of their allegedly pacifying effects, directors as different as Ken Loach in Britain and the late Ousmane Sembène in Senegal have continued to address class injustices through the resources of narrative. Beyond this concern with politically engaged cinema, however, a class-oriented approach can find suggestive things to say about aspects of representation in almost any film. What are the ideological implications of how the contemporary English working class is portrayed in Andrea Arnold's *Fish Tank* (2009), say, or how princes of American neoliberal finance are represented in such films as *Margin Call* (2011) and *The Wolf of Wall Street*? In close textual study, as throughout work in the discipline, class should remain a fundamental analytical term for film studies, rather than one to be regarded as hopelessly obsolete or inappropriate. Looking ahead to the remainder of this chapter, however, it is crucial now for film studies to explore the multiple articulations of class with other ideological registers. As Chuck Kleinhans puts it: 'Today Marxism seems most dynamic when it combines its analysis of class with an analysis of gender, race, national, postcolonial, and other issues raised by progressive social–political movements' (1998: 111). The thinking here chimes with Beller's own, since in *The Cinematic Mode of Production* he includes himself in a constituency of 'antiracist feminist Marxists' (2006: 291).

STOP and THINK

- Compared with categories of gender, sexuality and race, the concept of class might appear antiquated or superseded, as rusted in the West as the factories in which it was once openly articulated. To what extent would you resist this proposition? Is sensitivity to class politics an important element of your worldview and, more specifically, of your film criticism?

- Explore how cinema has framed a particular class and its relations with other social fractions. You might, for example, assess a selection of film representations of the English working class produced during the past three decades that extends from Terence Davies's *Distant Voices, Still Lives* (1988) to recent work directed by Clio Barnard, and that includes such titles as *Raining Stones* (1993), *Brassed Off* (1996), *The Full Monty*, *Billy Elliot* (2000), *Vera Drake*, *Four Lions* (2010), *Tyrannosaur* (2011) and two films by Shane Meadows: *Dead Man's Shoes* and *This Is England* (2006).

• These films differ markedly in genre (from broad comedy to drama, even melodrama) and in form (from social – indeed socialist – realism to playful experiment and openly advertised artifice). Consider, in these and other cases, the relationship between films' formal and stylistic regimes on the one hand and their ideological positions, specifically their class politics, on the other.

A very short history of gender in film studies

The beginnings of feminist film studies

Questions of *masculinity* have long been important to film spectators: simply recall, from Chapter 7, the hysteria of fans in 1926 following the death of male screen icon Rudolph Valentino. In academic film studies, however, gender-oriented criticism initially concerned itself instead with issues raised by the cinematic representation of women. Writers early in the 1970s extended to film 'second-wave' feminism's keen investigation of patriarchal bias and female stereotyping, with a number of US-based feminists aiming to do for this medium what Kate Millett had done for literature in her vital book *Sexual Politics* (1970). This *images of women* approach, as it came to be known to differentiate it from later strands of feminist film criticism, was inaugurated in 1973 with the publication of Marjorie Rosen's *Popcorn Venus: Women, Movies, and the American Dream*; a year later came Joan Mellen's *Women and Their Sexuality in the New Film* and, most influentially, Molly Haskell's *From Reverence to Rape: The Treatment of Women in the Movies*. Haskell organises her book by decades in film history, but the underlying trajectory is, dispiritingly, from an oppressive decorousness in Hollywood's early representation of women to blatant rape fantasy in films such as Sam Peckinpah's *Straw Dogs* (1971). A chapter on post-1974 US cinema, incorporated in the book's second edition in 1987, speaks of an 'Age of Ambivalence', which suggests modest improvement in Hollywood's sexual politics but not enough to prompt Haskell to retitle her study.

For all their trailblazing importance, this trio of books has an awkward, even embarrassing place in feminist film studies. They have frequently been criticised for demonstrating a naive under-standing both of social reality and of the operations of films them-selves in responding to that reality. The representatives of the images of women 'school' tend to show little awareness that the social world we inhabit is always in the process of being *constructed* by multiple, competing interests; instead, their assumption is 'that a pre-existing referent exists fully formed, simply waiting to be represented' (Buckland, 2012: 118). Similarly, Haskell, Mellen and Rosen frequently neglect to consider the complex *work* done upon these social materials by the films they discuss: rather than being endowed with what Warren Buckland terms 'its own materiality, its own signifying power' (2012: 119), each film is treated in less dynamic fashion as a depository of pre-existing images or reflec-tions of women, variously to be judged 'positive-correct-accurate' or – more likely – 'negative-incorrect-inaccurate' (Buckland, 2012: 117). A lack of engagement with psychoanalysis also means that, compared with other feminist criticism, the account given in these three books of female film spectatorship lacks richness and nuance.

Nevertheless, to read this strand of feminist film studies now is to recover a sense of its invigorating qualities. Conceptually under-developed though it may be, the tradition of image-critique which it initiated is not yet exhausted but continues to shape the work of women, as well as members of subordinated classes and racial, ethnic and sexual minorities, who deplore existing representations of themselves and demand more 'positive' ones. Haskell, Mellen and Rosen also write with a polemical urgency that is not always apparent in more thoroughly academicised feminist film studies. While it is crucial not to succumb to facile anti-intellectualism here, it can also be said that this sort of campaigning prose is crucial to the success of any political struggle. A book like *From Reverence to Rape* has the rhetorical power to raise its readers to anger and, potentially, activism. Here, for example, is Haskell's withering dismissal of the

supposedly 'great women's roles' of Anglo-American cinema in the
1960s and early 1970s: 'Whores, quasi-whores, jilted mistresses,
emotional cripples, drunks. Daffy ingenues, Lolitas, kooks, sex-
starved spinsters, psychotics. Icebergs, zombies, and ballbreakers.
That's what little girls of the sixties and seventies are made of'
(1987: 327–8).

Theories of the spectatrix

In 1989, a special issue of the radical film journal *Camera Obscura*
appeared under the title of 'The Spectatrix'. This new verbal coinage indicates how feminist film critics, going beyond the primary
interest that Haskell, Mellen and Rosen had taken in on-screen
images of women, came increasingly to regard the female spectator's situation as a locus of both theoretical inquiry and political
intervention. The most influential text in this alternative wave of
feminist film studies is Laura Mulvey's essay 'Visual Pleasure and
Narrative Cinema', first published in *Screen* in 1975, collected in
book form by Mulvey in 1989 and long a staple of anthologies of
film theory.

Mulvey develops a deeply pessimistic, even morbid account
of the female spectator's position as it is engineered by narrative
cinema. She considers the interlocking in mainstream film of three
kinds of 'look': the characters' looks at each other in the diegesis
(narrative), the camera's look at the characters and, finally, the spectator's look at the screen. Although she allows that these variously
situated gazes may co-exist in a state of 'shifting tension' (1989: 19),
she tends not to dwell upon such instabilities but goes on instead
to argue that, for male subjects at least, the three looks are liable
to be continuous with one another and mutually reinforcing. Thus
a male character in the diegesis prompts a camera movement or
editing transition by gazing towards a female; the resulting image
of her is then, in an uninterrupted visual relay, gazed upon by the
male spectator. Mainstream cinema is, according to Mulvey, constituted by a depressingly binary logic whereby 'pleasure in looking has been split between active/male and passive/female' (19).
Offering the male spectator what seems to be a reassuring image
of his own potency, the male character embodies action and asserts
mastery of the gaze (see Figure 26 for an instance where this is made

26 The male gaze at its most lethal: looking at women through the lens of the misogynistic photographer/killer in *Peeping Tom* (1960), directed by Michael Powell

murderous); by contrast, the on-screen woman can only connote '*to-be-looked-at-ness*' (19). Unlike her male counterpart, then, the woman spectator is left in an invidious position, with her most obvious choice being masochistic identification with a passive female object of desire.

The success of those able to assert *the male gaze*, whether they are situated on-screen or seated in front of it, actually represents a recovery from potential crisis. For while the male subject is indeed, in Mulvey's argument, the source of the gaze, she suggests at points in the essay that what he looks upon has the potential to induce panic rather than pleasure. Specifically, in psychoanalytic terms, the anxiety he faces is that of castration: the female body – so central to the visual repertoire of mainstream cinema – affords an ominous 'image of the bleeding wound' (Mulvey, 1989: 14). Faced by the need to avert such devastation of patriarchal authority, mainstream film turns, according to Mulvey, to two strategies: *voyeurism* and *fetishistic scopophilia*. The first of these operations involves a frequently sadistic treatment of the on-screen woman that is expressed by her narrative trajectory as well as her visual representation, and may gratify male characters and spectators alike. Scopophilia, on the other hand, refers to morbid sexual excitation by looking, and the specifically fetishistic variant identified by Mulvey is apparent when parts of the woman's body or props associated with her become abstracted as objects of psychic investment (here we return to Angelina Jolie's lips, mentioned in Chapter 7 in the context of male spectators' responses to female stars).

A number of critics have argued that Mulvey overstates the power of visual and narrative devices of these kinds to assuage castration anxiety. Male character and spectator alike may subsist in a condition more lastingly precarious than Mulvey's theory of mainstream cinema's patriarchal force is usually willing to acknowledge. Only occasionally does the essay allow that some narrative films, at least, may function to *undermine* voyeurism and fetishistic scopophilia, rather than uncritically reproducing them. Mulvey mentions in this context Hitchcock's *Rear Window*, *Vertigo* and *Marnie*, all of them readable as explorations of the perils besides the pleasures of the male gaze. Such instances of narrative cinema's capacity for auto-critique, however, are insufficient to redeem the institution in Mulvey's eyes. The section of her 1989 book in which 'Visual Pleasure and Narrative Cinema' was collected is called 'Iconoclasm', and she speaks frankly there about wanting to smash mainstream film because of the depth and reach of its patriarchal logic. Synchronically, then, with her earliest theoretical writing, she made a series of films with Peter Wollen – *Penthesilea* (1974), *Riddles of the Sphinx* (1977) and *Amy!* (1979) – that aimed to 'jam' normal cinematic looking and to render customary narrative immersion impossible, thereby making a space for the elaboration instead of a feminist consciousness. These works employed the strategies of avant-garde or experimental cinema, and were exhibited outside commercial circuits. Other feminist filmmakers produced similar interrogatory work, showing it in venues where the film texts themselves were frequently supplemented by printed materials, lectures and talks, and consciousness-raising discussions among spectators.

Yet feminist *counter-cinema* of the 1970s was problematical as a political option. By virtue of its suspicion of the mainstream's pleasures, it risked striking an austere, even puritanical note, and was often in danger of speaking a filmic language comprehensible only to elite fractions of cineastes rather than to the mass female audience that was its intended constituency. Thus a good deal of the feminist film criticism that comes after Mulvey's 'Visual Pleasure' essay is concerned more with mainstream films, attempting to find here the production of an empowered or, at least, a less drastically compromised female spectatorship. Mulvey's own later writing ventures at least some way in this direction. In 'Afterthoughts on "Visual Pleasure and Narrative Cinema" Inspired by King Vidor's *Duel in the Sun* (1946)', for instance, she utilises another part of Freudian theory to suggest that it may be possible after all for women viewers to identify non-traumatically with active male protagonists in film. As they do so, they return imaginatively to a 'phallic' phase of sexuality, a primal location open to both male and female subjects but, Freud argues, abandoned by the latter in their passage to conventional feminine identity. Nevertheless, again expressing her sense of the limitations of mainstream cinema, Mulvey goes on to argue that phallic identification of this kind can only be fleeting for the female spectator: 'for women (from childhood onwards) trans-sex identification is a *habit* that very easily becomes *second nature*. However, this Nature does not sit easily and shifts restlessly in its borrowed transvestite clothes' (1989: 33).

Where transvestism offers Mulvey a resource for conceptualising female spectatorship, *masquerade* fulfils this function for Mary Ann Doane. In 'Film and the Masquerade – Theorising the Female Spectator', an important essay first published in *Screen* in 1982, Doane utilises feminist work on *the performed quality*, rather than biological rootedness, of femininity. To think of this gender performance in terms specifically of masquerade is charged with liberating potential: 'The masquerade, in flaunting femininity, holds it at a distance. Womanliness is a mask which can be worn or removed' (1991: 25). In appropriating this model for film studies, Doane argues that the female spectator may only be masquerading as conventionally feminine, rather than occupying this gender position uncritically and irrevocably, when she identifies with the passive womanliness displayed on screen. However, in a later piece, 'Masquerade Reconsidered: Further Thoughts on the Female Spectator', Doane sounds more cautious about the political effectiveness of performing such blatant femininity. Intended as a strategy enabling women to survive oppressive patriarchal definitions of them, masquerade may only be, as Doane writes, 'an anxiety-ridden compensatory gesture' (1991: 38). Like transvestism for Mulvey, masquerade for Doane certainly affords female spectators a little more room for manoeuvre. Both conceptions, however, function only to enlarge the perimeters of a cage or prison; feminist psychoanalytic study of cinema tends, for all its diagnostic power, to leave intact a sense of patriarchal rule.

Problems of psychoanalytic feminism

While psychoanalytic feminism is far from exhausted as an intellectual tradition in film studies, it has been subjected to scrutiny from several perspectives. Cognitive theorists, seen earlier in this book privileging audiences' conscious responses over unconscious ones with regard to the processing of both film music and film narrative, have been active too in challenging feminist psychoanalytic models of the spectatrix. Here a representative contribution is Flo Leibowitz's essay, 'Apt Feelings, or Why "Women's Films" Aren't Trivial', included in the major counter-psychoanalytic anthology *Post-Theory* (1996). Leibowitz shares some common ground with psychoanalytic feminists in assuming the importance of that body of female-centred melodramas produced in Hollywood either side of World War II. However, her discussion of why these films matter to audiences bypasses processes of concern to psychoanalysis, such as masochism, and stresses instead the ethical interest of their portrayals of female suffering and self-sacrifice. For Leibowitz, strong audience identification with these women is achieved *consciously* rather than unconsciously; it also runs across sexual divisions, with this response available to males watching as well as to females:

> there is a limit to the degree these films are gendered. Both men and women can feel sad when rotten things happen to nice people, which is what happens in these films, and in that respect the term 'women's film' is a misnomer. Certainly the point of view of a film is in the film. But [Leibowitz's essay has] assumed that gender isn't an intrinsic part of point of view, and that the gendering of imaginative pleasures is not intrinsic to imagination. (1996: 227)

Although Leibowitz signals an affinity with feminist concerns by taking as her topic such a women-oriented genre, she deviates from feminism itself in propositions such as this one. However, film theorists identifying themselves explicitly as feminist have also sought to redirect critical attention from unconscious to conscious aspects of spectatorship. The African American feminist bell hooks made a vital intervention in this area with her essay 'The Oppositional Gaze: Black Female Spectators' (first published in 1992 and anthologised frequently since). Here hooks argues that the most influential analyses of the spectatrix are deeply flawed, replicating the racial blind spots of mainstream cinema itself: 'Feminist film theory rooted in an ahistorical psychoanalytic framework that privileges sexual difference actively suppresses recognition of race, reenacting and mirroring the erasure of black womanhood that occurs in films' (2009: 264). Interweaving high-theoretical discourse with reports of her own and her community's cinemagoing, hooks suggests that, in viewing mainstream films, black female spectators may develop an 'oppositional gaze' with respect to the screen that withholds *all* types of identification (whether sadistic or masochistic, cross-dressing or masquerading). Crucially, however, the work they do as film viewers is not simply negative and antagonistic. In hooks's summary, black women's spectatorship of this oppositional kind also involves a reconstructive dimension, imaginatively preparing different scripts of race and gender from those fashioned for them: 'We do more than resist. We create alternative texts that are not solely reactions. As critical spectators, black women participate in a broad range of looking relations, contest, resist, revision, interrogate, and invent on multiple levels' (2009: 271).

Something like an extended test of the viability of hooks's thesis was conducted by Jacqueline Bobo in *Black Women as Cultural Readers* (1995). Bobo considers in detail here responses by both academic critics and ordinary spectators to Spielberg's *The Color Purple* (1985). Like many other critics, Bobo registers her serious reservations about this film, notably for its transformation of the militant racial, gender and sexual agendas of Alice Walker's source-text into occasions for uplifting sentiment. However, while groups of African American women with whom Bobo discusses the film at length are certainly not oblivious to its political lacunae, it is striking that they nevertheless respond to it warmly, finding it instructive and empowering with regard to their own negotiations of black femininity (see Figure 27). There is evidence here for the reconstitutive

27 The question of black female spectators: *The Color Purple* (1985).
African American women viewers have testified to feeling empowered by
the film

element of hooks's oppositional gaze, reading across or through
a film to uncover progressive possibilities. The case of *The Color
Purple*, as Bobo writes, 'allows analysts to understand that audiences are not always the unthinking receivers of media messages
but have the ability to manipulate their reactions in very distinctive
ways' (1995: 97). Again, then, we witness a swerve in feminist film
studies away from a prioritising of the unconscious and towards a
concern with women's conscious, revisionary spectatorship. Bobo
is also committed in her work to *ethnographic* methods, challenging
the model of a unitary viewing position constructed by a film text
by doing fieldwork with particular female viewers. Such intellectual
practice is, of course, not restricted to African American scholars but has proved productive elsewhere in feminist film studies.
Recall from Chapter 7 Jackie Stacey's ethnographic recovery of the
responses of older English women to Hollywood's female stars of
mid-century.

Recent decades in film studies, then, have seen a pluralisation of
feminist methodologies in contrast to the predominantly psychoanalytic moment of the 1970s and 1980s. While psychoanalysis remains
an important resource, it is now more likely to be co-ordinated
with approaches including ethnographic ones, as sketched above;

similarly, that earlier concern to theorise the feminine viewing position that is generated by mainstream cinema has, quite substantially, given way to research into specific female spectatorships, with heightened attention to their fragmentation by differences of race, sexuality and class. However, none of these references to the emergence of projects and priorities other than those favoured by Mulvey's generation of militant theorists of the male gaze should be taken as signs that a specifically feminist film studies is now superfluous, even outmoded. The term *post-feminist* is as mischievous, even dangerous, applied to film studies as when it is used with regard to Western society at large. As Karen Hollinger writes, 'feminist film studies is not only still alive and well, but has, in fact, become much more heterogeneous, dynamic, and open in its scope' (2012: 19). The critical study from which these words come exemplifies this expanded subject range by pursuing feminist concerns into such areas as cinematic adaptations of novels.

Masculinities in film

Serious study of cinema's staging of masculinity is not a recent innovation. As pioneering in this field as she was in work on film's representation of women, Joan Mellen published *Big Bad Wolves: Masculinity in American Cinema* in 1977, evaluating in particular men's images in westerns and cop films. A number of conceptually more advanced articles and books followed, including Steve Neale's attempt to carry across elements of Mulvey's psychoanalytic approach in his essay 'Masculinity as Spectacle: Reflections on Men and Mainstream Cinema' (published by *Screen* in 1983). And the sense of a nascent, promising field of inquiry was evident by the time Steven Cohan and Ina Rae Hark co-edited *Screening the Male: Exploring Masculinities in Hollywood Cinema* in 1993. Subsequently, however, and particularly in the last decade, there has been an explosion of interest in the figure that John Beynon calls 'cinematic man' (2002: 64). If masculinity itself is arguably now in crisis in the West, *masculinity studies*, by way of compensation, is in vigorous health. Faced by profound changes in patterns of labour and domesticity, and by the entrenchment of feminist gains, contemporary American masculinity struggles to renew itself; this sense of exhaustion, however, is not shared by scholarship on contemporary

US masculinity on screen, which is currently in a phase of virile productivity, the last few years alone seeing the publication of such books as *Contemporary Hollywood Masculinities: Gender, Genre, and Politics* (2011), *Millennial Masculinity: Men in Contemporary American Cinema* (2012), *Masculinity and Film Performance: Male Angst in Contemporary American Cinema* (2013) and *Contemporary Masculinities in Fiction, Film and Television* (2015). And lest discussion of screen masculinities be perceived as replicating the Hollywoodcentrism that weakens genre studies and star studies, this line of inquiry has lately been globalised: witness the geographical range covered by titles such as *Masculinities in Contemporary Argentine Popular Cinema* (2012), *Men and Masculinities in Irish Cinema* (2013), *Stars and Masculinities in Contemporary Italian Cinema* (2014) and *Masculinity in the Golden Age of Swedish Cinema* (2014).

The plural noun in the titles of many of these books is significant. Whereas earlier critics tended to regard masculinity as an enduringly stable category – 'monolithic' and 'unperturbed', in Cohan's and Hark's words (1993: 3) – contemporary writers foreground instead a sense of its multiplicity and plasticity. Current gender theorists, notably Judith Butler, have decoupled masculinity and femininity from male and female biology respectively, reimagining them as cultural productions. If womanliness is a masquerade, as we saw above, so too is 'manliness'. Masculinity is from this perspective *dramaturgical*, its status akin to that of a theatrical performance that, at least in theory, might be enacted by females as well as males. Other metaphors are also available to capture this sense of the contingent and inessential in our gender identities: Murray Pomerance, for example, speaks of gender as 'sartorial', suggesting that masculinity, like femininity, is a set of clothes to be put on and taken off at will (2001: 307).

Productive as these figures of theatricality and costume are, they risk ignoring *inequalities* among the rival constructions of masculinity that will co-exist in any society. Beynon is alert to such hierarchisation, referring to the struggle in particular social conjunctures between 'hegemonic masculinity' and 'subordinate variants' (2002: 16). Screen masculinities themselves, as was discussed in Chapter 7, often contribute to the reproduction and glamorisation of culturally dominant models of how to look and act like a man. In other moments, of course, cinematic masculinity may work to undo this hegemonic form and to propose alternatives. At the time of his death in 1926, Rudolph Valentino was hugely popular with audiences, yet viewed by some sections of US opinion as suspiciously exotic and androgynous, threatening the well-being of traditional American masculinity. By contrast, a closer fit existed in mid-century between the popular screen masculinity of John Wayne and the gender norms of US society at large. The hypermasculinity of Schwarzenegger, Stallone and other muscular screen icons of the 1980s has, as considered above, a politically ambiguous status. If it aimed to restore the potency of a blue-collar American masculinity that had declined from 'hegemonic' to 'subordinate' in the face of such developments as the Vietnam War, the waning of manufacturing industry and the rise of a 'feminised' consumerism, the very strenuousness or excess of its efforts proved destabilising, with its fetishistic displays of the male body oddly mimicking the iconography of gay porn.

As the current popularity of stars such as Vin Diesel and Dwayne Johnson indicates, the hypermasculine has certainly not disappeared from US cinema. The superhero movie, assessed in Chapter 5, also functions as an arena for spectacular hypermasculine display. Care is needed here, however, since, in franchises such as the Batman and Iron Man films, the 'hard bodies' on screen are not self-fashioned by the heroes but donated to them by engineers and armourers: inside Barman's Kevlar suit or Iron Man's gleaming carapace is a more fragile representative of the masculine, prone to both physical trauma and psychological instability. Even in superhero films, then, as well as more broadly in contemporary US cinema, the hypermasculine has to compete with masculinities that scale back physical force and offer emotional expressiveness instead. Increasingly, qualities of sensitivity, nurturing, even vulnerability that are conventionally coded in the West as feminine may float away from women themselves and be appropriated by men on screen as part of an expanded male repertoire. Of course the opposite might also occur, with the cultural stock of masculinity open to female adoption (an appropriation represented in American cinema by figures extending from Sigourney Weaver's Ripley and Linda Hamilton's Sarah Connor, say, to Jolie's

Lara Croft and Chloe Grace Moretz's Hit-Girl). The politics of this latter development requires careful evaluation. For while Mulvey concedes that, through the figure of the strong, 'phallic' woman, 'the power of masculinity can be used as postponement against the power of patriarchy' (1989: 37), she goes on to suggest that this is a problematical option, one simply putting a female face on aggressive masculinity rather than doing away with it altogether.

If one task for this area of film studies is thus to assess the flow of screen masculinities across sexual dividing lines, another is to invest more heavily in surveys of masculinity in diverse national cinemas. The geographical range of some book titles cited above suggests that things have improved markedly since the beginning of the century when Beynon was able to write, quite reasonably, that 'There is a problem in looking at masculinity in other places because most of the literature about masculinity is about British and American men by British and American men and women' (2002: 62). Much more work remains to be done, however. What, for example, are the hegemonic and subordinate forms of masculinity in Iranian cinema? In Nigerian, or Brazilian, or Polish, or Australian cinemas? And how are such national masculinities reshaped by contact with Hollywood, or by the border-crossings that characterise cinema in the era of globalisation?

STOP and THINK

- Assess the strength of the claim by Mulvey and other feminists that the gaze of mainstream cinema is gendered masculine and functions in the interests of patriarchy. Do films you have watched bear out this thesis of the wielding of scopic power by male characters and male spectators alike, or do they complicate, or even contest, the notion of patriarchal rule over the visual?
- To what extent do *males* on screen suffer – or solicit – the fate of 'to-be-looked-at-ness' which Mulvey reserves for females? Where, and with what consequences?
- Consider the range of your identifications with characters in narrative film. Does identification tend to respect sexual divides, so that female spectators identify principally with

on-screen females, and male with male? Or is this too rigid as a model to capture our engagement with protagonists in film? Are there at least some instances in which lines of sexual difference are breached, so that, in temporarily cross-dressing fashion, male spectator becomes aligned with female character, and female with male? And with what consequences? Assess whether fluid identifications of this sort are liable to occur more frequently in some genres than in others.

Queering film studies

Interest in lesbian, gay, bisexual and transgender (LGBT) representation in film is currently supported by an institutional apparatus of academic books and journal articles, university courses and conferences, and dedicated film festivals. The earliest work that appeared on these subjects, however, was piecemeal and individualistic, even frankly idiosyncratic. A significant precursor volume is Parker Tyler's *Screening the Sexes: Homosexuality in the Movies* (1972). Tyler was an innovative poet and novelist, besides wide-ranging film critic; his interests in non-Anglophone and American avant-garde cinemas ensured that this book devoted considerable space to Andy Warhol's underground films, for instance, or the Italian director Federico Fellini's arthouse work. Allied to a vivid prose style, Tyler's eclectic set of examples generated fandom rather than a broad constituency of readers. More publicly visible, then, as an overview of homosexual cinematic representation was Vito Russo's book, *The Celluloid Closet: Homosexuality in the Movies*, published first in 1981, revised in 1987 and also adapted as a documentary for the screen in 1995. Like the early feminist film study of Haskell, Mellen and Rosen, Russo's study tends towards *image-critique*. In exhaustive detail, he documents largely coded film representations of homosexuality and interprets them, on the whole, as reflecting homophobic structures in society at large.

The Celluloid Closet performed valuable work in restoring a gay and lesbian dimension to classical Hollywood. From 1930 to 1968, US cinema was subject to the dictates of the Motion Picture Production Code (colloquially, 'the Hays Code'). The representation of certain activities, including adultery and murder, was drastically curtailed; other behaviours – including miscegenation and profanity – were excised from the screen entirely. But although the Code comprises a veritable lexicon of conservative America's phobias, it nowhere utters the word 'homosexuality'; instead, this is implied by vague formulations such as 'sex sins' and 'impure love' ('The Motion Picture Production Code of 1930 (Hays Code)', 2006: n.p.). Even as the Code exiled the homosexual from American screens, however, the fierceness with which it did so hinted at anxiety, a fear that policing action of this sort might not be fully successful. And, indeed, Russo uncovers much evidence of homosexuality in classical Hollywood's output – not openly avowed, to be sure, but readable nevertheless in narrative enigmas, or modes of actor performance, or selections in costume and hairstyle. The activity of decrypting in *The Celluloid Closet* tends not to be affirmative, though, but instead uncovers on the screen the signs of a virulently prejudicial society.

Despite important legal and cultural victories in recent decades for the LGBT community, Russo-style critique of its negative stereotyping by mainstream cinema has not disappeared. In 2013, for instance, the twenty-fifth anniversary of *School Daze* (1988) prompted an LGBT activist to enter into dispute on Twitter with the film's director, Spike Lee, regarding its alleged homophobia (Savali, 2013, n.p.). Other writers, however, influenced by *queer theory* (more on this intellectual formation below), have distanced themselves to an extent from Russo's form of film criticism. Rather than finding on screen uniformly degrading homosexual stereotypes, they activate a different sort of spectatorship that opens up spaces for queer pleasures. In doing so, they indicate that the sexual orientations of the gaze may be much more fluid and diverse than a model such as Mulvey's permits. Particular stars have proved to be important sites of erotic investment by non-straight audiences and critics. One notable example here is Rock Hudson, whose outing as gay following his death from AIDS in 1985 prompted spectators to revisit and, indeed, to rewrite a body of screen performances that had once seemed irredeemably heterosexist (not least the series of sex comedies he made alongside Doris Day in the late 1950s and early 1960s). Similarly, knowledge of the actor Montgomery Clift's troubled sexual identity complicates his status as a male pin-up of the postwar period and ensures that his work on screen generates, from a queer perspective, lively critical interrogations and subversive audience fantasies.

Queer readings of films are eclectic in their choices of primary material. Understandably attracted to the genre of the melodrama for its uncontainable excesses (Hudson performed in melodramas, too, during the 1950s), they also take an interest in categories such as the western, the war film and the action movie. These genres are heterosexually framed – even homophobic – and yet, suggestively, constituted by dramas of men together. It is, of course, important to pause before routinely eroticising all same-sex bonds on the screen; here, awareness of the concept of the *homosocial* is crucial. The queer theorist Eve Kosofsky Sedgwick identifies homosociality in any social location where same-sex relationships are endowed with the highest emotional and symbolic value. Far from being eroticised, instances such as these may present themselves as militantly and programmatically anti-homosexual (in a movie context, consider the anxiety in many war films that a particular soldier's alleged or perceived homosexuality will damage platoon morale and efficiency). In a striking move, however, Sedgwick also undermines the stability as a binary opposition of 'homosocial/homosexual', evoking instead 'the potential unbrokenness of a continuum between homosocial and homosexual – a continuum whose visibility, for men, in our society, is radically disrupted' (1985: 1–2). This insight can be carried across from the literary contexts that principally concern Sedgwick and mobilised in our analysis of male friendships in individual films – even entire genres – that flaunt a no-nonsense heterosexuality. And, though Sedgwick suggests that divisions between erotic relationship and homosocial bond are anyway more permeable for women, the conceptual framework she develops may also be applied productively to female buddy films. For instance, a lively debate has taken place over whether it is legitimate to construe the relationship between Thelma and Louise in Ridley Scott's 1991 film as characterised by lesbian desire, or if that would be inappropriately to eroticise a form of sisterliness.

Writers now on questions of LGBT representation in film are not restricted to activities of decoding or reading against the grain. Instead, they may engage in assessment of recent work where

members of sexual minorities appear openly: prominent examples from Hollywood itself would include *Philadelphia* (1993),
Milk (2008) and *A Single Man* (2009). Later, this chapter's case
study is *Blue Is the Warmest Colour* (2013), a successful French film
recounting a passionate lesbian relationship. Other critics in this
field are concerned with evaluating the achievements and legacies
of 'New Queer Cinema', a wave of filmmaking roughly dated to
the mid-1980s onwards and including the work of US and British
directors such as Todd Haynes, Derek Jarman, Isaac Julien, Jennie
Livingston, Rose Troche and Gus Van Sant. This body of films
is characterised by great formal variety, extending from camp to
intellectual self-consciousness or from narrative obliquity to melodramatic excess. Given this diversity in form, it is unsurprising
that, while sharing a concern with LGBT representation, the 'New
Queer Cinema' is politically heterogeneous also. The name given
to this loose cinematic grouping, however, suggests its correlation
with queer theory, a form of radical thinking which over the same
period has reconfigured many artistic and intellectual enterprises.
Queer theorists actually resist as fixed and limiting that definition
of 'gay' as the opposite of 'straight' that underpinned a previous
homosexual identity politics; instead, they argue that *all* sexual
identities are multiple, mutable, always in process. Thus a much
greater range of sexual orientations, positionalities and behaviours
than previously might now be construed as queer:

> Queer was not only meant to acknowledge that there are many differ-
> ent ways to be gay or lesbian, but also to encompass and define other
> sexually defined minorities for whom the labels 'homosexual' and/
> or 'heterosexual' are less than adequate: bisexuals, cross-dressers,
> transgendered people, interracial couples whether homosexual or het-
> erosexual, disabled sexualities, sadomasochistic sexualities whether
> homosexual or heterosexual, etc. Even heterosexuals can be queer
> – the so-called *straight queer* – because queer as a theoretical concept
> encompasses all human sexual practices while rejecting the opposing
> binary hierarchies of sexuality and gender that currently govern our
> understanding of them. (Benshoff and Griffin, 2009: 339)

Queer theory has had liberating effects on both the criticism
and the practice of cinema. Filmmaking itself under its influence
is polymorphously perverse, conjuring up a plurality of sexual

and gender identities far in excess of the permutations traditionally authorised by straight society. Employing the instruments of
queer theory, critics have also done valuable work in rewriting in
terms of transgressive erotics seemingly conservative films from
classical Hollywood and elsewhere. Nevertheless, queer theory also
incurs certain costs, both political and intellectual. Given our particular remit, we can set to one side the broader social question of
what happens to gays and lesbians themselves, and their specific
causes, in view of the dizzying expansion of categories of queer-
ness apparent from Benshoff's and Griffin's catalogue. From the
narrower perspective of film studies, however, there is the issue
of to what extent models of queer cinema and queer cinema criticism recently influential in the West can, or should, be exported
to non-Western situations. Certainly, the hallucinatory, charged
scenario of *Tropical Malady* (2004), a film by the gay Thai director
Apichatpong Weerasethakul, lends itself to interpretation in these
terms. In some other Asian societies, however, or in parts of Africa,
to attempt a queer reading of an old national classic or to put on
screen erotic experiences other than those of normative heterosexuality is liable to have punitive consequences.

STOP and THINK

- Setting to one side for the moment the expansive properties of the term 'queer', explore what it is that constitutes a
  gay or lesbian film. If the criterion of subject matter seems
  most important, then the canon would include representations of same-sex erotic experience by directors of heterosexual orientation themselves: Robert Aldrich's *The Killing
  of Sister George* (1968), or John Sayles's *Lianna* (1983), or
  Stephen Frears's *Prick Up Your Ears* (1987). Or, of course,
  Ang Lee's *Brokeback Mountain*. Some of these works, not
  least Aldrich's, tend to circulate phobic rather than affirmative visions of homosexuality. An alternative principle of
  selection, then, would determine that gay and lesbian film
  is produced only by filmmakers self-identifying as gay and
  lesbian. This raises a number of questions, however. Firstly,
  is it necessarily the case that movies on these themes by

gay and lesbian filmmakers will be more progressive or militant in their sexual politics? To argue this would be problematical, naively deriving a fixed ideological commitment from the mere fact of someone's socio-cultural positioning. Second, what should we do with particular films by gay and lesbian filmmakers that are not conspicuously organised by LGBT themes: Van Sant's remake of *Psycho* (1998), say, or his *Promised Land* (2012)? Is a distinctively gay or lesbian authorship still decipherable in the formal and narrative design of these films (recalling Chapter 5's point about significant emphases or fractures in films directed by women)?

• Taking a number of films in which same-sex relationships are paramount without being conspicuously eroticised, evaluate Sedgwick's thesis that there is a continuum, rather than a clear division, between the homosocial and the homosexual. Together with war films and westerns, many action franchises organised around supportive male duos suggest themselves for analysis here. What *is* the sexuality of 'the buddy movie'? And how useful, analytically speaking, is the term *bromance*?

Race and ethnicity in film studies

In 'How to Play Indians', a brief but subversive text, Umberto Eco writes that one way by which Native Americans can alleviate the 'dire' social conditions they face is to enter the film industry as actors and extras. Here is part of his catalogue of actions they will need to perform in order to succeed as 'movie Indians':

Attacking the Stagecoach

4. In any attack on a stagecoach, always follow the vehicle at a short distance or, better still, ride alongside it, to facilitate your being shot.

5. Restrain your mustangs, notoriously faster than coach horses, so you won't outstrip the vehicle.

6. Try to stop the coach single-handed, flinging yourself on the harness, so you can be whipped by the driver and then run over by the vehicle.

7. Never block the coach's advance in a large body. The driver would stop at once. (Eco, 1995: 218)

Wittily, Eco demonstrates how Native Americans have been traduced and diminished through their representation in decades of Hollywood movies. Instead of being permitted to manifest the strategic calculation and tactical nous apparent from the historical record, they have traditionally been confined on screen to idiocies such as those listed here.

'How to Play Indians' stands as a relatively small-scale contribution to the work of image-critique that, as with coverage of gender and sexuality, dominated initial responses by critics and activists to race and ethnicity in film and continues to be important. Screen caricaturing of Native Americans has been a cause of angry protest at least since an upsurge of indigenous people's activism in the US during the 1960s. Contemporaneously, forceful critiques began to emerge of cinematic stereotypes of African Americans. Here a significant early contribution was made by Donald Bogle in *Toms, Coons, Mulattoes, Mammies, and Bucks: An Interpretive History of Blacks in American Films*, a book cited in the previous chapter that was first published in 1973 and entered its fifth edition in 2015. Bogle's thesis is that mainstream US cinema has restricted African Americans on screen to a demeaning repertoire of five character-types: the compliant *Tom*, the buffoonish *Coon*, the tragic *Mulatto/a*, the smothering, sentimental *Mammy* and the violent, predatory *Buck*. Besides enabling him to memorialise the depressingly stunted careers of earlier generations of black actors, Bogle's typology has potential applications to recent and contemporary African American screen representation. To look at the middle phase of Eddie Murphy's career, say, is to experience anxiety that an actor who was so invigorating and edgy in early films such as *48 Hrs.* (1982) was in danger of rehabilitating the figure of the Coon in roles including the Nutty Professor (1996, 2000). Similar points could perhaps be made about parts played by Martin Lawrence. And even if they prove unwieldy in certain cases, Bogle's categories are still very helpfully utilised early in a film's interpretation. Take *The Butler* (2013), for instance, which, from its title onwards, threatens to resurrect the compliant Tom. Ultimately, however, the

film's central figure is not confined to that position, removed from
it both by the affective richness of Forrest Whitaker's performance
and by a narrative that shows his deepening engagement with black
political struggle.

This form of analysis of African American and Native American
stereotypes in film has been adapted for use by many other racial
and ethnic communities across the world. Consider, for example,
Italian American exasperation at the persistence of the gangster in
screen portrayals of this ethnic grouping, or contemporary Arab
American and Arab vigilance against Hollywood's representation of
the cruel terrorist, or Scottish objections that Disney Pixar's *Brave*
(2012) trades in outdated national types, deriving many of its characters from 'Celtic Cliché Central Casting' (McMillan, 2012: n.p.).
Kazakh officialdom, too, entered into the mode of image-critique in
objecting to what it took to be ethnic stereotyping by Sacha Baron
Cohen in *Borat: Cultural Learnings of America for Make Benefit
Glorious Nation of Kazakhstan* (2006).

Like the practice of registering and resisting gender and sexual
stereotypes, this critique of images of race and ethnicity has served
valuable purposes. Not the least of its achievements has been to put
race and ethnicity themselves firmly on the agenda of film studies, countering their earlier neglect by dominant paradigms such as
1960s auteurism and 1970s psychoanalysis. Robert Stam acknowledges, too, the legitimacy of demands by disadvantaged racial and
ethnic communities that, in the interests of 'representational parity',
they be given more 'positive' film versions of themselves (2000:
275). Simply recall from earlier in this chapter the exhilaration
felt by black female spectators at encountering in *The Color Purple*
what they perceived as inspirational African American women –
neither Mammy nor Mulatta, to use Bogle's terms. However, Stam
also uncovers the conceptual and political deficiencies of racial
and ethnic 'image studies'. In the first instance, to appeal for more
'positive' representations of a particular community tends to assume
that that community is monolithic, fully formed rather than always
in process, and that it can be straightforwardly expressed and epitomised by characters on screen. Furthermore, as Stam argues, an
image-studies approach may be quickly appeased by provision on
screen of 'positive' figures from a given racial or ethnic grouping,

and thus fail to go on to interrogate 'larger configurations of power' in film's narrative and stylistic regimes (2000: 276). None of this, it should be stressed, is to declare obsolete a concern with stereotypes. If it is to be effective, however, such analysis must become, as Isaac Julien and Kobena Mercer put it, 'conjunctural' or 'context-oriented', seeking above all 'to explain how and why certain ethnic stereotypes are at times recirculated' (2002: 361).

Racially and ethnically sensitive approaches to film, however, are not confined to the negativity of image-critique. Books, journals, festivals, DVD/Blu-ray series and other resources have been devoted to identifying and consolidating traditions of filmmaking by racial and ethnic minorities. Symptomatic here might be attempts to construct canons of Black British and British Asian films, or to identify a lineage of African American-authored films to set against Hollywood's 'plantation aesthetic'. Work such as *Smoke Signals* – written, produced and directed by Native Americans – prompts optimistic thoughts of a whole range of counter-cinemas originated and managed by minority populations. But while it is important to continue campaigning for an extension of filmmaking opportunities across racial and ethnic lines, this should not be regarded as a guarantor in itself of more radical material on screen. To claim that progressive images of a given community are inevitable if only they could be produced by a filmmaker sharing its skin pigmentation or its socio-cultural location is to succumb to *essentialist* thinking (in Chapter 6, similarly, we saw that it is important not to conflate female and feminist film authorship). This line of argument, in fact, has worrying affinities with racism itself, homogenising the minority population under discussion and ignoring how it is fissured by differences of class, gender, sexuality and so on.

The debate occasioned by Spike Lee's 1992 biopic of Malcolm X serves to illustrate that racial identity in itself does not predetermine a particular stance on questions of racial politics. After this film had been provisionally allocated to the liberal white director Norman Jewison, Lee fought hard to take it over, arguing that only an African American filmmaker could do justice to such a key figure in black history. While the film he eventually delivered is well regarded for its dissemination of Malcolm's life and thought to a contemporary mass audience, bell hooks, a figure of interest to us already in this chapter, states baldly that 'there is no visual standpoint or direction in *Malcolm X* that would indicate that a white director could not have made this film' (2006: 183). Her critique of conservative, domesticating elements in the film's treatment of its radical subject is well judged. Less compelling, however, is hooks's own essentialist implication that blackness and whiteness in the US each come equipped with a singular, unalterable viewpoint. Recent scholarship on race has demonstrated persuasively that there is no clear correlation of this sort between epidermal colouring and ideological position.

There is another strand in contemporary critical thinking about race that is proving highly suggestive for film studies: namely, an intensified concern with the category of *whiteness*. Often regarded in the past as a non-race or a neutral non-racial point in relation to which the racial identities of others reveal themselves, white is now to be conceptualised as a racial category also. As Richard Dyer writes at the start of *White* (1997), the founding text of *whiteness studies*, 'race is not only attributable to people who are not white, nor is imagery of non-white people the only racial imagery' (1997: 1). As with the emergence of masculinity studies, discussed above, suspicions might be voiced that this new intellectual field opens up precisely at a time when its subject enters into social crisis (thereby, perhaps, representing an attempt to maintain symbolic privilege even in the face of material losses). Excitingly, however, whiteness studies has prompted reinvestigation of many cultural phenomena, including key elements of film stylistics. While Dyer also engages in his book with painting and photography, his primary formation as a film scholar ensures that topics he chooses to discuss are of interest to us here. He uncovers, for instance, a hierarchical racial politics in the very framing and lighting of actors' faces on screen (not least in the aesthetic regime of classical Hollywood). There is, he writes, a 'practice of taking the white face as the norm, with deleterious consequences for non-white performers' (1997: 98). The white actor's face takes on as a result a heightened luminescence that, if only subliminally, prompts the spectator to endow him or her with a heightened moral status relative to performers of other races, given the greater shadowing of *their* features. In another chapter, Dyer considers displays of the muscular white male body in the *peplum*, an Italian genre which he glosses as 'adventure films centred on heroes drawn from classical (including Biblical) antiquity' (165). Audience attention is drawn in these instances to muscularity not in isolation but in conjunction with whiteness, the latter again brought out by filmmakers' choices of lighting and actor positioning. Analysis of this kind, co-ordinating aesthetic observation with political interrogation, has been carried on in Dyer's wake by other scholars of whiteness in film. There is, then, increased onus on us in our thinking about any film's racial politics to be sensitive to white and its meanings.

STOP and THINK

- In the study of race and ethnicity in film, critique of stereotypes has a long, pugnacious history. Assess whether it is still needed by considering recent cinematic images of a particular race or ethnic community. You might consider, for example, how the Japanese are represented in a series of Hollywood films of the twenty-first century, including *Pearl Harbor* (2001), *Kill Bill: Vol. 1*, *Lost in Translation* (2003), *The Last Samurai* (2003), *Memoirs of a Geisha*, *The Fast and the Furious: Tokyo Drift* (2006), *Emperor* (2012) and *47 Ronin* (2013). Do these works reproduce or dismantle Hollywood's earlier, 'Orientalist' repertoire of images of the Japanese (fanatical, sadistic killers; inscrutable masters of samurai wisdom; women of mysterious, exotic allure)? Even if they dislodge these stereotypes, do the films generate a new set of clichéd portrayals of the Japanese instead?

- Earlier in this chapter, we saw how psychoanalysis has complicated the sexual politics of film spectatorship, opening up the possibility of cross-gendered identification between viewer and character. By analogy, to what extent is *cross-racial* or *cross-ethnic* identification achieved in our filmwatching? If such mobility across racial and ethnic lines does occur, are its effects inevitably – and durably – positive? Or are the consequences limited? Is it possible that migration of this kind happens only in the regulated time and place of film spectatorship, with no discernible impact upon our thinking and practice in the world beyond the screen?

- 'Racism often travels in gangs, accompanied by its buddies sexism, classism, and homophobia' (Shohat and Stam, 2014: 22). Test this proposition with regard to a number of films.

Case study: *Blue Is the Warmest Colour* (2013)

Very near the start of *Blue Is the Warmest Colour*, a scene takes place in a literature class at a French high school. Adèle, played by Adèle Exarchopoulos, listens as one of her classmates reads aloud some words from their set text: *La Vie de Marianne*, an eighteenth-century novel by Pierre de Marivaux. 'I am a woman', the passage reads: 'I tell my story'. Placed so early in the action, this quotation serves to disclose the project of the film itself, for here too is a woman's story – or, more accurately perhaps, *two women's stories*, since central to Adèle's own narrative is Emma (Léa Seydoux), an older art student with whom she has a passionate sexual relationship (Figure 28). Discussion of the politics of *Blue Is the Warmest Colour* might begin with this moment in the classroom and consider who, exactly, is telling the film's story of intimate female experience. Just as Marianne in the novel the class is reading is ventriloquised by a male writer, so the two female protagonists within the film seem, on the face of it, to be male-authored: the director here is the Franco-Tunisian Abdellatif Kechiche. Judgements about authorship become more complex, however, when we note first of all that both Kechiche's

28 Representing lesbianism: Léa Seydoux and Adèle Exarchopoulos in *Blue Is the Warmest Colour* (2013)

co-screenwriter and the creator of the graphic novel on which the film is based are women. Moreover, when *Blue Is the Warmest Colour* won the prestigious Palme d'Or at the Cannes Film Festival in 2013, the jury awarded the prize not only to Kechiche but to Seydoux and Exarchopoulos, thereby ascribing to the actresses co-authorial responsibilities (in the process, dealing another blow to auteurist models of film creation).

Several controversies generated by this film, however, centre upon the director as if he were indeed wielding an auteur's power. A number of technicians complained that Kechiche created a 'bullying' atmosphere on set, besides violating the French Labour Code by insisting on overlong working days (Schmidlin, 2013: n.p.). Whatever the truth of these allegations, the episode valuably reminds us that political questions may be raised by conditions in filmmaking, rather than being restricted to content on screen. In a separate complaint, Seydoux and Exarchopoulos identified themselves as victims of the director's patriarchal as well as class dominance. According to their testimony, Kechiche 'ranted and raved at them as he sought to achieve optimum realism' during shooting not only of the couple's sexual encounters but of the harrowing scene of their break-up (Child, 2013a: n.p.). Sexism, if the actresses' account is credible, persisted in the film's mode of production even as it was frequently challenged on screen itself.

While these concerns about class and gender relations in the making of *Blue Is the Warmest Colour* should not be trivialised, they will be set aside in the remainder of this section so as to explore the ideology of the film's narrative and spectacle. How, for example, should we evaluate politically the several scenes of lesbian sexual activity? These are frank to a degree unusual in movies of wide commercial release. Linda Williams describes them as '*relatively* explicit' and as belonging to a category she calls 'hardcore eroticism' in order to differentiate it from pornography on one side and R-rated Hollywood cinema on the other (2014: 15). Nevertheless, the film's lesbian sequences have not escaped charges by some commentators that they mimic the look of pornography. The female critic Manohla Dargis, in a review for *The New York Times*, writes of the prevalence in these scenes of 'tasteful, decorous poses', a 'prettified, aestheticized' quality that runs counter to the film's realist aesthetic elsewhere (2013: n.p.). Julie Maroh, author of the graphic novel on which Kechiche based the film, is more outspoken still in her critique, describing the sequences as 'a brutal and surgical display, exuberant and cold, of so-called lesbian sex, which turned into porn' (Child, 2013b: n.p.).

Leaving to one side some incoherence in Maroh's terms ('surgical' and 'exuberant', for example, are ill-matched companions), it is suggestive that she goes on to object to these scenes for their implicit appeal to heterosexual male spectators – or, as she says, 'guys […] busy feasting their eyes on an incarnation of their fantasies on screen' (Child, 2013b: n.p.). Maroh is, in effect, drawing here upon the Mulveyan theory of the male gaze, proposing that even as the film's narrative inscribes female agency its spectacle diminishes women and restricts them to conveying 'to-be-looked-at-ness'. Despite her status as originator of the source-text, however, Maroh's voice is not the only one that should be heard in this debate. Linda Williams worries that responses to these scenes indicate that some female viewers 'have become pleasure-phobic in the wake of feminism' (2014: 12) and effectively are asking for the erasure of women from erotic sequences on screen in case these result, among other things, in the gratification of a heterosexual male audience. Yet sexual episodes in *Blue Is the Warmest Colour* may generate unpredictable and diverse pleasures, including, despite Maroh's doubts, the enjoyment of lesbian spectators. In addition, it should be acknowledged that Kechiche's mise-en-scène and editing tend to impede rather than simply to reward voyeurism. The women's bodies are often shown cropped or awkwardly framed or in low-key lighting, countering that sense of decorous display to which Dargis objects; in other shots, they are tangled together, so that body parts can no longer be securely attached to recognisable individuals. This is certainly not to say, however, that feminist concerns of the sort valuably brought into film studies by Mulvey and others should be suspended with regard to the framing of women here. One sequence is especially troubling, as the camera travels slowly over the naked Adèle's body while she poses as Emma's artistic model. If initially the shot appears to be subjectively motivated, this argument is rendered unsustainable both by the difference between Emma's positioning and that of the camera, and by the disparity between the single, comprehensive gaze of the portrait artist on the one hand and the camera's creeping, tantalising disclosure of Adèle's body on the other.

Like the film's visual aesthetic, its narrative design is traversed by both progressive and reactionary currents. While lesbianism often figures in mainstream pornography as brief and titillating digression from an otherwise implacably heterosexual script, here it acquires normative status. Adèle's first sexual experience in the film is masturbatory, but mediated by fantasies of Emma rather than of any heterosexual partner; the unsatisfactory encounter with a male classmate that follows is thus bracketed and diminished in importance by scenes of lesbian commitment. Similarly, when, distracted by loneliness, Adèle sleeps with a male colleague near the end of her relationship with Emma, these scenes are neither shown nor endowed with any emotional significance. Nevertheless, any account of the film's sexual imagination also has to reckon with the fact that lesbianism registers as a potentially tragic destiny. After the fateful break-up – an episode, by the way, in which Emma descends into sexist language, calling her lover a 'whore' and a 'slut' – Adèle is portrayed as emotionally emptied, barely sustained by her growing professional identity as a nursery school teacher. Even two scenes of cleansing by water, first at the beach and then under the shower, fail to revive her fully. And the closing scenes of *Blue Is the Warmest Colour* evoke Adèle's solitariness, rather than any prospect of sociable existence. Visiting Emma's latest art show, she wanders around for a time quite aimlessly, while desultory murmurs are heard on the diegetic soundtrack; the film's final sequence shows Adèle outside the gallery, walking first towards the camera and then away from it into a future that threatens to be marked by a sense of irreparable loss. 'With you, it's all or nothing', Emma said to her during the happy period in their relationship; here, at the end, given Adèle's solitary, receding figure, it appears to be nothing.

An ideologically sensitive reading of *Blue Is the Warmest Colour* should also attend to the entanglements of gender and sexuality on the one side with concerns of race and class on the other. The film is marked by a relaxed multiculturalism, with both Adèle and Emma interacting sociably with figures from minority ethnic backgrounds

(Adèle's supportive male classmate, for instance, or fellow demon-strators on the leftist protest marches in which both women take part). Note also how the sense of a racially and ethnically pluralist France is communicated stylistically by occasional incorporation of steel drums on the soundtrack. However, if race does not figure in the film as a source of social tension, this is not true of class: ultimately, in fact, it is class disparities that destroy the relationship between Adèle and Emma. Kechiche is highly sensitive to inequalities in the economic and cultural capital that the two women command. Thus a dinner party at which Emma's parents serve oysters and speak of art is followed, almost in schematic fashion, by one at Adèle's house that features a homely spaghetti bolognaise and conversation laced with lower-middle-class economic realism. While Adèle's friends gossip about boyfriends, those of the older Emma include a suave gallery owner and a PhD student working on the early-twentieth-century Viennese painter Egon Schiele. A class hierarchy structures the lovers' relationship itself: Adèle, besides operating during a party as an overworked cook and scullery maid, is also rendered socially subservient by sitting often as Emma's model and thus serving as an object of representation rather than as someone endowed with representational privileges herself. One response to these disparities would be to suggest that Kechiche succumbs here to a tendency in mainstream film representation of lesbians: Karen Hollinger refers to a long-running imperative 'to make the lesbian relationship con-form to heterosexual romantic norms by accentuating differences between the lovers rather than sameness' (2012: 141). Yet while such reasoning is conceivably applicable to *Blue Is the Warmest Colour*, an alternative argument would return to this chapter's starting point in the interweaving of multiple ideological registers. The viewer of this film is prompted to recognise that sexuality is not discrete from other political sites, such as class, but is complexly connected to them.

Selected reading

General

Benshoff, Harry M. and Sean Griffin (2009), *America on Film: Representing Race, Class, Gender, and Sexuality at the Movies*, 2nd ed. (Chichester: Wiley-Blackwell).

Despite the exclusive US focus, a very productive way into this chapter's concerns: wide-ranging, clear, attractively organised, and including many case studies.

Codell, Julie F. (ed.) (2007), *Genre, Gender, Race, and World Cinema: An Anthology* (Malden, MA: Blackwell).

Ample collection of gender- and race-oriented studies, discussing films ranging in provenance from Hollywood to Iran and Hong Kong.

hooks, bell (2009), *Reel to Real: Race, Sex and Class at the Movies* (New York: Routledge).

Invigorating responses by this major African American feminist writer to a wide range of films and film issues, including Tarantino's *Pulp Fiction* and Spike Lee's work; contains, too, the key essay, 'The Oppositional Gaze: Black Female Spectators'.

Class

Beller, Jonathan (2006), *The Cinematic Mode of Production: Attention Economy and the Society of the Spectacle* (Hanover, NH: Dartmouth College Press).

Remarkable contribution to Marxist film aesthetics, attempting to track the inequalities of national and global class systems into the cinematic image itself: demanding, provocative, highly rewarding.

Dave, Paul (2006), *Visions of England: Class and Culture in Contemporary Cinema* (Oxford: Berg).

Bold, stimulating attempt to restore class to centre-stage in film studies.

James, David E. and Rick Berg (eds) (1996), *The Hidden Foundation: Cinema and the Question of Class* (Minneapolis: University of Minnesota Press).

Should be supplemented by newer materials listed here, but an historically important volume, featuring essays on class in US, Soviet and Chinese cinemas; includes, too, an earlier version of James's essay, 'Is There Class in this Text?'

Leigh, Mary K. and Kevin K. Durand (eds) (2013), *Marxism and the Movies: Critical Essays on Class Struggle in the Cinema* (Jefferson, NC: McFarland).

Very timely collection: begins with studies of Fritz Lang's *Metropolis* (1927), from Weimar Germany, but otherwise pursues questions of class across US film from Chaplin's *Modern Times* (1936) to James Cameron's *Avatar* (2009).

Gender studies

Clover, Carol J. (1992), *Men, Women and Chainsaws: Gender in the Modern Horror Film* (London: BFI).

Perhaps the best-titled book in film studies: a sophisticated, stimulating study of the psychodynamics of our spectatorship of the slasher and rape revenge sub-genres.

Grant, Barry Keith (2011), *Shadows of Doubt: Negotiations of Masculinity in American Genre Films* (Detroit: Wayne State University Press).

An excellent companion volume to Shary below, given its concern largely with masculinities in earlier Hollywood cinema.

Hollinger, Karen (2012), *Feminist Film Studies* (Abingdon: Routledge).

Warmly recommended for its lucidity, judiciousness and commitment: helpfully tests with regard to particular films a series of models from feminist film studies.

Kaplan, E. Ann (ed.) (2000), *Feminism and Film* (Oxford: Oxford University Press).

Very generous, well-contextualised sampling of feminist theoretical and critical writings on cinema, dating from the early 1970s to the end of the twentieth century.

Mulvey, Laura (1989), *Visual and Other Pleasures* (Basingstoke: Macmillan).

Includes not only 'Visual Pleasure and Narrative Cinema', but revisions of the argument in such other pieces as 'Afterthoughts on "Visual Pleasure and Narrative Cinema" Inspired by King Vidor's *Duel in the Sun* (1946)' and 'Notes on Sirk and Melodrama'.

Radner, Hilary (2011), *Neo-Feminist Cinema: Girly Films, Chick Flicks, and Consumer Culture* (New York: Routledge).

Interrogatory readings of a series of US films oriented around young metropolitan women, beginning with *Pretty Woman* and concluding with *Sex and the City: The Movie* (2008).

Shary, Timothy (ed.) (2013), *Millennial Masculinity: Men in Contemporary American Cinema* (Detroit: Wayne State University Press).

Lively, wide-ranging essays on popular US cinema's stagings of masculinity in the past two decades.

Thornham, Sue and Niall Richardson (eds) (2013), *Film and Gender*, 4 vols (Abingdon: Routledge).

Colossal research resource, suited only to a library's budget: offers encyclopaedic coverage of gender concerns discussed more succinctly in other studies listed here.

Queer studies

Besides the general titles listed below, see also the lively individual studies published in Arsenal Pulp Press's 'Queer Film Classics' series.

Benshoff, Harry M. and Sean Griffin (eds) (2004), *Queer Cinema: The Film Reader* (London: Routledge).

Very useful collection of essays, demonstrating the impact of queer approaches upon such key domains of film studies as authorship, genre and spectatorship.

Benshoff, Harry M. and Sean Griffin (2006), *Queer Images: A History of Gay and Lesbian Film in America* (Lanham, MD: Rowman and Littlefield).

Needs supplementing by international materials, but thorough and insightful with regard to queer cinema in the United States.

Doty, Alexander (2000), *Flaming Classics: Queering the Canon* (London: Routledge).

Striking reinterpretations from a queer perspective of six films: *The Cabinet of Dr. Caligari* (1920) from Germany; *The Red Shoes* (1948) from Britain; and *The Wizard of Oz*, *The Women* (1939), *Gentlemen Prefer Blondes* (1953) and *Psycho* from the US.

Mennel, Barbara (2012), *Queer Cinema: Schoolgirls, Vampires, and Gay Cowboys* (London: Wallflower).

Helpful, economical introduction to the queer tradition in cinema, ranging historically from Weimar Germany to *Brokeback Mountain*.

Rich, B. Ruby (2013), *New Queer Cinema: The Director's Cut* (Durham, NC: Duke University Press).

Valuable collection of essays and reviews by the critic who coined the term 'New Queer Cinema' in 1992.

Race and ethnicity

Bloodsworth-Lugo, Mary K. and Dan Flory (eds) (2013), *Race, Philosophy, and Film* (New York: Routledge).

Wide-ranging collection, exploring questions of ethics, knowledge and politics raised by the framing of race in films that include *Avatar*, *The Help* (2011) and *Monster's Ball* (2001).

Bobo, Jacqueline (1995), *Black Women as Cultural Readers* (New York: Columbia University Press).

Fascinating example of ethnographic reception studies: as well as chapters on *The Color Purple* discussed above, explores audience evaluation of the experimental African American feminist film *Daughters of the Dust* (1991).

Dyer, Richard (1997), *White* (London: Routledge).

Foundational contribution to whiteness studies; extends to other
aesthetic fields, such as painting and photography, but packed with
insights into the privileging of whiteness across film's registers – from
narrative organisation to the lighting of actors' faces.

Izzo, David Garrett (ed.) (2014), *Movies in the Age of Obama: The Era
of Post-Racial and Neo-Racist Cinema* (Lanham, MD: Rowman and
Littlefield).

Contributors assess the politics of race in a range of films produced since
Barack Obama's first election success in 2008, including *The Butler*, *The
Great Gatsby*, *The Help* and *The Hunger Games*.

Shohat, Ella and Robert Stam (2014), *Unthinking Eurocentrism:
Multiculturalism and the Media*, 2nd ed. (Abingdon: Routledge).

Updated edition of a book indispensable for its analytical finesse, polemical urgency and global sensibility; it tracks racist and imperial tropes
across films of very wide provenance, and assesses the chances for an
anti-racist cinema.

Sim, Gerald (2014), *The Subject of Film and Race: Retheorizing Politics,
Ideology, and Cinema* (London: Bloomsbury).

Includes case studies, but especially useful for reflecting more generally
on what might comprise a 'critical race film studies'.

Vera, Hernán and Andrew M. Gordon (2003), *Screen Saviors: Hollywood
Fictions of Whiteness* (Lanham, MD: Rowman and Littlefield).

Attempts to bring to visibility Hollywood's construction of whiteness,
through case studies of many films from *Gone with the Wind* to *The
Matrix*: suggestive and accessible.

Online resources

Geena Davis Institute on Gender in Media, http://seejane.org/.

Website of an organisation founded by Hollywood actress Geena Davis
in 2007 that aims to document, interrogate and correct gender imbal-
ances and stereotypes in film and television.

JUMP CUT: A Review of Contemporary Media, www.ejumpcut.org/home.
html.

Indispensable, densely packed online journal, founded in 1974 to explore
questions of class, race and gender in cinema (and TV and video).

'The Movies, Race and Ethnicity', www.lib.berkeley.edu/MRC/
EthnicImagesVid.html.

Maintained by the University of California, Berkeley, this website provides a very helpful bibliography and filmography pertaining to film
representations of many races and ethnicities.

9

Film industries

Where should film studies direct its focus or place its emphasis? Historically, the discipline has devoted its greatest energy to analysis of the particularities of film texts themselves. More recently, however, some scholars in the field have sought to distance themselves from this critical practice, with the co-authors of *Global Hollywood 2* even characterising it as 'textual reductionism' (Miller et al., 2005: 43). A text more likely to cite the *F.T.* than *E.T.*, this book on the export drive of contemporary Hollywood argues that, while attention to films' formal specificities should not be relinquished, it must be co-ordinated with 'an account of *occasionality* that details the conditions under which a text is made, circulated, received, interpreted and criticised' (Miller et al., 2005: 41–2). In previous chapters, we have already reflected this new, expansionist enterprise in film studies: recall, for example, Chapter 3's interest not only in a film's composed soundtrack but in ambient noise during its reception in various sites, or Chapter 5's discussion of how 'generic communities' try to endow their definitions of film categories with cultural power. This chapter and the next, however, offer more sustained, systematic *extra-textual* analysis. Chapter 10 gravitates towards the last three items on Miller et al.'s agenda for a reconfigured film studies: namely, the geographically and historically dispersed activities of 'receiving', 'interpreting' and 'criticising' that take place during film consumption. In this chapter, by contrast, we explore the production and distribution of films, their 'making' and 'circulating'. An overview of Hollywood, cinema's hegemonic site of production, is followed first by discussion of two major non-Anglophone cinemas, then by assessment of changes that have occurred in film production and distribution in the context of an increasingly globalised media economy.

Film studies will be seen in this chapter to be edging closer to *business studies*. It should be clarified at the outset, however, that showing an enhanced interest in diagrams of studio ownership or graphs of film exports does not mean the abandonment of detailed work on films themselves. 'Text' remains as integral to discussion as 'context'. There can, anyway, be no clear separation of these levels or dimensions of analysis: product placement in a film – holding a little too long a shot of the protagonist's car or watch or laptop – is only a particularly visible instance of the enfolding of commercial imperatives into textual composition itself.

Hollywood

For Mitsuhiro Yoshimoto, film studies in its current phase stands condemned as 'a distinctly mono-cultural discipline in which Hollywood cinema dominates more than ever' (2006: 257). While globalisation is making increasingly possible 'a polycentric imagining of the world, where no single centre monopolises the production and circulation of audio-visual images' (257), Yoshimoto argues that such dispersal or decentring is not reflected in film studies itself. Instead, the discipline is prone to a 'false universalism' (260), applying unduly to multiple cinemas around the world the commentary it generates on the single case of Hollywood. Thus to begin a discussion of film industries with Hollywood, rather than with a different example from globally scattered production, would seem to further the already advanced Americanisation of film studies. However, there are compelling reasons for still electing to start in this way. The first of these acknowledges, quite ominously, the unmatched global penetration of Hollywood cinema: while no claim is made here for its aesthetic richness or thematic complexity relative, say, to Taiwanese or Argentine film, its superior economic and cultural power should be registered. More encouragingly, however, Hollywood will emerge in this chapter as a richer, less parochial object of inquiry than Yoshimoto allows. The geography of Hollywood production is transnational, certainly not to be circumscribed by the boundaries of the United States. If popular American cinema has always looked to stars and directors from elsewhere in the world as potential sources of renewal, the flow of creative personnel in the era of globalisation has grown both more intense and more complex (in Chapter 7 we saw that contemporary non-US stars often do not take one-way tickets when relocating to Hollywood for work on particular projects).

'Classical' Hollywood

Southern California was already a site of wide-ranging entrepreneurial activity when the film industry, drawn by factors including low land prices and the availability of dry, sunlit conditions for year-round shooting, arrived there early in the twentieth century. Previously, most filmmaking in the US had occurred nearer the financial hub of New York City; however, westward cinematic migration was rapid and wholesale. In 1909 the innovative director D. W. Griffith relocated from the East to Hollywood, a small settlement on the fringes of Los Angeles, and in 1913 Cecil B. DeMille, future maestro of Roman and biblical epics, began his career there by shooting a western, *The Squaw Man*. A cluster of studios of varying scale gradually cohered into what critics in retrospect would call 'classical' Hollywood, a system of filmmaking usually regarded as operating from the end of World War I into the 1950s.

Several terminologies applied to Hollywood's first phase have undergone critical scrutiny. In *The Classical Hollywood Cinema* (1985), by David Bordwell, Janet Staiger and Kristin Thompson, 'classical' appears without scare-quotes; instead, the authors argue, Hollywood films of this period are governed by codified principles of composition that suggest parallels with the classicism of other art forms. For rival scholars, however, 'classical' is suspect as the principal descriptive term for Hollywood in this (or any other) era because of its primarily stylistic and formal connotations and its effacement, therefore, of this cinema's sheer money-making drive. In *Hollywood Cinema* (second edition, 2003), Richard Maltby proposes the alternative of 'commercial aesthetic', a phrase which, usefully, does not overlook the artistic sensibility of popular American cinema, but stresses an irrepressible profit motive. A number of writers have also questioned how adequate it is to use 'the studio system' as a synonym for this phase of Hollywood's history, given that the term risks detaching production from those other branches of the film industry by which the major companies maintained their grip over markets in the US and beyond. The so-called 'Big Five' – MGM, Paramount, RKO, Twentieth Century Fox and Warner Bros – were, in the language of business theory, examples of *vertical integration*: they controlled not only film production but also channels of distribution and, through ownership of many of the most profitable cinemas in America, exhibition. At a lower level of corporate organisation, the 'Little Three' – Columbia, United Artists and Universal – produced and distributed films but had to rely upon deals with the larger studios to get them on to lucrative screens. Still further below were the tenants of 'Poverty Row': small companies like Republic and Monogram – the latter the dedicatee of Godard's *Breathless* – which owned no distribution or exhibition facilities, but produced westerns and other low-budget genre movies.

By their mode of making films, the studios of the classical Hollywood era invite at least partial analogies with contemporaneous industries of mass-production. Suitably adjusted and glamorised, the practices of the newly designed assembly line indeed seemed transferable to film manufacture. Thus each film project advanced through a series of specialist units housed within the same organisation. Items of fixed capital such as sets were efficiently adapted for repeated use; even stars – seemingly less malleable – were, as noted in Chapter 7, rationalised, typically tied into exclusive seven-year deals with particular studios and reduced to personas replicable across a body of screen work. According to Hollywood's many critics, such streamlined, industrial-scale output designed for maximum commercial gain was ill equipped to generate subtle and distinctive art. One of the most devastating critiques was presented in *Dialectic of Enlightenment* (1944), by the German Marxists Theodor Adorno and Max Horkheimer. Observing classical Hollywood closely while living in the United States as political refugees, Adorno and Horkheimer took it to be representative of the twentieth-century 'culture industry', sharing the tendencies of other media forms such as popular music and radio broadcasting to standardise public expression and manufacture passive respondents. Like the car industry, Hollywood ruthlessly suppressed questions of quality or value in favour of a logic of quantity:

> That the difference between the models of Chrysler and General
> Motors is fundamentally illusory is known by any child, who is fas-
> cinated by that very difference. The advantages and disadvantages
> debated by enthusiasts serve only to perpetuate the appearance of
> competition and choice. It is no different with the offerings of Warner
> Brothers and Metro Goldwyn Mayer. But the differences, even
> between the more expensive and cheaper products from the same
> firm, are shrinking – in cars to the different number of cylinders,
> engine capacity, and details of the gadgets, and in films to the differ-
> ent number of stars, the expense lavished on technology, labor and
> costumes, or the use of the latest psychological formulae. (Adorno
> and Horkheimer, 2002: 97)

From this perspective, variations of genre, narrative and form
among classical Hollywood's output are distinctions without a
difference. A social problem picture of the 1930s is functionally
equivalent to a musical of the late 1940s; a gangster film is identical
to a comedy. The same aesthetic structures and same reactionary ideology are lodged in each film made within this system of
film production. Here, however, Adorno and Horkheimer depart
from one tradition of Marxist criticism by scourging a strand of
popular culture without simultaneously attempting to salvage its
progressive potentials. Though their case is made pungently, it
derives from what Maltby identifies as a 'vulgar Marxist' position
that structures many studies of this particular cinema: 'Hollywood's
enslavement to the profit system means that all its products can do
is blindly reproduce the dominant ideology of bourgeois capitalism' (Maltby, 2003: 45). Even if much of classical Hollywood's
output indeed leans ideologically towards conservatism, its films
may still, at times, transmit radical or utopian possibilities. The
same is true of the re-engineered system that emerged in Hollywood
after drastic industrial, economic and social changes occurred in the
late 1940s and early 1950s.

'Post-classical' Hollywood
In 1948 the power of the major Hollywood studios was severely
weakened by a US Supreme Court judgement against Paramount.
Independent exhibitors had alleged monopolistic behaviour by
those studios which owned cinemas as well as production and

distribution interests; they objected in particular to such practices as *block booking*, whereby exhibitors in the independent sector were required to buy a slate of a major studio's films in order to obtain those likely box office successes which they really wanted. The uncoupling of highly profitable exhibition activities from production and distribution in the wake of the court ruling was to have a significant impact upon many Hollywood studios. Yet even before this legal verdict, there were signs of trouble for the American film industry. US audience figures had, in fact, peaked in 1946; under way was a decline in cinema attendance that would become precipitous in coming decades until the beginnings of revival in the late 1970s. Various reasons have been offered for this national loss of the cinemagoing habit. The most facile suggestion is that movies were simply ousted by their precocious sibling, television. However, numbers of cinema spectators had begun to fall well before the time of widespread TV ownership. It is more persuasive to look to larger structural changes in the United States, notably rising levels of postwar affluence that precipitated a flight from urban centres well equipped with cinemas to new suburbs that lacked this amenity. In addition, as Geoff King notes, money that once went on film nights was increasingly diverted into providing for the large numbers of baby-boom children, or distributed across a wider range of leisure activities, including DIY and gardening (2002b: 25).

Scholars still debate the extent to which 'post-classical' Hollywood differs from the mode of film production consolidated in the first half of the twentieth century. Maltby argues that the nature of the product, at least, was fairly unchanged: if two films made in Hollywood almost eighty years apart are juxtaposed, they will still 'have more in common with each other than either does with contemporary European art cinema, documentary, or avant-garde film' (2003: 8). Yet for other writers, the specifications of post-1950 US popular cinema are so altered from what came before as to amount to a paradigm shift. Without discounting the important continuities between an older, integrated Hollywood and a modern, decentred one, we evoke here a number of breaks in their respective forms of corporate organisation, business modelling and textual composition.

1. *Corporate organisation*. Declining audience figures, loss of control over exhibition and a scaling-down of production left the once-autonomous Hollywood studios vulnerable to takeover bids. For a period, they offered a source of glitz to companies in entirely unrelated fields: in 1969, the acquisition of Warner Bros brought much-needed glamour to Kinney National Services, a corporation known principally for its ownership of car parks and funeral parlours. Subsequent takeovers or mergers, however, have repositioned film studios more plausibly. The withering away of corporate regulation under Reaganomics in the 1980s even permitted some return to the classical era's vertically integrated pattern, with a major wave of cinema acquisition by Hollywood's production companies. But a more common move has been towards *horizontal integration*: increasingly, the old studio names figure as specialist filmmaking units in multi-media conglomerates also comprising music, publishing, TV, internet, amusement park and other entertainment interests. Thus Columbia is currently the film production arm of an agglomerated business structure headed by the Japanese electronics giant Sony; Warner Bros is positioned within the multi-media corporation Time Warner; and so on. The diffuse holdings of these companies, delivering entertainment to numerous platforms, indicate some waning of the traditional film object's power within the leisure economies of the US and beyond.

2. *Business modelling*. While right from its inception Hollywood has sought to exploit any ancillary commercial opportunity, box office returns themselves remained central to the business model of its classical era. Now, however, to a greater extent than other studios worldwide, Hollywood companies construe moviemaking as 'the creation of "filmed entertainment" software, to be viewed through several different windows and transported to several different platforms maintained by the other divisions of diversified media corporations' (Maltby, 2003: 190). Thus the revenue of today's Hollywood film derives not only from moneys paid by cinema audiences but from the cinema experience's near-infinite prolongation and repurposing in such other exploitable formats as DVD and Blu-ray, computer games, soundtrack albums, TV and online screenings, amusement park

rides and numerous promotional tie-ins. In many cases, the base metal of poor viewing figures for a film at the multiplex may still be alchemised into gold by such multi-media synergies.

Besides looking to exploit extra- or post-theatrical revenue streams, Hollywood producers have come increasingly to rely for profits upon box office performance abroad. To return for a moment to a film discussed earlier, *Inception* earned $292 million during its run in US cinemas, but $532 million in foreign markets ('*Inception*', 2014: n.p.). This ratio of 65:35 with respect to foreign and domestic grosses, respectively, is by no means exceptional for contemporary Hollywood films. A visit to the Box Office Mojo website on 23 August 2014, for instance, disclosed that in the first fifty-six days of its theatrical exhibition *Transformers: Age of Extinction* had garnered $243 million domestically as against $811 million worldwide ('*Transformers: Age of Extinction*', 2014: n.p.). This is a striking ratio of 77:23 in favour of foreign grosses, and, as with the figures for *Inception*, indicates the high degree of global transmissibility of spectacle-driven and action–adventure films, given what Franco Moretti terms their 'abrogation of language' relative to more voluble genres such as comedies and dramas (2013: 97). Audiences abroad are also able now to view Hollywood's products much more rapidly than before. The domestic model of TV-advertised *saturation* release of a film – emergent in the mid-1970s, largely replacing an earlier pattern of gradual, or *platform*, release (major cities first) – has been internationalised; the launch of blockbusters, in particular, is now a synchronised worldwide event. As well as a practical measure to deter video piracy, this move indicates Hollywood's contemporary modelling of itself as a global rather than national cinema.

3. *Textual composition*. Classical Hollywood's model of filmmaking – in which pre-production, production and post-production were all carried out in-house – has yielded to a looser, more devolved process (encouraging some commentators to cite the film industry as part of a general shift from Fordist to flexible, post-Fordist forms of manufacture). Hollywood production now is best viewed not as operation of an assembly line but as differentiated involvements in a range of niche projects. Developers

of a film idea seek to elicit major studio interest with a particular *package*: a given star's or director's guaranteed participation, say, or an already familiar narrative property (adapted from a popular novel or – as with the superhero films – a comic book). The level of the studio's financial commitment and creative intervention, however, will fluctuate markedly from case to case.

Several writers have argued that this loss of centralisation in contemporary Hollywood's production regime is replicated in the sorts of films it makes. Compared with classical Hollywood's highly integrated narratives, its current products are, for these scholars, characterised by a high degree of *disaggregation*: storytelling is subordinated to the display of lavish spectacle or the showcasing of elements with high synergistic potential, such as a film's sampled musical score. Justin Wyatt speaks of Hollywood's turn to 'modular' filmmaking in *High Concept: Movies and Marketing in Hollywood* (1994). Though touching on other film industries besides that of the US, Allan Cameron uses similar language more recently in *Modular Narratives in Contemporary Cinema* (2008). Yet, as already suggested above in Chapters 5 and 6, this thesis is overstated. While contemporary Hollywood indeed gives a new prominence to hyperkinetic visuality and to sonic overload, this should not be taken to imply the exhaustion of narrative drive. The concept of modular filmmaking extrapolates too quickly from a handful of blockbusters or event films, and prematurely consigns to history a storytelling mode that is one of the distinctive markers of Hollywood production and a source of continuity across its classical and post-classical periods.

STOP and THINK

- In arguing for a film studies freed from exclusive attention to the qualities of the film text itself, Miller et al. observe that 'Institutions do not have to be arid areas of study, and the links to everyday life are real' (2005: 43). Do you agree that the discipline is enriched by consideration of commercial, industrial and legal questions (raised, for example, by Hollywood's place in cinema's global economy)? Are there risks, as well as rewards, in this redesigned film studies? How, exactly, should discussion of a film's formal details be articulated with analysis of the data we gather from sources such as studio archives and newspaper financial pages?

- Maltby argues that a sense of American specificity or locality is diminished within the output of contemporary, globalised Hollywood, potentially devolving cinema's task of national investigation to more marginal filmmaking cultures in the US. Assess, then, the extent to which Hollywood constitutes a *national* cinema, comparable, say, to Egyptian or Swedish or Turkish cinemas.

Beyond Hollywood: two examples

Reinforcing Yoshimoto's point above about the pre-eminence of Hollywood in the study of film industries, Stephen Crofts writes, with pointed understatement, that 'Film scholars' mental maps of world film production are often less than global' (2006: 53). Periodically, it is true, certain non-Anglophone cinemas have been taken up in Britain and the United States as the focus of research activity and high-school and university curricula. Older examples include Soviet montage, German Expressionism, Italian neo-realism, postwar Japanese film and the French New Wave; newer equivalents might be the rich cinemas of Iran or Brazil. Such signs of cinematic cosmopolitanism should be welcomed, but only up to a point. In the first instance, these gestures beyond Hollywood clearly represent only a start in compiling a much-needed atlas of world film production: vast areas of the globe remain relatively unmapped, at least by Anglophone branches of the discipline. Where is the coverage in English of Peruvian film, or Moroccan, or Icelandic? Second, those cinemas in other languages that have been selected for widespread attention are typically marked by formal innovation and/or political radicalism that may then be used as sticks with which to beat Hollywood's purportedly conservative aesthetic. As a result, more *popular* or *generic* production even from nations falling within the gaze of Anglo-American film studies may continue to be neglected: thus with regard to France, for example, there are many studies of Godard's deconstructions of narrative cinema but notably less scholarship on Parisian comedies or adaptations of French literary classics.

This section offers a modest example of the cartography of production that is required by Anglophone film studies. Again, the question of selectivity arises: just two non-Hollywood cinemas are considered and, for reasons of space, only briefly. Countless other filmmaking centres might have been chosen: why not study stylistic and industrial practices in Finnish cinema, for example, or in the hugely prolific cinema of Nigeria, the unimaginatively dubbed 'Nollywood', where the regime of rapid, improvisatory shooting, editing on cheaper digital equipment and straight-to-video distribution perhaps holds lessons for cinemas of the future elsewhere? Nevertheless, the brief studies presented here of Bollywood and Hong Kong will allow us not only to register some of their distinctive features but also to raise questions of sub-national, national, regional and global film cultures that will be developed later in the chapter.

Bollywood

While Bollywood has an increasingly global reach, it is also an instance of *sub*-national cinema. There is a regrettable tendency by onlookers outside India to regard the output of this tradition of popular Hindi filmmaking as the totality of the nation's film production. The reality is very different, as Kush Varia reminds us: 'India has so many cinematic traditions which all deserve to be differentiated from one another and awarded their own legitimacy, definitions and study' (2012: 4). Thus Bollywood's productivity is matched by the fertility of many other filmmaking centres in India, which utilise various regional languages and sometimes very different formal idioms. Without pretending to exhaustive listing, reference might be made to the cinema of Malayalam-speaking Kerala in India's south-west, to the popular Telugu and Tamil film industries of the south-east, and to Bengali art cinema from the north-east – home of India's most internationally known director to date, Satyajit Ray.

Even in the face of these rival traditions, Bollywood's employment of Hindi, India's official language, might still seem to endow it with attributes of a national cinema. Again, however, it is important to make things more complex, this time by bringing out how Bollywood film is less an expression of Indian cultural autonomy than a *hybrid* form, interweaving multiple Indian and non-Indian influences. Its base, the city of Mumbai (formerly Bombay), is described in Salman Rushdie's novel *The Moor's Last Sigh* (1995) as India's pre-eminent multicultural site, all the way back to its beginnings as 'the bastard child of a Portuguese-English wedding': 'In Bombay all Indias met and merged. In Bombay, too, all-India met what-was-not-India, what came across the black water to flow into our veins' (2006: 350). Such crisscrossings can be observed in the subjects and forms of Bollywood itself. This is certainly not to deny the powerful shaping force of native cultural and religious traditions, notably Hindu epic and drama. *Raja Harischandra* (1913), the first extended narrative film to be made in India, is based on part of Hinduism's sacred text, the *Mahabharata*; ever since then, the *mythological* – cited in Chapter 5 as among non-US film genres – has remained part of Bollywood's output. In addition, this cinema's visual tradition of 'an erotic economy of the look and the counterlook' between spectator and spectacle has been linked by scholars to Hindu religious convention, replicating the practice of *darshan* which requires rapt contemplation of an object of veneration (Mishra, 2002: 9). Complicating cultural nationalist accounts of Bollywood's formation, however, this strikingly frontal mode of presentation of key figures or items also borrows from other, non-Hindu forms of staging, including Parsi drama and British proscenium arch theatre. Similarly, any thoughts of Bollywood's national autonomy have to reckon with this cinema's acquisitiveness with respect to the products of global film: genres from elsewhere such as the martial arts picture and the western (both Hollywood and 'spaghetti') have often been freely appropriated and repurposed.

If the heyday of the 'cinema of attractions' in the United States was quite short-lived, as we saw a number of writers suggesting in Chapter 4, its Bollywood equivalent has proved much more durable. Without repressing the pleasures of narrative, Bollywood has nevertheless tended to abstract and prioritise instances of the visual and vocal spectacular. Colour saturates many of its films, carried in costumes or in other details of mise-en-scène, such as the purple, pink and yellow pigments that make a polychromatic curtain of the screen during a festive scene from *Sholay* (1975; see Figure 29). Star

29 A festive scene from the Bollywood film, *Sholay* (1975). Imagine also the colours (and the music)

performance itself is 'spectacularised', with the camera dwelling upon the kinetic feats and expressive repertoires – or simply the bodies – of key actors and actresses. Set-pieces of music and dance, too, may become detached not only from plotting but even from unities of time and space precious to other, realist cinemas. This disarticulation or 'modularisation' of its formal elements has frequently made Bollywood an object of critique, not least among Indian intellectuals. Mumbai-born Rushdie himself speaks, at times, for this culture of distaste. Writing enthusiastically about *The Wizard of Oz*, he makes a qualitative distinction between this product of popular US cinema on the one hand and Bollywood films on the other, the latter striking him as 'trashy' and yielding a dubious pleasure akin to 'the fun of eating junk food' (1992: 13). At the same time, however, Rushdie has been drawn in his fiction to expressions of the irrepressible vibrancy of Bollywood. The narrator of *The Moor's Last Sigh*, for example, evokes it, in all its lavishness and generic intermixture, as an 'Epico-Mythico-Tragico-Comico-Super-Sexy-High-Masala-Art' (Rushdie, 2006: 148).

Bollywood has also struggled for critical reputation because of its dependence upon *melodrama*, an artistic mode that in the West is suspected of such vices as vulgarity and feminisation. Employing a term used by the French film theorist Christian Metz, Mishra writes that 'Bombay Cinema is itself a genre that is primarily a sentimental melodramatic romance [...] it is a grand syntagm (*grande syntagma-tique*) that functions as one heterogeneous text' (2002: 13). Mishra's totalisation of Bollywood output is instructive to a degree, helping us to identify a melodramatic strain running through an otherwise expansive generic array. Nevertheless, it is vital to see not only Bollywood's synchronic or systemic character but also its *diachronic* aspect, its mutability across time.

Three particular changes in this cinema might briefly be noted. In the first instance, Bollywood has increasingly embraced higher production values: indicative here is that *Lagaan: Once Upon a Time in India* (2001), a major success in the West besides India, initiated a tendency for films to use synchronised sound, rather than post-production recording. Second, Bollywood's thematic remit has widened, making it at times a cinema of troubling social inquiry. Thus *My Brother ... Nikhil* (2005) explores homosexuality and AIDS in India during the 1980s; *Black* (2005), *Iqbal* (2005) and *Barfi!* (2012) utilise different narrative structures and stylistic repertoires to consider the nation's treatment of people with disabilities; while *Love, Sex and Betrayal* (2010), in the words of one critic, 'paints a very bleak and dark portrait of kinship and gender relations in urban North India' (Ganti, 2013: 215). Third, Bollywood is much more than ever a cinema to be understood *globally* rather than nationally (or sub-nationally). Besides internationalising its networks of distribution and exhibition so that films may be viewed outside India in numerous venues and formats, including theatrical exhibition in multicultural cities, cable TV screenings and DVD releases, it has globalised its production process also. Recent examples of this deterritorialised Bollywood filmmaking include *Singh Is Kinng* (2008: set in Australia), *Kites* (2010: set partly in Las Vegas and Mexico) and *My Name Is Khan* (2010: set in the United States). The 'frictional trajectories inscribed in [Bollywood's] name' (Govil, 2008: 212) are increasingly apparent as, both aesthetically and economically, it is implicated in relations with other cinemas worldwide.

Hong Kong

Hong Kong cinema resembles Bollywood in several respects, while differing significantly in others. From its beginnings with *Stealing the Roasted Duck* and *Right a Wrong with Earthenware Dish* (both 1909), it too, like Bollywood, has shown a capacity for incorporation of heterogeneous influences: what David Bordwell calls 'a scavenger aesthetic' (2000: 11). Besides borrowing across its history from American musicals, French crime thrillers and the Cantonese movie tradition in China itself, Hong Kong filmmaking also includes among its intertexts such historically and geographically disparate extra-cinematic materials as classic ghost stories, Chinese martial arts novels and computer graphics (Bordwell, 2000: 11). It is liable, too, to cannibalise the contemporary Hollywood blockbuster: sequences from such successful American action films as *Speed* and *Die Hard* (1988) were rapidly recycled by the lower-budget Hong Kong system.

Writers on Hong Kong cinema, like those on Bollywood, have sometimes shown a tendency to totalise its output and perceive it as constituting 'a genre [...] one heterogeneous text' (to recall Mishra's description above of the formal unity of popular Hindi film). These observers take Hong Kong's cinematic rationale to be vivid scenes of action and violence, relatively unpinned from narrative. Where Bollywood defines itself through the foregrounded song and dance routine, Hong Kong, from this perspective, proffers the chase sequence and the extended combat showcasing attributes of strength, athleticism and quick-wittedness. Yet to speak only of the spectacular, hyperkinetic properties of Hong Kong cinema would be misleading. If Wong Kar-wai's *The Grandmaster* (2013), for example, has traces of the 'circus aesthetic' that for Bordwell characterises Hong Kong cinema (2000: 220), other work by this director, notably *Chungking Express* (1994) and *In the Mood for Love* (2000; see Figure 30), is far removed from the stylistic norms of the action movie. Although the action genre, broadly defined, is crucial to both the domestic and the foreign profitability of Hong Kong film, it hardly exhausts the totality of production. Critical space should also be made for recognition and evaluation of what Esther Yau calls this cinema's 'mundane, esoteric, womanist, queer, and communitarian moments and voices' (2001: 25). One of the several risks of construing the Hong Kong film tradition as solely a line of descent of action stars from Bruce Lee through Jackie Chan, Chow Yun-Fat and Andy Lau to Jet Li is that it is unduly *masculinising*. If

30 An alternative to action cinema in Hong Kong: Tony Leung and
Maggie Cheung in the melancholy romance, *In the Mood for Love* (2000),
directed by Wong Kar-wai

this critical narrative were to prevail, attention would be withheld
from a significant strand of films in other genres made by Hong
Kong's female directors, a line extending from older figures such as
Mabel Cheung, Ann Hui and Clara Law, active since the 1980s, to
younger filmmakers including Heiward Mak.

Hong Kong cinema should be located in a series of concentric
spaces. On the narrowest of these geographical scales, it has accrued
the status of a *national* film industry. Though open, as we have seen,
to a dizzying array of stylistic and thematic models from elsewhere,
it traditionally seemed able to absorb or 'indigenise' these without
fatal damage to a distinctive local identity. In earlier decades, at least,
local cinemagoers' taste tended to favour home-produced work, to
the extent that major Hollywood successes including *Mrs Doubtfire*
(1993), *Forrest Gump* (1994) and *The Lion King* (1994) failed at the
Hong Kong box office (Bordwell, 2000: 34). As well as national
in its spatial definition, however, Hong Kong film should also be
understood as *regional* in its sphere of influence. Its most complex
neighbourly relations, of course, are with the People's Republic
of China (not least since 1997, when Beijing assumed sovereignty
over Hong Kong at the end of British colonial rule). But stylistic,

industrial and commercial ties exist with other nations in the region: with Taiwan as a source of finance, for example, or with Japan as not only a significant market but also as home of an important competitor industry. Confirming Yau's sense also of the complex 'ethnoscape' of Hong Kong cinema (2001: 11), its creative personnel are likely be drawn from throughout Pacific Asia – sometimes from Australasia, too, as in the notable case of the cinematographer Christopher Doyle, born in Sydney, who has worked not only with Wong Kar-wai but with other filmmakers of Hong Kong.

Any mapping of Hong Kong cinema must inscribe it, finally, in a *global* media economy. In evaluating the consequences for the local industry of this positioning, it is important to avoid the twin extremes of uncritical celebration and morbid pessimism. Undeniably, though, filmmaking in Hong Kong has suffered during the past two decades, its share of both local and regional markets damaged by the incursions of an aggressively exporting Hollywood. As a result, production has dwindled in volume to fewer than fifty titles per annum; previous euphoria about Hong Kong as the 'true rival' to US cinematic hegemony (Moretti, 2013: 95) now seems misplaced. Even so, the current terms of film trade are by no means entirely weighted in favour of the United States. A model of *colonisation in reverse* might usefully be applied here. While, in classic imperial fashion, Hollywood's products have penetrated not only auditoria in Hong Kong but the imaginations of local spectators, so, reciprocally, Hong Kong film is in various ways now near the heart of Hollywood. Inelegantly, but usefully, Bordwell refers to a contemporary 'Hongkongification of American cinema' (2000: 19). Evidence of this would start with US recruitment of actors like Jackie Chan and directors like Tsui Hark, Ringo Lam and, above all, John Woo. Hollywood's films have been increasingly stencilled, too, by Hong Kong stylistics, as instanced by the choreography of combat in the *Matrix* trilogy (1999-2003) or *Kill Bill: Vol. 1*. And if Hong Kong cinema has long been adept in quickly adapting the Hollywood blockbuster, this process was reversed in 2006 when Martin Scorsese's *The Departed* transposed to Boston the Hong Kong hit *Infernal Affairs* (2002). All of this reverse colonisation comes at a price, perhaps, confirming an action-oriented perception of Hong Kong or appropriating Hong Kong's film resources chiefly in order to renew Hollywood and thereby boost its export potential, including in East Asia itself. Nevertheless, such transactions valuably remind us that globalisation in the film economy is not simply a narrative of inexorably spreading US dominance.

STOP and THINK

- The claim was made above that many people's maps of world film production tend to be patchy rather than comprehensive. Drawing upon your own spectatorship and reading, construct a personal cartography of world cinema. Which parts of this map are filled in in reasonable detail? Which areas, by contrast, are outlined only sketchily, or even left blank? Suggest reasons for this geographical variance.
- Stephen Crofts writes that loss of 'the culturally specific' is threatened when films imported from other centres of production are viewed without the support of 'cross-cultural contextualisation – a broadly educational project' (2006: 53). Review, in the light of his remarks, your own experience of watching films from outside your own nation and language. To what extent was contextual framing of the sort referred to here part of your spectatorship?
- Jean-François Lyotard argues that, in the postmodern West, cultural tastes are not restricted by national demarcations but instead are disposed towards materials of very diverse provenance: 'Eclecticism is the degree zero of contemporary general culture' (1984: 76). From our narrower perspective, is eclecticism the 'degree zero' of contemporary *film* culture? Bordwell indicates that it might be when he posits the capacity of spectators now to experience 'Japanese *anime*, Indian melodramas, Italian horror, Mexican masked-wrestler films [and] Indonesian fantasies' (2000: 96). From this perspective, films of heterogeneous non-Anglophone origins are liable, again, to lose any sense of cultural particularity and to be valued in the West principally for their capacity to refresh palates jaded by Hollywood. But perhaps this is too bleak an assessment, and neglects not only cultural expansions but political reconstructions that may occur as spectators in

Portsmouth or Portland venture beyond domestic film products? Offer your own assessment of the costs and benefits of
eclectic, transnational film consumption.

National and transnational film

'Having a nation', writes the political philosopher Ernest Gellner,
'is not an inherent attribute of humanity [...] nations, like states,
are a contingency, and not a universal necessity' (2006: 6).
Conceptually speaking, nations are fragile, owing their existence to
contentious acts of fabrication rather than to historical inevitability.
Nevertheless, while still hoping to devise alternative categories in
which people might be positioned, Gellner has to acknowledge the
nation's material effects, including its importance to anyone's sense
of identity: 'A man without a nation defies the recognised categories
and provokes revulsion' (6).

By analogy, can we imagine a film that has no country? A film
that, as Gellner wishes eventually to happen to individuals themselves, is not primarily identified as belonging to one or other of
those politico-spatial domains called 'nations'? In film studies, as
in political philosophy, it is advisable to assert the contingency of
national categorisation. For there is nothing inevitable or unimprovable about the current tendency to attribute films to particular
nations, as happens in contexts ranging from magazine listings and
festival programmes to academic book series that take as their subject 'Australian' or 'French' or 'Mexican' cinema. Valentina Vitali
and Paul Willemen remind us that early in the twentieth century, at
least, a film's point of national origin was not a significant concern
for distributors and exhibitors – or, indeed, for audiences themselves: 'The main way of differentiating product lines was provided
by the name and, eventually, by the reputation of companies that
produced films in different national territories' (2006: 1).

The category of the nation, Andrew Higson suggests, may
actually not be what is required by a geographically focused film
studies. As he argues, 'the contingent communities that cinema
imagines are much more likely to be either local or transnational
than national' (2006: 23). Rather like the concept of genre discussed
in Chapter 5, then, that of the nation risks being simultaneously

too large and too small for the discipline's needs. At one extreme it lacks the power of magnification necessary to recognise *intra*-national filmmaking cultures. How adequate is a unitary category of 'Belgian cinema', for example, when considering the work of the Dardenne brothers, with its carefully specified placement in French-speaking Wallonia rather than Dutch-speaking Flanders? Or how productive is the idea of 'Spanish cinema' when faced by a distinctive Basque film tradition that in recent decades has benefited from increases in local infrastructural support, generating work by directors such as Julio Medem and Montxo Armendáriz? At the other geographical extreme, the category of the nation is too small to account for certain itineraries of film production, distribution and exhibition. Other, larger cinematic cartographies suggest themselves in these instances. Thus ethnic and linguistic commonalities in adjacent states may allow some national cinemas to achieve *regional* status (as with Mexican film's periods of hegemony in Central America). Alternatively, ties of history and culture across truly global spaces can produce *diasporic* films such as *Bombón: El Perro* (2004), which is set in Patagonia in Argentina and directed by the Buenos Aires-born Carlos Sorin, but is an Argentine/Spanish co-production that has circulated throughout the Spanish-speaking world.

Yet even as the nation's impoverishing effects on film studies are pointed out, the category's indispensability should also be acknowledged (something that happened, too, with the idea of genre in Chapter 5). In a manner comparable to Gellner's recognition of the enduring power of the nation in political philosophy, Higson, from within film studies, allows for its 'helpfulness as a taxonomic labelling device, a conventional means of reference in the complex debates about cinema' (2006: 16). To attribute films to particular nations may be politically enlivening as well as conceptually leaky. Most importantly, it can allow us to identify sites of resistance to the directly colonial or otherwise overbearing force of other nation-states. As noted in Chapter 8, certain countries in the developing world that lack the resources to build substantial indigenous film industries remain largely at the mercy of others' cinematic representations: thus there are more positive things to do with a film labelled 'from Chad' or 'from Paraguay' than piously to point out that nations are artificial constructs. Similarly, films described as 'Palestinian' – including *Beyond the Sun* and *Spider Web*, both directed in 2010 by Saleem Dabbour – should not elicit in the first instance stern lessons from political philosophers about the category of the nation. Instead, given the following observations by actor-director Mohammed Bakri, the consolidation of a Palestinian cinema would be cause for political optimism: 'We have no film schools and we have no studios. We have no infrastructure because we have no country' (Brooks, 2006: n.p.).

A focus upon films' national origins is a handy way of disclosing shifts in cinematic power. At various times, film industries other than that of the United States have been globally pre-eminent. Mihir Bose records that in 1907 40 per cent of films shown in the US were from one Paris studio alone. French cinema was still dominant three years when, of the feature films released in Britain, 'thirty-six [were] from France, twenty-eight from the US, and seventeen from Italy, well ahead of the fifteen from Great Britain and four from Denmark, Germany and elsewhere' (Bose, 2006: 61). Such a modestly proportioned US film industry was not destined to last, of course. Miller et al.'s book, *Global Hollywood 2* is a finely detailed study of the mutually reinforcing commercial, legal and political strategies by which the hegemony of popular American cinema has been achieved during the twentieth and early twenty-first centuries (the authors briskly reject any suggestion that such global dominance is owing to the films' quality alone). The correlative of Hollywood's upsurge has been a drastic shrivelling of many 'national' or 'indigenous' film industries elsewhere. Among the more dismal facts uncovered by Miller et al. is that, from 1945 to 2000, the combined European film industries declined in size by eight-ninths (2005: 10). Elsewhere, as we have seen, even a self-confident indigenous film culture like Hong Kong's proved vulnerable to an increasingly globalised Hollywood.

Nevertheless, it is important not to absolutise the power of the United States in today's world cinematic system. Both earlier in this chapter and in Chapter 7, evidence of the involvement of other nations in Hollywood production has already served to counter the bleakest diagnoses of cultural imperialism. Whether providing finance capital or plausible locations or creative personnel, these other countries, at least to an extent, 'de-Americanise' American film. If such developments are certainly not all benign – Hollywood often redirects production and post-production abroad so as reduce labour costs and sideline trade unions – they are nevertheless not without progressive potential. Hollywood's 'Hongkongification' was noted above, with its exhilarating as well as disquieting effects. Similarly ambiguous is a post-2000 *Latinisation* of popular US cinema. During this period, a number of directors who made their reputations in Central and South America have been drawn to work in Hollywood. Consider here just one representative trajectory. The Mexican director Guillermo Del Toro first made his name with work done in his home country, particularly short horror and fantasy films and the vampire feature *Cronos* (1993). These gaining him a reputation north of the border, also, he was recruited by Hollywood, initially to direct the sci-fi horror film *Mimic* (1997) and subsequently to make films that include *Blade II* (2002), the two *Hellboy* movies and *Pacific Rim* (2013). From one perspective, a cinematic itinerary like Del Toro's might look like neo-colonial appropriation to revivify a flagging domestic film product (the *Hellboy* series, for example, recalibrates the superhero movie's parameters); from another position, however, it holds out the prospect of lodging an outsider mentality, a developing-world sensibility, within popular US cinema itself.

In a bold utopian gesture, Elizabeth Ezra and Terry Rowden have proposed that contemporary cinema be understood as 'borderless' (2006: 5). They turn for evidence not only to the migrant careers of current directors, stars and other creative figures but to the recent circulation of films themselves through spatially dispersed markets. If Hollywood blockbusters have crossed borders agilely, then so too have a number of art or genre films of non-Anglophone provenance, including from Brazil *City of God*; from Mexico *Amores perros*, *Y tu mamá también* (2001) and *Biutiful* (2010); from India *Monsoon Wedding* (2001); from China *Crouching Tiger, Hidden Dragon* and *Hero*; from South Korea *Oldboy* (2005); from France *The Artist* (2011); from Germany *Downfall* (2004) and *The Lives of Others* (2006); and so on. However, it seems premature to be welcoming – or deploring – the arrival of a completely cosmopolitan cinema: in a film context, the national has not yet given way to this extent to the *trans*national. Indeed, Ezra and Rowden moderate their initial optimism by acknowledging that the degree of 'cinematic mobility, like human mobility, is determined by both geopolitical factors and financial pedigree' (2006: 5). Uneven distribution of cultural and economic power determines not only the movements of stars, directors and other filmmakers but also the potential of particular films themselves to travel beyond their places of origin.

Suggestively, Ezra and Rowden write that transnational flows are apparent not only industrially (in modified systems of film production and distribution) but *textually* also (in the narrative concerns of an increasing number of films). Migration and diaspora have become prominent 'as themes within transnational cinema texts themselves' (Ezra and Rowden, 2006; 7). This is very true of the film that provides this chapter's case study.

Case study: *In This World* (2002)

Still tragically topical more than a decade after its release, *In This World* narrates the difficult, often covert journey of two Afghan youths from a refugee camp in northern Pakistan towards their intended destination of London. A red line periodically traced on a map indicates Jamal's and Enayatullah's progress (see Figure 31):

31 Geographically mobile cinema: *In This World* (2002). Note also the dissolve here, with a shot of a landscape giving way to the map

overland from Pakistan to Iran and Turkey; by boat to Italy; then, following the death of Enayatullah at sea, Jamal's onward travel to France by train and, finally, to England clinging to the underside of a lorry. Apart from relatively brief scenes in an Istanbul cutlery workshop, the docks at Trieste, the Red Cross refugee camp at Sangatte, near Calais, and a London mosque and café, the film is set in Asia. English is heard only occasionally on the soundtrack, mainly when a voiceover near the start informs the audience about the numbers and the suffering of refugees; instead, the dominant languages are Pashto and Farsi. The cast is drawn from non-professionals encountered along this cross-border itinerary, especially from Pakistan, Iran and Turkey.

Given this cosmopolitanism of theme and personnel, can *In This World* be described, with any plausibility, as a *British* film? Something to support such attribution is the country of origin of both the director Michael Winterbottom and the writer Tony Grisoni. However, this is flimsy ground on which to base an argument for any film's national identity: by the same token, *Casablanca* (1943), directed by Michael Curtiz, is a Hungarian movie, and *Troy* (2004), directed by Wolfgang Petersen, part of German cinema tradition. For more convincing evidence of *In This World*'s Britishness, we might turn to the fact that much of its funding was supplied by the BBC and the UK Film Council. Yet in assessing questions of national provenance, the criterion of financing or production is also quite rickety: after all, David Lynch's surreal *Inland Empire* was substantially funded by the Paris-based Studio Canal Plus, yet that does not make it 'a French film' in the way we might apply this term to *Amélie* (2001) or to the comedies of Jacques Tati.

Attempting to find a more compelling rationale for national designation of films than those just considered, Paul Willemen argues that 'the issue of national cinema is [...] primarily a question of address, rather than a matter of the filmmakers' citizenship or even of the production finance's country of origin' (2006: 36). If this yardstick is applied, *In This World* seems 'addressed' to a British – and, more broadly, Western – audience, seeking to advance its understanding of the catastrophic human displacements caused by US military and diplomatic action in Afghanistan following 9/11. Though the English-language voiceover features only briefly, its positioning in a formative early moment might be taken as a clue to the film's intended constituency.

Despite this rhetorical orientation towards the West, it is tempting for a moment to consider *In This World* as an instance of *'developing world' cinema*. Aesthetically, politically and industrially, it observes protocols of liberationist filmmaking in immiserated, subjugated parts of the globe as these were codified in manifestos such as 'For an Imperfect Cinema' (1969) by the Cuban director and screenwriter Julio García Espinosa and 'Towards a Third Cinema' (1969) by the Argentine filmmaker-theorists Octavio Getino and Fernando Solanas. Winterbottom's film largely forgoes high-budget glossiness and thus respects Espinosa's demand for a kind of aesthetic poverty that echoes the destitution of the people put on screen. While sunsets and sand dunes lend richness to the colour palette of *In This World*, there are also sparsely lit night scenes, instances of staccato camerawork and, throughout, no evidence of fetishisation of the perfect image. The film might similarly be aligned with Third Cinema, which, as Getino and Solanas theorise it, refuses both the commercial mainstream and an auteurist or art tradition of filmmaking associated principally with Europe. Though a fictional narrative, *In This World* has the atmospherics of undercover, propagandist documentary. Guards patrolling the snowy frontier between Iran and Turkey at night are viewed, as if surreptitiously, through infra-red equipment; some interior locations are scarcely lit at all, carrying suggestions of an attempt to avoid detection by the authorities. The sense of engagement with topical concerns is advanced by use of exclusively non-professional performers, playing characters quite adjacent to their 'real' selves. Winterbottom also filmed with a very small crew, housed in the first instance in a rented Pakistani bus: in this sense he fulfilled the imperative of both 'imperfect' and 'Third' cinemas that distance should be minimised between on the one hand the guild of film specialists and on the other the poor, dislocated peoples who are the objects of representation.

Persuasive though it is, however, the case for *In This World* as comparable to liberationist cinema of the developing world should in the end be resisted. Both textually and contextually, the film is marked still by First World privilege. To begin with, it is the product of a well-established filmmaking centre (albeit one that is, by Hollywood standards, modestly resourced); the BBC's involvement also guarantees it TV exposure to supplement its screening in spaces mainly identified with what Getino and Solanas call 'Second Cinema'. In a documentary accompanying the film's DVD edition, Winterbottom also reports that while the itinerary of filming usually resembled as closely as possible that followed by refugees travelling clandestinely from northern Pakistan to Europe, the crew's life was sometimes made more comfortable by use of flights to replace overland portions. Here, again, is evidence of an adequately funded production rather than that hand-to-mouth practice evoked by Third Cinema's theorists. This relative privilege can, at moments, be detected in the text itself. Although the use of infra-red photography, for example, aptly suggests at the narrative level an operation of insurgent counter-surveillance, it also cannot help but speak at the *formal* level of the filmmakers' technological advantages.

Terms of economic and cultural trade favourable to the West are most apparent when considering the film's very subject matter. Winterbottom, Grisoni and their UK-based collaborators enjoy a latitude of movement that is not available to the refugees whose lives they document sympathetically. As David Farrier writes, *In This World* is structured by a concern with *border-crossing*, 'but this crossing has significantly different implications for filmmaker and subject' (2008: 226). It is also the case that the geographical range of these Western filmmakers is unlikely, at present, to be replicable by many of their Pakistani or Iranian counterparts. The transnationalism of *In This World* is thus politically ambiguous, connoting ongoing inequalities as well as progressive commitments. Here a general point made by Ella Shohat and Robert Stam is instructive. They argue that, where First World filmmakers appear to possess a greater ability than their peers in the developing world 'to float "above" petty nationalist concerns', this is not owing to their richer imaginations, but, much more materially, because they can 'take for granted the projection of a national power that facilitates the making and the dissemination of their films' (2014: 285). Directors, producers and screenwriters in the developing world, by contrast, frequently lack the 'substratum of national power' on which to base internationally expansive projects (285). Without wishing to affiliate

In This World with 'the imperial imaginary' that Shohat and Stam critique so forcefully, it can still be observed that the film's movements through impoverished, unstable parts of Asia are licensed by the economic and cultural capital of the nation from which it emerges.

However, it would be unfair and misleading to conclude discussion at this point. A more positive way to think about *In This World* derives from a distinction made between two types of transnational or cosmopolitan imagination by the critics and documentary film-makers John Hess and Patricia R. Zimmermann. On one side is 'corporatist transnationalism' (2006: 99), usually associated with giant, profit-maximising companies that extend across national boundaries, in the process threatening local economic and cultural forms ('global Hollywood' itself is a striking instance of such transnationalism). On the other side, however, is the resistant practice Hess and Zimmermann call 'adversarial transnationalism' (99), a mode of cross-border engagement that affiliates with those dispossessed by the catastrophic military adventurism and economic colonialism of the late twentieth and early twenty-first centuries. If *In This World* cannot, in the end, be a bona fide film of the developing world, it may still be seen as founded on adversarial transnationalist principles. For example, it represents travel across borders as trauma rather than as First World-style leisure (radically different in this respect from one of Winterbottom's most recent projects: the 2014 BBC TV series, *The Trip to Italy*, starring Steve Coogan and Rob Brydon). And while London still serves as a destination, Jamal's arrival there is treated cursorily: the city is now less an imperial centre than a node in a complex global network. The film's closing credits, too, are set against patches of irregularly painted wall that, from a certain perspective, look like maps and so suggest the protagonist's ongoing displacement rather than any sense of settled location. Again, redeploying terms cited a moment ago from Ezra and Rowden (2006: 5), it must be acknowledged that Jamal's 'human mobility' is circumscribed at the same time that the 'cinematic mobility' of *In This World* itself is considerable. But if the film cannot in the end undo all of the privilege accorded by its production origins in the affluent West, it is nevertheless politically valuable for laying bare the ravages of contemporary corporatist transnationalism. Winterbottom has advanced this critical project in several later films, including *The Road to Guantánamo* (2006), co-directed by Mat Whitecross, and *A Mighty Heart* (2007).

Selected reading

Hollywood

Bordwell, David, Janet Staiger and Kristin Thompson (1985), *The Classical Hollywood Cinema: Film Style and Mode of Production to 1960* (London: Routledge).

Work of classic status itself, though its understanding of older Hollywood cinema has been revisited and challenged by later writers such as Maltby.

King, Geoff (2002), *New Hollywood Cinema: An Introduction* (London: I. B. Tauris).

Well-informed, judicious and enjoyable account of New Hollywood's industrial, stylistic and ideological departures from – and continuities with – the classical era.

McDonald, Paul and Janet Wasko (eds) (2008), *The Contemporary Hollywood Film Industry*.

Very helpful collection on contemporary Hollywood's industrial organisation and process; includes case studies of its exploitation of ancillary markets and its penetration of particular nations ranging from France to New Zealand.

Maltby, Richard (2003), *Hollywood Cinema*, 2nd ed. (Malden, MA: Blackwell).

Close to the last word on Hollywood's 'commercial aesthetic', describing minutely this cinema's industrial, technological, ideological, formal and stylistic specifications.

Miller, Toby, Nitin Govil, John McMurria, Richard Maxwell and Ting Wang (2005), *Global Hollywood 2* (London: BFI).

A densely researched, politically engaged account of Hollywood's global dissemination – and, more optimistically, of attempts worldwide to develop forms of cinematic 'counter-power'.

Miller, Toby (ed.) (2009), *The Contemporary Hollywood Reader* (Abingdon: Routledge).

Very substantial collection, offering expanded coverage of areas discussed in McDonald/Wasko and also featuring fuller analysis of film texts themselves.

Neale, Steve (ed.) (2012), *The Classical Hollywood Reader* (Abingdon: Routledge).

Rich, comprehensive volume: an excellent chronological counterpart to the collections on contemporary Hollywood by McDonald and Wasko, and Miller.

Bollywood

Dudrah, Rajinder Kumar (2006), *Bollywood: Sociology Goes to the Movies* (Thousand Oaks, CA: Sage).

Sophisticated exploration not only of Bollywood films themselves but of their multiple sites of reception, including in the Indian diaspora.

Ganti, Tejaswini (2013), *Bollywood: A Guidebook to Popular Hindi Cinema*, 2nd ed. (Abingdon: Routledge).

Lucid and helpful introduction.

Kavoori, Anandam P. and Aswin Punathambekar (eds) (2008), *Global Bollywood* (New York: New York University Press).

Wide-ranging, stimulating collection of essays on Bollywood as, in the editors' words, 'a space of cultural production and expression that is now decidedly global'.

Mishra, Vijay (2002), *Bollywood Cinema: Temples of Desire* (New York: Routledge).

Combines enthusiasm and erudition, Western-originated film theory and local knowledges, in exploring conceptual, formal and ideological questions raised by Bollywood over some seventy years.

Varia, Kush (2012), *Bollywood: Gods, Glamour and Gossip* (London: Wallflower).

Like Ganti's book, offers a clear, up-to-the-minute overview of this prolific cinema.

Hong Kong

Bordwell, David (2000), *Planet Hong Kong: Popular Cinema and the Art of Entertainment* (Cambridge, MA: Harvard University Press).

Bordwell in unbuttoned mood, attending to specifics but also taking Hong Kong cinema – especially its action genres – as exemplifying the vitality of popular film more broadly.

Kam, Louie (ed.) (2010), *Hong Kong Culture: Word and Image* (Hong Kong: Hong Kong University Press).

This collection on mutations of Hong Kong culture following Chinese repossession in 1997 also discusses literature, music and performance art, but devotes considerable space to the situation of cinema now.

Marchetti, Gina and Tan See Kam (eds) (2007), *Hong Kong Film, Hollywood and the New Global Cinema: No Film Is an Island* (Abingdon: Routledge).

Unfortunate subtitle, but a lively, wide-ranging collection of essays on the itineraries followed by Hong Kong film through many other cinemas and cultures.

Stringer, Julian (2007), *Blazing Passions: Contemporary Hong Kong Cinema* (London: Wallflower).

Succinct and accessible: a very convenient starting point.

Teo, Stephen (1997), *Hong Kong Cinema: The Extra Dimensions* (London: BFI).

Lucid, chronologically ordered account of the first nine decades of Hong Kong production.

National and transnational film

Besides the broad-focused studies listed below, consult also individual titles published in Routledge's 'National Cinemas' strand and Indiana University Press's 'New Directions in National Cinemas' series.

Durovicová, Nataša and Kathleen Newman (eds) (2010), *World Cinemas: Transnational Perspectives* (New York: Routledge).

Excellent collection, handily including not only analyses of specific cases but five contributions on, more generally, 'the geopolitical imaginary of cinema studies'.

Ezra, Elizabeth and Terry Rowden (eds) (2006), *Transnational Cinema: The Film Reader* (London: Routledge).

Essays registering the impacts of transnationalism everywhere from the film text itself to fan cultures and contexts of production: strikes a judicious balance between critique and optimism.

Hjort, Mette and Scott Mackenzie (eds) (2000), *Cinema and Nation* (London: Routledge).

A valuable book, bringing together case studies of the film cultures of Indonesia, Poland, Turkey and other countries with general reflections on questions of cinema and nation.

Naficy, Hamid (2001), *An Accented Cinema: Exilic and Diasporic Filmmaking* (Princeton: Princeton University Press).

Fascinating explorations of a body of formally varied and politically complex work by filmmakers from the developing world: mediates very productively between contextual and textual specificities.

Nagib, Lúcia, Chris Perriam and Rajinder Dudrah (eds) (2013), *Theorizing World Cinema* (London: I. B. Tauris).

Stimulating collection that mixes globally dispersed film-specific studies with broader discussions of national, regional and world cinemas; productively read in dialogue with Durovicová and Newman above.

Stafford, Roy (2014), *The Global Film Book* (Abingdon: Routledge).

Impressive more for breadth than depth, perhaps, but a clear, up-to-the-minute introduction to the diversity of global cinema.

Vitali, Valentina and Paul Willemen (eds) (2006), *Theorising National Cinema* (London: BFI).

Impressively wide-ranging collection, covering many national cinemas as well as testing the continuing viability of notions of 'the national' in an era of increasingly globalised film production.

Online resources

'Cinema Statistics', UNESCO Institute of Statistics, www.uis.unesco.org/culture/Pages/movie-statistics.aspx.

Valuably presents information on world film production and consumption, including the most recent statistics on nations' varying cinematic outputs.

'History of Hollywood', www.hollywoodfilmoffice.org/history.php.

Practically oriented resource for local filmmakers, but includes a helpful timeline of Hollywood's history.

Mediático, http://reframe.sussex.ac.uk/mediatico/.

Excellent resource, administered by Sussex University, that collects research and news 'on Latin American, Latino/a and Iberian media cultures'.

10
Film consumption

Where and how we watch films

Here is a moment from the start of *The Moviegoer* (1961), a novel by
the American writer Walker Percy:

> It reminds me of a movie I saw last month out by Lake Pontchartrain.
> Linda and I went out to a theater in a new suburb. It was evident
> somebody had miscalculated, for the suburb had quit growing and
> here was the theater, a pink stucco cube, sitting out in a field all by
> itself. A strong wind whipped the waves against the sea-wall; even
> inside you could hear the racket. (Percy, 1998: 4)

Binx Bolling, the moviegoer who narrates the novel, eventually gets
round to a description of what the cinema was showing: 'The movie
was about a man who lost his memory in an accident and as a
result lost everything' (4). Noticeably, however, before turning to
these textual matters, he establishes in some detail the geographical, architectural and social co-ordinates of this act of moviegoing.
While the cinemas Binx attends later in the novel are generally in
busy districts of New Orleans, this first one, by contrast, has an
unpopulated, semi-rural location. The building itself is not an inert,
affectless backdrop to his film-watching but, as 'a pink stucco cube',
positively engages the senses with its colour, texture and shape. No
clear demarcation exists here between exterior and interior spaces:
the auditorium is a *liminal* zone, mixing the film's soundtrack with
the loud noise of waves crashing outside. And just as the film text
loses some of its autonomy in the face of these peculiar environmen-
tal conditions, so its privilege is further weakened by the evidence

Binx provides of moviegoing's social contingencies. He is at the cinema, after all, as part of an attempt to seduce his secretary.

This episode from *The Moviegoer* serves as a reminder of what film studies has all too frequently excluded from its field of inquiry: namely, the complex spatial and social architectures within which any act of film consumption occurs. As Gabriele Pedullà writes: 'The reflections of a small number of architects excepted, the movie theatre has remained the great lacuna in twentieth-century film theory' (2012: 5). This blind spot is unfortunate because, throughout the history of film exhibition, spectators' desires and responses have not been governed exclusively by the contents of the screen. Ian Christie reminds us that film's very first patrons, in fact, had powerful *extra-textual* motivations: 'They went to the biograph, the cinematograph, the moving pictures, the nickelodeon: it was a *place* and an *experience* long before identifiable works and their makers emerged to claim their niche in history' (1994: 8). The only difficulty with this formulation is that it might imply that valuing the *space* and the *occasion* of spectatorship alongside or even above engagement with the film text itself is something which disappeared as soon as increased attention was paid to such textual elements as star, director and genre. On the contrary, spectators continue today to invest powerfully in the very sites of reception.

Film studies, as Pedullà indicates, has been slow to acknowledge that spectatorship is *variably situated*, meaning that there is a dearth of detailed cartographies of film consumption. The theoretical models that in Chapter 8 we saw prevailing in the discipline during the 1970s tended to set aside as conceptually unimportant the particularities of different viewing spaces and thus to shrink the scene of reception to a line connecting the projected image and the viewer's rigidified gaze. While this approach yielded sophisticated accounts of the absorptive power of spectacle, they came at a price. The positing of a uniform, textually constructed viewing position represses, among other things, awareness of unequal access to the very places of consumption in which that textual operation must occur. For some African American cinemagoers of the 1930s, say, forced to use a rear door to reach a racially segregated balcony or obliged to attend separate screenings along racial lines at inconvenient times, the idea that specificities of reception space can be ignored when calculating film's ideological effects would have seemed odd indeed. Focus solely upon the screen also neglects a host of other geographies that are encountered during film consumption. Consider, for example, the sumptuous lobby of a 1930s 'picture palace', or the multiplex's out-of-town location amidst arterial roads and retail parks, or the familiar contours of the living-room in which much film-watching now occurs.

There is abundant recent evidence, however, that film studies is rectifying this historical reluctance to 'place' spectators in any detail. The last few years have seen the emergence of what has been termed 'the new cinema history', with publication of a series of substantial volumes both theorising and performing study of globally dispersed instances of film consumption (see, for example, the texts edited by Richard Maltby and colleagues that feature in this chapter's 'Selected reading'). A pioneering contribution to the field was made slightly earlier in *The Place of the Audience: Cultural Geographies of Film Consumption* (2003), by Mark Jancovich and Lucy Faire, with Sarah Stubbings. This book plots the history of film exhibition in Nottingham in the English Midlands – from early screenings in fairgrounds and churches to the latest multiplexes – and argues forcefully that a text-centred approach to spectatorship cannot account for all of the meanings and connotations which cinemagoing has accrued. At times, the authors go very far in effacing the specificities of film texts themselves: particular movies that played at the Metropole, say, vanish in accounts of what this cinema signifies as a built space. While the book suitably corrects an exclusively textual model of spectatorship, then, it risks substituting another sort of one-sidedness, thereby not following consistently Henry Jenkins's thoughtful proposal that film consumption studies should be attentive to 'the relationship between the films' content and their consumption contexts' (2000: 178).

Annette Kuhn's *An Everyday Magic: Cinema and Cultural Memory* (2002), a text mentioned several times already in this book, comes closer to fulfilling Jenkins's programme. Like Jancovich et al., Kuhn is indebted to work in cultural geography and demonstrates heightened sensitivity to film reception sites (in particular here, the picture palaces and neighbourhood fleapits of prewar Britain).

However, extra-textual interest of this sort is subtly interwoven with detailed attention to the texts being consumed. Kuhn traces, for example, the effects of musicals starring Fred Astaire and Ginger Rogers upon spectators' movements and behaviours in off-screen spaces during the 1930s. As well as blending cultural geography and textual criticism, *An Everyday Magic* also draws upon *ethnographic* evidence derived from a series of interviews carried out by Kuhn with older people recalling their cinemagoing experiences. Given this crisscrossing of methodologies, her book is a striking early example of the '"mixed genres" of writing' that Jenkins suggested would characterise the emergent study of film consumption (2000: 177).

This is an opportune moment to assess the value of ethnography in studies of how we consume film. Like *An Everyday Magic*, the book by Jancovich, Faire and Stubbings gets close to its subjects for some of its evidence, drawn in this instance from questionnaires given out by the authors to contemporary Nottingham filmgoers. Both of these recent texts, however, differ markedly in their understanding of an ethnographic approach from that apparent in one of the few early attempts to reckon with film audiences. Here we are referring to the Mass-Observation project to gather information about Britain's cinemagoing habits at the time of World War II. If one of the tools used during this research was a questionnaire allowing spectators to record their own thoughts on the cinema experience, another was fieldwork in which the observer resembles nothing so much as an anthropologist encountering an unfamiliar tribe. Take this representative extract from 'Report on Cinema Queue' (May 1940): 'As the queue moves forward those men behind obs. [observer] who had been talking to a man by the kerb have to talk louder to make themselves heard [...] They are exchanging trivialities, "What are you doing with yourself?" "Seen Bert lately?" and so on' (Richards and Sheridan, 1987: 190). This blatantly externalised perspective on cinemagoers is resisted in the work of current scholars.

Nevertheless, Richard deCordova has questioned the merit even of sensitive, self-conscious uses of ethnography within film consumption studies. Like the research in anthropology from which it takes its protocols, an ethnographic approach to film audiences raises the issue of how 'the subjects of this research can escape becoming its object, constituted in an interpretive gesture by the researcher in relation to his/her agenda, identity, and desires' (deCordova, 2002: 160). Besides this problem of unequal observer/observed relations, ethnographic work on film audiences carries other risks. Jancovich, Faire and Stubbings rightly point out that it may on occasion generate aberrant results because of 'an over-concentration on fan cultures', leaving more 'casual' spectators relatively unstudied (2003: 27). Even an inclusively designed ethnography, however, studying a range of audiences, cannot yield much information about the commercial forces normally responsible for film exhibition, and so is of only partial value to research into film as an industry. A cultural geographic approach to spaces of film consumption may also be deficient in this respect, liable to dwell upon the surface particularities of these sites while neglecting to consider the organised economic interests that usually govern them. Nevertheless, it is this chapter's contention that, integrated where necessary with other approaches like textual analysis and political economy, both cultural geography and ethnography with respect to audiences offer exciting possibilities for film studies. What follows are, first, brief surveys of a range of film consumption sites – pre-theatrical, theatrical and post-theatrical – and then, echoing the work on Nottingham's exhibition history considered above, a case study of film-watching in one particular town.

Cinema before cinemas

Jancovich, Faire and Stubbings write that 'film consumption has never been fully defined or fixed, but has been in a constant process of contestation and transformation' (2003: 37). If currently there seems a plurality of film reception sites – from the IMAX theatre to the screen of a mobile phone watched in transit – this was no less true of the medium's earliest period. With the quite tardy development of specialised exhibition venues – the *OED*'s earliest instance of 'cinema' used in an architectural context comes from *Punch* magazine in 1913 – films at first were 'forced to seek hospitability elsewhere' (Pedullà, 2012: 30) and were shown in a heterogeneous array of pre-existing spaces.

Before turning to consider some of the sites in which films were projected to collectives of people, however, a word should be said about a still earlier development. Prefiguring possibilities in our own spectatorship now, the very first film consumption of all was undertaken by a relatively solitary figure, rather than by a crowd. Parlours equipped with Thomas Edison's coin-operated Kinetoscope machines opened in the United States from 1894: individual patrons peered into the interior of this device as brief footage of a popular entertainer or everyday scene spooled by, illuminated by a filament bulb. A little later, the Kinetophone emerged, representing something of an upgrade as a phonograph was built into the machine and thereby allowed some sound to be synchronised with the visual content. But although these inventions enjoyed a brief vogue, their modelling of film consumption as an individual rather than mass activity doomed them to obsolescence. The cinematograph devised in France by the Lumière brothers had the distinct advantage of configuring film for public exhibition rather than peephole spectatorship; as Louis Lumière wrote: 'the projected images may be viewed by a large number of spectators all at once' (Rittaud-Hutinet, 1995: 32–3).

Film was highly mobile during this early period across sites where projection to a large audience was possible. When the Lumières demonstrated their cinematograph at the Salon Indien of Paris's Grand Café on 28 December 1895, the occasion was conceived less as populist amusement than as scientific edification for the bourgeoisie: class – and imperial – privilege was amply evidenced by the venue's décor of elephant tusks and finely carved bamboo. Soon, however, the Lumière cinematograph attracted patrons who came not to appreciate its optical specifications but to be amazed by the sheer novelty of the images it projected. Film's gravitation here towards popular rather than elite culture was accelerated by its exhibition shortly afterwards in sites of mass entertainment, including fairgrounds, amusement parks, travelling shows, and also vaudeville theatres where it featured on a very varied bill of fare alongside songs, recitations, acrobatics and performances by trained animals.

While dedicated to popular entertainment, however, many of these spaces were still subject to class stratification. Some evidence for this is supplied in Rudyard Kipling's short story 'Mrs Bathurst' (1904) – incidentally, a preternaturally early fable of the dangers of becoming transfixed by the screen. Taking place in a circus in Cape Town and alternating with other amusements like 'the performin' elephants' (Kipling, 2011: 337), film exhibition as described in this text has democratic, even carnivalesque connotations. Nevertheless, the venue is not free of status differentiation: one character, fretting over his 'so-called finances', is only willing to enter the more expensive 'shillin' seats' when a friend pays for him (336). Social inequality of this sort was also to be seen in the *nickelodeons* that represent an important stage in film's progress towards specialist exhibition sites. These enterprises emerged in the US from 1905 and were usually housed in 'a converted cigar store, pawnshop, restaurant, or skating rink made over to look like a vaudeville theatre' (Gomery, 1992: 18). Providing wooden chairs or benches in front of a smallish screen in a sparsely decorated room, nickelodeons had the trappings of cheap, working-class entertainment (deriving their name – as did their British equivalent, *penny gaffs* – from a relatively low admission charge). Yet research by Douglas Gomery and other historians has shown that to consider the nickelodeon simply as a plebeian space is to neglect the fact that then, as now, film consumption was traversed by social differences. While nickelodeons attracted the nickname of 'democracy's theatre', they were frequently located in the wealthier districts of American cities such as New York.

Cinema spaces

Purposefully constructed venues of film exhibition – *cinemas*, in other words – began to supplant improvised, often ramshackle sites like nickelodeons shortly before World War I. The subsequent century of cinema-building in the West has generated many variants, including picture palaces, humbler neighbourhood picture houses, art cinemas, multiplexes and IMAX theatres. An adequate evaluation of the significance of these diverse sites would require many full-length studies. Ideally, research in this area will resist Occidentalist bias and also produce comparative geographies and ethnographies of film consumption around the world. With space limited, however, this section focuses upon two of the most important spaces of Anglo–American cinemagoing.

'Optical fairylands'

Robert C. Allen writes that many of the sites in which films are currently consumed in the West are 'phenomenologically impoverished' (2002: 304). He is particularly struck by the contrast between the functional, shed-like multiplexes of today and the lavishly designed picture palaces that emerged in the US, Britain and elsewhere from the 1910s onwards. The latter were 'spectacles of consumption in themselves' (Jancovich, Faire and Stubbings, 2003: 114), their dazzle rivalling or even outstripping the spectacular properties of what was on screen (see an example in Figure 32). Picture palaces appealed to patrons' senses by an amalgamation of exotic exteriors (flamboyantly recycling Egyptian, Gothic, Greek, Italianate and other building styles), cathedral-sized foyers and auditoria, and opulent internal decoration, with few expenses

32 The 'picture palace': the Trocadero Cinema Theatre, Elephant and Castle, London

spared on carpeting, mirrors, chandeliers and paintings. As the German cultural theorist Siegfried Kracauer wrote in 1926: 'to call them *movie theatres* [...] would be disrespectful' (Kracauer, 1995: 323). Instead, they were, in his words, 'optical fairylands' and 'palaces of distraction' (323).

The critical tenor apparent in that last phrase, in particular, runs through many accounts of cinemagoing produced by cultural commentators and political militants during the first half of the twentieth century. For Kracauer, picture palaces of the type he saw in Berlin were not so much utopian spaces as sites for the reproduction of reactionary politics. With organised religion declining in the West, these cinemas supplied in Marxian terms fresh opiates for the people, their architecture evoking 'the lofty and the *sacred* as if designed to accommodate works of eternal significance – just one step short of burning votive candles' (1995: 327). While Kracauer acknowledges the role played by film *contents* in shaping the conservative social values of the 'Little Shopgirls' or 'Little Miss Typists' frequenting the cinema – note his gendered and class-inflected terms for gullible audiences – he also insists on the determining effects upon the spectator of the place and experience of cinemagoing itself. The very design of the picture palace colludes with textual content to induce a kind of political torpor in its patrons. C. Day-Lewis – father of multiple Oscar-winner Daniel – makes a similar point in a 1938 poem, 'Newsreel'. As Europe was starting to burn, the cinema space functioned, in Day-Lewis's sardonic words, as 'the dream-house', its immersive darkness representing 'a fur you can afford' (1992: 270).

Critiques of this sort from the heyday of the picture palace accord with recent work by a number of scholars on the ideological risks carried by such an opulent cinema space. Historians of film consumption including Miriam Hansen and Judith Mayne have characterised the shift from the nickelodeon era to that of the picture palace as a kind of political fall. Where the rougher-hewn nickelodeons and penny gaffs allowed for boisterous collective spectatorship – perhaps even for an alternative 'public sphere' in which socially marginalised subjects, such as women and immigrants, could find a place – the grander cinemas that came afterwards instituted a more conformist mode of film consumption.

Although free to marvel at the splendid fixtures and fittings, the spectator at the picture palace was also subject to certain protocols (a precursor to that *disciplinisation* of the contemporary multiplex patron to be considered in the next section). As an example, audience conversation while a film played – an aspect of nickelodeon culture – was generally frowned upon in the newer, more controlled exhibition spaces.

There is, however, something one-sided about accounts of the picture palace as an agent of political conservatism. To begin with, this critique rests upon a suspect idealisation of the reception conditions that came earlier: historians have sometimes pointed out that the talk which occurred in the nickelodeon was not necessarily progressive, but also liable to be trivial or even to reinforce existing social prejudices. And if the nickelodeon was actually capable of generating a range of political effects, then so, too, was the picture palace. As Dudley Andrew writes: 'Unquestionably a space of ideological inculcation, the movie theater nevertheless let popular politics develop' (2010: 68). Kuhn is similarly nuanced in her evaluation, situating the picture palace in both 'a real and accessible world' with depressingly constrictive boundaries *and* in 'the worlds of fantasy and imagination' (2002: 141). In juxtaposition to the figure of the Little Shopgirl hypothesised by Kracauer – a simple dupe of the picture palace's grandeur – Kuhn proffers actual cinemagoers of the 1930s whom she interviewed in their old age. One of her most vivid witnesses was Muriel Peck: 'To go to the Astoria was like going to wonderland [...] The décor was Moorish [...] High up there were doors and balconies which were illuminated during the interval and one fully expected a beautiful princess to emerge with her prince' (Kuhn, 2002: 141). Was Peck a victim of the increasing commodification of the cinema experience? Perhaps. Was she a solitary dreamer, rather than the communally engaged figure whose absence underpins Kracauer's and Day-Lewis's critiques of picture palace spectatorship? Maybe. But to adhere only to this negative perspective would be as facile as it is insulting. The sense of wonderment that Muriel Peck and other spectators experienced as they left behind straitened everyday circumstances and entered the early twentieth-century picture palace was, in its small way, a model for any utopian politics.

'Gated communities'

While some observers, as we have seen, regretted the raucous nick-elodeon's displacement by the picture palace, many more recorded a deep sense of loss at the picture palace's own supersession by another wave of cinema-building. The *multiplex* – consisting in the first instance of an unostentatious concrete box, and containing not one but many screens – emerged in the United States during the mid-1960s. Gomery records that the first 'fourplex' opened in Kansas City in 1966, the first 'sixplex' in Omaha, Nebraska in 1969 and the first 'eightplex' in Atlanta in 1974 (1992: 97). Since then, the number of cinema screens under a single roof has continued to multiply, culminating in the post-1990 *megaplex* that often houses twenty or more auditoria (each relatively small in capacity compared with the single screen of the picture palace). This model of cinema design has been streamed to many other nations: for example, the UGC Ciné Cité in Paris currently has nineteen screens, while the Event Marion Megaplex in Adelaide, Australia, has twenty-six. Given the national origin of this cinema type, debates over the arrival of a multiplex in non-US localities have often taken as one of their themes the desir-ability or otherwise of an increased Americanisation of public space. Jancovich, Faire and Stubbings report that Nottingham's local press described plans for the city's first multiplex in 1988, not with out-right hostility, as an 'American invasion of the city' (2003: 201). Before cultural geographers and ethnographers explore the multi-plex's negotiation by its users, then, it is important to take a politi-cal economy approach that will show the involvement of powerful corporations in the worldwide proliferation of cinemas of this type. This trend, however, should no longer be understood simply as a manifestation of US economic and cultural imperialism. For while US-based cinema chains, such as Cinemark Theatres, have certainly continued to make significant incursions abroad, other leaders in this field have origins elsewhere. Cinépolis, for instance, is Mexico-based, owning cinemas not only in its homeland but throughout Latin America and India, and even in the United States; while AMC Theatres of Kansas is now a subsidiary of the Chinese entertainment and leisure conglomerate Dalian Wanda.

The multiplex offers a very different version of public space from the picture palace. Where the latter was located at the heart of a town or city, multiplexes are often situated near traffic nodal points in outlying districts, and thus especially accessible to spectators with cars. With its generally functional architecture and décor, this type of cinema also seems unlikely to appeal to its users as an object of imaginative investment. Sixty years on, Muriel Peck could still vividly recall the fountain and marble flooring in the foyer of her favourite picture palace; their contemporary multiplex equivalents – not quite such propitious materials for nostalgia – might be a prairie of beige carpet and a life-size cardboard cut-out of Harry Potter. In addition, the multiplex lobby typically contains video game machines, posters for forthcoming attractions and, of course, the refreshment stands.

At the multiplex, the spectator is positioned as a consumer not only of film but of a whole array of other products. It is important not to overstate the novelty of this: the earliest cinemas had their merchandising lines, too, selling drinks and snacks and sheet music of songs featured on-screen. In an intensification of the process, however, the newest, largest multiplexes effectively decentre the film-watching activity itself and recast it as part of a larger retail and recreational experience. Consumer opportunities are accompanied by regulations, prompting Charles Acland to find resemblances to a 'gated community' in a venue such as Universal CityWalk in Orlando, Florida, which situates a multi-screen cinema in an integrated, controlled environment of shops, restaurants and bars (2003: 149). An example closer to home for the British reader is the StarCity complex in Birmingham, opened in 2000 by George Clooney and Mark Wahlberg, and currently housing a twenty-five-screen cinema alongside such other attractions as Chinese, Indian and Mexican eateries, a bowling alley, a mini-golf course and a casino with 12,000 square feet of gaming space. Here, as elsewhere in the multiplex era, cinemagoing has been relocated from the public sphere of city streets surrounding the picture palace to a privatised consumer zone from which the non-purchasing classes are largely absent.

As with the picture palace, however, it is important not to hyperbolise any statement of the multiplex's regressive tendencies. For a start, StarCity preserves within its consumer enclave traces of older, carnivalesque sites of film exhibition: funfairs and firework displays are held there, offering a more democratic experience than is available in other parts of the venue. In addition, the space is not racially encoded as all-white. Reflecting Birmingham's multicultural population, the site's restaurants offer food ranging from halal meat to Indian vegetarian cuisine, while the cinema itself regularly includes Bollywood movies on its programme. Even if these practices might still be read pessimistically as merely extending the consumer class beyond its traditional white caucus – simply varying the racial identity of that 'bourgeois (cinemagoing) subject' that Acland argues is produced by multiplexes (2003: 202) – they are nevertheless progressive when juxtaposed with a white monoculture of film consumption earlier, or elsewhere, in Britain.

A plausible account of the politics of the multiplex experience will be nuanced, rather than either blandly optimistic or morbidly despondent. Consider, for instance, the relationship between discipline and freedom in this type of cinema. While the multiplex experience might seem a whirl of unfettered consumption, it also requires the spectator to submit to various forms of monitoring and control. Again, this is not unprecedented: earlier cinemas may have had only a rudimentary disciplinary apparatus at their disposal – a manager scrutinising patrons, an usher insisting on silence in the auditorium – yet they still sought to check the most libertarian spectatorship. However, it is possible to detect in the multiplex a significant increase in institutional power over filmgoers:

> The policing of ushers, the presence of security cameras, the regiment of scheduling, and the overt appeals to decorum in film trailers (feet off the seat in front, no talking, cell phones and pagers off, etc.) are indices of the intense interest in encouraging civility and reducing the prospects for impromptu (and economically unproductive) interventions. (Acland, 2003: 231–2)

To this list might be added newer warnings on-screen about punishments for video piracy. Perception of the multiplex's authoritarian regime leads Acland, somewhat uncritically, to espouse the radical potential of forms of indecorum, such as talking on the phone or resting feet on the seat in front. These behaviours, after all, seem more calculated to bolster a complacent egotism than to establish bonds of sociability. Nevertheless, there is something salutary about Acland's attempt to redeem the multiplex for a progressive politics, to uncover vivid collective experience in a sort of space that critics have often written off as merely functional and capitalistic. Even if multiplexes suggest a public sphere in decline from the riotous communality of some earlier film exhibition sites, they still gather strangers together and thereby signify faintly, in Acland's words, 'a dream of global collectivity' (2003: 243). Like the picture palaces that Rebecca Solnit wonderfully calls 'island republics' (2003: 245–6), the multiplex continues – albeit imperfectly and intermittently – to produce an experience of solidarity that evokes an alternative to dominant social forms.

STOP and THINK

- Evaluate the proposition that film studies should take into account not only what is watched, but *where* and *how* consumption takes place. How enriching of the discipline – or limiting upon it – do you judge extra-textual research of this kind to be? How should it be integrated with study of film texts themselves?

- Ethnographies of film consumption gather evidence from viewers themselves (for example, by making use of questionnaires and interviews). What strike you as the strengths and weaknesses of the various instruments or methods employed in such research? Given that an ethnographic approach to spectatorship brings into closer than usual contact the people being studied and the people doing the studying, are any conceptual or ethical problems raised by the researcher's role?

- Try an experiment in which you observe closely how spectators behave in any cinema (to avoid threats of litigation – or violence – it may be preferable to perform this exercise on a group of friends). Aim to log behaviours with all the zeal and thoroughness of the Mass-Observation project described earlier. What is usefully discovered about film consumption by such ethnographic scrutiny? But, also, what might be missed?

- Earlier, it was noted that an adequate study of film

consumption must be *global* in scope. In his travel book
Jesting Pilate (1926), Aldous Huxley made a pioneering contribution to comparative consumption studies, describing
how he came across a Hollywood film being screened at 'an
open-air picture show' in Batavia (now Jakarta, capital of
Indonesia) (1994: 138). Huxley is properly attentive to the
interactions here of text and context: 'The violent imbecili-
ties of the story flickered in silence against the background
of the equatorial night. In silence the Javanese looked on'
(139). Follow in Huxley's footsteps and offer a detailed
assessment of film consumption practices you have observed
outside your native society.

Home looking

In thinking about where, exactly, films are consumed, it is important not to be restricted by the four walls of exhibition venues themselves. Although a film is shown in an art cinema, say, or a multiplex
auditorium, the space of its reception is actually much more diffuse
and variegated than this. Consumption of *The Lego Movie* (2014),
for example, is liable to be extended across a number of extra- or
post-theatrical settings: the bar afterwards in which you discuss
the film's pleasures with friends, or the university seminar room in
which you develop a Marxist feminist reading of the father's role
as 'the Man Upstairs', or the internet forum on which you post
a piece of fan fiction about unsuspected fantasies of the character
Wyldstyle. Even such an expansive listing of sites, however, needs
supplementing if it is to capture the consumption space of certain
films. Take controversial works from *A Clockwork Orange* (1971)
and *Last Tango in Paris* (1972) through *The Last Temptation of
Christ* (1988) and David Cronenberg's *Crash* (1996) to *The Human
Centipede (First Sequence)* (2009) and *A Serbian Film* (2010). In
each of these cases the film circulated through the geographies of
parliamentary and council debate, newspaper editorialising, forums
of public opinion (latterly online), and so on. It was 'consumed' by
people who may have watched little – or none – of it.

Having acknowledged the diffuseness of post-theatrical film
consumption, however, space here allows detailed consideration of

only one, increasingly important site of spectatorship: *the home*. In a short but evocative essay, 'Leaving the Movie Theater' (1975), Roland Barthes juxtaposes cinematic viewing with the experience of watching a film on TV at home. The dark, comfortable space of the cinema, with its large screen and magnified sound, draws him into a state of hypnotic immersion, 'a veritable cinematographic cocoon'; domestic spectatorship, by contrast, holds 'no fascination; here darkness is erased, anonymity repressed; space is familiar, articulated (by furniture, known objects), tamed' (Barthes, 1986: 346). Here, too, the 'eroticism' Barthes associates with the cinema by virtue of mingling with strangers is 'foreclosed' (346). Barthes is, of course, writing at a time before development of home theatre systems equipped to fill a living-room with enormous, high-definition images and all-enveloping, multiplex-quality sound. However, his celebration of the cinema auditorium's immersive pleasures damns in advance the very phenomenon of domestic film consumption, which will always be compromised in his eyes by familiar surroundings, mundane distractions and, not least, by *light*.

But while appreciating Barthes's erotics of the cinema space, it is important not to accept without argument his thesis that domestic film consumption is necessarily impoverished. Nor is assent mandatory to the American cultural commentator Susan Sontag's assertion that 'The conditions of paying attention in a domestic space are radically disrespectful of film' (1996: n.p.). Evaluation of home spectatorship touches upon questions of psychology, sociology and economics, and thus requires a patient accumulation of detail rather than mobilisation of a simple spatial binary in which the cinema is good and the home is bad. Here Barbara Klinger's book *Beyond the Multiplex: Cinema, New Technologies, and the Home* is instructive. Klinger resists 'the value-laden dichotomy that has continually regarded home film exhibition through a comparative lens' (2006: 3). Complainants about the loss of film's absorptive power in domestic screenings forget that cinemas, too, with the distractions of talking patrons and crackling popcorn, do not always enfold the spectator into a blissful, womb-like environment. Klinger also addresses the somewhat different argument that watching films at home produces a passive, even anaesthetised spectator; she suggests, on the contrary, that 'All viewers – including couch potatoes – are

implicitly active', even if it has to be acknowledged that home viewers' engagement with the screen 'does not necessarily translate into
a progressive political position' (2006: 11).

Where Barthes is primarily concerned with the experiential quality of domestic spectatorship, an alternative account might start,
more hard-headedly, with its *economics*. As noted in Chapter 9,
Hollywood has for some time understood that theatrical screening
of a film, far from being an end in itself, is simply one stage in the
film's packaging and repackaging for different exhibition formats.
Much of this profitable reformatting is, of course, for domestic
consumption. At first, viewers at home were restricted to tuning
into movies as they were broadcast on terrestrial television: film
industries, not least Hollywood, had quickly conquered their hostility to this upstart medium, recognised an exploitable market when
they saw one and, from the 1950s, begun selling their backlists for
TV screening. The later emergence of cable networks – some housing dedicated movie channels – raised the price that studios could
charge for their works to be shown in a home setting. Increasingly,
however, consumption by home spectators has been beholden less
to corporate scheduling decisions and has taken the form of rent-
ing, purchasing or downloading films made available in a number
of portable formats. The video recorder emerged during the 1970s
and gradually became an indispensable consumer item; as early as
1992, revenues from the sale or rental of films in videocassette form
outstripped cinema box office returns in the United States. And
although one of the videocassette's several successor technologies –
the laserdisc – endures mainly as a specialist archiving medium,
there has been a mass-market triumph for two others: the DVD (or
digital video/versatile disc) and, latterly, the Blu-ray disc that is
better equipped for high-definition image resolution.

As artefacts, the videocassette, DVD and Blu-ray disc are ambiguous in their ideological implications. Although they hold out the
promise of individualised film consumption – short-circuiting corporate disciplines that govern a film's exhibition at the cinema – it
would be unwise to take them as signs of the consumer's sovereign
power. In a point that applies also to the later Blu-ray enthusiast,
Klinger points out that the DVD collector is subject to and even,
in a sense, constructed by continuous marketing initiatives by the

movie and audio-visual equipment industries: 'Solipsism is central to the pleasures and the paradoxes of collecting: considered a most private, even eccentric, activity, collecting is unavoidably tethered to public enterprises and discourses' (2006; 89). Yet while we should acknowledge the mighty commercial operations driving home consumption of DVDs and Blu-ray discs, and also the more recent (authorised) downloading of films, this should not entirely govern our evaluation of home spectatorship. For the domestic viewing of films in these formats brings new pleasures and knowledges, at least some of which are potentially progressive. In the first instance, the compressing of information on DVDs and Blu-ray discs allows spectators access not merely to the feature presentation itself but to an array of extra materials, which may, for example, contextualise a film in ways denied the cinema viewer. Second, these formats, together with downloads, have made the home spectator's screen a place potentially of greater textual variety than any theatrical venue. As well as increasing the circulation possibilities of locally made independent or avant-garde work, they help to internationalise exhibition, significantly extending spectatorship for films from around the world that have little or no prospect of securing theatrical release outside their own countries. Third, the portable formats open up possibilities for spectators of renegotiating and reordering – even, in a sense, rewriting – the films they watch (a topic for further discussion in the Conclusion).

Competing assessments have also been given of the sociability of watching films at home in DVD and Blu-ray form or as downloads. Particularly where domestic spectatorship is supported by a personal device such as a laptop, tablet or smartphone, there is a suggestion by some commentators that it scarcely counts as a *social* activity at all. In Pedullà's striking phrase, 'watching a film came to resemble a traditionally individual activity such as silent reading' (2012: 66). The disc or download is construed from this perspective as the preserve of a privatised viewer, someone detached from the interpersonal bonds of cinemagoing and now taking solipsistic pleasure not only in the film texts themselves but in the expensive audio-visual or digital hardware that plays them to optimal specifications. But while this portrait has a certain truth, it is also unsustainable as a generalisation about contemporary domestic spectatorship:

the new technologies support a much broader range of experiences than simply elitist, individualist connoisseurship. On many occasions, watching films in these ways may actually foster communality with partners, friends, families, even larger social groups. It need not, then, erase that sense of collectivity which is historically represented by the crowd gathered at a cinema. There is further cause here to challenge a simplistic politics of exhibition spaces and to argue specifically that engaged home spectatorship of a film on DVD, say, with family or friends is richer in collective life than something like a mid-afternoon multiplex screening in which the few spectators present sit islanded in solitude across the auditorium.

It is important, finally, not to overstate the extent of separation between home and cinema as loci of film consumption. Certainly, a dedicated audience will be recruited by each of these venues: on the one hand, the older or disabled spectator who is attracted by home consumption; on the other, the devotee of superhero films who wishes to see them scaled-up and amplified in cinema conditions. For the most part, however, film consumers are likely, as occasion demands, to move fluidly between spaces rather than to be confined to one or the other. The home has thus not replaced cinemas, but co-exists with them in a complex economy of film reception. There is, in fact, no unilinear history of exhibition sites; instead, modes of film spectatorship are repeated across the nineteenth, twentieth and twenty-first centuries, albeit recurring in different technological guises and with different social, psychological and economic implications. On the one hand, the privatised reception of films today that is possible via an electronic device recapitulates the ethos of the pre-theatrical Kinetoscope or Kinetophone; on the other, current exhibition practices such as the incorporation of multiplexes in retail and leisure complexes are oddly reminiscent of that earlier, carnivalesque period when films sat alongside rival forms of the spectacular.

STOP and THINK

• Consider what happens when you watch at home a film already viewed at the cinema. What difference does it make to relocate spectatorship of *Interstellar* (2014), say, from the IMAX auditorium to a laptop in your room? Are you still viewing the same film, as theorists of textual continuity regardless of variations in exhibition format would argue; or should we actually speak of *a new text*? Are any differences you detect traceable to the mode of exhibition itself, such as the consequences of shrinking a multiplex-scale image? Or do differences arise because of circumstances of home spectatorship, including light (rather than the cinema's darkness), distraction (rather than an ethos of compulsory concentration) and textual segmentation (as against the cinema's mode of continuous viewing)?

- In 'Leaving the Movie Theater', Barthes is restricted by existing technology and conceives of home consumption of films as occurring only via the living-room TV. This activity is, for him, an agent of ideological conservatism: 'television *doomed* us to the Family, whose household instrument it has become – what the hearth used to be, flanked by its communal kettle' (1986: 346). However, compare this account of repressive home spectatorship with your own experiences of domestic film consumption. Itemise the various forms of domestic film-watching available now and assess the sorts of social life – or *anti*-sociability – associated with them.

- As suggested above, it is unwise to conclude that contemporary spectators express an absolute preference for *either* the cinema *or* the home as a place of film consumption: many people oscillate instead between the two venues (each of these exhibition spaces having, of course, multiple permutations). Analyse and account for your own movements across the broad geography of film spectatorship.

Case study: film consumption in Loughborough

Robert C. Allen describes the benefits that may accrue to someone uncovering the archaeology of cinemagoing in his or her own locality: 'A student can be wonderfully empowered by becoming the world's leading expert on the history of film exhibition in Shelby, NC' (2002: 305). In the hope of such reward, then, a brief history is offered here of film consumption in Loughborough in the English Midlands. The results of this research are interesting more for their typicality than their distinctiveness. A provincial town known principally for engineering, hosiery, pharmaceutical production and, since 1966, for its university, Loughborough's population stood at 21,000 in 1901, 38,000 in 1961 and almost 60,000 in 2011; despite its relatively small size, however, the town has supported a mixed and, at times, prolific cinematic economy.

The history of film exhibition in Loughborough follows, almost schematically, the broad lines of development sketched earlier in this chapter. Initially, films in the town had a transient, itinerant life, being shown not in any permanent space but in 'the travelling phantoscope and other shows which appeared at the November Fair' (Jones, 2002: 18). Here, as elsewhere, film's earliest exhibition fostered associations of popular diversion, rather than rarefied art. These connotations persisted in Loughborough even as more durable venues were found (beginning with the Town Hall, or Corn Exchange, where screenings started in 1902). The ready convertibility to film exhibition of sites of other entertainments was also apparent in Loughborough just before World War I when a short-lived roller-skating rink, near the present-day location of the university, was repurposed as a cinema under the name of the New Playhouse. Film's high importance to the town's cultural economy during this period can be gauged, too, by the appearance on the front page of the local newspaper, the *Echo*, of advertisements for current showings. The New Playhouse's programme at the end of January 1914, for example, included *The Pit and the Pendulum* (1913), an adaptation of Edgar Allan Poe's short story by the pioneering female director, Alice Guy; softening this suggestion of audience terror, however, the cinema's advert also featured a promise of free tea and biscuits to matinée customers.

In September 1914, however, Loughborough's first purpose-built cinema opened: the Empire, situated near the marketplace. For some decades subsequently, this modestly sized town housed several cinemas in competition with each other. Besides the Empire and the New Playhouse, filmgoers could choose to visit Vint's Electric Hippodrome (opened in 1910) or, a little later, the Victory (opened in 1921). The Victory secured a decisive market advantage late in 1929 when it became the first cinema in the town technically equipped to screen films with optically encoded soundtracks, as opposed to films that were rendered rudimentary and partial 'talkies' by the playing of synchronised phonograph discs in the auditorium.

In Loughborough, however, as universally, film consumption had other determinants besides the textual product itself. Reports and advertisements retrieved from the archives of the local paper, and spectators' memories as transcribed by local historians, collectively put great stress on the attractions of the screening spaces themselves. Thus an advert for the Empire in the *Echo* of 11 September 1914 drew prospective patrons' attention to the ornamentation of both the building's exterior ('beautiful illuminants' to light the façade) and its interior ('white and rich gold'). When the Empire was expensively reconstructed some two decades later as the *New* Empire – rendering it a picture palace or, in another term common in this period, a *super cinema* – the building was presented as a major pleasure in itself, rather than as a merely functional site of film projection. The *on-screen* spectacle was certainly acknowledged in a souvenir programme printed to mark the new cinema's grand opening on 30 March 1936: the steadiness of the projected image was emphasised, for example, while customers were notified that the New Empire's General Manager will be 'pleased to give you any information you may require in connection with films, stars or film production generally, as he is a recognised authority on all matters cinematic' ('New Empire Super Cinema, Loughborough', 1936: 17). Nevertheless, the drift of this promotional material hints that the spectacular was lodged still more vividly in the building's Art Deco frontage, its lavish foyer, its exuberant auditorium décor, even in the high specifications of its heating and cooling systems. Similar attentiveness to the gratifications afforded by an entertainment space itself was apparent in the design and fitting-out of Loughborough's second lavishly appointed Art Deco cinema: the Odeon, which opened only eight months later in November 1936.

Mervyn Gould suggests, however, that by comparison with the adulation accorded the New Empire's opening, the local paper's response to the establishing of the Odeon was slightly muted. Perhaps, he speculates, this lowered enthusiasm was 'because it was the second Super of the year, or a national circuit house instead of a local independent' (1994: 69). Reference here to varying forms of cinema ownership reminds us of how crucial it is to incorporate economics in discussion of film exhibition in Loughborough (or, indeed, anywhere else). Certainly, as Richard Maltby acknowledges, 'social and cultural histories of specific cinema audiences' are subjects central to the emerging field of study devoted to film consumption (2011: 3). Yet an adequate research programme, Maltby contends, will extend beyond these 'ethnographies of cinemagoing' (16) and consider also phenomena that include 'the commercial activities of film distribution and exhibition' (3). Even when concerned with film-watching in a specific place such as Loughborough, then, scholarship should not be bound by 'the idiosyncrasies of the local microhistorical narrative' (Maltby, 2011: 16), but should register those regional, national and indeed global forces of production, distribution and exhibition that effectively shape both the viewing choices of the town's film patrons and the spaces in which viewing occurs.

Taking its cue from these remarks, analysis of the commercial imperatives directing film consumption in Loughborough might start with the detail of the Odeon's ownership, since this meant that the cinema's programming was not locally designed but the outcome of decisions made by a chain at national level. However, it is not only in this nationally owned cinema that signs can be discerned of the Loughborough spectator's subjection to commercial regimes. Attempts to organise local audiences were clearly made by Charles K. Deeming, managing director of the Universal Car Company. While local rather than national in provenance, Deeming's corporation nevertheless exerted a controlling grip on film consumption in the town from the 1930s onwards by owning the Victory and New Playhouse cinemas as well as the New Empire. Moreover, the way in which it conceived of the New Empire valuably alerts us to the fact that current modelling of film consumption as simply one node in an extended retail experience is not an innovation but actually a reactivation, or repackaging, of older commercial practices. Thus the *Echo*'s report of 3 April 1936 advised patrons of sources of gratification in the new cinema other than the film text itself, pointing out that 'it would be possible without leaving the building to have a meal, to see a first-class screen entertainment and then to proceed to the ballroom for a dance'. Uncovering evidence such as this is not intended to reduce audiences in Loughborough, or elsewhere, to the condition of consumerist zombies, transiting uncritically or without friction among a host of retail options: the tenor of this chapter, as of this book more generally, has been to argue against any such modelling of the neutered or easily pacified spectator. Nevertheless, it is important, too, not to overstate the autonomy of audiences, and recognition of the commercial patterns and drives that underlie cinemagoing in a community like Loughborough contributes to this work.

Since World War II, the history of Loughborough's cinemagoing, like that of cinemagoing elsewhere in the West, is one largely of decline. From a peak in 1946 of 1,640 million cinema visits annually, audiences in Britain fell drastically, so that the equivalent figure in 1960 stood at only 501 million ('A Century of Change', 1999: 26). Unsurprisingly, far fewer screening spaces were required. In Loughborough, the Victory closed its doors in 1967 and the Odeon, by then renamed the Classic, followed in 1974 (although the building remains, housing a bingo hall). The New Empire thus achieved monopoly status in the community as a film exhibition space (albeit a monopoly of significantly lower commercial value than would once have been the case). This cinema underwent multiple name changes as, reflecting the increasingly precarious economics of film exhibition, it passed through a series of corporate ownerships. Thus it became the Essoldo in 1954, the Curzon in 1972, the Classic in 1973, the Curzon again in 1974, and then the Reel in 2001 until acquisition by the Odeon group in 2011. The cinema's hegemony has been seriously challenged, however, by Cineworld's opening in 2016 of an eight-screen multiplex near the town centre; in modest local imitation of an entertainment complex like Birmingham's StarCity, cinemagoing here is combined with other consumer pleasures, notably eating out (its restaurant franchises include Nando's and Pizza Express). Whereas earlier in its history Loughborough was able to support a multi-cinema economy, it remains to be seen how long the present-day Odeon, housing six screens and a single pizza restaurant, will be able to resist this powerful competitor.

Finally, in keeping with arguments developed earlier in this chapter, it should be emphasised that attention to cinemagoing in Loughborough tells only part of the story of the town's film consumption. Anyone wanting to reconstruct the exhibition history of the New Empire, say, can draw readily upon the sorts of

archival material identified by Maltby as available to this strand of
film studies: 'theatre records, newspaper reviews, the trade press
and business correspondence' (2011: 17). Also accessible are the
oral testimonies of local cinemagoers, as recorded by historians like
Mervyn Gould. However, it is a requirement of the new studies of
film consumption that practitioners range more widely and more
ingeniously than before in search of sources of evidence. Thus, in
Loughborough's case, historians need to find ways of measuring
film consumption on the university campus, including screenings
organised by the long-running Film Society and also those timeta-
bled as part of degree programmes in several disciplines. Similarly,
work should be done to map and evaluate incidences of home consumption of film in the town. For every person in Loughborough
who went to the Odeon to watch *The Inbetweeners 2* in September
2014, there was, after all, a local resident or student choosing to
watch something quite different via a host of platforms or devices
at home. A major challenge for film consumption studies now is to
develop the means of capturing such informal, multiply situated
spectatorships.

Selected reading

Acland, Charles R. (2003) *Screen Traffic: Movies, Multiplexes, and Global
    Culture* (Durham, NC: Duke University Press).
    Vividly written, searching assessment of the impact upon cinemagoing of
    post-1980 shifts in film production, distribution and exhibition.
Barber, Stephen (2010), *Abandoned Images: Films and Film's End* (London:
    Reaktion).
    Remarkable book that moves outwards from the sites of derelict cinemas
    in Los Angeles to reflect, without morbidity, on the 'nature and status of
    film' now.
Biltereyst, Daniel, Richard Maltby and Philippe Meers (eds) (2012),
    *Cinema, Audiences and Modernity: New Perspectives on European Cinema
    History* (Abingdon: Routledge).
    Informative studies of many local sites of film consumption, the volume
    functioning as a European-centred companion volume to the same edi-
    tors' *Explorations in New Cinema History* (see below).
Gomery, Douglas (1992), *Shared Pleasures: A History of Movie Presentation
    in the United States* (London: BFI).

Densely researched account of film exhibition in the US from Kinetoscope parlours to the era of home video: industry-centred, but an indispensable resource.

Jancovich, Mark and Lucy Faire, with Sarah Stubbings (2003), *The Place of the Audience: Cultural Geographies of Film Consumption* (London: BFI).

Fascinating, meticulously researched account of changing spaces of film consumption in Nottingham: questionable for its diminished interest in films themselves, but a major contribution to audience studies.

Klinger, Barbara (2006), *Beyond the Multiplex: Cinema, New Technologies, and the Home* (Berkeley: University of California Press).

Important study of what is now, in many nations, the principal site of film consumption; avoids both a morbidly pessimistic and an uncritically celebratory tone.

Kuhn, Annette (2002), *An Everyday Magic: Cinema and Cultural Memory* (London: I. B. Tauris).

Wonderfully rich, often moving exploration of British cinemagoing in the 1930s, articulating ethnographic and cultural geographic approaches with sensitivity, too, to films' textual details.

Maltby, Richard, Daniel Biltereyst and Philippe Meers (eds) (2011), *Explorations in New Cinema History: Approaches and Case Studies* (Chichester: Wiley-Blackwell).

Rich, globally expansive collection, with many of the essays bearing upon questions of film consumption in very different venues (from Australian garden suburbs, say, to New York's underground arts scene).

Pedullà, Gabriele (2012), *In Broad Daylight: Movies and Spectators After the Cinema*, trans. Patricia Gaborik (London: Verso).

Excellent, erudite book, exploring aesthetic and political questions raised by the increasing consumption of films on individual devices, rather than as part of an organised cinema audience.

Waller, Gregory A. (ed.) (2002), *Moviegoing in America: A Sourcebook in the History of Film Exhibition* (Malden, MA: Blackwell).

Absorbing collection of contemporaneous reflections on the first century of US film exhibition by journalists, architects, management gurus and others.

Online resources

Cinema Theatre Association, http://cinema-theatre.org.uk.

Home page of the UK-based Cinema Theatre Association: besides information on and images of British cinemas, includes links to resources on cinemas worldwide.

Eyles, Allen, 'Cinemas and Cinemagoing', www.screenonline.org.uk/film/
   cinemas.
   Helpful, multi-part overview, hosted by the BFI website, of changing
   contexts of film exhibition in Britain from the end of the nineteenth
   century.

Conclusion:
film studies and the digital

By way of conclusion, we turn first of all to a text cited much earlier in this book: Peter Wollen's 'An Alphabet of Cinema' (in Wollen, 2002). Writing very early in the twenty-first century, Wollen was prescient in making one of his alphabetical selections: 'O', he says, 'is for Online' (2002: 13). He goes on to indicate that the digital will leave its imprint, if that is not too concrete a term to apply to this technology of the virtual, upon all domains and levels of film. Thus transformations will occur in film production itself, since 'Digital technology is changing the whole nature of image-capture, allowing images to be changed, combined and appropriated' (13). Similarly, film exhibition will be drastically reconfigured: if 'film as a collective spectacle will continue', movies will also, Wollen anticipates, be distributed to a range of venues not requiring the traditional gathering together of a crowd. Finally, freed, at least to an extent, from the requirement to consume films according to routines and sequences prescribed by others, the spectator, too, will be decisively remodelled: 'When cinema goes online, we will be able to download films and simultaneously summon up clips from other films for comparison, background information from research libraries and archives, even out-takes that we can use privately to make our own revised versions of sequences' (13).

In the years since Wollen wrote these words, the 'successive substitutions of the digital for the analog' (Rodowick, 2007: 184) have become ever more extensive. If it is still a little premature to speak of film as now 'a digital art' (Wollen, 2002: 13), it is nevertheless one that is significantly and increasingly digitising. For our purposes, it is important to acknowledge that the changes wrought by the digital upon film production, exhibition and consumption bring into question, perhaps even into crisis, key assumptions and protocols of film studies as these developed and cohered in the second half of the twentieth century. Something should, then, be said here about the effects upon our discipline of film's digitising condition.

The growth of the digital requires us to rethink with particular urgency the relationship of film to the real. For enthusiasts and detractors alike in the nineteenth century, the power of photography as a medium consisted in the fact that the operation of light upon chemical emulsions on a filmstrip left behind an imprint, or indexical trace, of whatever really had passed in front of the camera lens. While film itself has offered a playground to illusionists all the way from the pioneering Frenchman Georges Méliès to contemporary Hollywood's special effects designers, its own photochemical origins mean that it too, as an art form, has traditionally carried with it the promise of the real (or, from a more jaundiced perspective, reality's taint). In a memorable phrase, David Thomson writes of film as 'scooping up the momentary appearance of things, like a blood sample at a crime' (2005: 100). As Chapter 1 noted, a belief that film is defined and empowered as a medium by transcriptions of reality itself underpins the critical writing of André Bazin, Siegfried Kracauer and many others.

Compare the tropes mobilised by that earlier wave of film theorists with a passage written much more recently by Dudley Andrew. While, for Andrew, the 'magic' of film still exists, it is of a different order from the happy accidents that once occurred during shooting as a result of photochemical processes. Instead, he argues, 'The magic has migrated to the computer, where soundtracks are additive concoctions of scores of tracks, and pictures are composited, not composed' (2010: 6). To put it more bluntly still, as Andrew does, 'the digital has shifted attention from shooting to postproduction' (5). Of course, the faith in film's indexical power that is exhibited by writers such as Bazin and Kracauer is unlikely wholly to disappear even as increasing numbers of the images we look at on screen are generated by computer rather than produced photographically in any simple or unassisted way. At the same time, however, more and more people are likely to lose the habit of taking cinematic images to be unimpeachable evidences of the real. As one of its key tasks in the future, film studies will need to explore the resulting 'structures of feeling' (to borrow a term from the cultural theorist Raymond Williams).

It should not be thought that filmmakers themselves have responded with equal enthusiasm to digitisation. Some older figures who are wedded to a tactile notion of cinema – to sensuous encounters with celluloid, not least in the editing suite – react with dismay to the rise of odourless, non-touchable digital video. Andrzej Wajda, the eminent Polish director, deplores what he sees as the sheer facility of digital production and post-production: 'video is a technique that offers no resistance [...] This means you work without tension, without the familiar atmosphere of being on the edge, constantly at risk' (1989: 43–4). More recently, in the excellent American documentary *Side by Side* (2012), filmmakers including Christopher Nolan and his regular director of photography Wally Pfister are to be seen choosing film over digital video for what they perceive as the former's superior visual expressiveness. Even in this impartially titled movie, however, they are in a minority, outvoted by directors, editors and cinematographers who speak of being drawn to digital for the support it lends to a form of filmmaking that is characterised by speed, flexibility and ease of revision. Elsewhere, the US director Robert Rodriguez tells a linear narrative of technological progress to rationalise his own movement away from shooting on traditional film: 'any filmmaker who compares film and digital on-set will suddenly look at their film camera like it's a lead brick or an old vinyl LP record' (McKernan, 2005: 125–6).

There is, however, no such thing as a uniform digital aesthetic in contemporary cinema. While many current filmmakers share a commitment to utilising digital technology, the work they produce varies considerably in form and intent. At one end of the spectrum are the saturated colours and exquisite pictorial details of such films as *Life of Pi* and *The Great Gatsby*; at the other are the reduced palettes and rougher, improvisatory looks of films including *Winter's Bone* and the Turkish *Once Upon a Time in Anatolia* (2011). If some filmmakers have abandoned analogue formats in a quest for stylistic density, others have done so with quite different motivations. Holly Willis writes of the 'rejuvenation of activist media' enabled

by quicker, less expensive shooting and editing on digital videotape (2005: 96). Thus a number of directors of documentaries have
embraced the new technology in insurrectionary mode, launching
guerrilla-style strikes against the versions of public events proposed by mainstream information networks. Instances here include
Dylan Avery's quartet of home-made *Loose Change* films (2005–9)
that challenge the official US narrative of the 9/11 attacks. Such
increased enfranchisement of filmmakers can also, with caution, be
posited at a global level. The emergence of relatively cheap digital
movie cameras and desktop editing programs, coupled with distribution routes based around DVDs and downloads, potentially gives
opportunities for making documentaries and features not only to
marginal groups inside Western nations that already boast cinema
industries but to people in countries historically subordinate within
the world cinema system.

Besides taking account of changes in production enabled by digital technology, film studies should consider shifts also in exhibition.
The eight years between publication of the first and second editions
of this book have seen, in less economically powerful nations as well
as in the wealthy West, the near-universal equipping of cinemas
with digital projectors. Whereas companies once had to provide
exhibitors with multiple, expensive prints of the films to be shown,
now delivery is effected digitally (including by sending films as files
to cinema computers). The result is a standardisation of the spectacle on screen: whereas individual analogue copies of films were
subject to small variations that emerged during projection, digitisation erases such particularities and guarantees a uniform viewing
experience from Montreal to Manchester. For some spectators, of
course, this is regretted as a sanitising of film consumption.

Even in cinemas newly kitted out with digital technology, however, audiences are still subject as before to inexorably unfolding
spectacle. Gabriele Pedullà writes vividly, if a little melodramati-
cally, of the cinema spectator's lack of freedom. Once the projector is set in motion at the designated screening time, he writes,
it proceeds 'with the somber obstinacy of fate' (2012: 113). Or,
again: 'Everything is already written. For the audience, in movies,
fate advances at a rhythm of twenty-four frames per second [...]
implacable, merciless, unstoppable' (106). Strikingly, however,

Pedullà and many other critics have found digital spectatorship in *non-theatrical situations* to be much more mobile and liberatory. The DVD or Blu-ray viewer at home, for example, may skip freely between segmented chapters of a film, introducing discontinuity and even reversibility into a previously rigid narrative structure laid down by the filmmaker; he or she can also transit back and forth between the film itself and a repertoire of other images. This room for manoeuvre leads Pedullà to speak of 'the invention of the spectator-projectionist' (2012: 113). Choosing a metaphor from elsewhere in the world of film that has greater implications of creativity, Anne Friedberg argues that the viewer in such situations 'becomes a *montagiste*, editing at will with the punch of a fingertip, "zipping", "zapping" and "muting"' (2000: 447).

Film studies should set itself the task of pursuing the aesthetic, cultural and ideological questions raised by the emergence of Pedullà's spectator-projectionist or Friedberg's spectator-editor. For at least two reasons, uncritical celebration of this remodelling of the viewer should be avoided. A sober note is sounded in the first instance by Victor Burgin, who compares the home viewer's rapid image-switching with an early form of radical spectatorial activity. If contemporary practice in some ways mimics French Surrealist efforts to disrupt narrative sequence in film by dropping in and out of a series of cinemas – an activity mentioned above in Chapter 4 – it lacks the Surrealists' psychological experiment and political intent; as Burgin writes: 'The decomposition of narrative films, once subversive, is now normal' (2004: 9). Secondly, a culture of zipping and zapping threatens to dissolve the film experience itself in a much larger image stream, recalling in the process how the medium emerged late in the nineteenth century alongside a host of other visual technologies. Many people, of course, will not be nostalgic about such a development. Nevertheless, the shift from a culture of sustained attention to film images to more fleeting engagement with them, or from a practice of concentration to an ethos of distraction, may not be without costs.

Film studies should, in general, be vigilant in the face of celebratory, even utopian accounts of film production, exhibition and consumption in the digital age. A suitably cautious note is struck by Holly Willis at the end of her largely positive report on digital developments. She points out that, while filmmakers and viewers alike have the chance in the contemporary media system to be the manipulators of new technology, they also face the prospect of being the manipulated: 'as we experience new forms of digital media, we are also being configured by new forms of digital media; and as much as we enjoy the power and freedom they offer, it behooves us to be cognisant of the systems of power and control that they allow over us as well' (2005: 97). Just as the ideologically neutral material of celluloid supported a vast range of positions and purposes over the course of the twentieth century, so twenty-first-century digital video will also be multiple rather than singular in its cultural and political effects. Despite euphoric manifestos of the sort that always accompany any technological breakthrough, digitisation's progressiveness cannot be assumed in advance. If this is a technology that facilitates such things as nimbler, sassier documentaries, it is also one liable to appropriation by commercial film industries for the production of ever more lavish and overpowering spectacle.

Selected reading

Balcerzak, Scott and Jason Sperb (2009, 2012), *Cinephilia in the Age of Digital Revolution: Film, Pleasure and Digital Culture* (New York: Columbia University Press).
  Two timely volumes, tracking digital developments in film through many contexts and across several nations.
McKernan, Brian, *Digital Cinema: The Revolution in Cinematography, Postproduction, and Distribution* (New York: McGraw-Hill, 2005).
  A handy, accessible source of technical information that also includes interviews with such pioneers of digital filmmaking as George Lucas and Robert Rodriguez.
Shaw, Jeffrey and Peter Weibel (eds) (2003), *Future Cinema: The Cinematic Imaginary after Film* (Boston: MIT Press).
  Compendious exploration of post-celluloid filmmaking, including assessment of its continuities with earlier marginal practices within cinema.
Sickels, Robert C. (2011), *American Film in the Digital Age* (Santa Barbara: Praeger).
  Attentive to digitisation's reconfiguring both of American film texts themselves and of contexts of production and reception in the United States.

Willis, Holly (2005), *New Digital Cinema: Reinventing the Moving Image* (London: Wallflower).

An excellent introduction: succinct, well-informed and with a sharp argumentative edge.

Online resources

Makhmalbaf, Samira (2000), 'The Digital Revolution and the Future Cinema', n.p., www.iranchamber.com/cinema/articles/digital_revo lution_future_cinema.php.

Reflections on digital developments by this Iranian filmmaker, claiming they presage 'the death of Hollywood production and not the death of cinema'.

Manovich, Lev (1995), 'What Is Digital Cinema?', pp. 1–27, http:// manovich.net/index.php/projects/what-is-digital-cinema.

Prescient, lucid reflections on the challenge posed by digital to 'the very identity of cinema'.

'On Digital Cinema, Special Effects, and CGI Studies' (2011), Film Studies for Free, 2 January, http://filmstudiesforfree.blogspot.co.uk/2011/01/ on-digital-cinema-and-cgi-studies.html.

Gathers together links to an extensive array of academic articles on film's digitisation.

Further reading

Books listed below supplement those already cited in each chapter's 'Selected reading'.

Reference

Barrow, Sarah, Sabine Haenni and John White (eds) (2015), *The Routledge Encyclopedia of Films* (Abingdon: Routledge).
A generous collection of essays on two hundred films from diverse times and places.

Cook, Pam (ed.) (2007), *The Cinema Book*, 3rd ed. (London: BFI).
Enlarged, updated edition of a well-established guide to film studies: more internationalist than its precursors.

Donald, James and Michael Renov (eds) (2008), *The SAGE Handbook of Film Studies* (Thousand Oaks, CA: Sage).
Substantial resource, helpfully subdivided into three sections on global film industries, key critical paradigms, and major questions in film studies.

Hayward, Susan (2013), *Cinema Studies: The Key Concepts*, 4th ed. (Abingdon: Routledge).
Valuable dictionary-style text, offering substantial glosses on terms extending alphabetically from 'action movies' to 'zooms'.

Kuhn, Annette and Guy Westwell (2012), *Dictionary of Film Studies* (Oxford: Oxford University Press).
An excellent resource: thorough, lucid, internationally minded.

Thomson, David (2014), *The New Biographical Dictionary of Film*, 6th ed. (London: Little, Brown).
Fulfils its reference function by including filmographies of countless directors and stars, but more notable still for its eloquent, provocative assessments of them.

Film theory and criticism

Badiou, Alain (2013), *Cinema*, ed. Antoine de Baecque, trans. Susan Spitzer (Cambridge: Polity).

Brings together thirty passionate and searching pieces on film by one of France's foremost philosophers.

Bazin, André (2005), *What Is Cinema?*, Vol. 1, ed. and trans. Hugh Gray (Berkeley: University of California Press).

Important reflections on the nature and meaning of film by this major French critic: essays include 'The Ontology of the Photographic Image' and 'The Evolution of the Language of Cinema'.

Bazin, André (2005), *What Is Cinema?*, Vol. 2, ed. and trans. Hugh Gray (Berkeley: University of California Press).

Another significant volume by Bazin, this time featuring more specific studies of films and filmmakers (including several pieces on Italian neo-realism).

Bordwell, David and Noël Carroll (eds) (1996), *Post-Theory: Reconstructing Film Studies* (Madison: University of Wisconsin Press).

Historically important collection of essays seeking to map out routes for film studies beyond – or around – 'Grand Theory'.

Branigan, Edward and Warren Buckland (eds) (2014), *The Routledge Encyclopedia of Film Theory* (Abingdon: Routledge).

Compendious volume on issues in film theory spanning the alphabet from 'affect' to 'voice'.

Braudy, Leo and Marshall Cohen (eds) (2009), *Film Theory and Criticism: Introductory Readings*, 7th ed. (New York: Oxford University Press).

Very generous sampling of a century of theoretical writings on cinema: best read alongside an overview of the field such as Stam's *Film Theory: An Introduction*.

Carroll, Noël (2008), *The Philosophy of Motion Pictures* (Malden, MA: Blackwell).

Lucid and engaging volume, addressing fundamental questions in film studies, such as film's 'medium-specificity' and its status as art.

Cavell, Stanley (1979), *The World Viewed: Reflections on the Ontology of Film*, 2nd ed. (Cambridge, MA: Harvard University Press).

A 'kind of metaphysical memoir' comprising Cavell's recollections of and reflections on film, this is a book that new generations of scholars are turning to productively.

Colman, Felicity (2014), *Film Theory: Creating a Cinematic Grammar* (New York: Wallflower).

Careful, suggestive exploration of the problematics of producing theoretical writing on an audio–visual medium such as cinema.

Cubitt, Sean (2005), *The Cinema Effect* (Cambridge, MA: MIT Press).

Rewarding, historically wide-ranging investigation into what, precisely, 'cinema does'.

Deleuze, Gilles (2005), *Cinema I: The Movement-Image*, trans. Hugh Tomlinson and Barbara Habberjam (London: Continuum).

Provocative reflections by one of twentieth-century France's major philosophers on the distinctiveness of cinematic perception.

Deleuze, Gilles (2013), *Cinema 2: The Time-Image*, trans. Hugh Tomlinson and Robert Galeta (London: Bloomsbury).

Companion volume to *Cinema 1* that considers the complexities of cinematic treatment of time and memory: dense, absorbing, open to dispute.

Elsaesser, Thomas and Malte Hagener (2010), *Film Theory: An Introduction Through the Senses* (New York: Routledge).

Fascinating book, tracking to and fro between specific films and moments in film theory in order to address the question: 'What is the relationship between the cinema, perception and the human body?'

Metz, Christian (1991), *Film Language: A Semiotics of the Cinema*, trans. Michael Taylor (Chicago: University of Chicago Press).

Epochal attempt to read the production of meaning in film in the light of theories of the sign derived from linguistics.

Miller, Toby and Robert Stam (eds) (2000), *Film and Theory: An Anthology* (Malden, MA: Blackwell).

Should be supplemented by newer texts, but offers encyclopaedic, globally informed commentaries on key areas of film studies.

Nannicelli, Ted and Paul Taberham (eds) (2014), *Cognitive Media Theory* (New York: Routledge).

While extending also to TV and video games, this book explores the cognitive processes, both of reason and emotion, engaged by spectators of film.

Rosenbaum, Jonathan (2010), *Goodbye Cinema, Hello Cinephilia* (Chicago: University of Chicago Press).

Generous anthology of work by this important American critic who is poised between journalism and academia, and who also proselytises for film on his website.

Rushton, Richard and Gary Bettinson (2010), *What Is Film Theory?: An Introduction to Contemporary Debates* (Maidenhead: Open University Press).

Helpful volume, explicating key developments in film theory during the past forty years.

Stam, Robert (2000), *Film Theory: An Introduction* (Malden, MA: Blackwell).
Thorough overview of film studies from its beginnings to 2000, written
with zest and an argumentative edge.

Turner, Graeme (2006), *Film as Social Practice*, 4th ed. (Abingdon:
Routledge).
A well-established study, taking a clear approach to film in its variously
formal, ideological and institutional dimensions.

Wood, Michael (2012), *Film: A Very Short Introduction* (Oxford: Oxford
University Press).
A lovely book: miniature, as the subtitle says, but elegant, witty and
continuously thoughtful on film's aesthetics and economics.

Film history

Abel, Richard (ed.) (2005), *Encyclopedia of Early Cinema* (Abingdon:
Routledge).
Comprehensive, easily searchable volume on film from the 1890s to the
1910s.

Armes, Roy (2006), *African Filmmaking: North and South of the Sahara*
(Edinburgh: Edinburgh University Press).
Good, lucid book situating a number of African cinemas within diverse
historical and aesthetic contexts.

Berghahn, Daniela and Claudia Sternberg (eds) (2010), *European Cinema in
Motion: Migrant and Diasporic Film in Contemporary Europe* (Basingstoke:
Palgrave Macmillan).
Studies of border-crossing in multiple, contemporary European cine-
mas: helpfully read alongside the longer European histories of Ezra and
Fowler below.

Diawara, Manthia (2010), *African Film: New Forms of Aesthetics and Politics*
(Munich: Prestel Verlag).
With its emphasis upon work of the past two decades, this volume can be
read productively alongside Armes's broader survey of African cinema.

Eleftheriotis, Dimitris and Gary Needham (eds) (2006), *Asian Cinemas: A
Reader and Guide* (Edinburgh: Edinburgh University Press).
Substantial volume, exploring developments in Asian cinemas that range
geographically – and formally – from Turkey's to that of Taiwan.

Enticknap, Leo (2005), *Moving Image Technology: From Zoetrope to Digital*
(London: Wallflower).
Starts with an unpromising sideswipe at 'Freudian claptrap', but settles
into a well-informed, accessible account of evolving technologies of film
production and exhibition.

Ezra, Elizabeth (ed.) (2004), *European Cinema* (New York: Oxford University Press).

Valuable essays on developments in a range of European cinemas from film's beginnings to the start of the twenty-first century.

Fowler, Catherine (ed.) (2002), *The European Cinema Reader* (London: Routledge).

A good companion for Ezra's book above: includes key manifestos from twentieth-century European filmmaking, besides contemporary scholarship on many national cinemas.

Galt, Rosalind (2006), *The New European Cinema: Redrawing the Map* (New York: Columbia University Press).

A study that, given its post-1990 and 'post-national' orientations, joins Berghahn and Sternberg in entering productively into dialogue with the books edited by Ezra and Fowler.

Gomery, Douglas and Clara Pafort-Overduin (2011), *Movie History: A Survey*, 2nd ed. (New York: Routledge).

Helpful volume, comprehensive in both its period coverage and its geographical range.

Grainge, Paul, Mark Jancovich and Sharon Monteith (2007), *Film Histories: An Introduction and Reader* (Edinburgh: Edinburgh University Press).

Invaluable collection, interpreting its remit generously and exploring not only film's aesthetic evolution but also the histories of its exhibition, marketing and consumption.

Guynn, William (ed.) (2011), *The Routledge Companion to Film History* (Abingdon: Routledge).

Follows a series of short chapters on aspects of film's development with a dictionary of critical terms.

Hart, Stephen M. (2015), *Latin American Cinema* (London: Reaktion).

Combines comprehensiveness and economy in narrating Latin American cinema's history from the late nineteenth century to the present.

Moran, Albert and Errol Veith (2009), *The A to Z of Australian and New Zealand Cinema* (Lanham, MD: Scarecrow Press).

Valuable resource that assembles detailed chronologies and alphabetised inventories of these two cinemas (treated here as related but distinct).

Ross, Steven J. (ed.) (2014), *Movies and American Society*, 2nd ed. (Chichester: John Wiley & Sons).

Extends chronologically from the earliest US film production to today's 'global' Hollywood, and usefully brings together contemporary documents with recent critical essays.

Teo, Stephen (2013), *The Asian Cinema Experience: Styles, Spaces, Theory* (Abingdon: Routledge).

Productively read alongside Eleftheriotis and Needham above: engaging and wide-ranging, if open to critique for its hypothesis of a unified Asian cinema.

Thompson, Kristin and David Bordwell (2009), *Film History: An Introduction*, 3rd ed. (New York: McGraw-Hill).
Like the authors' *Film Art*, this is scholarly and eloquent (and sumptuously illustrated).

Withall, Keith (2014), *Studying Early and Silent Cinema* (Leighton Buzzard: Auteur).
Clear, accessible introduction to this phase of film's history.

Online resources

Reference

Box Office Mojo, http://boxofficemojo.com/.
  Important repository of statistics on films' US and global revenues.
British Film Institute, www.bfi.org.uk.
  Major portal to film archives, educational materials and sources of cinema information.
Internet Movie Database, www.imdb.com.
  Despite its commercial trappings, a valuable resource, enabling rapid retrieval of information on films and filmmakers.
Moving Image Gateway, http://bufvc.ac.uk/gateway/search. php?subject=Film+Studies.
  Includes links to several hundred web resources of interest to film researchers.

Film theory and criticism

Bright Lights Film Journal, http://brightlightsfilm.com/.
  Lively, eclectic film journal – published online since 1995 – that, in its own words, aims to 'combine popular and academic styles, with humor and progressive politics tossed into the mix'.
Film-Philosophy, www.film-philosophy.com.
  Stimulating online journal that responds both to philosophers thinking about film and to films as doing philosophy in their own right.
Off Screen, http://offscreen.com/.
  Engaging, accessible, globally oriented journal that features essays, interviews and book and film reviews.
Scope: An Online Journal of Film and Television Studies, www.nottingham. ac.uk/scope.

Housed by the University of Nottingham, and featuring detailed book reviews and good articles on all aspects of film studies.

Senses of Cinema, www.sensesofcinema.com.

Australian online journal, published quarterly: especially attentive to its own national cinema, but includes articles written with brio on topics of international range.

Film history

'BFI Screen Online: The Definitive Guide to Britain's Film and TV History', www.screenonline.org.uk.

Rich collection of material on British film (and television) from the late nineteenth century to the present.

References

Acland, Charles R. (2003) *Screen Traffic: Movies, Multiplexes, and Global Culture* (Durham, NC: Duke University Press)

Adorno, Theodor (2001), *The Culture Industry: Selected Essays on Mass Culture*, ed. J. M. Bernstein (Abingdon: Routledge)

Adorno, Theodor and Hanns Eisler (2007), *Composing for the Films* (London: Continuum)

Adorno, Theodor and Max Horkheimer (2002), *Dialectic of Enlightenment: Philosophical Fragments*, ed. Gunzelin Schmid Noerr, trans. Edmund Jephcott (Palo Alto: Stanford University Press)

Allen, Robert C. (2002), 'From Exhibition to Reception: Reflections on the Audience in Film History', in *Moviegoing in America: A Sourcebook in the History of Film Exhibition*, ed. Gregory A. Waller (Malden, MA: Blackwell), pp. 300–7

Altman, Rick (1999), *Film / Genre* (London: BFI)

Altman, Rick (2004), *Silent Film Sound* (New York: Columbia University Press)

Altman, Rick (ed.) (1992), *Sound Theory / Sound Practice* (New York: Routledge)

Andrew, Dudley (2010), *What Cinema Is!: Bazin's Quest and Its Charge* (Chichester: Wiley-Blackwell)

Arnheim, Rudolf (1997), *Film Essays and Criticism*, trans. Brenda Benthien (Madison: University of Wisconsin Press)

Astruc, Alexandre (1968), 'The Birth of a New Avant-Garde: La Caméra-Stylo', in *The New Wave*, ed. Peter Graham (London: Secker and Warburg), pp. 17–23

Aumont, Jacques (1987), *Montage Eisenstein* (Bloomington: Indiana University Press)

Babington, Bruce (2001), 'Introduction: British Stars and Stardom', in

British Stars and Stardom: From Alma Taylor to Sean Connery, ed. Bruce Babington (Manchester: Manchester University Press), pp. 1–28

Badiou, Alain (2013), *Cinema*, ed. Antoine de Baecque, trans. Susan Spitzer (Cambridge: Polity)

Bakhtin, M. M. and P. N. Medvedev (1978), *The Formal Method in Literary Scholarship: A Critical Introduction to Sociological Poetics*, trans. Albert J. Wehrle (Baltimore: Johns Hopkins University Press)

Barenboim, Daniel (2009), *Everything Is Connected: The Power of Music* (London: Phoenix)

Barthes, Roland (1977), *Image – Music – Text*, trans. Stephen Heath (New York: Hill and Wang)

Barthes, Roland (1986), *The Rustle of Language*, trans. Richard Howard (Oxford: Blackwell)

Batchelor, David (2000), *Chromophobia* (London: Reaktion Books)

Baudry, Jean-Louis (2004), 'Ideological Effects of the Basic Cinematographic Apparatus', in *Film Theory and Criticism: Introductory Readings*, 6th ed., eds Leo Braudy and Marshall Cohen (New York: Oxford University Press), pp. 355–65

Bazin, André (2005a), *What Is Cinema?*, Vol. 1, ed. and trans. Hugh Gray (Berkeley: University of California Press)

Bazin, André (2005b), *What Is Cinema?*, Vol. 2, ed. and trans. Hugh Gray (Berkeley: University of California Press)

Beller, Jonathan (2006), *The Cinematic Mode of Production: Attention Economy and the Society of the Spectacle* (Hanover, NH: Dartmouth College Press)

Benjamin, Walter (1999), *Illuminations*, ed. Hannah Arendt, trans. Harry Zohn (London: Pimlico)

Benshoff, Harry M. and Sean Griffin (2009), *America on Film: Representing Race, Class, Gender and Sexuality at the Movies*, 2nd ed. (Chichester: Wiley-Blackwell)

Beynon, John (2002), *Masculinities and Culture* (Buckingham: Open University Press)

Bickerton, Emilie (2009), *A Short History of Cahiers du cinéma* (London: Verso)

Bobo, Jacqueline (1995), *Black Women as Cultural Readers* (New York: Columbia University Press)

Bogle, Donald (2001), *Toms, Coons, Mulattoes, Mammies, and Bucks: An Interpretive History of Blacks in American Films*, 4th ed. (New York: Continuum)

Bordwell, David (1985), *Narration in the Fiction Film* (London: Methuen)

Bordwell, David (1997), *On the History of Film Style* (Cambridge, MA: Harvard University Press)

Bordwell, David (2000), *Planet Hong Kong: Popular Cinema and the Art of Entertainment* (Cambridge, MA: Harvard University Press)

Bordwell, David (2006), *The Way Hollywood Tells It: Story and Style in Modern Movies* (Berkeley: University of California Press)

Bordwell, David and Kristin Thompson (2010), '*Inception*; or, Dream a Little Dream within a Dream with Me', Observations on Film Art, n.p. www.davidbordwell.net/blog/2010/08/06/inception-or-dream-a-little-dream-within-a-dream-with-me/ (accessed 6 August 2014)

Bordwell, David, Janet Staiger and Kristin Thompson (1985), *The Classical Hollywood Cinema: Film Style and Mode of Production to 1960* (London: Routledge)

Bose, Mihir (2006), *Bollywood: A History* (Stroud: Tempus)

Brooks, Xan (2006), 'We Have No Film Industry Because We Have No Country', *The Guardian*, 12 April, n.p. www.theguardian.com/film/2006/apr/12/israelandthepalestinians (accessed 10 September 2014).

Buckland, Warren (2012), *Film Theory: Rational Reconstructions* (Abingdon: Routledge)

Buckland, Warren (2014), 'Introduction: Ambiguity, Ontological Pluralism, and Cognitive Dissonance in the Hollywood Puzzle Film', in *Hollywood Puzzle Films*, ed. Warren Buckland (New York: Routledge), pp. 1–14

Buñuel, Luis (1985), *My Last Breath*, trans. Abigail Israel (London: Flamingo)

Burgin, Victor (2004), *The Remembered Film* (London: Reaktion)

Burkeman, Oliver (2006), 'Mission Over for Mister Impossible', *The Guardian*, 24 August, n.p. www.theguardian.com/media/2006/aug/24/marketingandpr.film (accessed 3 January 2014)

Carroll, Noël (2008), *The Philosophy of Motion Pictures* (Malden, MA: Blackwell)

Caughie, John (ed.) (1981), *Theories of Authorship: A Reader* (London: Routledge & Kegan Paul / BFI)

'A Century of Change: Trends in UK Statistics since 1900' (1999), House of Commons Library Research Paper 99/111 www.parliament.uk/documents/commons/lib/research/rp99/rp99-111.pdf (accessed 13 March 2014)

Chatman, Seymour (1990), *Coming to Terms: The Rhetoric of Narrative in Fiction and Film* (Ithaca: Cornell University Press)

Child, Ben (2013a), '*Blue Is the Warmest Colour* Director Hits Back after

Actor Complaints', *The Guardian*, 6 September, n.p. www.theguardian. com/film/2013/sep/06/blue-is-the-warmest-colour-director-hits-back (accessed 18 June 2014)

Child, Ben (2013b), '*Blue Is the Warmest Colour* Sex Scenes Are Porn, Says Author of Graphic Novel', *The Guardian*, 30 May, n.p. www.theguard ian.com/film/2013/may/30/blue-warmest-colour-porn-julie-maroh (accessed 18 June 2014)

Chion, Michel (1994), *Audio-Vision: Sound on Screen*, ed. and trans. Claudia Gorbman (New York: Columbia University Press)

Chion, Michel (2009), *Film, a Sound Art*, trans. Claudia Gorbman (New York: Columbia University Press)

Christie, Ian (1994), *The Last Machine: Early Cinema and the Birth of the Modern World* (London: BBC Educational)

Clark, Virginia M. (1987), *Aldous Huxley and Film* (Metuchen, NJ: Scarecrow Press)

Cobb, Jasmine Nichole (2014), 'Directed by Himself: Steve McQueen's *12 Years a Slave*', *American Literary History*, 26, 2: 339–46

Cohan, Steven and Ina Rae Hark (1993), 'Introduction', in *Screening the Male: Exploring Masculinities in Hollywood Cinema*, eds Steven Cohan and Ina Rae Hark (London: Routledge), pp. 1–8

Collins, Jim (1995), *Architectures of Excess: Cultural Life in the Information Age* (New York: Routledge)

Comolli, Jean-Luc and Jean Narboni (2004), 'Cinema/Ideology/Criticism', in *Film Theory and Criticism: Introductory Readings*, 6th ed., eds. Leo Braudy and Marshall Cohen (New York: Oxford University Press), pp. 812–19

Cooke, Mervyn (2008), *A History of Film Music* (Cambridge: Cambridge University Press)

Crofts, Stephen (2006), 'Reconceptualising National Cinema/s', in *Theorising National Cinema*, eds Valentina Vitali and Paul Willemen (London: BFI), pp. 44–58

Dargis, Manohla (2013), 'Seeing You Seeing Me: The Trouble with *Blue Is the Warmest Color*', *The New York Times*, 27 October, n.p. www. nytimes.com/2013/10/27/movies/the-trouble-with-blue-is-the-war mest-color.html?pagewanted=all&_r=0 (accessed 18 June 2014)

Day Lewis, C. (1992), *The Complete Poems*, ed. Jill Balcon (Palo Alto: Stanford University Press)

deCordova, Richard (2002), 'Ethnography and Exhibition: The Child Audience, the Hays Office, and Saturday Matinees', in *Moviegoing in America: A Sourcebook in the History of Film Exhibition*, ed. Gregory A. Waller (Malden, MA: Blackwell), pp. 159–69

Derrida, Jacques (1992), *Acts of Literature*, ed. Derek Attridge (New York: Routledge)

Dick, Bernard F. (2002), *Anatomy of Film*, 4th ed. (Boston: Bedford / St Martin's)

Dilley, Whitney Crothers (2009), 'Globalization and Cultural Identity in the Films of Ang Lee', *Style*, 43, 1: 45–64

'Directive 2006/116/EC' (2006), Official Journal of the European Union, 1–7 http://eur-lex.europa.eu/legal-content/EN/TXT/PDF/?uri=C ELEX:32006L0116&from=EN (accessed 3 March 2014)

'Directive 2011/77/EU' (2011), Official Journal of the European Union, 1–5 http://eur-lex.europa.eu/LexUriServ/LexUriServ.do?uri=OJ:L: 2011:265:0001:0005:EN:PDF (accessed 3 March 2014)

Doane, Mary Ann (1991), *Femmes Fatales: Feminism, Film Theory, Psychoanalysis* (New York: Routledge)

Donnelly, Kevin J. (2005), *The Spectre of Sound: Music in Film and Television* (London: BFI)

Dyer, Richard (1997), *White* (London: Routledge)

Dyer, Richard (1998), *Stars*, 2nd ed., with supplementary chapter by Paul McDonald (London: BFI)

Dyer, Richard (2002), *Only Entertainment*, 2nd ed. (London: Routledge)

Dyer, Richard (2004), *Heavenly Bodies: Film Stars and Society*, 2nd ed. (London: Routledge)

Eagleton, Terry (1983), 'Power and Knowledge in "The Lifted Veil"', *Literature and History*, 9, 1: 52–61

Eco, Umberto (1995), *How to Travel with a Salmon, and Other Essays*, trans. William Weaver (New York: Harvest)

Eco, Umberto, with Richard Rorty, Jonathan Culler and Christine Brooke-Rose (1992), *Interpretation and Overinterpretation*, ed. Stefan Collini (Cambridge: Cambridge University Press)

Eisenstein, S. M. (2010a), *Selected Works*, Vol. 1, *Writings, 1922–34*, trans. and ed. Richard Taylor (London: I. B. Tauris)

Eisenstein, S. M. (2010b), *Selected Works*, Vol. 2, *Towards a Theory of Montage*, trans. Michael Glenny, eds Michael Glenny and Richard Taylor (London: I. B. Tauris)

Eisenstein, S. M. (2010c), *Selected Works*, Vol. 3, *Writings, 1934–49*, trans. William Powell, ed. Richard Taylor (London: BFI)

Elsaesser, Thomas and Malte Hagener (2010), *Film Theory: An Introduction Through the Senses* (New York: Routledge)

'*The Equalizer*, Film' (2014), Facebook, n.p. www.facebook.com/ TheEqualizerOfficial (accessed 10 November 2014)

Ezra, Elizabeth and Terry Rowden (2006), 'General Introduction: What Is Transnational Cinema?', in *Transnational Cinema: The Film Reader*, eds Elizabeth Ezra and Terry Rowden (London: Routledge), pp. 1–12

Fairservice, Don (2001), *Film Editing: History, Theory and Practice* (Manchester: Manchester University Press)

Farrier, David (2008), 'The Journey Is the Film Is the Journey: Michael Winterbottom's *In This World*', *Research in Drama Education*, 13, 2: 223–32

Fitzgerald, F. (1990), *The Great Gatsby*, ed. Tony Tanner (London: Penguin)

Forster, E. M. (2005), *Aspects of the Novel*, ed. Oliver Stallybrass (London: Penguin)

Foucault, Michel (1977), *Language, Counter-memory, Practice: Selected Essays and Interviews*, ed. Donald F. Bouchard, trans. Donald F. Bouchard and Sherry Simon (Ithaca: Cornell University Press)

Friedberg, Anne (2000), 'The End of Cinema: Multimedia and Technological Change', in *Reinventing Film Studies*, eds Christine Gledhill and Linda Williams (London: Arnold), pp. 438–52

Gaddis, William (1985), *J R* (New York: Penguin)

Gage, John (1993), *Colour and Culture* (London: Thames and Hudson)

Gaines, Jane (1991), 'Costume and Narrative: How Dress Tells the Woman's Story', in *Fabrications: Costume and the Female Body*, eds Jane Gaines and Charlotte Herzog (London: Routledge), pp. 203–11

Ganti, Tejaswini (2013), *Bollywood: A Guidebook to Popular Hindi Cinema*, 2nd ed. (Abingdon: Routledge)

Gaudreault, André and François Jost (1999), 'Enunciation and Narration', in *A Companion to Film Theory*, eds Toby Miller and Robert Stam (Oxford: Blackwell), pp. 45–63

Gellner, Ernest (2006), *Nations and Nationalism*, 2nd ed. (Malden, MA: Blackwell)

'Gender Equality in Swedish Film' (2013), Swedish Film Institute, n.p. www.sfi.se/en-GB/Statistics/Gender-equality/ (accessed 17 August 2014)

Genette, Gérard (1980), *Narrative Discourse: An Essay in Method*, trans. Jane E. Lewin (Ithaca: Cornell University Press)

Geraghty, Christine (2000), 'Re-examining Stardom: Questions of Texts, Bodies and Performance', in *Reinventing Film Studies*, eds Christine Gledhill and Linda Williams (London: Arnold), pp. 183–201

Gibbs, John (2002), *Mise-en-scène: Film Style and Interpretation* (London: Wallflower)

Gilbey, Ryan (2002), 'Unmade Freds', *Sight and Sound*, 12, 1: 12–13

Giles, Paul (2013), 'A Good *Gatsby*: Baz Luhrmann Undomesticates Fitzgerald', *Commonweal*, 140, 12: 12–15

Gledhill, Christine (1991), 'Introduction', in *Stardom: Industry of Desire*, ed. Christine Gledhill (London: Routledge), pp. xiii–xx

Gledhill, Christine (2000), 'Rethinking Genre', in *Reinventing Film Studies*, eds Christine Gledhill and Linda Williams (London: Arnold), pp. 221–43

Gomery, Douglas (1992), *Shared Pleasures: A History of Movie Presentation in the United States* (London: BFI)

Gorbman, Claudia (1987), *Unheard Melodies: Narrative Film Music* (Bloomington: Indiana University Press)

Gould, Mervyn (1994), *Loughborough's Stage and Screen, Together with Coalville's and the Deeming Cinema Circuit* (Wakefield: Mercia Cinema Society)

Govil, Nitin (2008), 'Bollywood and the Frictions of Global Mobility', in *The Bollywood Reader*, eds Rajinder Dudrah and Jigna Desai (Maidenhead: Open University Press), pp. 201–15

Graham, T. Austin, Caleb Smith, John Irwin and Wai Chee Dimock (2013), 'What's Left to Say? Four Fitzgerald Scholars on Baz Luhrmann's *Gatsby*', *Los Angeles Review of Books*, 5 June, n.p. http://lareviewof-books.org/essay/whats-left-to-say-four-fitzgerald-scholars-on-baz-luhrmanns-gatsby (accessed 15 August 2013)

Grant, Barry Keith (2008), 'Man's Favourite Sport?: The Action Films of Kathryn Bigelow', in *Auteurs and Authorship: A Film Reader*, ed. Barry Keith Grant (Malden, MA: Blackwell), pp. 280–91

Gunning, Tom (2000), '"Animated Pictures": Tales of Cinema's Forgotten Future, after 100 Years of Films', in *Reinventing Film Studies*, eds Christine Gledhill and Linda Williams (London: Arnold), pp. 316–31

Gunning, Tom (2004), 'An Aesthetic of Astonishment: Early Film and the (In)Credulous Spectator', in *Film Theory and Criticism*, 6th ed., eds Leo Braudy and Marshall Cohen (New York: Oxford University Press), pp. 862–76

Gunning, Tom (2006), 'The Cinema of Attraction[s]: Early Film, Its Spectator and the Avant-Garde', in *The Cinema of Attractions Reloaded*, ed. Wanda Strauven (Amsterdam: University of Amsterdam Press), pp. 381–8

Hammond, Paul (ed.) (2000), *The Shadow and Its Shadow: Surrealist Writings on the Cinema*, 3rd ed. (San Francisco: City Lights)

Haskell, Molly (1987), *From Reverence to Rape: The Treatment of Women in the Movies*, 2nd ed. (Chicago: University of Chicago Press)

Hassler-Forest, Dan (2012), *Capitalist Superheroes: Caped Crusaders in the Neoliberal Age* (Winchester: Zero Books)

Heidbrink, Henriette (2013), '1, 2, 3, 4 Futures – Ludic Forms in Narrative Films', *SubStance*, 42, 1: 146–64

Hess, John and Patricia R. Zimmermann (2006), 'Transnational Documentaries: A Manifesto', in *Transnational Cinema: The Film Reader*, eds Elizabeth Ezra and Terry Rowden (London: Routledge), pp. 97–108

Higson, Andrew (2006), 'The Limiting Imagination of National Cinema', in *Transnational Cinema: The Film Reader*, eds Elizabeth Ezra and Terry Rowden (London: Routledge), pp. 15–25

Hillier, Jim (ed.) (1985), *Cahiers du cinéma: The 1950s* (London: Routledge and Kegan Paul)

Hillier, Jim (ed.) (1986), *Cahiers du cinéma: 1960–1968* (London: Routledge and Kegan Paul)

Hollinger, Karen (2012), *Feminist Film Studies* (Abingdon: Routledge)

hooks, bell (2006), *Outlaw Culture: Resisting Representations* (New York: Routledge)

hooks, bell (2009), *Reel to Real: Race, Sex and Class at the Movies* (New York: Routledge)

'*The Hunger Games*' (2014), Box Office Mojo, n.p. http://boxofficemojo.com/movies/?id=hungergames.htm (accessed 17 November 2014)

Huxley, Aldous (1994), *Jesting Pilate: The Diary of a Journey* (London: Flamingo)

'*Inception*' (2014), Box Office Mojo, n.p. www.boxofficemojo.com/movies/?id=inception.htm (accessed 13 June 2014)

Intellectual Property Office (2011), *Copyright: Essential Reading* (Newport: UK Patent Office)

James, David E. (1999), 'Is There Class in This Text?: The Repression of Class in Film and Cultural Studies', in *A Companion to Film Theory*, eds Toby Miller and Robert Stam (Malden, MA: Blackwell), pp. 182–201

Jancovich, Mark and Lucy Faire, with Sarah Stubbings (2003), *The Place of the Audience: Cultural Geographies of Film Consumption* (London: BFI)

Janouch, Gustav (1971), *Conversations with Kafka*, trans. Goronwy Rees (New York: New Directions Books)

Jarman, Derek (1995), *Chroma: A Book of Colour – June '93* (London: Vintage)

Jarvis, Brian (2004), *Cruel and Unusual: Punishment and US Culture* (London: Pluto Press)

Jenkins, Henry (2000), 'Reception Theory and Audience Research:

The Mystery of the Vampire's Kiss', in *Reinventing Film Studies*, eds Christine Gledhill and Linda Williams (London: Arnold), pp. 165–82

Jenkins, Henry (2013), *Textual Poachers: Television Fans and Participatory Culture*, rev. ed. (New York: Routledge)

'Jennifer Lawrence Actor/Director' (2014), Facebook, n.p. www.facebook.com/JenniferLawrence (accessed 16 November 2014)

'Jennifer Lawrence Charity Work, Events and Causes' (2014), Look to the Stars: The World of Celebrity Giving, n.p. www.looktothestars.org/celebrity/jennifer-lawrence#charities (accessed 16 November 2014)

'Jennifer Lawrence Says a Powerful Woman Exudes Confidence during New Dior Ad Campaign – Watch Here!' (2014), Just Jared, 16 September, pp. 1–5 www.justjared.com/2014/09/16/jennifer-lawrence-says-a-powerful-woman-exudes-confidence-during-new-dior-ad-campaign-watch-here/ (accessed 16 November 2014)

Jones, David (2002), *Loughborough: Living Memories of Your Town* (Salisbury: Black Horse Books)

Julien, Isaac and Kobena Mercer (2002), 'De Margin and de Centre', in *The Film Cultures Reader*, ed. Graeme Turner (London: Routledge), pp. 355–65

Kalinak, Kathryn (2010), *Film Music: A Very Short Introduction* (New York: Oxford University Press)

Keen, Suzanne (2003), *Narrative Form* (Basingstoke: Palgrave Macmillan)

King, Barry (2003), 'Embodying an Elastic Self: The Parametrics of Contemporary Stardom', in *Contemporary Hollywood Stardom*, eds Thomas Austin and Martin Barker (London: Arnold), pp. 45–61

King, Geoff (2002a), *Film Comedy* (London: Wallflower)

King, Geoff (2002b), *New Hollywood Cinema: An Introduction* (London: I. B. Tauris)

King, Geoff (2003), 'Stardom in the Willennium', in *Contemporary Hollywood Stardom*, eds Thomas Austin and Martin Barker (London: Arnold), pp. 62–73

Kipling, Rudyard (2011), *The Man Who Would Be King*, ed. Jan Montefiore (London: Penguin)

Kleinhans, Chuck (1998), 'Marxism and Film', in *The Oxford Guide to Film Studies*, eds John Hill and Pamela Church Gibson (Oxford: Oxford University Press), pp. 106–16

Klinger, Barbara (2006), *Beyond the Multiplex: Cinema, New Technologies, and the Home* (Berkeley: University of California Press)

Korcheva, Gabby (2011), 'Top 10 Bicycle Movies', *Momentum Mag*, pp. 1–11 http://momentummag.com/features/top-10-bicycle-movies/#next (accessed 12 May 2014)

Kracauer, Siegfried (1995), *The Mass Ornament: Weimar Essays*, ed. and trans. Thomas Y. Levin (Cambridge, MA: Harvard University Press)

Kracauer, Siegfried (1997), *Theory of Film: The Redemption of Physical Reality* (Princeton: Princeton University Press)

Kuhn, Annette (2002), *An Everyday Magic: Cinema and Cultural Memory* (London: I. B. Tauris)

Langford, Barry (2005), *Film Genre: Hollywood and Beyond* (Edinburgh: Edinburgh University Press)

Leibowitz, Flo (1996), 'Apt Feelings, or Why "Women's Films" Aren't Trivial', in *Post-Theory: Reconstructing Film Studies*, eds David Bordwell and Noël Carroll (Madison: University of Wisconsin Press), pp. 219–29

Leyda, Jay (1960), *Kino: A History of the Russian and Soviet Film* (London: Allen and Unwin)

Livingston, Paisley (1996), 'Characterization and Fictional Truth in the Cinema', in *Post-Theory: Reconstructing Film Studies*, eds David Bordwell and Noël Carroll (Madison: University of Wisconsin Press), pp. 149–74

Livingston, Paisley (2006), 'Cinematic Authorship', in *Philosophy of Film and Motion Pictures: An Anthology*, eds Noël Carroll and Jinhee Choi (Malden, MA: Blackwell), pp. 299–309

Luhrmann, Baz (2013), 'Baz Luhrmann Speaks on Directing *The Great Gatsby*', *Life and Times*, 4 April, n.p. http://lifeandtimes.com/director-baz-lurhmann-speaks-on-directing-the-great-gatsby (accessed 16 November 2013)

Lukow, Gregory and Steven Ricci (1984), 'The "Audience" Goes "Public": Inter-Textuality, Genre and the Responsibilities of Film Literacy', *On Film*, 12: 28–36

Lyotard, Jean-François (1984), *The Postmodern Condition: A Report on Knowledge*, trans. Geoff Bennington and Brian Massumi (Manchester: Manchester University Press)

McDonald, Paul (2003), 'Stars in the Online Universe: Promotion, Nudity, Reverence', in *Contemporary Hollywood Stardom*, eds Thomas Austin and Martin Barker (London: Arnold), pp. 29–44

McDonald, Paul (2013), *Hollywood Stardom* (Chichester: Wiley-Blackwell)

McKernan, Brian (2005), *Digital Cinema: The Revolution in Cinematography, Postproduction, and Distribution* (New York: McGraw-Hill)

McMillan, Graeme (2012), '*Brave* Old Worlds: Does Pixar Have a Problem with Stereotypes?', *Time*, 20 June, n.p. http://entertainment.time.com/2012/06/20/brave-old-worlds-pixars-stereotype-problem/ (accessed 11 August 2014)

McQueen, Steve and Henry Louis Gates, Jr (2013), 'Steve McQueen and

Henry Louis Gates, Jr. Talk *12 Years a Slave*, Part 2', *The Root*, 25 December, pp. 1–3 www.theroot.com/articles/culture/2013/12/_12_years_a_slave_director_steve_mcqueen_interviewed_by_henry_louis_gates.html (accessed 27 February 2014)

Maltby, Richard (2003), *Hollywood Cinema*, 2nd ed. (Malden, MA: Blackwell)

Maltby, Richard (2011), 'New Cinema Histories', in *Explorations in New Cinema History: Approaches and Case Studies*, eds Richard Maltby, Daniel Biltereyst and Philippe Meers (Chichester: Wiley-Blackwell), pp. 3–40

Mamer, Bruce (2014), *Film Production Technique*, 6th ed. (Stamford, CT: Cengage Learning)

Mannoni, Laurent (2000), *The Great Art of Light and Shadow: Archaeology of the Cinema*, trans. Richard Crangle (Exeter: University of Exeter Press)

Marcus, Laura (2007), *The Tenth Muse: Writing About Cinema in the Modernist Period* (Oxford: Oxford University Press)

Marx, Karl and Friedrich Engels (1967), *The Communist Manifesto* (Harmondsworth: Penguin)

Miller, D. A. (2007), 'On the Universality of *Brokeback*', *Film Quarterly*, 60, 3: 50–60

Miller, Toby, Nitin Govil, John McMurria, Richard Maxwell and Ting Wang (2005), *Global Hollywood 2* (London: BFI)

Millerson, Gerald (2013), *Lighting for Television and Film*, 3rd ed. (Burlington, MA: Focal Press)

Mishra, Vijay (2002), *Bollywood Cinema: Temples of Desire* (New York: Routledge)

Moretti, Franco (2005), *Graphs, Maps, Trees: Abstract Models for a Literary Theory* (London: Verso)

Moretti, Franco (2013), *Distant Reading* (London: Verso)

Morin, Edgar (2005), *The Stars*, trans. Richard Howard (Minneapolis: University of Minnesota Press)

Morrison, Toni (1988), *Beloved* (London: Picador)

Morson, Gary Saul (1981), *The Boundaries of Genre: Dostoevsky's 'Diary of a Writer' and the Traditions of Literary Utopia* (Evanston, IL: Northwestern University Press)

'The Motion Picture Production Code of 1930 (Hays Code)' (2006), n.p. www.artsreformation.com/a001/hays-code.html (accessed 1 October 2014)

Mulvey, Laura (1989), *Visual and Other Pleasures* (Basingstoke: Macmillan)

Mulvey, Laura (2006), *Death 24× a Second: Stillness and the Moving Image* (London: Reaktion)

Münsterberg, Hugo (2002), '*The Photoplay: A Psychological Study*' and *Other Writings*, ed. Allan Langdale (New York: Routledge)

Nannicelli, Ted and Paul Taberham (2014), 'Introduction: Contemporary Cognitive Media Theory', in *Cognitive Media Theory*, eds Ted Nannicelli and Paul Taberham (New York: Routledge), pp. 1–23

Narboni, Jean and Tom Milne (eds) (1972), *Godard on Godard* (London: Secker and Warburg)

Naremore, James (1999), 'Authorship', in *A Companion to Film Studies*, eds Toby Miller and Robert Stam (Malden, MA: Blackwell), pp. 9–24

Neale, Steve (2000), *Genre and Hollywood* (London: Routledge)

'New Empire Super Cinema, Loughborough: Souvenir Programme' (1936), Loughborough Library Local Studies Reference Collection

Oldham, Gabriella (2012a), *First Cut: Conversations with Film Editors* (Berkeley: University of California Press)

Oldham, Gabriella (2012b), *First Cut 2: More Conversations with Film Editors* (Berkeley: University of California Press)

Ondaatje, Michael (2002), *The Conversations: Walter Murch and the Art of Editing Film* (New York: Knopf)

Peacock, Steven (2010), *Colour* (Manchester: Manchester University Press)

Pedullà, Gabriele (2012), *In Broad Daylight: Movies and Spectators After the Cinema*, trans. Patricia Gaborik (London: Verso)

Percy, Walker (1998), *The Moviegoer* (New York: Vintage)

Perkins, V. F. (1972), *Film as Film: Understanding and Judging Movies* (Harmondsworth: Penguin)

Pidduck, Julianne (2006), 'The Transnational Cinema of Ang Lee', in *Asian Cinemas: A Reader and Guide*, eds Dimitris Eleftheriotis and Gary Needham (Honolulu: University of Hawaii Press), pp. 393–403

Polan, Dana (2007), *Scenes of Instruction: The Beginnings of the U.S. Study of Film* (Berkeley: University of California Press)

Pomerance, Murray (2001), 'Marion Crane Dies Twice', in *Ladies and Gentlemen, Boys and Girls*, ed. Murray Pomerance (Albany: State University of New York Press), pp. 300–16

Propp, Vladimir (1968), *Morphology of the Folktale*, 2nd ed., trans. Laurence Scott (Austin: University of Texas Press)

Richards, Jeffrey and Dorothy Sheridan (eds) (1987), *Mass-Observation at the Movies* (London: Routledge & Kegan Paul)

Rittaud-Hutinet, Jacques (ed.) (1995), *Letters: Auguste and Louis Lumière* (London: Faber and Faber)

Roberts, Randy and James S. Olson (1997), *John Wayne: American* (Lincoln: University of Nebraska Press)

Rodowick, D. N. (2007), *The Virtual Life of Film* (Cambridge, MA: Harvard University Press)

Rohdie, Sam (2006), *Montage* (Manchester: Manchester University Press)

Rushdie, Salman (1992), *The Wizard of Oz* (London: BFI)

Rushdie, Salman (2006), *The Moor's Last Sigh* (London: Vintage)

Said, Edward W. (1991), *Musical Elaborations* (London: Chatto and Windus)

Savali, Kirsten West (2013), 'LGBT Activist, Writer Calls Spike Lee's Film "Homophobic" On Twitter, Filmmaker Defends His Work', *NewsOne*, 12 March, n.p. http://newsone.com/2274769/spike-lee-school-daze-homophobia/ (accessed 16 March 2014)

Sayles, John (2003), *Thinking in Pictures: The Making of the Movie 'Matewan'* (Cambridge, MA: Da Capo Press).

Sayles, John and Gavin Smith (1998), *Sayles on Sayles* (London: Faber and Faber)

Schatz, Thomas (1981), *Hollywood Genres: Formulas, Filmmaking, and the Studio System* (New York: Random House)

Schatz, Thomas (1988), *The Genius of the System: Hollywood Filmmaking in the Studio Era* (New York: Pantheon Books)

Schmidlin, Charlie (2013), '*Blue Is the Warmest Colour* Crew bring Allegations of "Bullying" & "Anarchic" Over-Budget Production', *The Playlist*, 29 May, n.p. http://blogs.indiewire.com/theplaylist/blue-is-the-warmest-color-crew-bring-allegations-of-bullying-anarchic-over-budget-production-20130529 (accessed 18 June 2014)

Sedgwick, Eve Kosofsky (1985), *Between Men: English Literature and Male Homosocial Desire* (New York: Columbia University Press)

Seeley, William and Noël Carroll (2014), 'Cognitive Theory and the Individual Film: The Case of *Rear Window*', in *Cognitive Media Theory*, eds Ted Nannicelli and Paul Taberham (New York: Routledge), pp. 235–52

Sellors, C. Paul (2010), *Film Authorship: Auteurs and Other Myths* (London: Wallflower)

Sergi, Gianluca (2004), *The Dolby Era: Film Sound in Contemporary Hollywood* (Manchester: Manchester University Press)

Shingler, Martin (2012), *Star Studies: A Critical Guide* (London: BFI/ Palgrave Macmillan)

Shohat, Ella and Robert Stam (2014), *Unthinking Eurocentrism: Multiculturalism and the Media*, 2nd ed. (Abingdon: Routledge)

Silverman, Kaja (1988), *The Acoustic Mirror: The Female Voice in Psychoanalysis and Cinema* (Bloomington: Indiana University Press)

Sjogren, Britta (2006), *Into the Vortex: Female Voice and Paradox in Film* (Champaign: University of Illinois Press)

Smith, Jeff (1996), 'Unheard Melodies? A Critique of Psychoanalytic Theories of Film Music', in *Post-Theory: Reconstructing Film Studies*, eds David Bordwell and Noël Carroll (Madison: University of Wisconsin Press), pp. 230–47

Smith, Murray (2010), '*Engaging Characters*: Further Reflections', in *Characters in Fictional Worlds: Understanding Imaginary Beings in Literature, Film and Other Media*, eds Jens Eder, Fotis Jannidis and Ralf Schneider (Berlin: de Gruyter), pp. 232–56

Smith, Valerie (2014), 'Black Life in the Balance: *12 Years a Slave*', *American Literary History*, 26, 2: 362–6

Solnit, Rebecca (2003), *Motion Studies: Time, Space and Eadweard Muybridge* (London; Bloomsbury)

'Some Bicycle Films' (2011), n.p. www.ionet.net/~tslade/bikefilm.htm (accessed 12 May 2014)

Sontag, Susan (1996), 'The Decay of Cinema', *The New York Times*, 25 February, n.p. www.nytimes.com/1996/02/25/magazine/the-decay-of-cinema.html?src=pm&pagewanted=1 (accessed 11 December 2013)

Stacey, Jackie (1994), *Star Gazing: Hollywood Cinema and Female Spectatorship* (London: Routledge)

Stam, Robert (2000), *Film Theory: An Introduction* (Oxford: Blackwell)

Stam, Robert (2005), 'Introduction: The Theory and Practice of Adaptation', in *Literature and Film: A Guide to the Theory and Practice of Film Adaptation*, eds Robert Stam and Alessandra Raengo (Oxford: Blackwell), pp. 1–52

Stam, Robert, Robert Burgoyne and Sandy Flitterman-Lewis (1992), *New Vocabularies in Film Semiotics: Structuralism, Post-Structuralism and Beyond* (London: Routledge)

Strauven, Wanda (2006), 'Introduction to an Attractive Concept', in *The Cinema of Attractions Reloaded*, ed. Wanda Strauven (Amsterdam: University of Amsterdam Press), pp. 11–27

Stravinsky, Igor (1946), 'Igor Stravinsky on Film Music as Told to Ingolf Dahl', *Musical Digest*, 4–5: 35–6

Taylor, Lisa (2004), '"Baby I'm a Star": Towards a Political Economy of the Actor Formerly Known as Prince', in *Film Stars: Hollywood and Beyond*, ed. Andy Willis (Manchester: Manchester University Press), pp. 158–73

Taylor, Richard and Ian Christie (eds) (1994), *The Film Factory: Russian and Soviet Cinema in Documents, 1896–1939* (London: Routledge)

Thompson, John O. (1991), 'Screen Acting and the Commutation Test', in

Stardom: Industry of Desire, ed. Christine Gledhill (London: Routledge), pp. 183–97

Thompson, Kristin (2003), *Storytelling in Film and Television* (Cambridge, MA: Harvard University Press)

Thompson, Roy (1998), *The Grammar of the Shot* (Oxford: Focal Press)

Thomson, David (2005), *The Whole Equation: A History of Hollywood* (London: Little, Brown)

'Tom Cruise on Facebook and Twitter' (2014), n.p. http://fanpagelist. com/user/tomcruise#/profile_tweets.php?user=tomcruise (accessed 3 August 2014)

'*Transformers: Age of Extinction*' (2014), Box Office Mojo, n.p. www.box officemojo.com/movies/?id=transformers4.htm (accessed 29 April 2014)

Truffaut, François (2008), 'A Certain Tendency of the French Cinema', in *Auteurs and Authorship: A Film Reader*, ed. Barry Keith Grant (Malden, MA: Blackwell), pp. 9–18

Tupitsyn, Masha (2013), 'The Acting Personality: Just how "Authentic" Is Jennifer Lawrence', *Indiewire*, 4 March, n.p. http://blogs.indiewire. com/pressplay/the-acting-personality (accessed 16 November 2014)

Varia, Kush (2012), *Bollywood: Gods, Glamour and Gossip* (London: Wallflower)

Vincendeau, Ginette (2000), *Stars and Stardom in French Cinema* (London: Continuum)

Vitali, Valentina and Paul Willemen (2006), 'Introduction', in *Theorising National Cinema*, eds Valentina Vitali and Paul Willemen (London: BFI), pp. 1–14

Vonnegut, Kurt (2000), *Slaughterhouse-Five* (London: Vintage)

Wajda, Andrzej (1989), *Double Vision: My Life in Film*, trans. Rose Medina (New York: Holt)

Watson, Paul (2012), 'Approaches to Film Genre – Taxonomy/Genericity/ Metaphor', in *An Introduction to Film Studies*, 5th ed., ed. Jill Nelmes (Abingdon: Routledge), pp. 188–208

Weisz, Marni (2014), 'Kat Came Back', *Cineplex Magazine*, 15, 11: 32–4

Wexman, Virginia Wright (2003), 'Introduction', in *Film and Authorship*, ed. Virginia Wexman (New Brunswick, NJ: Rutgers University Press), pp. 1–18

Wiegman, Robyn (1993), 'Feminism, "The Boyz", and Other Matters Regarding the Male', in *Screening the Male: Exploring Masculinities in Hollywood Cinema*, eds Steven Cohan and Ina Rae Hark (London: Routledge), pp. 173–93

Willemen, Paul (2006) 'The National Revisited', in *Theorising National*

Cinema, eds Valentina Vitali and Paul Willemen (London: BFI), pp. 29–43

Williams, Alan (1984), 'Is a Radical Genre Criticism Possible?', *Quarterly Review of Film Studies*, 9, 2: 121–5

Williams, Linda (2014), 'Cinema's Sex Acts', *Film Quarterly*, 67, 4: 9–25

Willis, Holly (2005), *New Digital Cinema: Reinventing the Moving Image* (London: Wallflower)

Wollen, Peter (1998), *Signs and Meaning in the Cinema*, 4th ed. (London: BFI)

Wollen, Peter (2002), *Paris Hollywood: Writings on Film* (London: Verso)

Wood, Michael (2012), *Film: A Very Short Introduction* (Oxford: Oxford University Press)

Wyler, William (1947), 'No Magic Wand', *The Screen Writer*, 2, 9: 1–14

Yau, Esther C. M. (2001), 'Introduction: Hong Kong Cinema in a Borderless World', in *At Full Speed: Hong Kong Cinema in a Borderless World*, ed. Esther C. M. Yau (Minneapolis: University of Minnesota Press), pp. 1–28

Yoshimoto, Mitsuhiro (2006), 'National/International/Transnational: The Concept of Trans-Asian Cinema and the Cultural Politics of Film Criticism', in *Theorising National Cinema*, eds Valentina Vitali and Paul Willemen (London: BFI), pp. 254–61

Žižek, Slavoj (2008), *Violence: Six Sideways Reflections* (London: Profile Books)

Index

Note: page numbers below in *italic* refer to illustrations.